MICHAEL ZANDER

A MATTER OF JUSTICE

JUSTICE

THE LEGAL SYSTEM IN FERMENT

I.B. TAURIS & Co Ltd
Publishers
London

Published by
I.B. Tauris & Co Ltd
3 Henrietta Street
Covent Garden
London WC2E 8PW

British Library Cataloguing in Publication Data

Zander, Michael
   A matter of justice : the legal system in ferment.
   1. Law—Great Britain
   I. Title
   344.107   KD660

   ISBN 1–85043–040–3

Printed and bound in Great Britain by
Redwood Burn Limited, Trowbridge, Wiltshire

A MATTER OF JUSTICE

Contents

Introduction

It is a commonplace that the post-Second World War era has been a period of unprecedented change in Britain. But has the legal system remained impervious to this process of dramatic transformation? After all, lawyers and judges are thought to be deeply complacent and conservative, and the ways of the law are old-fashioned. The public's image of the law is that of the quill pen, Dickensian chambers, barristers and their wigs, briefs tied in pink ribbon. And with some reason. The processes of the law are slow, complex and costly. Laws and lawyers alike are stilted and long-winded. So is this not one area in which life goes on unperturbed as it always has done?

In many ways the picture is accurate. Lawyers and judges *are* mostly conservative and the law developed by the courts, being based on respect for precedents, is backward looking. No one would deny that the process is costly and slow. Yet, to judge at least from the number of official inquiries into every aspect of the system, it can hardly be said that the gibe of complacency is fair. Just about every aspect of the legal system has in recent years been subjected to independent inquiry. Since the 1960s there have been official committees to look into legal services, restrictive practices in the legal profession, the organisation of the courts, the rules of evidence, the prosecution system, police powers, jury trials, civil procedure, the condition of the statute book and the interpretation of statutes, to name only a few.

Moreover, the serried ranks of official reports issued by committees set up by Government are greatly outnumbered by the much larger number of studies and reports issued by private and non-official bodies. The representative organs of the legal profession (the Bar Council in the case of the Bar, the Law Society in the case of the solicitors' branch, and their sub-committees), for instance, have produced a mass of proposals on reform of the law, of the legal system and of the organisation of the profession itself. The solicitors' conveyancing monopoly, advertising rules of the two branches of the profession, monopolies over rights of audience, the internal organisation of the professional bodies, the machinery for complaining against lawyers, legal aid, the remuneration of lawyers, the rules on costs — each of these topics has been and remains in a state of upheaval. The ordinary member of the legal profession going about his avocation could be forgiven for losing track of the bewildering series of reports with their recommendations and decisions implementing some of these proposals. The momentum of events has been astonishing. The professional journals such as the *Law Society's Gazette*, the *New Law Journal* or the *Solicitors' Journal* have almost weekly carried accounts of some new development. Simply to keep abreast of events has been no easy matter.

Plainly, the fact that there has been so much restlessness about the law and the legal system signifies a measure of discontent. If, as many people say, the British* system is the best in the world, how is it that there has been such an outpouring of reform proposals? In truth, the international comparison made in statements that one system is better than others is largely meaningless. There is no way of evaluating a system as a whole in the international context without minute comparison of its component parts — a study that no-one has ever attempted, and that is too complex to be undertaken. It is difficult enough to form a view about the comparative merits of different systems on a single topic. To try to make such an assessment for so diffuse an enterprise as a legal system as a whole is impossible. Moreover, even if it could be done and even if one discovered that one's own system stood highest in the international league table, there would be little cause for complacency, since there would always be ample room for improvement.

The recent manifest concern for improving the legal system has been a feature of Governments of both Left and Right. Both

---

* There is in fact no such thing as a British legal system. The system is somewhat different in England and Wales, Scotland, and Northern Ireland. This book deals essentially with the system in England and Wales — styled for the sake of brevity as the English system.

Conservative and Labour Governments have set up major inquiries into aspects of the system and have implemented their findings. On occasion, a government of one party has even implemented proposals of an inquiry established by its predecessor of the opposing party. So the Heath Conservative Government gave effect to the recommendations of the Beeching Royal Commission which had been set up by Mr Harold Wilson; the Philips Royal Commission on Criminal Procedure was established by the Callaghan Labour Government but it was the Thatcher Government which implemented its proposals.

The fact that an inquiry is set up does not, of course, mean that it will result in proposals for reforms, nor that, if such proposals are made, they will be implemented — nor that, if they are implemented, things will necessarily improve. But the fact that in the past twenty or so years there have been so many major inquiries, official, semi-official and unofficial, into aspects of the legal system speaks for itself.

The purpose of this book is to trace and assess the great range of recent developments in the different parts of the legal system and to consider the present 'state of the art'. How is the system working? What proposals for making it work better are on the table? What are the prospects?

The aim has been to write for three distinct audiences — lawyers, law students and the lay reader who takes an interest in public affairs. This has created certain problems. The subjects covered are very broad — civil and criminal justice, the legal profession, judges, the legislative process, the jury, access to justice. Each could justify a whole book. To try to deal with such broad and complex topics each in a single chapter demands an uncomfortable degree of selectivity. Yet it seemed worthwhile to paint on a broad canvas and to try to identify the main themes of the contemporary picture. Inevitably much detail had to be overlooked. Even so, the layman may feel that sometimes there is more than he wants, whilst at other points the lawyer, and particularly the specialist, may have wished for more. Attempting to satisfy the different needs of readers with varying degrees of interest and knowledge is not entirely an easy matter.

The manuscript was finally completed in October 1987. Thanks are due to the publishers for getting the book out with such uncommon speed, and especially to Mrs Margaret Cornell for her painstaking and most efficient editing. This was particularly valuable since developments in the legal system occur at such a pace that writing a book about the system is like attempting to hit a rapidly moving target. I would also thank my secretary, Angela White, who somehow found time, in addition to all her other tasks, to render the manuscript into a fit state.

Michael Zander
London

1

The Legal Profession at Bay

The cry 'hang all the lawyers' has been a familiar refrain for centuries. Lawyers have never had a good press. But in the past two decades they appear to have had a particularly difficult time, and at present the profession seems in greater disarray than at any stage in the post-war era.

Paradoxically, at the very same time, the profession in England and Wales appears to be booming as never before, expanding its work in new directions, growing rapidly in size, and generally showing every sign of shaping up tolerably well to the rigours of a new, more competitive, era — whilst being castigated from without and tearing itself apart from within. This, in other words, is a period of great and unparalleled travail.

The extent of the recent and continuing boom in English legal services may be judged from the spectacular growth in the size of the profession. For most of this century there were approximately 2,000 barristers and 20,000 solicitors. But from the mid-1960s the numbers on both sides of the profession started to grow exponentially. In 1960 there were 1,919 barristers in private practice and 19,069 solicitors with practising certificates. By the time the Royal Commission on Legal Services reported in 1979 the number of barristers had more than doubled to 4,263 and the number of solicitors had grown to 33,964. By 1985 the respective numbers had swelled to 5,367 and 47,114. The increase in the size of the Bar has been mainly fuelled by an explosion in the number of cases in which legal representation has been available. In 1960, for instance, there were a mere 5,000 grants of legal aid for cases in the magistrates' courts; in

1985 the equivalent figure was 427,000. In 1960 there were some 12,000 grants of legal aid for trials in the higher criminal courts; in 1985 the figure was 116,000. In the case of the solicitors' branch of the profession the increase had more to do with the rise in the proportion of the population owning their own homes and the consequential rise in the numbers of conveyancing transactions. The number of mortgages granted rose from 387,000 in 1960 to 1,070,000 in 1985. The proportion of people owning their homes rose in the same period from 44 to 64 per cent.

In recent years most of the increase in numbers of solicitors has been accounted for by women recruits to the profession. Women rose from 6 per cent of admissions to the Roll in 1965 to 41 per cent in 1985, an astonishing change. In 1983/4, one in four assistant solicitors were women; a year later the proportion was one in three. By 1987 overall, 18 per cent of practising solicitors were women. In 1986/7 the number of women passing the Solicitors' Finals examination was for the first time greater than the number of men, and women's share of new articles registered reached exactly 50 per cent. But evidence was beginning to emerge that the career pattern of women was distinctly different from that of men.*

There has been a similar increase in the number of women at the Bar. In the early 1980s the Law Society was warning of the profession being overmanned, but by 1987 there was talk of a serious recruitment crisis. New admissions in the profession peaked at 3,500 in 1980. The five-year average from 1980 to 1985 was 2,700. But that seemed insufficient. By all accounts, the profession was still expanding and could absorb even more recruits.[1]

This period of remarkable growth has also been the period of greatest trauma for the profession. The modern period in which it has had to face a barrage of sustained and informed critical opinion began in the 1960s. Reflecting on this development in 1967, the late Morris Finer, QC (as he then was) said that the tide was running strongly against the legal profession but that it was wrong to think of it as a revolt of the masses. It was rather, he thought, a protest by politicians, social workers,

---

* Figures published in the Annual Statistical Report for 1987 showed that the proportion of women solicitors with practising certificates declines rapidly after the first year of admission to the Roll, with 36 per cent not holding a certificate after ten years as compared with 12 per cent of men. Also three times as many women as men *pro rata* remain as employed assistant solicitors ten years after admission (see *Law Society's Gazette*, 3 September 1987, p. 2446).

journalists, university teachers — in short, the makers of opinion.[2]

>They are in reaction against what they are coming to regard as the unjustified pretensions of the legal profession: its incompetencies in the role in which it has for centuries claimed a supremacy of abilities; its unwillingness or its ignorance of the means to adapt itself to the demands of modern life in general and the claims of the citizen of the welfare state in particular.

An echo of this was to be heard in an article published in July 1986 in which Dr Yvonne Cripps, of Emmanuel College, Cambridge, reported on her study of criticisms of all the professions commissioned by the Inter-Professional Group.[3] The professions, she said, had been dilatory in putting their case to the public. There had been a tendency simply to hope that the forces acting to change them would disappear, but instead they had intensified and increased. The published responses from the professions had been weak and 'the public might be forgiven for believing that the professions are more concerned to fight for increased fees and improved working conditions than to answer criticisms about their conduct and organisation'. They had so often focussed their arguments on issues which might seem to augment the well-being of professionals rather than of consumers. They had an excellent case to put to the public but they had to demonstrate the importance of their special role and status in the community. An analysis and revision of their own practices in the light of the public interest was an essential feature of this process.

The case for the lawyers is that they act as an invaluable resource for clients, steering them through their difficulties, mitigating the rigour of the law, mediating, fixing, negotiating, taking up the cudgels where cudgels are needed, but reaching compromises in disputes where that seems the wiser course. A good lawyer is not simply facilitator, counsellor, advocate, and general adviser, he may see ways of doing things and opportunities that would not have occurred to the client. His role can include a constructive and creative function, though most lay clients probably see little evidence of this. The legal profession in this country has not had as good a reputation for initiative and ingenuity as that, for instance, in the United States — and has paid the price of losing much business to competitors, notably accountants. On the other hand, it is probably true that although the profession as a whole tends to have a poor press, the relations between individual clients and their own lawyers are usually good and the client normally expresses himself as well pleased with the work done for him. The survey of use of lawyers' services done for the Royal Commission on Legal Services showed 67 per cent of clients expressing themselves 'completely satisfied', 17 per cent 'fairly satisfied', 7 per cent 'somewhat dissatisfied' and 6 per cent 'very dissatisfied'. This pattern of response is typical of the results of most such studies, although a poll of 5,000 businesses and companies in Sussex published in July 1987 produced 35 per cent of respondents dissatisfied with the quality of service from solicitors and 55 per cent who said they did not get value for money. In both respects accountants fared better with 20 per cent and 30 per cent dissatisfied.[4]

Traditionally, the legal profession has set great store by its independence and on the whole it has been left to get on with its own affairs. In the recent past, however, it has had to endure the indignity of repeated external inquiries. Between the mid-1960s and the end of the 1970s there were no less than four statutes dealing with aspects of legal services, the report of a committee on criminal legal aid, three reports of the National Board for Prices and Incomes and four reports of the Monopolies Commission, culminating in a Royal Commission on all aspects of the profession and legal services set up by Mr Harold Wilson in 1976.

The Royal Commission was chaired by a layman (Sir Henry, later Lord, Benson) and had a majority of lay members. It reported in January 1979 following the taking of voluminous evidence and lengthy consultation and deliberation. The profession viewed the whole process with the utmost disfavour and anxiety. From its point of view there were three crucial issues: the Bar's monopoly over the right to appear as an advocate (the 'right of audience') in the higher courts, the solicitors' monopoly over conveyancing work, and the division of the profession into barristers and solicitors. To its intense relief (and surprise) the Commission concluded not only that it was generally serving the public well but that in relation to the three issues of its concern the public interest would in each case be best served by a continuation of the *status quo*. It seemed that the profession had weathered the storm. When in 1983 the Government announced its acceptance of the report, both the Bar and the solicitors must have thought that, essentially, the long ordeal of external review and criticism was over. The Commission's report would be forgotten. (Amazingly, it was never debated in either House of Parliament!)

CONVEYANCING: AUSTIN MITCHELL'S BILL

Nevertheless, almost before the profession had had time to congratulate itself on what seemed like a miraculous escape, the battle began again. This time the onset of the series of threatening developments can be traced to a particular event on a particular date which will for ever be marked as a critical day in the history of the profession. In the autumn of 1983, Mr Austin Mitchell, Labour backbench MP for Grimsby, won a high position in the annual ballot for private members' legislation and was persuaded by the Consumers' Association and its legal adviser, Mr David Tench, to adopt its bill to allow licensed conveyancers to undertake conveyancing in regard to residential property in competition with solicitors. The Bill had its Second Reading on 16 December 1983. During the Second Reading debate, the then Solicitor-General, Sir Patrick Mayhew, announced that the Government opposed the Bill, though it did intend to set up a committee to see if anything could be done to simplify conveyancing procedure. However, to the dismay of the Law Society and to general astonishment, Mr Mitchell won a majority of 96 to 76 on the Second Reading. The Law Society had failed to mobilise its supporters.[5]

The Government then had to decide how to react. The then Lord Chancellor, Lord Hailsham, urged that the Government oppose the Consumers' Association's bill, but Mr Norman Tebbitt, the hard man of the Right, and the Prime Minister persuaded the Cabinet to reject this advice. A deal was done with Mr Mitchell. Accordingly in February 1984 it was announced that Mr Mitchell would withdraw his bill and that the Government would instead bring forward its own bill to achieve broadly the same objective. It first set up an expert committee under Professor Julian Farrand, a Law Commissioner, and its first report[6] formed the basis for Part II of the Administration of Justice Act 1985. This provided for licensed conveyancers to undertake conveyancing work, subject to control by a new Council responsible for the code of conduct, prescribing educational and other qualifying requirements, and devising rules relating to insurance, compensation for victims of fraud, and disciplinary procedures*. Considering that Mr Mitchell's

---

* In August 1986 the Council announced the general education and training requirements and the transitional arrangements under which those with appropriate experience as conveyancers could obtain licences from the spring of 1987. Experienced conveyancers would be exempted from the full education and

Bill was the brainchild of the Consumers' Association, it was appropriate that the first chairman of the Council should be Mrs Rachel Waterhouse, Chairman of the Association.

With the announcement in February 1984 that the Government would implement the Austin Mitchell Bill, panic set in in the Law Society and the whole solicitors' branch of the profession. For many years conveyancing has accounted for something like half of all solicitors' income. The proportion varies between different types of firms; the smaller the firm, the greater the dependence on conveyancing. The Royal Commission found that single practitioners earned 60 per cent of their gross fee income from conveyancing, two to four partner firms, 54 per cent, five to nine partner firms, 49 per cent, and firms with more than ten partners, one third.[7] A survey carried out more recently by Messrs Peat, Marwick and Mitchell for the Law Society confirmed that, although the percentages had changed somewhat, loss of conveyancing income would be liable to have a devastating impact on the bulk of the profession. Domestic conveyancing was 46 per cent of the income of single practitioners and 41 per cent of two to four partner firms, compared with only 10 per cent for firms with more than ten partners — most of whose conveyancing is commercial and therefore not affected by the advent of licensed conveyancers.[8]

The Royal Commission had recommended by a clear majority of ten to five that the monopoly should continue. For the Commission the chief argument was that conveyancing represented the citizen's largest single consumer transaction, and it was vital that the legal work should not be botched. The safest thing was to leave it in the hands of the solicitors. Mrs Thatcher and the majority of her Cabinet, on the other hand, had been impressed by the argument that competition would bring down charges and that the work could be done with a sufficient degree of competence by persons specially licensed to do conveyancing.

---

training requirements but only if they could pass a two-part examination on law and conveyancing. They would also have to take a separate paper on accounts rules. (Of the 399 who sat the first examinations only 175 passed!) All licensed conveyancers would have to be properly insured and the Council was making appropriate arrangements for negligence and fraud compensation. (See *Law Society's Gazette*, 3 September 1986, p. 2530). For an assessment of the rules, see P. Kenny, 'How much licence do the new conveyancers have?', *Solicitors' Journal*, 17 July 1987, p. 958.

ADVERTISING

The almost immediate response by the Law Society to the Government's announcement was to abandon its long-held and deeply felt view that advertising by individual solicitors was unprofessional conduct. In 1977 in evidence to the Royal Commission the Law Society had said that the special relationship of trust between the lawyer and his client required the lawyer to refrain from practices acceptable in the market place.

In particular, while professional men constantly compete with one another in reputation for ability, they do not compete by way of advertisement and other methods familiar and unobjectionable in the business world. The Society believes that self-advertisement by individual solicitors is wholly inconsistent with the proper relationship between solicitor and client.

Like all the professions the lawyers resisted marketing themselves for fear of damaging their image.

In reality, in spite of these protestations, the Law Society had over a number of years gradually moved away from the strictest interpretation of this position. Already in the 1960s it started to engage in institutional advertising by printing some 13 million leaflets on what solicitors do, and in the succeeding years it financed several expensive television campaigns to tell the world how useful solicitors were. It persuaded the Government to publish annual regional directories of the firms undertaking legal aid work and tens of thousands of copies were distributed free of charge to public libraries, Citizens' Advice Bureaux and other referral agencies. These directories, which since 1984 have been produced by private publishers, Waterlows, and which are no longer confined to firms undertaking legal aid, contain a mass of detailed information about firms, their addresses, opening hours, members, and the work they do. From November 1983 the Law Society permitted local Law Societies to place 'tombstone' advertisements in the local press restating the information from the directory. But it was only with the impending debacle of the loss of the conveyancing monopoly that the Law Society abandoned its basic opposition to individual firms advertising.

On 21 June 1984, only a few months after the Government stated that it would implement Austin Mitchell's Bill, the Council of the Law Society announced that as from October solicitors would for the first time be permitted to advertise the range of services they offered to the public, and their charges. (Conveyancing fees used to be based on scales which were, in effect, both maxima and minima. In 1973 scale fees were abolished and solicitors were permitted to charge 'reasonable' fees. But price competition was dulled by the prohibition on advertising.) The press statement referred to the Government's announcement and added sourly that those who supported the decision 'could probably thank the Government for their success in the Council vote'. Advertising was not to be allowed on television, but radio and the national and local press as well as other means could be used, provided the advertisement did not bring the profession into disrepute or use 'knocking copy'.[9]

The profession did not easily acquiesce in the dramatic change of policy. At the AGM in July 1985 a resolution was moved that 'individual advertising by solicitors is contrary to the interests of both the public and solicitors'. The motion, which also called for a ballot, was defeated by the narrowest of margins — 3,420 votes to 3,407. The ballot which followed was almost as close — 13,528 for advertising, 11,246 votes against. The profession was clearly deeply divided on the issue. But it appeared to adjust reasonably quickly to the new situation and only a year later, in December 1986, the Council of the Law Society approved a wholescale further relaxation of the advertising and touting rules. The basic principle of the new Publicity Code is that a solicitor may now publicise his practice provided that he does not attract clients in a manner likely to impair his independence or integrity, or the client's freedom to instruct the lawyer of his own choice, or the solicitor's duty to act in the client's best interests, or the good repute of the profession or proper standards. Subject to these very general qualifications, he can use any form of media — television, direct mail shots, tee shirts, or, for that matter, sky writing. Firms may not, however, make unsolicited visits or telephone calls (as in promotion of double glazing); 'knocking copy' is still not permitted, nor can one mention success rates or even the names of clients without their consent. Otherwise just about anything goes.[10]

For the moment, however, the profession has on the whole reacted very cautiously to the new rules — though detailed descriptive articles in the legal press about firms and their individual members are now beginning to appear[11] and many firms have produced brochures about their operations. Some have been a little more adventurous. Pictons, a 17-partner firm in the Chilterns area, have used an advertisement on local radio featuring the voice of Willie Rushton:

> Pictons the solicitors are absolutely hopeless at cricket, terrible at tennis, appalling at light opera, awful at open heart surgery, and embarrassingly bad at synchronised swimming. . . . But then Pictons are frightfully good at dealing with legal matters. . . .

There then follows a short list of types of legal work and a stop-press flash: one of the partners has just become an expert in synchronised swimming!

Another wrinkle was added in summer 1987 when Landau and Cohen of Finchley and Edgware announced that they were sponsoring one of their client firms, the Clapton football team who play in the Vauxhall Opel League. The average gate at a home match was only 350 or so but the firm believed that the sponsorship (with the players wearing the firm's legend on their shirts) would be good for business. Meanwhile the South London firm Sandoms, with offices in Deptford, Peckham, Beckenham and South Norwood, became the first solicitors to advertise on London Transport buses. The firm was said in July 1987 to be running a conveyancing advertising campaign on 56 buses at a cost of £35 per bus per month. Liverpool solicitors Yaffe Jackson and Ostrin thought they were the first to use advertising hoardings.

A survey in 1987 of 350 firms revealed that just over half (55 per cent) had actually advertised in local or national magazines and newspapers. Only a quarter of those who had advertised in the press reported any perceptible increase in business but, somewhat surprisingly, over a half of them said that they would continue to advertise regularly or sporadically. A little over a third of the firms (37 per cent) had produced a brochure — in over half the cases after consulting some form of specialist advisers.[12] The brochure was used by most of them as something to be left in the waiting room but two-thirds also mailed it out on request and about one-third had undertaken a direct mailing campaign. Virtually all found it useful and something they intended to continue.

The battle to try to increase legal services through better promotion is still in its infancy. The profession is besieged by articles in practitioners' journals from advertising experts selling their wares. Advertising through local radio, or even in local newspapers, may seem undesirable to most firms. But promotional brochures about the firm, newsletters and leaflets to clients about developments in the law, and even direct mail targeted at distinct potential client categories, may all come to be normal. It is not yet clear, however, whether advertising will have the effect of redistributing the work already available or whether and, if so to what extent, it will generate new business. Since there is a great unmet need for legal services, it would seem very probable that it will actually help to bring in new clients, as well as possibly giving some competitive advantage to those who go in for this form of self-aggrandisement.

One concrete result of advertising in the United States, where it has been permitted since 1977, has been the development of 'legal clinics' — on the model of supermarkets — offering routinised legal services at rock-bottom prices achievable through high turnover. The clinics concentrate on divorces, wills and personal injury work.[13] Contrary to what might be expected, low-cost operations do not necessarily threaten standards. A survey of one of the oldest clinics, Jacoby and Myers, revealed that divorces costing half the normal going rate nevertheless resulted in significantly higher child support for wives. Clients rated the clinics higher than ordinary practices on measures such as promptness, interest and concern about their problems, explaining matters to them, and charges. At the time of the research the firm had 16 offices and ran a heavy television campaign which attracted 2,500 new clients per month.[14] Although there is no sign yet of any such developments in this country, it would be surprising if something resembling the clinics did not gradually emerge.

The mere threat of increased competition, long before either the first licensed conveyancer appeared or the relaxation of the advertising rules could have had any impact, appears to have had the effect of bringing conveyancing charges down remarkably. Already in January 1985 the Consumers' Association stated that, although estimates varied as to how much solicitors' charges had been reduced, it could be by up to one-third. The Farrand Committee in its second report in January 1986 was of the opinion that conveyancing charges had gone down appreciably. Bearing in mind that conveyancing accounts for so huge a proportion of solicitors' work, this is plainly a serious development for the profession — and correspondingly welcome for the public. It certainly bore out the view of those in the Thatcher Cabinet who thought that a dose of competition for solicitors might not come amiss.

It does not follow, however, that the fears of the profession regarding a likely loss of business will come to be realised. This obviously depends on how many licensed conveyancing firms emerge and by how much they will be able to undercut the cost of services provided by solicitors. Early indications were not unduly frightening. The number of licensed conveyancers, at least initially, seems likely to be only a bare hundred or two[15] and many will probably be employed by solicitors. (In fact some actually are solicitors!) Interviews by Peat Marwick and Mitchell in 1986 with a sample of solicitors showed that none of them regarded licensed conveyancers as a threat. Fees quoted by the existing licensed conveyancers were considered by many firms to be no lower than those charged by solicitors. It seems improbable therefore that a handful of licensed conveyancing firms will succeed in wresting much business away from the more than 7,000 firms of solicitors. According to the Peat Marwick survey, greater competition appeared to be coming from sole solicitor practitioners who were undercutting larger firms as a way of surviving.[16]

BANKS AND BUILDING SOCIETIES AS THE COMPETITION

The real longer-term danger to solicitors in the conveyancing field is, however, not so much the licensed conveyancer but banks and building societies and possibly other financial institutions offering conveyancing services to their customers through qualified solicitor employees. Hitherto this has been prohibited under the rule that prevents solicitors from sharing profits with non-lawyers. When the Government first announced its intention to abolish the monopoly, it said that it would permit solicitors employed by banks and building societies also to undertake conveyancing. The Law Society mounted a desperate rearguard action to defeat this proposal.[17] It feared that these institutions with their massive financial resources would be able to undercut solicitors' charges and permit clients to pay for their conveyancing over a period of years as part of the mortgage transaction. Bank charges for probate work are higher, not lower, than those of solicitors but for all that the Law Society made considerable play with the fear that the ordinary high street solicitors' office would be forced to the wall by such unfair competition. *The Times* of 31 May 1984 quoted a senior Law Society Council member, Mr Tony Holland, as saying:

A nationwide network of 7,500 solicitor firms would be replaced by a powerful cartel of 15 financial giants. Solicitors' offices will close, contract or amalgamate, leaving large sections of the country without easy access to legal services other than conveyancing.

The chief argument the Law Society deployed, however, was that to permit the bank or building society to engage in conveyancing would lead to an inevitable conflict of interest where it was also the lender in the purchase of the property.[18] It was this argument that eventually prevailed. The Government announced in December 1985 that it had been persuaded that banks and building societies should only be permitted to offer conveyancing services where they were not the lending institutions. In a written parliamentary answer, the Solicitor General stated that 'the Government is not satisfied that lending institutions could safely be permitted to offer both conveyancing and a loan in the same transaction'. It therefore proposed 'to prohibit lending institutions from providing conveyancing either directly or through a subsidiary company in which they hold a majority stake, to those who are also borrowing from them'.[19]

It is not easy to see why banks and building societies would wish to offer conveyancing services to persons who are not their mortgage clients; for the time being therefore, this serious potential threat has been averted. But the Building Societies Act 1986 allows banks, building societies and other financial institutions to undertake conveyancing, and the 'conflict of interest' restriction on which the legal profession is relying is only in the regulations made under the Act.[20] This means that it would be a simple matter for a future government to change the regulation — and to open the profession to the sharp winds of competition from giant financial institutions.

It seems hardly credible that this will not happen at some time in the not too distant future. Banks and building societies have already moved into the field of estate agency. Hambros, the Prudential, Lloyds Bank and the Nationwide Building Society have each, for instance, bought hundreds of estate agency outlets. The chief motive for this development was the hope that it would enable them to provide not merely house purchase but also mortgage finance, life assurance, general insurance and pensions contracts. Estate agent offices could become 'one-stop money shops'. Conveyancing services would be another part of the potential package of services. Even without a change in the conflict of interest rule, it may be possible for lending institutions to get round the regulations by the expedient of offering conveyancing through separate companies in which they have an equity limited to, say, 5 per cent. The legal profession is thus facing an exceedingly troublesome and uncertain future in this vital area of its work.

CONFLICT OF INTEREST

In grappling with these problems, the Law Society in 1986 published a consultation paper on proposed changes in the Practice Rules governing solicitors. Draft rule 1.1 identified as fundamental the solicitor's independence and integrity and the client's freedom to instruct a solicitor of his own choice. But draft rule 1.4 contemplated that solicitors should be permitted to be employed by building societies, banks, estate agents and other institutions to provide conveyancing services to the public. This sparked off a fierce debate amongst solicitors. In the eyes of some critics in the profession, these two principles were in irreconcilable conflict.[21]

> The commercial reality will be that clients will not be free to instruct solicitors of their choice. Solicitors will not be independent or able to preserve their integrity. There will always be an inherent conflict between the solicitor's duty to the client and to the employer. Inevitably, the solicitor's main regard will be to the protection of the employer's interests.

In their view, only if solicitors were banned by the Law Society from working for financial institutions providing conveyancing services could the independence of the profession be maintained. The institutions would still be able to employ licensed conveyancers or barristers to do their conveyancing but the solicitors' profession would have retained its soul.[22]

Walter Merricks, formerly a law centre solicitor, writing in December 1986 as Secretary of the Law Society's Professional and Public Relations Committee, asked whether it would really be desirable for solicitors' firms to be swallowed up by large commercial institutions offering all sorts of legal services.[23] The way the institutions had gobbled up the estate agents showed that this was not an entirely fanciful notion. Could the spirit of the lawyer's independence survive the corporation of the large institutions, profit targets, work-flow formulae, the promotion hierarchy and all the rest of it? Was the future for big City firms to become part of large financial conglomerates, while the more successful provincial practices became wholly-owned subsidiaries of banks, building societies or insurance companies?

Independent practitioners trying to start up in practice and looking for overdraft facilities might find banks only prepared to loan funds in return for an equity stake in the firms and a veto on unprofitable legal aid work. All these criticisms were sufficiently powerful for the Committee responsible for drafting the new rules to withdraw for the time being the proposal regarding employment of solicitors by financial institutions for the provision of conveyancing services.

But the critics objected equally, and for the same basic reason, to the Law Society's draft rule 1.3 that solicitors in private practice should be allowed to have 'arrangements' with banks, building societies, estate agents and others. The essence of an arrangement is that the solicitor would introduce work to the institution or vice versa, for the *quid pro quo* of mutual referral. As a result the solicitor could lose his independence.

When the issue came to be debated by the Council of the Law Society at its meeting in December 1986 the argument raged for over five hours. Those in favour of the new draft code argued that it was necessary to equip solicitors to compete in the world in which they found themselves. Covert arrangements already existed and could not be policed. The non-enforceability of the existing rules was unfair to the law-abiding firm. In the end, the Council did not approve the proposed draft rule permitting 'arrangements', and the matter was accordingly put off for further consideration at a later date.[24]

PROPERTY SELLING BY SOLICITORS

The solicitors' profession and the Law Society have also been reacting to a variety of fast-moving developments in the property-selling business. Since the end of the conveyancing monopoly became certain, the air has been thick with new ideas for marketing legal services in the property field. New computerised systems for conveyancing have been developed and widely adopted by solicitors' firms. It is clear that almost every aspect of conveyancing and related transactions lends itself to a high degree of computerisation. Solicitors are actively exploring ways of providing a comprehensive house transfer system. Instead of having to trail from estate agent to solicitor to building society and having to orchestrate their fragmented array of services, the lay client, it is suggested, should be able to go to one place and one person who will for an inclusive fee offer a package of services embracing virtually everything that is needed by the consumer when buying or selling a house.[25] A

National Association of Solicitors Property Centres was established in April 1984 to promote such centres — following the
Scottish system where solicitors have for a long time been
permitted to undertake estate agency work.[26] Interest was such
that by December 1984 no fewer than 1,300 solicitors' firms had
joined the new association.[27] The Law Society found it difficult
to know quite how to respond to this new venture and issued
guidance which held the situation for the time being.[28] A
number of such ventures popped up in different parts of the
country.[29]

MULTI-DISCIPLINARY PARTNERSHIPS

Then at the end of April 1987 solicitors received a wide-ranging
paper prepared by John Hayes, the dynamic new Secretary
General of the Law Society ('Multi-disciplinary Partnerships
and Allied Topics'), which canvassed a series of fundamental
questions that now faced the profession. They were asked to
express a view on the following points: whether solicitors should
be permitted to form limited liability companies;* whether non-
partners in solicitors' firms should be allowed to share in the
profits; whether 'arrangements' for the introduction of business
should continue to be prohibited; whether parts of a solicitors'
practice should be capable of being 'hived-off'; whether institutions employing solicitors should be allowed to provide legal
services to the public; and whether solicitors should be allowed
to form partnerships with non-lawyers.

The paper referred to recent developments and to the threat of
competition from members of other professions, notably accountants.

> The vast increase in accountants' work, including their
> associated management consultancy practices, has made them
> the major employer of graduates in this country (about 10 per
> cent of all graduates each year now are recruited by
> accountants). . . . [C]ompared even to the most sophisticated
> City solicitors' practices, the largest international accoun-
> tancy firms provide such a range of services as to be de facto
> multi-disciplinary firms.

The rationale for the proposed changes in the rules was said to

---

* The Royal Commission on Legal Services in 1979 had been in favour of
permitting solicitors to incorporate with limited but not with unlimited liability
(para. 30.22-24).

be the desire of clients to have an 'all-in service'.

The Council had recently decided that solicitors could limit their liability for negligence by contract and would shortly consider on what terms solicitors should be allowed to incorporate.[30] (The Law Society of Scotland had just allowed Scottish solicitors to practise in limited liability companies.) But the further question was whether non-solicitors should be allowed to hold the equity in such companies so that solicitors could be controlled by non-solicitor shareholders. (Can one imagine the public holding shares in Slaughter and May, Allen and Overy and other great City firms?)

The disadvantage of the existing rules, the paper argued, was that they restricted solicitors from offering an all-in service and thereby competing more effectively. But relaxation of the rules risked the integrity and reputation of the profession. It might be legitimate to change the rules to permit a solicitor to employ specialists who were not solicitors — such as surveyors or accountants. The solicitor would still be responsible and accountable for the work done. But forming partnerships with non-solicitors created the danger that lower standards might become accepted — especially if the non-lawyer partners were in the majority, though there could be a rule requiring that solicitors be in a majority.

The paper raised for consideration the question whether 'arrangements' whereby solicitors get work on a regular basis from certain intermediaries such as banks or building societies threatened their independence. It asked whether solicitors should be permitted to 'hive-off' part of their business — property selling, mortgage broking, insurance investment — which had some commercial attraction and might be an alternative to multi-disciplinary partnerships, but which could lead to the fragmentation of the profession.

The Royal Commission on Legal Services in its 1979 Report had been against multi-disciplinary partnerships. The equivalent Royal Commission for Scotland had disagreed with this recommendation. The Director General of Fair Trading, in a report published in August 1986[31] ('Restrictions on the Kind of Organisation through which Members of Professions May Offer their Services'), sided with the Scottish Royal Commission.

In sending the discussion paper to the solicitors' profession at the end of April 1987, the then President of the Law Society, Sir John Wickerson, stated that the issues reviewed were 'perhaps the most fundamental to have faced solicitors since we emerged as an independent self-regulating profession in the last century'. In view of this, the time allowed for discussion was not over long. The profession was given three months until 31 July to respond, with a view to the Council of the Law Society taking decisions in the autumn.

There is no doubt that the profession is deeply divided and deeply troubled by these developments. The Social Democratic Lawyers Association, for instance, found itself unable to agree either on the issue of multi-disciplinary partnerships or on whether banks and building societies should be allowed to provide conveyancing services for borrowers. The majority saw a risk of inter-professional partnerships possibly leading to a substantial reduction in the services now provided by solicitors. Partnerships with estate agents would tend to become estate agents providing conveyancing services. This would seriously undermine the viability of firms providing comprehensive legal services, which would be contrary to the public interest.[32] If firms of solicitors and accountants acted as both auditors and solicitors to a business, there was an increased risk of a conflict of interest and a reduced ability of one professional adviser acting as watchdog vis-à-vis the other. At the top end of the market, there was a risk that the big multinational accountants' firms (which already had large legal departments) would convert themselves into multi-professional mega-firms which would buy up the best legal talent for the exclusive (and very expensive) use of themselves and their large clients. The first formal response to the Law Society's paper came in July 1987 from the Young Solicitors' Group which in a lengthy memorandum called for mixed partnerships, incorporation with unlimited liability, and permission for solicitors to share profits with employees and to make arrangements for the introduction of business. The young solicitors claimed that for the profession to insist on traditional rules to preserve its 'independence', might result in its becoming independent but irrelevant. It would lose business to competitors.

According to *The Times* of 6 August 1987, the first soundings from the profession indicated, however, a narrow majority against allowing solicitors to form mixed partnerships with members of other professions. The Law Society was therefore said to be considering an alternative 10-year survival strategy that would be put to the Council in November 1987. It was said that the package would include relaxation of the rules on conflict of interest, methods to recoup work lost to accountants by enabling solicitors to provide financial advice to clients on a fuller basis, and techniques to enable them to advertise more effectively. It would examine the profession's technology and the case for a national electronic communications network so that solicitors could link up with each other, and with banks, building societies and bodies such as the Land Registry.

The battle raging amongst solicitors for the soul of the profession seems bound to go sooner or later in favour of those urging relaxation of the traditional rules. The competitive pressures seem overwhelming and the tide of events is sweeping the profession along into new and uncharted waters. *The Times* of 2 June 1987, for instance, reported that thirteen leading provincial firms of solicitors were planning a joint television advertisement for use in each of the ITV regions. (The first television advertisement by a solicitor had been shown the previous week — a 20-second film produced for less than £10,000 by the Carlisle firm, Burnetts, to be run 32 times on Channel 4 and Border Television.) The conservative position has to a large extent been undermined by recent changes which would have been unthinkable even a short time ago. The conservatives now feel on the defensive and increasingly believe they are fighting a losing battle.

The effects of these developments on the lay public are impossible to predict at this stage. The Peat Marwick study on conveyancing charges published in January 1987[33] suggested that firms of solicitors had not yet seriously considered what the impact of increased competition might be in future years. Those best placed to succeed were obviously those where partners showed entrepreneurial flair and a willingness to compete. For larger firms, of more than three partners, this meant diversifying their business base into new areas of work such as litigation or commercial work. For smaller firms and sole practitioners, it meant focussing on domestic conveyancing and reducing costs through improving operating efficiency. Those most likely to be affected by the growing pressure on conveyancing income and increased competition were the smaller firms that were not able to broaden their business base nor to reduce overheads in line with falling profit margins. Increasingly, mergers might be the only way they could survive.

Mergers between firms seem recently to have become more common at both ends of the market. Mergers at the bottom of the market receive little publicity. At the top end the most spectacular development was the recent merger of the two City giants, Clifford Turner and Coward Chance. The formation of a new firm, Clifford Chance, with 146 partners and total staffs of around 1,300 was announced on 1 May 1987. A medium-sized provincial merger announced during the same period was that between Mills and Reeve of Norwich and Francis and Co. of Cambridge. The new firm, Mills and Reeve Francis, would have 35 partners and some 250 staff — making it the largest firm not only in East Anglia but one of the largest firms anywhere in the country outside London. News of mergers is now a regular and frequent occurrence.*

However, in spite of all these developments, not only has the profession continued to grow in size but, in the three-year period 1984-6, sole practitioner firms, which are probably most at risk from the threat of fiercer competition, actually grew by 9 per cent (from 2,506 to 2,744) compared with an overall growth in the period in the number of firms of 3 per cent (from 7,575 to 7,833). The other category to expand rapidly was that of the largest firms. Those with eleven or more partners grew in the period 1984-6 by 8 per cent (from 298 to 321) and firms with over twenty partners increased from 63 to 71 (13 per cent) in the one year 1985/6 with the corresponding number of principals increasing by 20 per cent. Broadly therefore the indicators were that the smallest and the largest firms were getting more numerous with the large firms getting larger. But the average-size firm still had only 3.2 principals.

The geographical distribution of private practices is skewed heavily toward London. In 1986 London, with 14 per cent of the population, had 26 per cent of the solicitors' firms. The South generally, with one third of the population, had 31 per cent of the firms, whilst the North, with 53 per cent of the population, had only 43 per cent. Gross fee income for the year 1985/6 was up 10 per cent from £2 billion to £2.3 billion (or 8 per cent per principal from £81,000 to £88,000). Fee income likewise favours London which in 1985/6, with 31 per cent of the firms (sic), had 42 per cent of the gross fee income. Growth in London was at

---

* Arrangements short of merger are also developing. Five of the largest firms outside London established 'M5' in the 1970s on the basis that all were linked by the M5 motorway. Burges Salmon of Bristol, Wragge and Co. of Birmingham, Mills Reeve and Francis in East Anglia, Bond Pearce in Devon and Booth and Co. of Leeds share a variety of services. First it was simply a pooling of management ideas. Then they started joint training seminars and conferences. The annual joint conference in 1987 was attended by over 200 staff members. They are beginning to pool legal research. They produce common up-dating materials for clients. They are pooling developments in computers, electronic communication and information technology generally. In 1987 they started collective recruitment advertising. (See C. Christian, 'M5: Driving in the right direction?', Solicitors' Journal, 7 August 1987, p. 1056.)

double the rate of the North and Wales, with the rest of the South doing only slightly better than the North.*

THE TWO BRANCHES OF THE PROFESSION AT EACH OTHER'S THROATS

All these extraordinary and unexpected developments flowed directly from Austin Mitchell's short Bill threatening the solicitors' conveyancing monopoly. But the threat to the monopoly also had effects in quite different directions. Almost immediately after the Government stated in February 1984 that it intended to take over Mr Mitchell's Bill, the Law Society announced on 27 March that the Council had 'decided to press for the removal of the barristers' monopoly of rights of advocacy in the higher courts'. This was to strike at the heart of the arrangements governing the divided profession. The lay public tends to believe that they are based on a differentiation between advocates (barristers) and office lawyers (solicitors). But this is too simple — for many barristers spend little time in court, while some solicitors do a great deal of advocacy in the lower courts and in tribunals. The real basis of the distinction is that barristers have the monopoly of appearing as advocates and of being appointed to the bench in the higher courts, whereas solicitors have the monopoly of the right of direct relations with the lay client. The client must therefore take his problem to a solicitor. It is only in a small minority of cases that the matter goes on to a barrister — either because the case requires advocacy in the higher courts where the solicitor has no right to appear or because the solicitor feels that he should go to a barrister because his own office cannot provide sufficient expertise to deal with the problem. (In fact only about 4 per cent of all matters that go to solicitors reach a barrister.)

Until recently, the two branches of the profession broadly agreed that the division was in the public interest, whilst the view from outside tended rather to the opinion that the division was wasteful of both effort and clients' money. (Why pay two lawyers when one would suffice?) The question was put to the test of a full-scale inquiry for the first time in the form of the

---

* The figures come from the increasingly valuable annual report prepared for the Law Society and published annually in the *Law Society's Gazette*. The report is compiled by Mr P.G. Marks, a member of the Council of the Institute of Statisticians. The 1987 figures were published in the *Gazette* for 3 September 1987, p. 2446 and the Law Society's *Annual Statistical Report*, 1987. For previous years see 26 September 1984, p. 2609; 16 October 1985, p. 2903; 29 October 1986, p. 3257.

Royal Commission on Legal Services set up by the Wilson Labour Government. The Commission was widely expected to give the thumbs down to the divided profession. But instead, in their 1979 Report, the fifteen commissioners unanimously expressed themselves convinced that the existing arrangements were for the best. This was actually not wholly surprising. Both sides of the profession argued for the continuation of the *status quo* and there was no very significant weight of informed opinion to the contrary.

In regard to the Bar's monopoly over the right of appearing as advocates in the higher courts, however, the Royal Commission was split down the middle; it opted for continuation of the *status quo* by only eight votes to seven. For the Bar the new threat to its rights of audience was crucial. It had just managed to scrape home in 1979. But now, only a few years later, here was the Law Society using the anticipated blow to its conveyancing monopoly as a reason to attempt to re-open a question which the Royal Commission had seemingly concluded. The Bar's response was pained. On 2 April 1984 it put out a statement noting with regret 'that the Law Society has once again thought it necessary to raise the issue of solicitors' rights of audience'. It reminded the world that the Royal Commission had found that 'the public interest required that a specialist corps of advisers and advocates should be maintained' and had accordingly not recommended any change in the barristers' monopoly. The Government had accepted this view in its response to the Royal Commission's report. The Bar suggested acidly that 'There can be no sensible suggestion that the loss by the solicitors profession of the conveyancing monopoly alters the well settled public interest in any way'.[34]

At first it seemed as if the move by the Law Society had been ill-advised — it appeared petulant, even childish. The Government seemed unlikely to move to give solicitors better rights of audience. Conveyancing affects millions of ordinary citizens and is an issue which excites the media and may influence voters. Who can appear as an advocate in the higher courts, by comparison, looks simply like a demarcation dispute between the lawyers. In fact, the Government gave the Bar the reassurance it needed in the debates that took place during 1985 on the Prosecution of Offences Bill, which was designed to establish a new national Crown Prosecution system under the Director of Public Prosecutions. The Bar was desperately concerned that crown prosecutors might be given a right of audience in the crown court where at present barristers have a

monopoly.* The Government assured the Bar that it had
nothing to fear on this account.[35] Lawyers working for the new
service (which was established in 1986) were to have no right of
audience in the crown court.

Nevertheless, before the end of 1985 the Bar was again in a
state of acute anxiety. This time its rights of audience were
challenged by the ample figure of Mr Cyril Smith, the Liberal
MP, who wanted to have his solicitor read to the High Court the
terms of the settlement of a libel action brought against him and
Radio Trent by twenty-five other Members of Parliament. On
18 October 1985, the judge, Mr Justice Leonard, held that he
had no authority to allow a solicitor to appear before him, and
on 11 December this was confirmed on appeal by the Court of
Appeal. However, Sir John Donaldson, Master of the Rolls,
giving judgment for the Court of Appeal, stated that the judges
of the High Court as a collegiate body could change the rules
regarding rights of audience.[36] A few weeks later on 13 January
1986, the judges duly met to consider proposals from the two
sides of the profession. After some delay the Lord Chief Justice,
Lord Lane, announced on 9 May on behalf of all the High Court
and Court of Appeal judges that the rules were to be changed to
allow solicitors to appear in formal and uncontested matters.[37]
Two working days later, on 13 May, three solicitors made legal
history by being the first to appear in open court in the High
Court as spokesmen for their clients, robed and in winged collars
(though without the barrister's wig). Appropriately, the first
case to be heard was the libel action brought by the 25 MPs
against Mr Cyril Smith. This therefore gave solicitors a foot in
the door. It is clear, however, that the Law Society is by no
means satisfied. (It described the event as 'only a small step
forward', and a disappointment.)

In fact, five months earlier, on 22 January 1986, the Law
Society had published a discussion paper proposing that the
Bar's monopoly over the right of audience should either be
abolished or radically modified. The document, inoffensively
entitled 'Lawyers and the Courts: Time for some Changes',
represented a revolution in Law Society thinking. For decades
the official line from the Law Society headquarters in Chancery
Lane had been implacably opposed to any steps toward
unification of the two branches of the profession. In the case of

---

* The Crown Prosecution Service employs both barristers and solicitors but for
the purposes of the rules about rights of audience they are all treated as
solicitors regardless of their actual professional status.

the Bar, this was obvious self-interest. In the case of the Law Society, it represented partly the sense that solicitors up and down the country benefitted from having a specialist Bar available and partly a realisation that few solicitors would in practice want to avail themselves of the opportunity of appearing as advocates in the higher courts. But less tangibly it also reflected the historic relationship between the 'senior' and the 'junior' branches of the legal profession. The solicitors have always been treated by the Bar as inferior and had accepted their position. They were drawn from the middle classes whereas the Bar tended to be upper middle class. The barrister had been to university which, until the 1960s, was relatively rare for solicitors. The Bar was defined by the system as the senior branch. (The solicitor always comes to the barrister and not vice versa. A barrister is not even permitted to go to a solicitor's office for a conference.) Even highly competent and experienced solicitors would defer to counsel. The barrister might or might not deign to take the solicitor into his confidence on how he intended to approach the presentation of the case in court. If not, it would not occur to the solicitor to inquire, let alone to suggest that the barrister discuss the matter with him. The barrister was in charge and ran the case. The solicitor did not literally tug his forelock, but that was the traditional feel of the relationship between the two branches.

From the 1960s this began to change. Increasingly solicitors and barristers had been at the same schools and the same universities. By the 1980s the overwhelming majority of solicitors were graduates. In fact, so many of the ablest graduates were becoming solicitors that the Bar had felt obliged to set up a committee to inquire into the matter.* The solicitors' branch began to feel intellectually and socially stronger, and its economic and numerical strength grew. But although the official rhetoric pretended that the two branches were on equal terms, the actual day-to-day relationship continued (and to an extent still continues) to reflect something of the old feelings. The fact

---

* In its report in May 1985 the committee found that the Bar was experiencing difficulties in attracting recruits of the right calibre, but the evidence does not in fact entirely support this conclusion. The Bar's intake seems to include significant numbers of graduates with Firsts and Upper Seconds (see Jolyon Jenkins, 'Can the Bar still get the cream?', Law Magazine, 10 July 1987, p. 26). According to the Law Society's Annual Statistical Report for 1987, 51 per cent of those going to train as solicitors had First or Upper Second Honours degrees compared with 45 per cent of those going to train as barristers. However, the Bar was attracting marginally more Firsts. (Law Society's Gazette, 3 September 1987, p. 2447.)

that the Law Society came out in a plain and unvarnished claim against the Bar's monopoly was therefore an event of real significance, marking an end to the long tradition of deference. The junior branch still respected the independent Bar and was genuinely content to have it survive, albeit in a severely slimmed-down form, but it was no longer afraid to stand up for itself and to claim its full entitlement.

The discussion document called for common education for all lawyers, followed by two or three years in the office of a general practitioner. During that time, the lawyer would have the right to appear as an advocate only in the lower courts or tribunals. After that all lawyers, it was suggested, should have the same right of audience — and be eligible for any judicial appointment. Those who wished to practise as specialist advocates would be able to transfer to the Bar on passing certain tests. Clients would have direct access to barristers 'where that provides an efficient result and is what they require'. The report was not an official Law Society document but it came from the Law Society's important Contentious Business Committee.

The Bar's reaction was angry. The then Chairman of the Bar, Mr Robert Alexander, QC, said immediately that 'the proposal would destroy the Bar as we know it'. It would 'seriously weaken the whole administration of justice' to which the Bar was integral. If, as the discussion paper accepted, a separate Bar should continue, why should all solicitors have a right of audience in all courts? 'It simply doesn't make sense and emphasises the regrettable fact that these are self-serving proposals.'[38] And when the Bar issued its considered response to the Law Society's document in June 1986 the tone was still unusuallly blunt. 'Any objective reading of the proposals,' it said, 'ought to lead to their outright rejection.' They were 'self-contradictory, contain new and unjustifiable restrictive practices and are ill thought out and unspecific in respects which are fundamental to any sensible discussion of them'.[39] The Bar rejected each of the Law Society's arguments.

Commenting judiciously on the arguments advanced by both sides, the *New Law Journal* concluded that neither was capable of being impartial as to the needs of the public interest.[40] 'The fact is that both documents are partisan statements in which self-interest is paramount.' Each claimed to have the solution nearest to the public need, but these protestations had to be accepted with caution. Both sides of the profession were more concerned about survival than about the public interest. Both sides made frequent good sense. Neither was wholly convincing.

Probably there were no final answers. Some cases benefitted from the solicitor's greater knowledge about the case and his greater involvement. Others benefitted from the barrister's independence and detachment. The same was true of the argument over the costs of different models, or the argument over specialist skills.

> One searches in vain in the Bar's submissions for any admission that barristers' standards of expertise in advocacy leave anything to be desired. . . . Badly prepared, poorly argued cases are unhappily too frequent. . . . The fact remains that many barristers cannot by the kindest stretch of the imagination be classed as specialists.

It was mainly because the present system gave exclusive access to some courts to a branch of the legal profession which labelled itself as specialist but whose members were not always so, refusing access to specialists from the other branch, that demands for change had reached their present level. But it was unlikely, the *Journal* suggested, that the exchanges between the two branches of the profession would produce the correct remedy.

The tone of these exchanges was so sharp that the leaders of both sides were becoming alarmed at the impression created in the wider public. The result was the announcement on 15 April 1986 of a joint committee on the future of the legal profession to be chaired by Lady (Mary) Marre, a former distinguished Citizens' Advice Bureau worker and former member of the Lord Chancellor's Legal Aid Advisory Committee. The new committee (which was initially proposed by the Bar) comprised five barristers, five solicitors and five 'independent' members. The membership was impressive (it included both the Chairman of the Bar and the President of the Law Society) and its remit appeared broad enough to cover any problem of concern to the two branches of the profession.[41] But, given the irreconcilable nature of the differences between the two sides, it was unclear what such a committee could hope to achieve. It was expected to be in existence for some two years. It would not attempt to repeat the Royal Commission's laborious exercise nor did it originally intend to take evidence — though later it changed its mind on this. Nor would it have any research capacity of its own. Even given Lady Marre's formidable capacities, it seemed an initiative unlikely to do little more than buy time and settle relatively minor issues. Agreement on the major disputes between the two branches seemed unlikely,* though there is a possibility that the committee might eventually produce a majority report, with the independent members siding with the viewpoint of either the barristers or the solicitors. But, even then, whether changes resulted on issues such as rights of audience would depend on government reaction.

On 28 May 1986 the then Lord Chancellor, Lord Hailsham, warned at a conference of the Bar that mutual hostilities between the two branches of the profession were a recipe for disaster. His own strongly held opinion, he said, was that the divided profession should be preserved, and he did not see a case for extending solicitors' rights of audience further.[42] But the Law Society was arguing to officials in the Lord Chancellor's Department that, if economy and efficiency were to be achieved in work conducted out of the public purse, solicitors should be given a right to appear as advocates in crown court cases. Research had shown that in 96 per cent of guilty and 79 per cent of not-guilty pleas the client saw his barrister for the first time on the morning of the trial.[43] This was so plainly unsatisfactory that it would be better if solicitors could deal with such cases.[44]

The Bar meanwhile let it be known that it was considering, tit-for-tat, whether and in what circumstances some kinds of lay clients such as accountants should be permitted to instruct barristers direct without the intervention of a solicitor. The two branches had already agreed in a statement at the end of April 1986 that a barrister appearing in the magistrates' court need not be attended by a representative of the solicitors' firm (often an out-of-work actor) if, in all the circumstances, it was reasonable to have him conduct the case on his own.[45]† The question of direct access by lay clients to barristers is, however, a different issue. In November 1986 the Law Society said that it thought this problem should be referred to the Marre Com-

---

* A more flexible approach than usual was revealed, however, by the former Chairman of the Bar, Mr Robert Alexander, speaking at the Bar's annual conference in September 1986. It might be possible, he thought, for some solicitors to be specially licensed by circuit judges and magistrates to conduct crown court cases, so as to ensure that it was 'the competent solicitor advocate who gained access to the courts' (*The Times*, 20 September 1986). This at least was not the Bar's traditional root and branch opposition to solicitors' rights of audience in the crown courts.

† According to *The Times* of 12 August 1987 the Bar was in the process of unilaterally deciding to extend this to crown court cases. If true, this would be of considerable significance — symbolically even more than in practice. The Law Society would be wholly opposed to such a development unless it resulted in extended rights of audience for solicitors.

mittee. In the meanwhile, however, it did not welcome the proposal.[46] (What was sauce for the barrister goose was apparently not sauce for the solicitor gander.)

The arguments over the divided profession, rights of audience and the Bar's monopoly over judicial appointments at the higher level will rage on. There are many strong points to be made on each side of each of these issuess.[47] Most people seem to come to these questions with minds that are already made up and impervious to persuasion. It does not seem useful to rehearse the opposing contentions here, the more so since it is improbable that the issues will in the end be decided by the weight of argument. They tend to be issues on which there is little in the way of solid evidence for or against — e.g. whether abolition of the restrictive practice will affect standards, costs, or availability of services. The answers tend to be based on guesswork guided by impression and conviction. There is little prospect either that the contending parties will come to agree. What is clear is that, although, at the beginning of the 1980s, in the aftermath of the Royal Commission's report, these issues appeared from a practical point of view to be dead, they are now very much alive. They have come alive unexpectedly because of the impact of the impending threat to the solicitors' conveyancing monopoly. Now the yeast is working and there is no way of knowing how the existing arrangements may have changed further by the end of the decade, let alone the end of the century. It seems obvious, however, that the trend is running in the direction of further reform.

Not that Mrs Thatcher's Government is likely to move far in the direction of reform on these matters. It seems unlikely that the new Lord Chancellor, Lord Havers, will take a very different view from his predecessor. The Legal Aid Efficiency Scrutiny Committee which reported to the Lord Chancellor in June 1986 (p. 62 below) suggested in relation to criminal legal aid in the crown courts that, although there might be a case for retaining the Bar's monopoly in regard to not guilty pleas, it was more difficult to see why solicitors should not have a right of audience in guilty plea cases (which represent over 60 per cent of the total.) The Bar's argument that such simple cases were needed as training for their youngsters was 'from the legal aid point of view not a good reason'. The Committee estimated that extending solicitors' rights of audience would save around £1 million a year.[48]

But the Government rejected the Scrutiny Committee's proposal. The White Paper on Legal Aid published in March

1987 stated: 'The Government does not intend to extend rights of audience in the Crown Court. This would be contrary to the view, accepted by the Government, of the Royal Commission on Legal Services.' Given that the same Government had first accepted and a few years later rejected the view of the Royal Commission on the solicitors' monopoly in regard to conveyancing, the argument was perhaps less than persuasive. But clearly for the time being at least the matter is closed — though if a majority of the Marre Committee agreed that solicitors' rights of audience should be extended, the whole issue would be reopened. (In October 1987 Lady Marre herself said that in her view solicitors should be eligible for appointment to the High Court bench — an indication of her general views on the demarcation dispute.)

It would be equally surprising, however, if the Committee concluded that the independent Bar should be scrapped. The probability must be that somehow or other the English Bar will contrive to survive — if only because there are so many barristers passionately devoted to its survival and such large numbers of solicitors who find it convenient to use its services. Even if the restrictive practices protecting the Bar are abolished, many solicitors will find it convenient as well as congenial to continue to instruct counsel partly to take advantage of greater expertise and partly to shelter behind his skirts.

The best model for the English situation is possibly that of New Zealand where lawyers all qualify as barristers *and* solicitors and can then decide to practise as both or as barristers or solicitors only. Only QCs are limited by not being able to practise as solicitors. There is a small separate Bar, but both lawyer and client have maximum freedom to choose the arrangement that suits them best.[49] Even if a legislative magic wand were waved over the English profession translating all lawyers into a single category, it seems certain that some, and perhaps many, of those who are now barristers would announce that they intended to fight the reform by the simple expedient of accepting instructions only from other lawyers — as happened in Australia in 1891 in the State of Victoria.[50] If there were enough solicitors and lay clients willing to continue to use the separate Bar it is difficult to see how this could be prevented.

REFORM AT THE BAR

Most of the dramatic events of the past few years have concerned the solicitors' rather than the barristers' branch of the profession, but the Bar too has been caught up in a series of recent important developments. In 1986 it voted for a package of internal reforms recommended by the Rawlinson Committee, the gist of which was to oust the judges from their traditional position at the centre of the management of the profession. The new constitution which came into force on 1 January 1987 created the General Council of the Bar, a wholly elected body, in place of the previous Senate which consisted of a mixture of elected barristers and barristers and judges appointed by the four ancient and powerful Inns of Court. Under the new arrangements the powers of the Inns of Court (exercised through a new Treasurers' Council consisting of treasurers and other benchers of the Inns) were reduced in essence merely to referring matters back to the Bar Council with the requirement that they be passed by a two-thirds majority if they were to bind the Inns.[51]

As a result of other reforming measures the Bar now has the services of an expanded and reorganised secretariat* paid for out of subscriptions which for the first time are compulsory.[52] The Campaign for the Bar (launched by a group of disaffected barristers who claimed that the former Bar Council did not sufficiently perform the narrow trade union role of promoting and defending the barristers' position vis-à-vis both the solicitors' branch and the Government) succeeded in getting its entire slate of candidates elected to the Bar Council in both 1985 and 1986. The campaign's founder, Robin de Wilde (hence the 'Wilde bunch'), made it clear that the campaign's main focus would be a more aggressive stance on such issues as rights of audience for solicitors, and pursuing solicitors who were late in paying barristers' fees. The blunt, no-nonsense approach of the campaign was expressed by de Wilde in his manifesto. In his view the policy of the old Bar Council was 'a mixture of appeasing the Law Society and taking care not to upset any other body such as the Lord Chancellor's Department or the Treasury with occasional yelps of surprise when the profession is threatened by anyone'. The character and style of many of those traditionally elected and co-opted to the Bar Council left a good deal to be desired, in his opinion. 'Some consider that their election is a method to ease judicial preferment.' Criminal legal

---

* The Law Society likewise revamped its secretariat. Mr John Hayes, the new Secretary General appointed in 1986, was a mere 41-year-old. Almost immediately on taking office he cleared out the old guard, reorganised the management structure and installed as his senior lieutenants a group of able young colleagues.

aid was 'a scandal'. The criminal Bar was being 'destroyed' by the Treasury and the bureaucracy.[53]

The rise of the Wilde bunch phenomenon (their style and approach reflecting naked self-interest — no more old-fashioned *noblesse oblige*) marks an important development in the Bar's history, with a major division between specialist practitioners earning huge incomes and the bulk of the Bar dependent on legal aid and other work paid for out of public funds, who increasingly feel under threat.* A survey of barristers in criminal work showed the 1984/5 notional net annual income before tax of London barristers of five to nine years experience at a median of £12,500 and for those with ten to fifteen years experience £15,900. The equivalent for barristers in the provinces was £11,900 and £14,700.[54] (If the earnings of those at the criminal Bar are really as low as the survey suggested, it is surprising that so few seem to be leaving the profession. Maybe the figures were not in fact quite accurate.)

At the same time there are practitioners earning literally hundreds of thousands of pounds per annum. A brief fee covering preparation of the case and the first day in court in a medium heavy five-day case these days can be as high as £10,000. In a really heavy case lasting a few weeks it will often be much higher. It was reported in 1984 that Mr Justice Leggatt, a High Court judge who had been injured in a car accident whilst Chairman of the Bar, claimed lost earnings of £1,000 a day for the 163 days he was incapacitated.[55] In 1987 it was said that one of the 35 QCs employed in the amazing litigation following the collapse of the International Tin Council had his brief marked at £150,000 with daily refreshers of £1,500. The case was scheduled to last six weeks.† The other QCs were

---

* The Bar's remuneration survey done for the Royal Commission on Legal Services showed that no less than 43 per cent of the Bar's income came from public funds — 19 per cent from criminal legal laid, 16 per cent from prosecution work and 8 per cent from civil legal aid. There are no more up-to-date figures, but even if the proportion of publicly funded work has gone down as private sector fees have moved sharply ahead, it undoubtedly remains very high.

† Press estimates of the fees in the sensational libel action brought by Mr Jeffrey Archer, author and former Deputy Chairman of the Conservative Party, suggested that Mr Robert Alexander for Mr Archer may have earned £150,000. The *Law Magazine* (7 August 1987, p. 9) assessing these figures said the brief fee would have been in the £15,000 to £20,000 range with daily refreshers of £1,000. The trial lasted three weeks. On that basis he would have earned some £30,000 or possibly £35,000 — far less than the press had suggested but still not bad for what the *Law Magazine* suggested was 'a relatively simple case'. Counsel for *The Star*, Mr Michael Hill QC, it thought, collected some £25,000 to £30,000 and the junior barristers some £10,000.

thought to have fees 'in the same ball park'.[56] With earnings for some on such a grandiose and exorbitant scale, it is hardly surprising that the ordinary member of the Bar feels envious and disgruntled.

The militancy of the Campaign for the Bar enjoys massive support from rank and file barristers. Annual and extraordinary general meetings of the Bar in the past two or three years have been attended by upwards of a thousand barristers, and the tone has often been heated and far from gentlemanly. The atmosphere of such meetings would have been unthinkable a few years ago. The Bar Council has no alternative but to respond to this new more radical stance. The unprecedented legal proceedings brought in 1986 by the patrician Robert Alexander QC, as Chairman of the Bar, against the Lord Chancellor over the level of criminal legal aid fees was a sign of these new times.[57] He was driven by forces he could not control.

In a different domain the Bar was for the first time setting about tackling the acute accommodation crisis caused by a shortage of rooms in the traditional premises of the Inns. A survey in 1986 showed that ten per cent of London barristers were sharing a desk! Twenty sets of chambers had no waiting room. Gray's Inn had 1.35 barristers per room. In Inner Temple the figure was 2.14 per room.[58] For many years the only set of barristers to break the traditional unwritten rule that barristers must practise within the hallowed precincts were those of the radical peer Lord Gifford, who established chambers first in Lambeth and subsequently in Covent Garden. But recently others have begun to consider moving, and a dozen or so out of 200 sets of chambers have actually done so. Adrian Whitfield QC, Vice-Chairman of the Bar's Accommodation Committee, wrote in May 1987 how his own chambers had taken the plunge and moved to Fleet Street. They did not regret the move.[59]

> We look at our open-plan clerks room, our large hall, the rooms designed, wired and decorated to suit each tenant, the libarary/conference room, the parking spaces and the shower and wonder why anyone hesitates.

This policy found expression in the summer of 1987 in a historic decision of the Bar to change its accommodation policy. The Chairman of the Bar issued a statement on 15 June that the Bar and the Inns of Court had reached agreement on a policy to ensure the availability of sufficient accommodation for the practising Bar, especially in London. The two crucial elements were that the accommodation would if necessary be outside the precincts of the Inns and that the letting would be on open market terms rather than the traditional favoured basis whereby the Inns charged their barrister tenants less than commercial rents.[60] To a layman both parts of the new policy would seem natural and obvious. To any barrister both would represent a revolution. The finance for the new accommodation was to come from loans raised by the Inns of Court on their immensely valuable properties (estimated to be worth over £200 million) which are currently virtually unencumbered by mortgages. The Bar, a profession whose whole existence is predicated on its competence in giving advice, together with the judge-dominated Inns of Court, has for decades allowed an absurd accommodation crisis to drag on and has failed to utilise and deploy enormous assets which could have solved the problem years ago. The serried ranks of eminent barristers and senior judges between them behaved in this area like the proverbial little old widow. One cannot deny that the manner in which the Bar dealt with the accommodation problem in the twenty years since the crisis started in the 1960s throws serious doubt on its collective abilities and on its capacity for inventive or lateral thinking.

Another indication of the changed climate came in 1986 when a committee set up by the Bar recommended that its traditional antipathy to advertising and publicity should give way to a more modern approach. It proposed a Bar Directory giving details of the specialisations and qualifications of every member of the Bar, and this was approved by the Bar Council. It also wanted alterations in the Bar's Code of Conduct to allow chambers to publish brochures with similar information and comparable advertising in professional journals circulating to solicitors. This recommendation was too advanced, however, and was shelved for the time being.[61] It was then announced by the Bar Council that as from 2 March 1987 the Bar would withdraw credit facilities from solicitors who had failed to pay barristers' fees for over a year after reminders. (This was a direct result of the original campaign led by de Wilde.[62])

Another revolution taking place is that the Bar is increasingly taking active steps to try to recruit more able graduates from the universities and actually to offer them some form of remuneration in the early years of practice. Solicitors' articled clerks are these days paid something like a living wage and in large firms are remunerated handsomely from the outset. The Law Society's recommended minima for articled clerks differ by region. In 1986/7 the minima ran from £4,450 to £6,000. But the proportion of articled clerks who are paid the minimum varies also. In Central London it is well under 10 per cent. The upper quartile salaries in 1986/7 ranged from about £5,000 in the North to around £9,000 in Central London. In the largest firms an income of over £10,000 from Day One is now becoming quite common. The Bar cannot match this, but the Bar Council stated in June 1987 that the majority of new recruits now had some form of scholarship or other financial assistance from the Inns, or from chambers. The value of such awards is less than articled clerks get, but at least it helps to reduce the old complaint that only those with private incomes or parental support could go to the Bar.

The Bar Council is also looking afresh at the basic rules about professional organisation and fee sharing. The Chairman of the Bar announced in May 1987 that while the Bar adhered to the traditional rule that barristers could not form partnerships, it would in future permit 'purse-sharing' arrangements (e.g. pooling of fees and their distribution according to some agreed formula.) This represented a major departure.*

Another aspect of professional organisation receiving critical attention is the division of the Bar into Queen's Counsel and junior barristers — though this issue has not yet resulted either in a change of official policy or even the setting up of a Bar Council committee. Queen's Counsel (otherwise known as QCs or leaders or silks) represent about one tenth of the Bar. QCs are appointed by the Lord Chancellor to whom application is made. Many more apply than are appointed. The Lord Chancellor's senior officials then make exhaustive inquiries, mainly amongst judges, about the applicants to discover whether they are of the right calibre and of complete probity, and whether they are successful (evidence of income has to be submitted).[63] A junior barrister applies for silk for three main reasons. One is in order to earn more money; the fees charged by QCs are distinctly higher. Another is to lighten his work load; since QCs tend to get fewer, heavier cases and tend to act with a junior helping them, they can leave a lot of the legwork to the junior. The third is to get on to the profession's highest ladder and to join the pool from which High Court judges are selected. But taking silk is a

---

* Under the new arrangements solicitors would have to be informed that purse sharing operated in those chambers, and barristers in such chambers could not appear against each other nor in a case in which a member of chambers was judge. (See *Law Society's Gazette*, 27 May 1987, p. 1566.)

considerable professional risk since, if the gamble fails and one does not succeed in building up a new practice as a QC, a promising career will be blighted. One applies for silk usually in one's mid or late thirties or early forties at a point when financial and family responsibilities are usually multiplying. To have one's previously successful career marred at that point is extremely serious.

The Royal Commission on Legal Services came to the unanimous conclusion that the division of the Bar into two ranks of barristers should be retained, but there are beginning to be voices raised, even from within the profession, that it is against the public interest.[64] The Social Democratic Lawyers, for instance, in 1986 stated their opposition to it as an undesirable extension of state patronage which weakened the independence of the profession. Plainly a barrister with his eye on the main chance will avoid offending the Establishment lest he blot his copy book, but that would presumably be true anyway for anyone with ambitions to be a judge. A stronger reason for abolishing the status of silk is the inflationary effect it has on fees charged, and the catastrophic impact which failing as a QC has on an otherwise blameless career. But there is no sign that reform of the silk system is about to happen.

Nor is there any sign that the Bar is ready to tackle one of the most curious features of the organisation of the profession — the power and earnings of the barrister's clerk. Each set of chambers has to have a clerk; most have several. The clerk is not merely the valued office manager. He also negotiates the fees for his barrister principals and allocates the work when, as is often the case, it is not specifically earmarked for a named barrister or, equally common, the barrister who was booked for the case is unable to take it at the last moment because his previous case is not finished. The senior clerk takes a percentage of the barrister's fee — traditionally the shillings on the guineas, but today usually ten or, more often, five per cent. The result is that at least the senior clerk is usually earning far more than all but the most senior members of chambers. (*The Times* diarist PHS reported on 3 July 1987 that commuters on the 7.55 pm from Waterloo to Woking the previous evening had enjoyed the hospitality of a regular at the bar who was celebrating his retirement. His occupation: barrister's clerk; his age: 38. PHS returned to the matter on 17 July. His attention had been drawn to 'an extraordinary tax concession' negotiated by the Barristers' Clerks Association on behalf of the 300 or so senior clerks. This entitled them to receive any fees after retirement free of tax. No

wonder barristers' clerks retired at 38. The special privilege had
been agreed by the Treasury on the ground that the clerks were
subject to financial uncertainty (sic) as employees of a self-
employed profession which could not sue for non-payment.*)

The level of earning capacity achieved by the clerks is out of
all proportion to the work they do, and the power they exercise
over their principals is thoroughly unhealthy. Moreover, the fee-
fixing process, with the clerk having a direct financial interest
in the level of the fee, has a directly inflationary effect on the
overall level of fees. An experienced solicitor, Mr Geoffrey
Bindman, writing in *The Guardian* in April 1985 said that there
was little real competition as a result of the 'undisguised
collusion' between the clerks whose interest was to push fees up
not down. 'They may compete avidly for briefs but fees are
pushed up not down in what is in effect a cynical assertion of
monopoly power.' Far from objecting, as a distinguished former
judge, Sir Robert Megarry, has said, 'fees are the clerk's
business and counsel gratefully and trustingly leaves it to him'.
The clerk even exerts an influence over who becomes a member
of chambers; the notorious race, and to a lesser extent sex,
discrimination that still influences entry to chambers is partly
the result of the involvement of the clerks in the decision-
making. But the Bar finds it convenient to continue with the
system and to leave the clerks with their powers unchecked.
Apart from anything else, not many barristers would have the
courage, even if they had the will, to challenge the power of the
clerk who after all controls their fate.

Another Bar tradition which remains unaltered is that fees
covering preparation of the case and the first day in court must
be negotiated at the outset before the work has been done, and
that if in the event the case is settled and the work not done the
barrister is nevertheless entitled to his full fee. The rule used to
be that he was not even permitted to return any part of the
unearned fee, but this was amended to allow, but not require,
that the unearned fees be disgorged. However, as Geoffrey
Bindman in his same *Guardian* article confirmed, 'the fee is
obviously agreed on the assumption that the case will be fought,
but refunds are rarely offered if it is not'. This seems unethical
and unworthy of an honourable profession. In cases paid for out
of the public purse, the rule significantly requires payment after

---

* The diarist did not appear to know that barristers themselves enjoyed
precisely the same privilege until it was abolished by Mr Roy Jenkins as
Chancellor of the Exchequer in 1967.

the event on the basis of the work actually done.

One of the traditions of the Bar that is being changed, however, is the air of effete other-worldliness studiously cultivated in the past by the barrister's profession. Chambers are now a multi-million pound a year enterprise. The Bar has belatedly recognised the need for modern management style and for some effort in the direction of office efficiency. Like the solicitors' branch, the Bar is moving into the modern world in the field of computers, word processors and office management.[65] It has even appointed a public relations firm to assist it in presenting the right image.

IS THE FUTURE BLEAK OR ROSY?

The overall position of the legal profession at the end of the 1980s can therefore be said to be, on the one hand, fraught and traumatic and, on the other hand, flush and blooming. It all depends on one's perspective and one's impression of which way things will develop.

The 'pessimist' would say that the very existence of the two sides of the profession is in peril. The bulk of the solicitors' profession could be wiped out by the combined effect of licensed conveyancers, banks, building societies and other financial institutions sooner or later moving into conveyancing, large accounting firms swallowing the leading City firms, Treasury support for legal aid work collapsing, and lay agencies such as Citizens' Advice Bureaux taking over much legal advice. It cannot be long before computerised data bases available to the public at public libraries and similar outlets may make the need for a legal profession to give simple, standard advice unnecessary. One will go to the computer terminal, punch in the details of one's legal problem and the answer will come back as if from a high street bank cash facility.

The independent Bar for its part is obviously threatened by the increased specialisation by solicitors, by the extension of solicitors' rights of audience, by the Treasury's growing reluctance to finance the cost of public sector legal services, and by the possibility that crown prosecutors will gain rights of audience in the crown court and that a salaried public defender service will take over criminal defence work from private practitioners. In this scenario the only practitioners recognisably working like members of the Bar today would be a thin cadre of specialist advisers, acting as consultants advising the general body of the profession and very probably other professionals who would have the right of direct access.

The 'optimist', whilst recognising that the profession has problems generated by increased competition from within and without, will take a much rosier view. He will regard licensed conveyancers as unlikely to make much of a dent on the solicitors' share of the still lucrative conveyancing market. Banks, building societies and other financial institutions will either not be permitted to compete for conveyancing work or, if they are permitted, will prefer to stand back and leave the work to solicitors in private practice for fear of destroying the high street solicitors whose services they value for their clients. Solicitors may gain extended rights of audience but few will exercise them, and the bulk of the Bar will retain their existing share of the work. Advertising will have the effect of significantly increasing the volume of work coming into the profession. Lawyers will provide services for millions of ordinary citizens who at present fail to get the legal services they need even for acute legal problems. They will capture work back from the accountants. They will move even more broadly into international practice in the EEC and world-wide.

Which of these two very different sets of predictions is likely to be closer to the truth? The large City firms of solicitors are obviously totally unconcerned about the threat to the profit margins of provincial firms caused by the loss of the conveyancing monopoly. But even they are under pressure. The problem for them is not a shortage of work. There is masses of it pouring in. Financial conglomerations, takeover battles, mergers, privatisations, liquidations and all the other features of 'Big Bang' which under Thatcherism have turned London into the world's leading financial market have brought in an unprecedented volume of work that commands huge fees. The problem is rather the intensification of competition. Large companies and financial institutions increasingly like to have several firms of solicitors on their list. If one fails to produce an acceptable service they change to another. Life in the City firms used to be relatively leisurely. Today it is hectic. Much of the work is carried out under extreme pressure of time. Teams of highly specialised staff have to be ready to work through the night if need be, or risk losing the client. Specialisation is the norm — though even under the Law Society's new relaxed advertising rules it remains improper for a firm to claim specialist skills. The internationalisation of business has led many of the leading firms to open overseas branch offices, typically in New York, Hong Kong, Brussels, Paris, the Middle East, or Tokyo. Some firms have three or four overseas offices*.

City firms are in competition not only with each other but increasingly with the great Wall Street firms with their international practices, and even more with the large accounting firms which in the past few years have established themselves as all-round business advisers. For the moment the City firms are expanding rapidly; gross fee income is in tens or even hundreds of millions of pounds; partnerships are growing hugely; the future looks rosy. But competition is intense and the pace is hotting up.

In fact, competition with accountants threatens a much broader swathe of solicitors' firms than the large City firms which can in the end be expected to survive comfortably. Accountants have for years been scooping up work that might logically be thought to be lawyers' work — notably in tax advice but more generally in the commercial field. Now that accountants firms employ lawyers to provide legal advice to their clients the service they can offer is increasingly broader. According to *Accountancy Age* of 8 May 1986 the lawyers were losing, or had already lost, the competitive battle.

> They have lost the battle without so much as a shot having been fired. And with the lead which the accountancy profession now has there seems little chance of the lawyers clawing any of it back.

The greatest reason, the writer thought, was the attitude to competition.

> We will happily accept that the accountancy profession was hardly speedy in coming round to the idea of free and open competition among its members. But compared to the legal profession it has behaved like a cheetah pursued by a swarm of supersonic bees.

Certainly the profession has of late been devoting an immense amount of time and energy to internecine warfare. But the pressures on it are now fierce. There has, as the *New Law Journal* said editorially in November 1986, been much 'flounder-

---

* The overseas earnings of the legal profession rose from an estimated £19m. in 1975 to an estimated £88m. in 1985. The chief reason is thought to be the advent of Eurocurrency markets covering Eurobonds, syndicated credits, project finance and the financial activity they generate. In addition, there is still the traditional role of London as the place where maritime and commercial law disputes are resolved and for commercial arbitration. (See 'The Overseas Earnings of the Legal Profession', *New Law Journal*, 24 October 1986, p. 1018).

ing and confusion which has made the lawyer of the '80s the object of his own self-criticism and self-doubt as well as keeping him the continuing target of those sectors of the public for whom the law is always fair game'. Today's lawyer, the journal suggested, 'does not enjoy his forebears' inner confidence in his position and role in society.'

The remarkable changes of the past few years indicate that things are moving and that the profession is much more receptive to altering even rules, practices and arrangements which have been hallowed by time. But there must still be reason to doubt whether the two sides of the profession have adequately grasped the essential fact that they are being required to act genuinely in the public interest — not simply to mouth the slogan. There are still too many examples of a profession concerned first for its own well-being and only secondarily for the public. The professional codes of practice, for instance, still seem more concerned with control of competition than with protection of the client. A concern for raising standards of competence and performance is now manifest, but it has not yet gone very far. Changes have resulted more from buffeting by events than from forward planning. The squabbling between the two branches of the profession has been not merely unworthy of a great profession but too nakedly based on self-aggrandisement.

A profession that feels threatened is liable to behave defensively to protect its turf. There is much in the events of the past few years that displays this tendency. On the other hand, there are some signs of a profession that is beginning to come to terms with contemporary realities. Crystal-ball gazing at this precise moment is uncommonly difficult. But it would be surprising if the solicitors' drive for increased rights of audience did not succeed, if Treasury pressure on public sector legal fees let up, and if profit margins in domestic conveyancing were not further threatened by increased competition. It would be equally surprising if the independent Bar did not survive essentially in its present form, though possibly somewhat slimmed down. Almost certainly both sides of the profession will continue to be balkanised, with more and more specialist categories and groupings and vast divisions of income between those dependent largely on public sector earnings and those with private clients. Salaried public defenders to take over criminal defence work seem as unlikely as that the whole of legal aid will be handed to salaried poverty lawyers or, even less, to some form of national legal service. The computer and alternatives to law and the legal system notwithstanding, it is probable that the need for lawyers will continue to grow as society gets more and more complex. It seems safe to predict therefore that by the end of the century the lawyers will still be around — and in even greater numbers.

2

Access to Justice

The concept of justice has been central to civilisation from time immemorial. But it is only in this century that the concept of universal access to justice has been taken seriously. It was not until well into the twentieth century that Western democracies began to make genuine provision through legal aid schemes for citizens who lacked the means to secure the services of lawyers as legal advisers and advocates in legal proceedings.[1] Britain was foremost amongst them.

Today the problem of access to justice is seen to consist of a variety of issues — the extent of the use and non-use of lawyers, the scope of the legal aid scheme, the availability of other systems for financial assistance to those who need the services of lawyers, and alternative systems for providing legal services through non-lawyers and for avoiding the need for legal services through use of alternative techniques.

THE USE OF LAWYERS

If one poses at the outset the question who in England today goes to lawyers, the answer is surprising. A survey of nearly 8,000 households conducted for the Royal Commission on Legal Services revealed that over half of all people over the age of 18 (57 per cent) had used lawyers at some time during their lives[2] and that almost one-sixth (15 per cent) had been to a lawyer in the previous year, 1977.[3] The access to solicitors is naturally affected by the distribution of solicitors' offices. There are considerable variations from one part of the country to another. In 1983, the number of solicitors per 10,000 of population ranged from 8.7 in London and the South to 4.5 in the North with a national average figure for England and Wales of 6.6. Previous research has shown that the distribution of solicitors' offices is associated not, as one might expect, with the level of owner-occupier households but more with general levels of prosperity, as measured particularly with the level of retail sales in the area.* In the study done for the Royal Commission, the age group using lawyers the most was that between 25 and 34,[4] and men proved slightly more likely to use lawyers than women. Incidence of use was highest among those who lived in households whose head was in a professional job and lowest in households where the head was in semi-skilled or unskilled manual work. Taking all non-manual groups, use of lawyers during the year was 21 per cent, compared with 12 per cent for manual groups.[5] But when the question was changed to the use of lawyers over more than the one year in question the difference between socio-economic groups was much less marked — 67 per cent of those in non-manual households had used a lawyer at some time as compared with 51 per cent of manual households.[6] Moreover, when property matters were excluded, the class pattern was broadly similar. Most consultations were about property matters; such consultations were mostly made by those living in non-manual households; and, according to the Royal Commission, matters involving property accounted for most of the higher incidence of use among people of different types of households.[7]

From this evidence it appears that a high proportion of the population do in fact use lawyers, and, although there are differences between young and old, men and women, and social classes, they are to a considerable extent explained by differences in life cycle. Young people use lawyers more than the elderly because they are more likely to be buying and selling a home, or getting a divorce. So far as age differences are concerned, it does seem additionally that those now in the younger age group are probably using lawyers more than older people did themselves when they were under 35. As the Royal Commission stated, 'the incidence of use of lawyers' services has almost certainly risen over the past 20 to 25 years'.[8] The general increase in prosperity since the Second World War no doubt is also a factor in this growing use of lawyers.

---

* The figures were given in the 'Statistical Summary of the Solicitors' Profession', *Law Society's Gazette*, 26 September 1984, p. 2609, Table 8. See also Ken Foster, 'The Location of Solicitors', *Modern Law Review*, 1973, p. 1530.

Unfortunately, however, the fact that a large proportion of the adult population has used lawyers does not mean that all, or even most, of those who need lawyers for their legal problems get to see one. The research evidence shows that there is a substantial unmet need for legal services. The evidence is clearest in regard to personal injury cases, where a large-scale and sophisticated study was conducted over some years by the Oxford Socio-Legal Centre.[9] Personal injury cases are a peculiarly useful focus for a study of the unmet need for legal services because this is a field of work in which most firms of lawyers practise, legal aid is available, trade unions are active and there is likely to be widespread public knowledge of the fact that damages can be claimed for accidents which are someone else's fault. Also, both in road and in factory accidents, the person responsible for the injury would normally be covered by insurance and would therefore be worth suing.

The study was based on interviews with 12,217 households involving 35,085 individuals. They were asked about any injury or illness lasting two weeks or more in the previous twelve months or any accident in the previous four years. The final (weighted) sample produced 1,711 accidents, of which 455 were work accidents, 318 were road accidents and 938 were other accidents (in the home or at leisure or sport). The basic conclusion was stark. Damages were obtained by only 19 per cent of the victims of work accidents and 29 per cent of road accident victims. In the great majority — three-quarters of the one and two-thirds of the other — there was not even a claim for damages. So most of the victims of accidents in both these categories failed to make a claim. In fact, only one in three road accident victims actually consulted a solicitor, compared with about one in four work accident victims and one in fifty victims of other accidents.[10]

For all categories therefore the great majority of victims did not seek legal advice. The reasons are, of course, varied. For some, it is simple ignorance that they have the basis of a possible claim. For others who realise that there might be the basis of a claim, it is too much trouble, or the prospects of success are (rightly or wrongly) thought to be doubtful, or the likely delay or cost are thought to be too great, or they are intimidated by lawyers and their jargon and rituals. Some cannot face legal wrangles. Often there is worry about disturbing the existing relationship with an employer, or the accident victim thinks he has obtained sufficient financial compensation from his industrial injury benefit. For many

people the time following an accident is difficult enough without
voluntarily adding what are seen to be the extra strains of doing
something about getting compensation: ('I felt so poorly after the
accident . . . that I couldn't face doing anything'; 'I felt too ill to
be bothered. My mother died suddenly and what with the
accident and family troubles I didn't pursue the matter.')

The same phenomenon has been demonstrated in other
contexts. A study carried out by the present writer and
colleagues in three poor London boroughs showed that a failure
to take advice whether from a lawyer or anyone else in
situations where advice on a legal problem would seem to have
been indicated was very common. In certain types of case, such
as social security problems or consumer complaints, advice was
virtually never sought. In others, such as matrimonial problems
or matters involving landlord-tenant relations, it was sought
sometimes. But even in cases such as personal injury matters,
threatened eviction or making a will, there was a high
proportion of cases in which no advice at all was sought. The
only category of problem in which virtually everyone received
legal assistance was in the purchase of a house.[11]

There have been a variety of theories as to why people who
need legal advice fail to get it.[12] But none of them explain the
empirical facts that have been developed by research. These
show that, once property matters are excluded, the use of
lawyers is relatively uniform as between different social classes
and income categories, and, secondly, that the non-use of
lawyers is very high even amongst the relatively affluent. Also,
the use or non-use of lawyers is affected much more by the
nature of the problem than by individual personal characteristics. So, in house purchase virtually everyone uses a lawyer
regardless of social class or income; in consumer matters, on the
other hand, virtually no-one uses a lawyer regardless of social
class or income. In matrimonial matters or personal injury cases
many do and many do not use lawyers, but again personal
characteristics seem to have little or nothing to do with it. In
other words, there are areas of work in which the legal
profession functions effectively and on a considerable scale but,
even so, substantial numbers of those affected by the problem do
not seek the help of lawyers, whilst in other areas there is no
effective pattern of contacts between lawyers and potential
clients. Frequency of the problem arising is not the explanation.
Some very common legal problems have a high incidence of
lawyer use, while others do not. Conversely, some very
infrequent legal problems have a high frequency of lawyer use.

In house buying most people use lawyers probably because they imagine that they could not manage to do it themselves and they have not hitherto known of any alternative. In criminal cases the overwhelming majority of defendants who have a lawyer obtain one through legal aid; and they seem to get to hear of legal aid variously from a police officer, from a duty solicitor in the police station or the court, from a fellow prisoner, from official literature issued at the police station or the magistrates' court, from a court clerk or from the magistrates themselves. One way or another a large number of suspects seem to get to hear of legal aid — though a survey by the Lord Chancellor's Department[13] has shown that even in serious cases tried in the magistrates' courts a surprisingly high proportion of defendants do not have legal aid largely because they do not apply for it.* This suggests that although the networks of communication in the field of criminal legal aid are fairly extensive they are by no means perfect. Many people who probably need a lawyer in the magistrates' court still fall through the net.

In the field of personal injury cases, the Oxford study indicated that the crucial factor explaining the use or non-use of lawyers was the presence or absence of some form of lay person to suggest that the victim of the accident should take professional advice. More than two-thirds of those in the study who had consulted a solicitor said that the impetus to do so had come from another person. It seems 'that for most people who did attempt to claim damages, the informal discussions which took place before they sought formal legal advice were extremely important in providing or reinforcing the incentive to claim'.[14]

An analysis of these pre-legal discussions indicated that many who consulted a solicitor did so on the advice of people such as trade union officials, hospital personnel, local doctors, policemen, and advisers at advice bureaux, as well as relatives and friends. Work accident victims who were members of trade unions naturally consulted with their union and depended less than victims of other types of accidents on their social and

---

* The study in 60 magistrates' courts was of 3,000 cases, all of which involved either shoplifting, assault on the police, social security fraud, possession of cannabis or criminal damage. In the drugs cases the proportion who applied for legal aid was only 25 per cent, in shoplifting, 34 per cent; in criminal damage and social security fraud it was between 42 and 44 per cent. The highest proportion was in assault against the police where it was 76 per cent. Even there therefore nearly a quarter of all defendants did not apply for legal aid. (Lord Chancellor's Department, op. cit., Table 10).

family network. Road accident victims got assistance from the
police and from their own insurance companies, while victims of
other accidents depended more on the advice of doctors, relatives
and friends.[15] Often the person made the suggestion spontan-
eously without being asked by the injured person. Most accident
victims knew nothing of the legal aid and legal advice scheme.
Even amongst those who had made contact with a solicitor, only
a quarter actually knew of the legal advice scheme and fewer
than a half knew of the legal aid scheme.[16]

Going to a lawyer with a problem is not something that most
people do easily. Seeing a lawyer, like seeing a dentist, is felt to
be basically disagreeable because of the potential cost and a
variety of other discouraging factors. Even those who are able to
diagnose their problem as 'legal' and one in which a lawyer
might be able to help will probably need to be pushed or
encouraged to go. As the authors of the Oxford study said, 'The
"risk" of visiting a solicitor is only taken when the injured
person has been convinced, or reassured, from other sources
about the strength of his claim'. In the Oxford study no less than
84 per cent of cases brought to solicitors resulted in a claim
being made. It is improbable that victims of accidents could self-
diagnose the validity of their claims accurately in so high a
proportion of cases. The figure therefore suggests once again
that in the great majority of instances the victim of the accident
has previously taken advice from someone else before going to
the lawyer.

The implications of such findings for promoting improved
access to justice for citizens with legal problems are not wholly
comforting. Insofar as the citizen comes into contact with some
form of agency or official or other identifiable category of person
through his problem, information can perhaps be improved so as
to make it more likely that he will become aware of his legal
problems and of what he can do about them. So, in regard to
accidents, leaflets can be put in doctors' waiting rooms and in
hospitals, and medical staff and hospital almoners can be given
some minimal information about what constitutes the basis for a
claim which they could then pass on to their patients. Schemes
for free interviews for accident cases are in operation in many
local Law Society areas, and in June 1987 the Law Society
launched a nationwide Accident Legal Advice Service (ALAS)
based on a mention in the solicitors' regional directories, and
some 500,000 leaflets in public libraries, lay advice agencies,
community health councils, and DHSS offices plus a free postal
and telephone service. A 30-second commercial advertisement

was also to be run in major post offices.[17] But it seems that hospitals and doctors have been reluctant to display the leaflets.* Court clerks or officials in the local authority housing departments could be trained to find out whether users of the office have problems relating to, say, eviction or repairs. Social workers could be given better education in recognising legal problems and then helped to steer their clients toward appropriate advisers, whether lawyers or not.

But where the legal problem is one that simply occurs in the community and there is no-one who in the natural course of events would interview the person affected, it is not so easy to see how access to suitable advisers can be improved. For such situations, the best hope seems to be to train 'friends and relatives' — which is much the same as training the general public. Such a task poses huge problems. Advertising about the availability of legal advice and the essential elements of legal problems is costly and of doubtful efficacy. Even in the unlikely eventuality that the Government were willing to spend the vast amount of money needed to promote advertising that was both frequent and widely disseminated, it does not by any means follow that the ordinary citizen would pay much attention. Even those actually faced with the problem at the time may not be effectively reached by advertising — let alone those who at the time have no reason to be thinking of that category of problem. Advertising, leaflets, programmes of legal education for school children, lectures to community or youth organisations and similar activities no doubt all help to raise the level of consciousness about legal problems somewhat and to promote more use of the legal system by those with legal problems. But there is no likelihood that, either singly or in aggregate, they make a dramatic difference. It seems certain that whatever is done to promote knowledge about legal problems much ignorance will continue.

It should, of course, also be recognised that even those who are fully aware of the existence of a legal problem and of what can

---

* Research on the operation of the first of such schemes in Manchester showed that 42 per cent of those using the scheme had not thought about the possibility of trying to get compensation before they saw a leaflet or poster advertising the scheme. Also nearly two-thirds of accident victims using the scheme had never consulted a solicitor before. No less than 80 per cent of free interviews granted under the scheme resulted in some action being taken by solicitors to obtain compensation, but more co-operation was needed from hospitals and doctors. (Hazel Genn, *Meeting Legal Needs?*, SSRC Centre for Socio-Legal Studies, Oxford, 1982.)

be done about it may in the end choose not to bother. It is the right of the citizen to sit on his hands and do nothing rather than to enforce his rights. (Often that will in fact be the socially most responsible and sensible course.) But the hope is that as much as possible will be done to make the system accessible to the citizen, so that he can decide for himself whether he wants to try to find assistance for his problem.

Much ingenuity and effort have been expended in recent years to develop new techniques for addressing the problem of unmet need. The 1985-86 Report of the Lord Chancellor's Legal Aid Advisory Committee, for instance, devoted several pages[18] to the problem of legal services for those in rural areas, and for those who were unable to get to see a solicitor because of old age or physical disability. The report proposed that in such cases legal advice should be capable of being given by post or telephone or by home visits, for which travel costs would be reimbursed. A variety of methods including village link schemes, peripatetic advisers and mobile bureaux should all be used. New technology, the Committee suggested, could play a major part in providing legal services to outlying areas. The microfiche briefcase developed by the Citizens' Advice Bureaux gave instant access to a huge volume of information; the cordless telephone allowed for immediate follow-up action to be taken as it would be in an office. Advice services could be advertised on local radio and television. More phone-in programmes for giving advice could be developed. Voluntary organisations and even the general public could be given access to new systems for providing information on micro-computers.

> The combination of user friendly new technology, built up to reflect local needs, and the time sharing of local premises by different organisations, can provide an infinitely variable arrangement which could be adapted to local needs.[19]

COSTS

One critical factor in the availability of legal services is that they should be priced at a level that is within the reach of the citizen. The business community on the whole can probably afford its legal services, though it has to be said that the legal profession takes considerable advantage of this. The fees currently charged by, say, City firms of solicitors and leading barristers are so astronomically high that one is inclined to wonder whether even in a free market there is not some self-denying limit or external control on what professional people should feel able to charge. A person who is buying or selling a house knows that the lawyers will charge a substantial fee, which is absorbed, willingly or not, as one of the costs of the entire transaction. In litigation, a person advised that he has a good claim may be prepared, even if he does not have much money, to go ahead at his own expense, knowing that under the English so-called 'indemnity rule' of costs the bulk of his costs will be paid by the loser. If one has property to dispose of, the costs of a will are usually relatively low. Advice on tax affairs may equally save the client money.

But in most situations and for most people, going to a solicitor is felt to be so expensive that it does not quite seem worthwhile. The rates charged by lawyers range from, say, £25 to £30 an hour at the bottom of the range to as much as £200 or even more at the top. A leading Queen's Counsel can command a fee of £500 for an hour's conference. It is therefore not difficult to run up a bill of hundreds or even thousands of pounds and in a long litigated case costs can be in the tens and hundreds of thousands. (Press reports of costs at the end of a highly publicised trial are almost invariably grossly exaggerated, but even if they are reduced by a factor of two they still often represent astronomic figures. The press said that Mr Jeffrey Archer's libel action in July 1987 cost three quarters of a million pounds. The true figure, the *Law Magazine* suggested on 7 August 1987, was 'only' £300,000.) At such prices one might forgo the advantage of having the service of the lawyers.

For those who cannot afford to pay the costs there are various systems of support which may help. Where there is insurance or the backing of a trade union or other organisation able to take on the costs of the case, costs do not present a problem. In litigation, the trade union normally agrees to pay not only the costs of the client but, if he loses, also the costs of the winner. The client will therefore usually get free legal services — paid for out of members' weekly dues. Legal services provided by trade unions represent a very significant resource, though they are usually available only for matters arising out of the course of employment — mainly personal injuries.

So far as legal costs and damages insurance is concerned, this has for decades been a familiar part of policies of insurance for motorists and householders, but in that context the legal services covered are limited to a narrow range of potential hazards (falling chimney pots, colliding motor cars and the like). In recent years, however, insurance companies have increasingly tried to market policies covering a wide range of general risks in regard to legal problems arising for householders, consumers, employees, pedestrians for the uninsured costs of motoring and in some cases even as defendants in criminal proceedings. Several companies now offer this form of cover. The Law Societies of England and Wales and Scotland approved one such scheme in 1982 but many others are in existence. A useful ancillary service in many cases is the provision of a 24-hour telephone advisory service. Premiums vary according to the cover offered; the typical rate is at present around £70 for a policy that covers all the members of the family.* Some matters are excluded, such as matrimonial disputes, defamation, income tax or business problems. Most policies do not cover criminal cases and all have a limit on the amount of cover. The client has to be able to show that he has a reasonable chance of success. But once the insurers have approved, the client is normally entitled to use his own lawyers.

In Germany where such policies have been known for a long time, premium income for legal costs insurance is over £700 million a year. In the United Kingdom, where general legal expenses insurance only started in the 1970s, it is said to be around £25 million. But the insurance companies believe that there is great scope for expansion through policies sold both to individuals and to groups. It is not only the insurance companies and lawyers who will benefit. The ordinary citizen who previously would not have been able to afford competent assistance with his legal problem and who is not eligible for legal aid can now get the help he needs. To have legal aid, at least if one does not have to make any contribution, is usually sufficient protection. One has a wide choice of lawyers of all levels of seniority, the quality of work done should be reasonable, and win or lose there is nothing to pay. But anyone who is earning more than the national average is likely to be outside the legal aid scheme unless he has large numbers of dependants, and those in regular employment with wages that are around the average or less may have to pay a considerable contribution towards their costs. In the absence of contingent fee arrangements, a prepaid insurance scheme may at present be

---

* A variant announced by one company in March 1987 was for the premium (of £3.50 per client) to be paid by the solicitor. The client would get free membership of 'Lawclub' which would give him protection against legal fees, disbursements and costs of his opponent of up to £50,000 per case. (See *Solicitors' Journal*, 27 March 1987, p. 3981 and, generally, *New Law Journal*, 27 March 1987, p. 3981.)

the best available answer to the problem of the costs of legal services for the ordinary working population.

In the United States and several Canadian provinces some forms of litigation can be financed through contingent fee arrangements, under which the client agrees to pay the lawyer a percentage of the damages if he wins, but, if he loses, he pays nothing. Such arrangements are not permitted in either England or Scotland, though in Scotland a client is allowed to agree with his lawyer to pay a fixed fee if he wins but nothing if he loses. (He cannot, however, agree to pay a percentage of any recovery.) The objection to the contingent fees arrangement is that it gives the lawyer a financial stake in the outcome of the case which may tempt him into unethical conduct or to agree to a settlement of a case which ought to be contested so that he is certain of getting a fee. It can lead to overreaching when clients are asked to agree to an extortionate level of remuneration for the lawyer — though this can be controlled by rules. It may also have the disadvantage of inflating the overall level of damages, if courts give the plaintiff extra in order to pay his lawyers. (The danger of this is obviously greater in the United States where civil cases are still decided by juries than in England where damages are assessed by the judges.)

Until recently there has been virtually unanimous disapproval in England of contingent fee arrangements as practised in the United States.* The only exception has been for a scheme devised by JUSTICE (the British Section of the International Commission of Human Rights), under which successful plaintiffs would agree to pay a proportion of their damages into a Contingency Legal Aid Fund (CLAF). The fund would then meet the costs of the loser. The scheme would avoid the danger of the lawyer having a stake in the outcome of the case since he would be paid in any event. The scheme now has the support of the Law Society's Contentious Business Committee in a paper, 'Improving Access to Civil Justice', published in July 1987.

The Committee first rejected the 'straight' contingent fee system on the ground that it was not possible to overcome the ethical and consumer protection problems. Also, contingent fee systems seemed to bring out the worst in ambulance-chasing lawyers — as in Bhopal after the leak of poisonous gas in 1985 with American lawyers swarming round the victims of the

---

* In July 1987, however, the Young Solicitors' group suggested that contingent fees might be a valuable way of financing litigation where legal aid was not available. (See *Solicitors' Journal*, 17 July 1987, p. 956.)

disaster like bees round a honey pot. But having concluded that
contingent fees were not desirable, it went on to urge the merits
of the JUSTICE CLAF scheme which has been in operation in
Hong Kong since 1 October 1984. The main practical problem is
how to raise the money to finance the scheme in the early
stages. In Hong Kong the scheme (known as the Supplementary
Legal Aid Scheme) had received a loan from the Government of
$1 million. One way round the difficulty of building up the funds
relatively quickly might be to use the CLAF scheme for claims
not at present covered by legal aid — for instance, those brought
in industrial tribunals for compensation for unfair dismissal, or
race or sex discrimination (though there are very few of these).
In 1984, 32 per cent of all applicants before industrial tribunals
were unrepresented. CLAF might be used to reduce their
numbers. It could also play a role in claims under the Criminal
Injuries Compensation Scheme or before the Motor Insurers
Bureau.

The trouble with CLAF is that, if it were voluntary, it must be
doubtful whether enough plaintiffs would in fact agree to pay
into the fund. Most plaintiffs succeed in getting some damages
and then costs, and it is not obvious why anyone who is advised
that he has a good chance of success should insure himself
against the somewhat remote possibility of having to pay costs
by agreeing to join the CLAF scheme. This was in essence
conceded in the Law Society's paper when it admitted that the
levy on successful applicants in the industrial relations tribunal
cases might have to be as high as 30 per cent of the resulting
award. The authors recognised that this was 'sufficiently high to
be unattractive to many would-be applicants but it might be
worth offering as an option when the only alternative might be
not to pursue the case'. The trouble then, however, would be that
it would apply only to a minority of cases and there could never
be enough money in the fund to make it self-financing. The only
solution would be to make the contribution compulsory — which
would probably be unacceptable.

The Contentious Business Committee also investigated the
establishment of a form of mutual fund Fixed Costs Scheme
under which solicitors would pay a premium to insurers and any
individual client with a claim would pay a fixed sum to cover the
costs in the event of the case being lost. Like CLAF, this would
guarantee the lawyers their fees but it would be a fixed sum
payable in advance rather than a percentage payable after the
case was over. The premium and the fixed fee paid by the client
could be relatively low because in most cases the plaintiff would

win — in which case his costs would be borne by the loser. The amount could be varied depending on the actuarial experience with each category of litigation. On initial instructions the amount payable might be in the range of £25 to £75, which would cover costs incurred up to the issue of proceedings. Thereafter a larger sum, say in the £350-£550 range, would be payable as a lump sum. That would cover all costs payable, win or lose. The scheme, which would be entirely voluntary, could be adapted for use for a variety of categories of litigation. This seems a more attractive option than CLAF since it could be used in cases which do not generate damages. Also the overall cost to the litigant would be known from the outset, whereas under CLAF only a percentage figure would be known.

The Law Society's paper also suggested that the scheme could be used to deal with a long acknowledged gap in the legal aid scheme by permitting the financing of cases brought by groups of persons. At present these are excluded from legal aid because aggregation of the means of the members puts them outside the means test limits. Since under the scheme there would be no means test this problem would not arise, though the group case might be affected by the different principle that there would probably be an upper limit on the total cost of cases.

In the meantime the citizen does have other existing possibilities to help with the costs of legal services. If the client requires preliminary advice there is the admirable Fixed Fee scheme run for many years by the Law Society, under which solicitors give half an hour's diagnostic advice for £5 regardless of the client's means. Not all solicitors offer the service — and some of those who do are perhaps not keen that it should be too widely known since it is certainly run at a loss. But the Fixed Fee scheme is a way of bridging the inevitable gap between the client's felt need to see a solicitor and his reluctance because of unease at the likely cost. The profession runs the scheme partly as a social service and partly as a loss leader to get the client across the invisible barrier at the door of the lawyer's office. (The Scottish Law Society, which runs the same scheme, announced in July 1987 that in future there would be no charge at all for the first diagnostic interview and that solicitors would be allowed to advertise the fact.)

THE LEGAL AID SCHEME

For those of modest means a major contribution is, of course, made by the legal aid scheme. For decades the state has spent millions of pounds to provide access to justice for those who cannot afford the services of lawyers. (The overall cost in 1986 was £419.8 million gross or £341.7 million net.)[20] The English scheme has been in the forefront of the modern international movement to improve access to justice. It consists of three main parts: criminal legal aid, civil legal aid and legal advice and assistance.* The criminal legal aid scheme operates in both crown courts and magistrates' courts. Some half a million persons a year currently take advantage of the scheme. In the crown court virtually everyone who applies gets legal aid, and almost everyone does apply. The proportion of defendants with legal aid is therefore astonishingly high — around 98 per cent. It can be said that in the crown court there is effectively little, if any, unmet need for legal services, at least to the extent that lawyers are supplied for defendants regardless of whether they are pleading guilty or not guilty. Moreover, since virtually all serious criminal cases are handled under legal aid it follows that even the most senior members of the criminal Bar spend most of their time on legal aid work. The English legal aid scheme is not like that of many other countries around the world where legal aid is provided mainly by young and inexperienced lawyers.

The position in the magistrates' courts inevitably is different since they handle large numbers of very minor cases where legal aid would not be appropriate. Nevertheless the number of cases where legal aid is granted is now very high. On the other hand, there are surprisingly many instances where defendants in even relatively serious cases tried in the magistrates' courts do not apply for legal aid. The refusal rate by magistrates is low in all categories save that of summary offences.† One unmet need in magistrates' court cases is in the differential policy applied by different courts. It is clearly unsatisfactory that one's chances of getting legal aid should depend on the court at which one happens to be charged.

Legal aid is available for civil cases in any court, save for a few categories such as libel actions and election petitions. The

---

* There is also a sub-scheme known as 'Assistance by way of representation' (ABWOR) which enables a solicitor to represent his client in certain proceedings in courts or tribunals; and two statutory duty solicitor schemes — one introduced in 1983 to provide immediate assistance for unrepresented defendants in magistrates' courts and the other introduced in 1986 to provide advice for people detained in police stations.

† For indictable offences (279,700 applications), the rate in 1985 was 9 per cent, for juvenile court cases (45,200 applications) 6 per cent, whilst for summary offences (61,600 applications), it was 35 per cent. For committal proceedings (75,000 applications), it was 1 per cent.

applicant must show that he has reasonable grounds for taking or defending the proceedings and that overall it is reasonable for him to do so. He must also qualify on the means test which determines whether he is eligible and if so, whether he pays a contribution. (In 1985/6, 80 per cent had a nil contribution, and 5 per cent had to pay under £100; only 3 per cent were subject to a contribution of more than £500.) As many as one-fifth of all those offered legal aid decline the offer, usually because they are unwilling to pay the contribution required of them. By far the largest single category of cases supported from legal aid is matrimonial, with personal injury cases second, far behind (about half of all personal injury cases are legally aided), and after that a great variety of other types of cases.

The legal advice and assistance ('Green Form') scheme provides for oral and written advice, assistance with vetting or drafting of documents, negotiations, correspondence or any other help short of representation. This is currently utilised by close to a million people a year. In 1985 the payments to solicitors under the scheme amounted to £65 million as against receipts in the form of contributions from clients of only £2.9 million. Family matters (and in particular divorce and other matrimonial disputes) account for over two-fifths of all matters dealt with under this scheme; crime represents a further quarter.

In areas where they exist, another major source of help for legal problems is the law centre, an office funded by local and/or central government in which salaried lawyers provide services that are free to the client. Law centres, which have existed since 1970, attract young lawyers, often of a radical or unconventional cast of mind; their style tends to be less formal than that usual in private practice — 'lawyers in jeans'. They have been set up mainly in inner city areas of high deprivation. There are, however, only some fifty law centres — providing services that are complementary to, rather than in competition with, those provided by private practitioners. Much of the work of law centres is the one-to-one kind traditional between lawyers and clients but many law centres also devote considerable resources to work for groups. This frequently results in more activist lawyering than is customary in private practice and sometimes in activities that are politically controversial.

Originally, the Law Society and solicitors generally were apprehensive that law centres would provide unfair competition to local practitioners, especially those in the poorest areas where law centres would be set up. But under a concordat with the Law Society it was agreed in 1977 that law centres would refer on to private practitioners most ordinary legal aid work, and on that basis the two sectors have arrived at a harmonious working relationship.[21]

Law centres now enjoy a high degree of support from the legal profession,[22] the Citizens Advice Bureau movement, the Lord Chancellor's Legal Aid Advisory Committee[23] and from politicians of all parties. The problem they have faced recently, however, is the uncertainty of funding.[24] Local authority resources have been declining through a combination of rate capping, abolition of the Greater London Council and the metropolitan councils, and the general economic climate. The Royal Commission on Legal Services and the Lord Chancellor's Legal Aid Advisory Committee both agreed that law centres should be funded out of the public purse of central rather than local government. The former Lord Chancellor, Lord Hailsham, resisted this proposal, however, and refused to agree that his Department should take over and finance this new dimension in legal services. As a result, in 1986-87 the outlook for law centres became uncertain. But it seemed inconceivable that the law centre movement would in the end be allowed to founder for lack of the £2-3 million needed to keep it afloat. By comparison with the several hundred million being spent on the legal aid scheme, this is plainly a trivial amount.

HELP FROM NON-LAWYERS

Help for legal problems does not necessarily have to come from lawyers, however. The most important source of help provided by non-lawyers is the Citizens' Advice Bureaux (CABx), which exist up and down the country and which provide free advice on a vast array of problems. There are currently some 1,000 Bureaux employing about 2,500 paid and 22,500 unpaid voluntary workers. The number of matters dealt with in 1986/87 was no less than 6.7 million, the largest category being (significantly) social security problems (19 per cent). An estimated one third to one half have a legal component, which means that CABx with hardly a lawyer employee to their name are dealing with upwards of two million legal problems a year.

About half of all CABx use voluntary weekly rotas of local solicitors to supplement, free of charge, the advice given by their own staff. If the matter demands further assistance they are permitted to handle the clients from their office — providing that the scheme has the blessing of the Law Society and provided, of course, that the client wants it. But the overwhelming majority of problems that come to the CABx are handled by their own workers, most of whom have only the somewhat modest amount of training provided by the movement itself. Considering this, the overall level is remarkably high and they are generally regarded as an invaluable and major resource in the handling of legal problems. The Royal Commission on Legal Services recommended in 1979 that the CAB movement be the basis of the primary level of advice throughout the country. The central government grant to the movement in 1985-86 was a mere £7.1 million, and it has been estimated that local authorities provided about £16 million in direct financial support to bureaux.

In addition to CABx, there are probably 600 or more small advice centres run by a variety of organisations, some specialist (on debt problems, drugs, consumer affairs, immigration matters, housing, abortion etc.), some generalist. The citizens' need for advice seems to be rising exponentially. Green Form work more than doubled between 1979 and 1984. The number of Citizens' Advice Bureaux increased by over half in the decade from 1975 and the number of queries dealt with by Citizens' Advice Bureaux grew in that same period from under 3 million in 1975/76 to over 6 million in 1985/86. The reasons for this trend no doubt include a greater awareness of rights leading people to seek to challenge decisions which might earlier have been reluctantly accepted; the growing complexity of government legislation; the apparent increase in marital breakdown; an increase in the numbers tried for criminal offences, and the huge increase in the numbers of unemployed.

Many legal problems are dealt with not through the ordinary legal system but in Industrial Tribunals, Social Security Appeal Tribunals (which deal with National Insurance, Industrial Injuries, Supplementary Benefit and Family Income Supplement), Immigration Adjudicators and Immigration Appeal Tribunals and the like, which between them deal with tens of thousands of cases annually. With a few exceptions — the Lands Tribunal, the Employment Appeal Tribunal and the Mental Health Review Tribunal — legal aid is not available in tribunals. In the 1960s it was suggested that the procedure in tribunals was sufficiently simple for individuals to be able adequately to represent themselves. But during the past ten years it has been almost universally agreed that this is not so. The statistics show that those with a representative do significantly better than those without. Even a friend or relative is a more effective representative than a lay person appearing on his own. At present representation in tribunals is handled mainly by trade union officials, lawyers paid for by individual clients, advisory agencies, including in particular some Citizens' Advice Bureaux, and the broad category of 'friends and relatives'.

The Lord Chancellor's Legal Aid Advisory Committee, the Royal Commission on Legal Services and the Government's Legal Aid Efficiency Scrutiny Team all agreed that some form of state-aided representation in tribunals should be available for appropriate cases. The Royal Commission said that legal aid should be available for some cases, but its chief recommendation was that lay agencies such as Citizens' Advice Bureaux should be given public funds to improve their service to clients in tribunals, including representation. The Lord Chancellor's Advisory Committee in its 1982-83 report urged that legal aid should be extended to all statutory tribunals. The Legal Aid Efficiency Scrutiny Team argued in its 1986 report that a trained lay advocate would normally be perfectly competent to handle representation in tribunals and that lawyers would only rarely be necessary. State funds should be made available to contracting bodies able to provide the service needed. In most cases Citizens' Advice Bureaux would probably get the contract, but in some places other advice agencies or consortia of local solicitors might also make a bid.

The Government gave a dusty answer to these proposals. In its White Paper on Legal Aid published in March 1987 it would only go so far as to state that extensions through the legal aid scheme for representation in tribunals would be made 'where it is shown to be necessary and resources allow'. It was 'not clear that publicly funded representation is necessary for all tribunal proceedings'. A different approach, it suggested, would be to simplify tribunal procedure to make legal representation unnecessary. (This is almost certainly a vain hope.) The White Paper referred to the fact that the Lord Chancellor's Department had commissioned research into the effectiveness of representation at tribunals. 'Against this background the Government [did] not intend that there should be any general extension of publicly funded tribunal representation.'

The Government's Efficiency Scrutiny Team* also proposed a radical restructuring of the arrangements for legal advice

---

* The four members were respectively from the Treasury, the Lord Chancellor's Department, the Church Commissioners and the Prime Minister's Efficiency Unit.

generally.[25] It pointed to a lack of co-ordination in the existing arrangements. Some areas had a plethora of different agencies, whilst others had none. There was considerable overlap between the services provided by Citizens' Advice Bureaux and private practitioners and no-one was responsible for taking decisions as to the most effective deployment of the available resources. It recommended that legal advice which simply enabled the client to arrange his own affairs (on wills, conveyancing and probate) should no longer be available from public funds. It should similarly be unavailable for problems on which one could not get legal aid proper. This would eliminate it from defamation cases and minor traffic offences — though the report went much further by also excluding all non-imprisonable offences. Legal advice for other criminal cases should, however, continue to be available from private practitioners, though solicitors should in future receive reimbursement for only one hour's advice (as compared with the present approximate two hours' worth) before having to get authority to proceed, and such approval would have to be obtained from the magistrates' court and not from the legal aid authorities.

But the chief proposal was that the first port of call for the citizen should normally in future not be a solicitor but rather an advice agency, and in particular a Citizens' Advice Bureau. The Green Form scheme would be abolished. The Citizens' Advice Bureaux would take over the giving of first-line legal advice — though it was admitted that there would have to be a significant number of lawyers employed by the Citizens' Advice Bureaux to make this possible. Legal aid Area Directors should be made responsible for getting the best service possible within nationally laid down criteria as to access, competence of advisers, emergency advice arrangements and tribunal representation and within a budget allocated by the central administration, which should be taken away from the Law Society and run instead by a new Legal Services Board (with Area Officers) operationally independent of both Government and the profession but acting within guidelines agreed by the Government. These changes, the report suggested, would enable a significantly better service to be provided at a lower cost, which would permit substantial expansion for tribunal representation within existing resources.

This analysis and radical set of proposals was strongly challenged by the Law Society which said it would duplicate resources already developed by private practice; the service would be second-class because funding would be inadequate; it

would inhibit choice; and would create obstacles to the efficient
conduct of cases. Also, by taking away 'Green Form' work from
solicitors it might cause some practices to become uneconomic,
with the consequences that legal services would be reduced
where they were most needed.

According to the Law Society's cogently argued memorandum,
far from costing less, as the Scrutiny report envisaged, the new
proposals would cost more. But the danger was that the
Treasury would not respond to the needs created by the volume
of work. Instead of being demand-led, responsive as previously
to the numbers of clients requiring help, the new service would
be likely to be subject to a Treasury fixed ceiling, with the result
that the service provided would become less and less adequate
which would in turn result in longer and longer queues for it.
Estimates of the numbers of extra staff needed in Citizens'
Advice Bureaux were far too low. Clients' choice would be
restricted to the local advice agency instead of their being able
to select from amongst local solicitors' firms. At present, for
instance, a Greek could choose a firm that had a solicitor who
spoke his language; an Asian could go to an Asian solicitor. But,
according to the report's proposals, the advice agencies would
have a monopoly over giving legal advice under the state
scheme. In small towns there would be only one agency. How,
then, could both sides get assistance? Travel time would be
significantly increased. If it were expected that clients needing a
solicitor would first have to attend a Citizens' Advice Bureau,
clients in rural areas, in particular, would be put to enormous
inconvenience.

The Law Society also made the point that the Efficiency
Scrutiny Team's proposals would for the first time abrogate the
principle that a legally aided client should enjoy the same
service as a private client. The private client would be able to go
to the solicitor. The legally aided client would have to go to the
advice agency which would not have the right to issue legal
proceedings and would therefore be weakened in negotiating on
behalf of the client. Public legal services would be stamped
'second-class' not only by their inbuilt delay but also by the
disruption of negotiation and preparation. If, for instance, advice
bureaux had to handle the preliminary stages of personal injury
cases for clients entitled to legal aid they would inherit a huge
mass of work, and to little purpose. This work at present cost the
Exchequer nothing since the costs were paid by insurance
companies. Pre-litigation negotiations required knowledge of the
current levels of damages, which advice agencies would not

have. There was complaint that even solicitors were not as expert as they should be in personal injury litigation. This would be greatly compounded if the work was done by advice agencies instead. Extra costs would be incurred by the process of referral to solicitors who would be prevented from providing an all-round service to the client. The Efficiency Scrutiny Team's proposals would lead to a worse service to the public without achieving the Government's need for cost effectiveness.

After making all due allowance for the fact that the Law Society was seeking to retain many millions of pounds worth of work for solicitors, it clearly had very much the better of the argument. Its contentions were enormously strengthened when the Citizens' Advice Bureaux also basically rejected the Scrutiny proposals. The written response to the Scrutiny report from the National Association of Citizens' Advice Bureaux in September 1986 noted with suspicion that the real motive behind the proposal to transfer legal advice from solicitors to lay advice agencies was to save public money. 'The concern that goes with that is that access to legal services for our poor clients would be diminished ... and that the service would find itself forced to ration by queues.' Also how could the already hard-pressed CAB service cope with the mass of work that it would then have to handle? Relations with legal aid practitioners would be threatened. It was true that most legal aid work was concentrated in the hands of relatively few firms of solicitors. (The latest Legal Aid Annual Report showed that 831 solicitors firms, 7.5 per cent of the total, received 40.75 per cent of all payments under the Green Form and Advice and Assistance Scheme.) It was also true that the advice agencies already did far more legal advice work in some areas than solicitors. (Thus the CAB service dealt with over one million enquiries per year on social security compared with only 17,000 dealt with by solicitors under the Green Form scheme.) Nevertheless, NACAB said, it was concerned that the Scrutiny proposals were 'based on a fundamental premise that advice agencies are sufficiently well established and well distributed to assume this extra responsibility'. Unfortunately this was not so. The worry was that a major new responsibility grafted on to a service not yet properly developed could lead to a cut in legal services available to the poor.

At the CABx AGM on 23 September 1986 the proposals on legal advice were declared to be 'unacceptable' and NACAB was instructed to make this view the basis of its response to the Scrutiny.

The Scrutiny proposals were extensively criticised from many other quarters. Even the Legal Action Group (the important pressure group for improving legal services for the poor) which for years has been highly critical of the legal profession's performance in the field of legal aid and has repeatedly called for more lay involvement in the provision of legal services, was doubtful about the proposals.[26]

The Lord Chancellor's Legal Aid Advisory Committee gave the Scrutiny report a mixed reaction.[27] It welcomed its fresh approach and in particular its suggestion that there was a need for a co-ordinated approach to the provision of legal advice and tribunal representation making use of private practitioners and specialist and lay advisers, but it was concerned that abolition of the Green Form scheme might create gaps in the geographical provision of legal services and reduction in their quality and scope. It was against the idea that Area Directors would take appeals against refusals of legal aid, which it thought should be done by an independent person or body not an official. It was strongly against the restriction of legal advice in criminal cases to one hour's worth of work. The suggestion that advice could no longer be given in relation to non-imprisonable offences was 'arbitrary and misguided'. It saw no merit in the notion that opposing parties should be allowed to object to the grant of legal aid (even though this was now part of the Scottish scheme). It opposed the recommendation that contributions in civil cases should continue throughout the duration of the case, which it thought would deter litigants from accepting legal aid without any compensating advantages. The Committee expressed alarm at the proposal that in criminal cases contributions should be assessed at the end of a case and that means testing at the beginning of cases should be abolished. It supported the idea of a Legal Services Board, but hoped that the features of the comparable Scottish Board which appeared to allow directions from the Secretary of State would not be repeated for the Board for England and Wales. The Board should be independent of ministerial control.

The inquiry by the Efficiency Scrutiny Team was a *tour de force* carried out in a mere three months (from February to June 1986) by four officials, only one of whom had previously had any involvement in the legal aid scheme. It was hardly surprising that some of its proposals simply did not stand up to close examination. In particular, it cannot be pretended that implementation of the proposal to prevent clients from going to solicitors for legal advice will result in an improvement of the service provided to the public. The standard of work done by solicitors and their employees is, of course, variable, but the same could be said of advice agencies a high proportion of whose workers are part-time and semi-trained. If the burden of work undertaken by advice agencies were to be increased, the problem of quality of work would be correspondingly greater — especially if the work became more technical and complex. The present arrangements where the work of advice agencies, local solicitors and law centres to some extent overlap may be somewhat muddled, but it is difficult to see that the system proposed by the Efficiency Scrutiny Team would be an improvement in any terms other than the drawing of neat lines and the saving of money. The user of the services is likely to be considerably worse off.

The Government published its response to the Scrutiny Report in a White Paper at the end of March 1987 ('Legal Aid in England and Wales: a New Framework'). It stated that the considerable numbers receiving legal aid and legal advice and assistance clearly illustrated the success of the scheme in meeting its basic objective of ensuring that persons of small or moderate means received access to proper advice and to justice. The reason for the Scrutiny was that the Government was 'determined to ensure that legal aid [was] provided efficiently and effectively and that it [gave] the best possible value for the money spent'. The Government had decided that a new framework was needed for the management and operation of the scheme, which when fully carried into effect would save £10 million — not a large sum in the context of overall costs of the legal aid scheme and hardly worth all the upset caused by the Scrutiny report.

In regard to administration, the principal change would be the transfer of the running of the scheme from the Law Society to a Legal Aid Board which would act 'under the guidance of the Lord Chancellor'. (A similar Board has been established for Scotland under the Legal Aid (Scotland) Act 1986, and began operations in April 1987.) The Lord Chancellor would appoint the Chairman and members, who would be non-executive. He would also 'concur' in the appointment of certain key staff in senior positions. The Board would consist of both lawyers and non-lawyers. (In Scotland the Board consists of three practising solicitors, two senior barristers and a number of non-lawyers, including three accountants one of whom is the chairman. The numbers of accountants is plainly significant.) It may be deduced that the Government envisaged the Board being very

much under the control of the Lord Chancellor. How independent it might be allowed to be is highly questionable.* The
notion of its acting 'under the guidance' of the Lord Chancellor
is not encouraging — especially since there is no mention of an
intention that the Board should be independent. (In the Scottish
system the Board has no veto over regulations, though it has to
be consulted regarding them in draft.)

Detailed administration would be through the existing
network of Area Offices and the present staff. Initially the new
Board would simply take over the functions of the Law Society
in running the scheme. But gradually it would be given other
tasks so as to permit 'a more coherent approach to be adopted
towards the scheme than has hitherto been possible'. Thus it
might take over assessment of means from the Department of
Health and Social Security, decisions on the grant of criminal
legal aid (at present handled by magistrates' courts), and at
least some of the determination of lawyers' bills now carried out
for criminal cases by the courts. (In Scotland the Board does the
assessment of means, and has also taken over the grant and
refusal of legal aid in the lower criminal courts.)

In an ominous phrase the White Paper warned that the
Government would require the Board 'to set appropriate targets
for handling its business', and that these would then be
'carefully monitored'. The aim was to balance the interests of the
taxpayer and those of the applicant for legal aid. The position of
the Lord Chancellor's Advisory Committee, which over the years
through its annual reports has played a crucial role in analysing
the 'state of the art' and pointing directions for the future, would
be reviewed. No decision had yet been taken as to whether it
would continue its role or function after the establishment of the
Board.

The White Paper rejected the Scrutiny Team's main proposals
that the Green Form scheme should simply be abolished and
that virtually the whole of legal advice and assistance should be
transferred from solicitors to Citizens' Advice Bureaux. This
recommendation, the White Paper admitted, had 'provoked
considerable criticism'. It had been argued that the Scrutiny
proposals were unworkable because of the limited number of

---

* A consortium of organisations including the Law Society, the Bar, the TUC,
the National Consumer Council, the Advice Services Alliance and the Law
Centres Federation, wrote to the new Lord Chancellor, Lord Havers, in July
1987 urging that the Board should be 'independent of both the legal profession
and the government', and expressing the view that the Advisory Committee
should be retained.

advice agencies, the enormous burden of taking on the extra
work done by solicitors, the difficulty of defining what should be
done by solicitors and what by advice agencies, and possible
conflicts of interest if both sides were represented by the one
agency. The Government acknowledged that there was 'force in
some of these objections'. Nevertheless the Green Form scheme
could be improved 'to provide better service at lower cost'. The
Government was attracted to the principle of using the skills of
advice agencies 'especially to deal with those areas of work in
which their special experience is likely to be greater than that of
many solicitors in private practice'. It therefore intended to take
powers to enable the new Board 'to make alternative arrangements for the provision of advice and assistance for particular
categories of work where this would be a more efficient way of
providing the service'.

The Board would also be asked to consider the most cost-
effective way of providing advice and assistance, including
whether better use might be made of advice agencies. Once it
had made appropriate contractual arrangements for the provision of advice by other agencies, for instance on welfare benefits,
these would be excluded from the Green Form scheme. The
detailed arrangements might vary from area to area; they could
possibly be based on tenders for the provision of advice in a
particular locality. But the Government would 'need to be
satisfied that all areas of the country [were] fully provided for in
all types of work'. No transfer of work from solicitors to other
agencies would take place until after the detailed arrangements
had been worked out. This 'should avoid any risk of disruption to
the public and to those providing the advice'. Assistance with
conveyancing and with the making of wills would, however, be
excluded from the Green Form scheme, but there were no plans
for the time being to exclude other categories of work.

The White Paper proposed three other highly controversial
changes. One, as suggested by the Scrutiny Team, was to give
the opposing party the right to make representations against the
grant of legal aid, on the ground that this has a major impact on
the course of litigation and ought to be made against the
background of the fullest knowledge of the facts. This seems an
objectionable idea, since it is not clear what right one litigant
has to oppose funding of the other litigant's case. The second
proposed change, however, is a good deal worse. Instead of
contributions to civil legal aid being payable as now by twelve
monthly instalments they would, again as suggested by the
Scrutiny Team, be payable throughout the duration of the case.

This means that the litigant who embarks on litigation would have no way of knowing at the outset the extent of the contribution he might ultimately have to make. It would also penalise him directly for the delays in the system, and would therefore give even more leverage to his opponent to negotiate a settlement.

The third proposal was in regard to remuneration of the lawyers for legal aid work. Hitherto they have been paid on the basis of a statutory formula of fair remuneration for work actually and reasonably done. The level of remuneration has never been munificent, but it seems that the differential between legal aid rates and rates for work done in the private sector is now liable to grow even greater. The White Paper said that the Government would continue to have regard to the principle of fair remuneration for work actually and reasonably done, but it would also have regard to other claims on public funds. In a passage that seems alarming for the future development of legal services, the White Paper warns:

> The Government has to be fair to the taxpayer as well as to the practitioner. The Government does not consider that the rates for legally aided work should necessarily be the same as those for privately funded work.

Already the rates for legal aid work are sufficiently low increasingly to discourage practitioners from undertaking it.* In 1986 they also led to the unprecedented spectacle of legal proceedings being brought by both branches of the legal profession against the Lord Chancellor to challenge the latest proposed increase in rates for criminal legal aid. The legal proceedings led to negotiations and a higher increase, but at the expense of the introduction of standard fees for some categories of work.[28] If the rates decline relatively further, it is predictable that this tendency will accelerate and would-be clients will find fewer and fewer lawyers willing to take on legal aid work. This would be liable to depress the quality of work done under legal aid — turning it into a service that is, and is thought of, as second-class. There are also dangers in the proposal in the White Paper that legal aid work should be handled by panels of

---

* In October 1985 the largest legal aid practice in the country, Bowlings of Stratford in the East End of London, said that it was 'to a major degree pulling out of legal aid'. It was ceasing to do criminal legal aid and so far as possible, Green Form work including civil work in the magistrates' courts. In 1984 the firm had 17 legal aid fee earners; by November 1985 they would be only seven. (*New Law Journal*, 4 October 1985, p. 975.)

solicitors with specialist skills in each category of work. By definition that would have the effect of reducing the numbers of lawyers eligible to do the work and thereby of worsening the position of the indigent client.

In short, the White Paper was a bleak document with the hand of the Treasury written plainly all over it. It was certainly the most depressing official document on legal aid and legal services since the scheme was established in the late 1940s and became the model for developments in legal aid all over the world. There is not a word in it which could be said to indicate recognition of the fact that many citizens continue to suffer from inadequate access to justice. Some even fear that the message of the White Paper, combined with the Efficiency Scrutiny report, heralds the beginning of the end of the legal aid scheme — that the Treasury will squeeze and starve it of resources to such an extent that its use will start to decline dramatically.[29]

There can be no guarantee that these gloomy fears are unfounded. Certainly it is clear that the days when the cost of legal aid was allowed to grow rapidly appear numbered. (The 16.6 per cent cut in dependants' allowances in the legal aid means test announced in February 1986 was an unwelcome harbinger of this threat.) Between 1979/80 and 1986/87 the total legal aid bill grew from around £100 million to around £400 million, a rate of increase that was nearly three times as fast as that for public expenditure generally, and from 1986 to 1990 it was budgeted to rise five times as fast. The increase was by no means mainly attributable to rates of remuneration. One crucial cause is the rapid increase in the numbers of cases; there has, for instance, been a more than 50 per cent increase in crown court cases since 1979. But Lord Hailsham's description of legal aid costs 'cascading out of control' was seized upon by the Treasury — and the Efficiency Scrutiny report and the White Paper were the direct result. It is certainly impossible to predict how far the Treasury will seek to go in the medium or long term in reducing the scope of the existing scheme.

In Scotland under the 1986 Act a person who is tried in the lower criminal courts can get legal aid only in exceptional circumstances if he pleads not guilty, and then only if he applies within 14 days of pleading. If he pleads guilty he cannot get legal aid at all, and this applies even where he first pleads not guilty and then changes his plea. The application form for criminal legal aid has to be countersigned by a solicitor stating that he is prepared to accept the case. He must also answer whether he believes his client's proposed defence 'appears to be frivolous'. If any such changes were proposed to the English legal aid scheme they would be fiercely resisted by the profession and many others. The principle of legal representation for those who plead guilty as much as for those who plead not guilty has virtually become part of the constitutional balance between citizen and state. The strength of the convention was recognised recently in the arrangements for legal advice to persons detained in police stations under the Police and Criminal Evidence Act. At the very last moment it seemed as if the commitment to the provisions for free legal advice in police stations would be swept away by Treasury pressure, but after a considerable battle the then Home Secretary, Mr Leon Brittan, succeeded in preserving the provisions for free and non-means-tested legal advice for detainees.

The future will clearly see a continuing drive to achieve economies, a continuing battle between the legal profession and the Lord Chancellor's Department over rates of legal aid remuneration, and some changes in the evolving relationship between the lawyers and the lay advice agencies, notably the Citizens' Advice Bureaux. The future for the fifty or so law centres is uncertain. Probably they will survive precariously without either greatly expanding or declining in numbers at least over the next few years. The role to be played by the new Legal Aid Board will depend on the quality of those appointed as members and on the extent to which the Government allows them to play an independent role. It will also be affected by the extent to which all those concerned with the problem of access to justice maintain the pressure on the system.

During the 1960s and 1970s this movement became a significant force. The Legal Action Group as the chief pressure group in the field has now been joined by the Legal Aid Practitioners Group of solicitors, the Law Society, the Bar Council, the National Association of Citizens' Advice Bureaux and the broadly based Advice Services Alliance representing a variety of lawyer and lay services and agencies concerned with the provision of legal advice and services to the citizen. The Lord Chancellor's Legal Aid Advisory Committee through its legal services conferences and annual reports has itself become an important factor in maintaining the pressure in support of a continuance and gradual improvement in the extent of legal services. Officials in the Lord Chancellor's Department and, to a varying extent, successive Law Officers and Lord Chancellors have also on the whole shown a degree of commitment to the ideal of improved legal services. There is therefore a powerful constituency of support to oppose the Treasury.

It will be a continuing struggle. But the fears of those who see only reason to despair appear exaggerated. Certainly there are likely to be some extremely unwelcome cuts in the range and scope of services (as well as some cuts based on greater efficiency which may be justified improvements in the system). But given the political strength of the legal services movement in this country and the ingenuity and energy of its proponents, it would be surprising if the Treasury were able to effect any radical reductions in the scheme of state contribution to access to justice.

3

The Quality of Legal Services

One of the chief claims made by the professions is that they provide an assurance of quality of service. 'Come to the professional man for work of superior standard under stringent ethical controls' is the cry. The claim that the work done is of significantly higher quality has fuelled the legal profession's defence of monopolies and restrictive practices. Thus, according to the Law Society, if non-solicitors were permitted to undertake conveyancing, the general public would be at risk of charlatans and incompetents. Similarly, according to the Bar, if solicitors could appear as advocates in the higher courts, the standards of advocacy would fall dangerously. Moreover, the standards are backed, the professions claim, by elaborate safeguards and controls. But how far are these claims justified? Are the standards as high as is pretended? Are they high enough? How well do the safeguards operate?

ARE STANDARDS WHAT THEY SHOULD BE?

One way of trying to find out is to ask clients for their views. With the single exception of defendants in criminal cases,[1] this usually results in an overwhelming vote of confidence in the profession. As has already been seen (p. 8 above), the survey of lawyers' services carried out for the Royal Commission showed 84 per cent of clients expressing themselves satisfied, as against 13 per cent who had been dissatisfied. Admittedly, the respondents in that survey were all individuals. It may be significant that the survey of 5,000 businesses and companies published in 1987 (p. 8 above) showed a significantly higher proportion of dissatisfied customers. The ordinary lay person cannot be expected to have a sufficient grasp of the law and practice to be able to make an informed assessment of the quality of the work done for him by his lawyers. The fact that he has some grievance does not mean that the complaint is justified — any more than it demonstrates that it is not well-founded. It may or may not be. The mere fact that the client is satisfied or dissatisfied in itself proves nothing either way.

The views of companies or businesses or other 'repeat players' are intrinsically worth more just because they are likely to have a more informed view than the ordinary lay person. But even there considerable caution would need to be exercised before one could feel that any survey of client response was a reliable indication of the actual quality of the work done by the profession. No adequate study of this kind has yet been produced or even attempted.

A more reliable approach may be to ask insiders who know the system themselves. Occasionally, evaluations of the quality of work done by the legal profession do appear in print — usually in the form of encomiums from practitioners or former practitioners who have moved on to be judges. Such views tend to be mainly self-congratulatory. In a sense views which are critical may carry more weight, simply because they run so much against the conventional grain. In 1979, Mr Marcel Berlins, formerly Legal Correspondent of *The Times*, spent part of the period when *The Times* was not printed because of an industrial dispute knocking around the criminal courts to judge for himself, as he said, 'whether the standards of advocacy, knowledge and presentation exhibited by young barristers were declining as fast as many judges and senior lawyers had been telling me'. His visits were haphazard — he made no attempt at statistical validity. He went mainly to criminal trials in the magistrates' courts and crown courts in the London area. He deliberately avoided spectacular, widely publicised trials and concentrated on relatively run-of-the-mill cases which would not normally be the subject of great press or public interest (though many did involve serious offences attracting heavy penalties). His verdict was less than encouraging:[2]

I was appalled. It was not just that so many young barristers seemed incapable of forming a grammatically correct English sentence (and I am not talking about 'immigrant' lawyers). Much more distressing was the poor, sometimes inexcusable, standard of presentation of the lay client's case. I was present on two occasions when counsel managed to forget the crime with which his client had been charged. I saw more than one example of counsel clearly being unaware of the leading relevant case or the relevant piece of legislation. Mistakes about the detail and circumstances of the crime and in pleas of mitigation, about the defendant's age, occupation and personal circumstances were commonplace. I did not try to ascertain the reasons for the incompetence but it could not all have been the result of late briefs.

Mr Berlins is acknowledged to be an impartial and fair observer. His strictures on the mediocre standards of advocacy at the Bar have to be treated seriously.

A different example of the same genre of criticism is the two books written by Mr Michael Joseph on two major types of legal services. The first, *The Conveyancing Fraud* published in 1976, was written to denounce the racket, as he sees it, of conveyancing work done by the solicitors' profession. Michael Joseph is not only a solicitor but an experienced conveyancer, at that time of some 15 years standing, and a frequent contributor to legal journals. His book was the first detailed exposure of what solicitors actually do for their money in conveyancing transactions. The answer was very little and nothing that could not be done equally well or better at a fraction of the time and cost. The review of the book in the *Solicitors' Journal* recommended it to articled clerks as a guide to the mysteries of conveyancing.

Mr Joseph's thesis simply was that conveyancing was a gigantic put-on perpetuated from generation to generation by solicitors to their own huge profit. In most solicitors' offices the work to a great extent was actually done not by solicitors but by their unadmitted staff — legal executives. He analysed the two main components in the solicitor's work — pre-contract inquiries and post-contract investigation of title. The Law Society claimed that it was essential to consult a solicitor because of all the hidden dangers of buying a house. Only a solicitor, for instance, could discover whether there was a second mortgage, local plans to build a motorway, a concealed tenant or inconvenient water mains. Mr Joseph's retort was that in the overwhelming majority of cases there was nothing to discover ('there are seldom more legal rights connected with a house than with a cigarette lighter'). But, if there were any such rights, the chances were that the solicitor would not discover them, or if he did, the buyer himself could have done so equally well.

Preliminary questions asked by solicitors related only to the property in question and could not therefore discover anything about neighbouring properties. If the local authority had plans for the area, they would be revealed only if they had reached an advanced stage of fruition. One would do better, Mr Joseph suggested, to spend half an hour at the property and 10 minutes on the telephone to the local planning department than to address the large number of formal, standard and almost entirely valueless questions put ritually by the buyer's solicitor to the solicitor for the seller and to the local authority. The answers to these questions were *pro forma* and intentionally uninformative. (Those from local authorities were normally even printed.) They were prefaced with the statement that the answers were 'not guaranteed' and the wrong answers would, in any event, not be discovered until after completion, by which time it was too late.

After contract, the solicitor supposedly investigated title but again, Mr Joseph suggested, this was mainly a charade. Registration of title applied to over two-thirds of all properties. In such cases investigation of title consisted of checking to see that the seller's name was typed onto the Land Certificate. But even where the title was unregistered, according to Mr Joseph the amount of work involved was minimal. Title only needed to be proved for 15 years, which was normally simple. The Law Society warned about the danger of concealed tenancies but since the buyer's solicitor never actually visited the premises, for all he knew the house might be filled with concealed tenants. Mr Joseph suggested that in reality nearly all the important things were actually left to chance. The only reason that things normally worked out alright was that there was usually nothing that could go wrong. He calculated that the seller's solicitor probably spent an average of one and a half hours on the entire transaction and the buyer's solicitor some two hours. But by dragging the process out over three or four months the client was kept ignorant of how little work was involved.

Mr Joseph's strictures may have helped in the general process of undermining the solicitors' conveyancing monopoly which resulted in the 1985 Act permitting the work to be done by licensed conveyancers. But the new law did not abolish the monopoly, it merely enlarged it to include licensed convey-ancers. (In fact, it tightened up the monopoly by making it impossible for unqualified conveyancers to compete legally, whereas previously they had just about been able to find their way through the legal loopholes to offer a cut-price service. This has now been brought to a stop.) But conveyancing itself is virtually unchanged since Mr Joseph's book was first published. If his criticisms of the nature of the work done and the way it is done were true then (and they have never been refuted by the Law Society or anyone else), they remain true today. Nevertheless, although his book and others provide a guide to do-it-yourself conveyancing, it is not to be expected that many house buyers will have the patience and the confidence to do their own conveyancing and in practice the work will continue to be done in the main by the experts, except that computerisation has undoubtedly made it even less demanding than it was in the 1970s.

Mr Joseph then tackled another major slice of work done by lawyers in his second book cheekily entitled *Lawyers Can Seriously Damage Your Health*, published in 1984, which dealt with the way lawyers handle personal injury litigation. His method was to take three real cases, each a horror story, and to trace the fate of the victims in the hands of their lawyers.

Mr Jenkins had been injured whilst operating a machine in a factory. His first two firms of solicitors failed to inspect the machine. The third firm took 16 months before getting round to an inspection, by which time it emerged that the machine had been damaged when a crane dropped a heavy object on to it! It was therefore impossible to prove that the machine was in a defective condition at the time of the accident and Mr Jenkins lost his case.

Peter aged eight had lost his eye in a school playground accident when Ian, another eight year old, poked him in the eye with a broken car aerial a foot long. The solicitor failed to inspect the playground and, at first, did not get the statements of a number of boys who had seen the accident. Ian had been running around flicking mud with the aerial at other children — which could and should have been seen and stopped by a reasonably vigilant playground supervisor. The solicitor failed to appreciate the importance of this evidence and did not even send the statements to the Queen's Counsel whom he instructed. The QC advised that there were no prospects of success in an action for damages against the education authority and eventually, after much protest, Peter's parents were pressured by his lawyers to accept a paltry £1,000 for their boy's lost eye when in truth the claim was worth far more.

Tessa, the third example, was also eight when she suffered permanent brain damage after being struck by a van when starting to cross the road. Successive lawyers failed to see the vital importance of evidence of negligence by the van driver in the police reports of the accident and failed to investigate properly. The lawyers strongly advised acceptance of the insurer's first offer of £1,000 and later of £5,000. In the end, after a four-day hearing, the judge awarded damages of £40,000. The decision ultimately turned on questions put to a witness not by the lawyers but by the judge.

No less than 11 firms of solicitors and 10 barristers were involved in these three cases. Mr Joseph's vivid commentary suggests that almost without exception they were incompetent — or worse. They generated mountains of paper most of which proved useless in advancing the client's claim. Crucial and obvious steps in the investigation of the facts were repeatedly overlooked. Issues were misunderstood and muddled. Most of the actual work was done not by the solicitor himself but, as is common in many firms, by clerks (legal executives) who are often semi-trained, and who, in these cases, sought the advice of barristers at every turn. A barrister's advice is only as good as his instructions, and the instructions were generally inadequate and incomplete — as well as being concealed from the client.

Mr Joseph suggested that a reasonably competent investigator with a camera could have collected the necessary evidence in his cases in two or three days, whereas it took the lawyers two or three years. He painted a picture of 'a team of lawyers shunting the papers backwards and forwards to one another, with their windy instructions and counter-instructions and their formalistic nonsense under which, as like as not, the crucial issue of the case will lie forever buried'. In the particular cases he chose these strictures seemed well justified. This, of course, does not prove that lawyers normally handle their cases in so grotesquely incompetent a manner. Short of a detailed study of a random sample of actual cases there is no way of saying how typical or untypical they are. No such study has ever been done.

It was suggested to the Royal Commission on Legal Services that it would be most desirable for such a study to be undertaken but unfortunately the idea did not commend itself. Instead the Royal Commission contented itself with analysis of the survey of some 2,000 recent users of lawyers' services, with the 1,500 complaints sent to it by members of the public, with records of complaints about lawyers' services sent to the Law Society and to Citizens' Advice Bureaux, and with comments on quality from miscellaneous other sources. From all these data it concluded that '[M]ost legal work is transacted well and efficiently. Most clients are satisfied with the service they receive. The judiciary is in general able to rely on the quality of work performed in the courts.'[3] City institutions, including the Stock Exchange, the British Bankers' Association and the Committee on Invisible Exports, told the Commission that 'the legal services available in London are of a high standard; this attracts legal and other business from abroad which contributes to our invisible exports'.[4]

Nevertheless the Commission reported that

at the other end of the scale some clients find that the services offered by both barristers and solicitors are slow and inefficient, that their standards of administration are not up-to-date or effective and that legal knowledge and expertise, particularly in topics such as social welfare law, are deficient. While the quality of the service provided by the profession is adequate for many purposes, there are a number of areas where substantial improvements are needed.

It instanced delays, failure to keep clients informed, poor quality of instructions sent by solicitors to barristers, late return of briefs by barristers, pressure created by last-minute settlement negotiations and poor office administration.[5]

In the absence of any valid survey of the way different categories of legal work are done, the Royal Commission was not properly entitled to conclude that the norm was satisfactory; if Michael Joseph is right, the norm may be far from satisfactory. But this is, in one sense, by the way. It is accepted, as it must be, that standards are not, and can never be, beyond reproach. There will always be considerable room for improvement. If there were any doubt on the matter, the level of insurance premiums paid by solicitors would settle the matter. The gross annual insurance premiums paid by solicitors for negligence liability rose from £7 million in 1976 to £52.3 million in 1986. In the five years from 1981 to 1986 premiums increased by 250 per cent. When the Law Society went over to a self-insurance scheme in 1987 the initial premium was fixed at £69.5 million on the assumption that the losses against net contribution (expressed as a percentage) would be a minimum of 115 per cent.[6]* In other words, the volume of negligence claims is already huge and will no doubt get higher still. This hardly suggests that standards of competence are all they might be.

---

* It was reported in 1987 that around 5,000 claims were notified under the master indemnity policy in 1986, and that slightly over half resulted in some payment. Claims paid under the policy in 1986 averaged £14,000 (*Law Magazine*, 29 May 1987, p. 29).

SAFEGUARDING PROFESSIONAL STANDARDS

There are a great variety of mechanisms aimed directly or indirectly at the maintenance and raising of professional standards. They include the qualification procedure for lawyers, post-qualification training and specialisation, discipline and complaints machinery, negligence actions, and the promulgation of standards and ethical controls by the professional bodies.

Qualification — the academic stage. Almost all civilised countries require a lawyer to have a law degree. In England this has never been so and is still not so today.[7] The ancient universities of Oxford and Cambridge did not start to teach law on any meaningful scale until the late nineteenth century. They had, of course, taught Roman law, but the teaching of English law was left to the Inns of Court. The Inns provided a high standard of instruction until the mid-seventeenth century when, during the Civil War, their courses collapsed, not to be revived until two hundrd years later. During this long fallow period the universities provided virtually no legal training. Blackstone delivered his famous course on the Common Law at Oxford from 1753 but, after his resignation, the teaching of the subject languished. In 1800, the Downing Chair of the Laws of England was founded at Cambridge, but the subject did not flourish there either. When a Select Committee inquired into the state of legal education in 1846, it reported that 'no legal education worthy of the name is at this moment to be had'.[8] Legal education here, it said, exhibited a 'striking contrast and inferiority' to that 'at present in operation in all the more civilised states of Europe and America'.[9] Whereas in Berlin, for instance, there were fourteen professors teaching some thirty branches of the law to hundreds of students, in Oxford and Cambridge there appeared to be neither lectures, nor examinations, nor even any students in law.[10]

The Select Committee's criticisms led to changes. Both the universities and the profession began to bestir themselves. In 1852 Oxford established a B.C.L. degree, and in 1855 Cambridge started an LL.B. degree. Law faculties began at London University and in provincial universities as they were set up. By 1908, there were eight law faculties. They taught English law as one of the liberal arts, concentrating primarily on jurisprudence and common law subjects, with a strong admixture of Roman law. They were still at the stage of establishing that law was a fit subject for university education. They were short of funds and had difficulty in attracting students. Most of those who went to the Bar tended to read classics or some other non-law subject; solicitors were unlikely to go to university at all. The reputation of the law faculties in the profession was not high.

During the twentieth century, however, the position has gradually changed and in the past decade or so it has been transformed. The number of students undertaking law degrees in England and Wales rose from some 1,500 in 1938 to 3,000 in 1960, to 5,300 in 1970, to over 7,000 in 1974,[11] and by 1986 to some 14,000. A survey published in 1975 showed that there were thirty university law schools in the United Kingdom, plus nineteen polytechnics and other local authority maintained institutions offering degree courses in law.[12] The Ormrod Committee Report in 1971 recommended that the law faculties should expand so as to produce some 2,000 graduates per year.[13] In fact, by 1974-5, the universities and polytechnics in England and Wales were producing some 2,500 graduates[14] and by 1980 the figure had risen to over 4,000 where it has stayed.[15]

A Committee of the Law Society urged in 1968 that a law degree should be made compulsory and the recommendation was adopted by the Council of the Law Society. But the profession reacted negatively to the idea and in the event it was not translated into official policy. Nor has the Bar yet required a law degree, though it has now become the norm to take a degree in law at either a university or polytechnic. The Bar told the Royal Commission on Legal Services that, in 1975, 87 per cent of intending practitioners called to the Bar were graduates of British universities and that, of that number, 81 per cent were law graduates. The Law Society's equivalent figures were 77 per cent and 78 per cent. In 1984, 72.5 per cent of new solicitors were law graduates, 14 per cent were non-law graduates, 8 per cent were mature students and 5 per cent were former barristers, solicitors from overseas and other miscellaneous categories.[16] Graduates who do not take law degrees are normally required to take a one-year academic course given at the College of Law or a few polytechnics; this is supposed to give the non-law graduate the equivalent of the essence of the academic stage of legal education.

Most university and polytechnic law teachers would vehemently deny, however, that academic legal education has, or should have, any connection with the practice of law whether as a barrister or solicitor or in any other context. The tradition of English legal education is resolutely non-vocational and non-professional. Indeed, until the 1950s university law departments still quite commonly refused to teach such basic 'practical' subjects as company law or labour law, let alone tax law. In the past twenty or so years academic legal courses have broadened to include a wide range of such practical subjects, and even tax law is now taught at some universities. But there is no attempt to prepare students for practice. The function of the academic stage is taken to be to teach students to think as lawyers, to train their minds, and to give them a grounding in some of the basic subjects and a sense of the role of law in society. But whereas practitioners are largely concerned to interpret and apply legislation, law students by contrast spend most of their time with case law. Law teachers themselves rarely have much, if any, practical experience. Drafting skills are not taught at all. Even in regard to such basic 'academic' tasks as legal writing and research, the work required of most students is remarkably superificial. (Is there any valid reason, for instance, why law students should graduate from most universities without ever having been given an opportunity to write anything more substantial than the usual flimsy weekly essay? Surely, a requirement to write up at least one piece of research in a twenty to thirty-page paper should be an essential ingredient of every academic law course, if only as an exercise in a minimum level of scholarly attainment.) There are only one or two institutions where students get any opportunity to develop interviewing skills or the handling of real life cases under academic supervision.[17]

It may well be that a future practitioner would nevertheless normally be well advised to study law first at the university as the best means of becoming at least somewhat 'learned in the law'. But it cannot be pretended that the academic stage of legal training has any very direct connection with the establishment of proper standards of service of the public by the legal profession. A person who took a degree in classics and then studied his basic law in the one-year cram course at the College of Law or at one of the polytechnics could still hope to be an excellent practitioner; by the same token, someone who graduated with outstanding honours in his university degree course could turn out to be hopeless as a practitioner.

Qualification — the vocational stage. The vocational stage of training differs in its details for barristers and solicitors, but in essence it is similar. In both cases the would-be practitioner has to undergo a one-year institutional course run by the profession, followed by a period of in-training in the profession itself — as an articled clerk for solicitors and a pupil for barristers. The one-year institutional course is today a vastly better vehicle than it was in former times. Until the 1960s, the course run by both sides of the profession was heavily academic and far removed from the work done by practitioners. Nowadays both courses are at least geared to the needs of the future practitioner. No doubt considerably more could be done to make them effective. In particular, both are seriously deficient in not providing adequate training under supervision in handling through simulation exercises the range of basic transactions faced by young practitioners. To provide such exercises for some 1,000 Bar students and 3,000 solicitor students is simply too costly. But within their limits the courses are a serious contribution to the establishment of proper standards for the profession.

After the vocational course, and its very demanding concluding examination, comes the exposure to 'real life' in articles or pupillage. The quality of this experience is very variable — ranging from excellent to deplorable. It depends on the way the time is organised, on the relationship between the articled clerk or pupil and those responsible for his training, on what work he is asked to do and how it is supervised. Some articled clerks and Bar pupils get first-rate experience, others waste their time. The Ormrod Committee on Legal Education in its 1971 report thought that articles were so uneven in quality that it would be better to abolish them and put in their place a fully developed practical skills course, plus restricted practice for three years after qualification. At one point the Law Society itself agreed that articles should be abolished, but the profession did not accept this conclusion and it was abandoned. The Royal Commission was of the opinion that, with certain tightening up, the articles system could provide a sound basis for in-training. Some of the proposed changes have in fact been made, including a form of monitoring by Local Law Societies of articles through interviews with articled clerks to inquire as to the nature of the training received. Nevertheless, as Professor Roy Goode, an experienced solicitor, said in 1979:[18]

> the system of articles as a method of learning the trade is unstructured, wasteful and inefficient, even in a well organised firm which takes its responsibilities to its articled clerks seriously. The principal has neither the time or the pedagogic experience to lay out a complete office procedure in a systematic fashion nor to train his clerk in interviewing techniques.

What is distinctly missing in the whole process of qualification is the kind of integration of training that exists for medical students. The need for such integration was noted in 1971 by the Ormrod Committee:[19]

> The fact that the law degree has not attained a qualification status in its own right has also had far reaching results. The converse case in medicine has meant that medical faculties have always been obliged to make some provision for the vocational or practical aspect of the training of medical students, and have, therefore, had to remain closely associated with the practising profession. They have now acquired a dominating role in all stages of medical education, including the post-graduate field. Their professors are in active professional practice in the teaching hospitals, and there is a free two-way traffic between academic and hospital medicine. The law faculties, on the other hand, have become isolated from the practising profession... The traditional antithesis between 'academic' and 'vocational', 'theoretical' and 'practical', which has divided the universities from the professions in the past, must be eliminated by adjustment on both sides.

But, as Professor Goode gloomily said, 'these words, like the sower's seed, have fallen on stony ground'. Legal education is scarcely more integrated now than it was then.[20]

> There is still inadequate interplay between the academic and the practitioner; the Council of Legal Education [for the Bar] and the Law Society, though regularly exchanging views and information, continue to plough their separate furrows in the provision of vocational training for the law graduate; articles and pupillage remain substantially unchanged.

Continuing education and accreditation of specialisms. After qualification solicitors are subject to a restriction that prohibits them from practising on their own account for a further three years. During that period they must continue to work in someone else's office. There is no equivalent safeguard in the case of barristers. In fact, they can start to take their own cases after only six months of their normal one year of pupillage.

During the three-year period of restricted practice solicitors have, since 1984, also been under an obligation to attend a number of courses or lectures. The Law Society allocates a certain number of points to different types of lectures (depending on length and the subject matter) and the newly qualified solicitor can choose whatever combination he pleases, provided he gets his required number of 48 points in the three-year period. Only a half-day course on office management run by the Law Society is compulsory; the choice of the rest is up to the individual. The Law Society publishes twice yearly a directory of a vast array of courses and lectures offered by universities and polytechnics, by local Law Societies, the College of Law and a variety of other organisations. This new mandatory system has led to a great flowering of continuing education courses which are now increasingly being taken not only by newly qualified solicitors on a compulsory basis but also by older solicitors voluntarily. The costs generally are borne by firms.

Continuing post-qualification legal education on a voluntary basis has in fact been an established feature of life for solicitors for decades. The new system has simply put this concept on to a compulsory basis for those newly qualified. At the Bar, by contrast, formal continuing education is a new development. Continuing education of an informal kind is even more important at the Bar than for solicitors. The constant interaction between barristers over work problems, whether in chambers, over lunch in the Inns, or at dinner whilst on circuit, operates as a living and rich source of mutual support and education. But it has not until very lately occurred to the Bar that there was need for anything more formal and organised. In fact the Bar's evidence to the Royal Commission in 1977 actually went so far as to say: 'Little or no post-qualification education or training is undertaken on a formal basis. It is not generally appropriate to the circumstances of practice at the Bar.'[21] A decade later, however, the tune had changed. The Chairman of the Bar's new Professional Standards Committee wrote in May 1987 that the Bar was gradually working toward more formal (albeit for the time being purely voluntary) training after the Bar examinations.[22]

The 1986 Bar Conference,* the courses for barristers at the Institute of Chartered Accountants, the seminars run last year by the Council of Legal Education and the Bar European Group, this year's two day course for pupils which is to be run by the Bar Council at the end of June: these, I believe, are only precursors for a much greater involvement by the Bar in post-entry training which is likely to be a feature of the 1990s and for which the Bar must plan now.

* The Bar's first ever annual conference (as opposed to general meeting) was held in 1986. It was a great success and seems set now to become a regular annual event.

A different approach to the problem of standards is some form of further training leading to recognition of specialist qualifications. This is normal in the medical profession but until recently it has played no part in the field of legal services. Now, in various countries it is being tested as a way both to raise standards and to improve the match between the client with a problem and a practitioner with the appropriate skill. So far, the English approach has been very tentative. The first step was to allow solicitors to indicate the fields of work in which they were prepared to take cases in the Legal Aid Directory (which then became the Solicitors' List and the Solicitors' Regional Directory) and which, as has been seen, is published annually and distributed widely and free of charge as a way of informing advice and referral agencies, such as Citizens' Advice Bureaux, what work firms and their individual lawyers purport to undertake. But this involves no certification of competence, let alone of specialisation. It is simply a claim made by the firm, with no independent validation. The rules permitting solicitors to advertise since October 1984 are based on the same concept. Solicitors may state what work they do but they cannot lay claim to any specialist capacity.

In October 1984 the Law Society asked its Education and Training Committee to consider future policy on specialisation. Its remit was to make recommendations basically as between three different models: 'Low-level' schemes — where solicitors would simply indicate willingness to undertake an unlimited number of categories of work; 'Medium-level schemes' — where solicitors would be required to fulfil fairly modest conditions, for example, that they had been qualified for three years, had substantial experience in the relevant field, had engaged in a minimum number of hours of legal education and perhaps obtained references from persons known to be competent in that field; or 'High-level schemes' — where there would be some form of peer review of competence.

So far in England the experience has mainly been with 'low-level' types of scheme in the form of the rules about advertising and the Directory or Solicitors' List. But there are also several 'medium-level' schemes in existence. These are the panels recently set up by the Law Society to license solicitors for particular categories of work — the Mental Health Review Tribunal panel, the Child Care Panel and the Legal Aid (Duty Solicitor) panel. In the case of the Mental Health Review Tribunal, practitioners wishing to join the panel must be able to show that they are personally willing and able to conduct such cases, and that they have represented at least five clients before a Tribunal in the previous 12 months; they must also attend an approved course of instruction and an interview to satisfy interviewers of their suitability for such work. (The Panel in June 1986 has nearly 200 members.) Those wishing to join the Child Care Panel face similar requirements. Originally, the requirement of attending a training course applied only to those who lacked experience, but the Blom-Cooper Report on the killing of Jasmine Beckford led to a new rule that all solicitors wishing to have their names on the panel should be obliged to attend a training course, regardless of their prior experience. In April 1986 there were over 1,000 names of solicitors on the panel.[23] Membership of criminal legal aid duty solicitor schemes is assessed by local committees of practitioners. Applicants must regularly practise in criminal defence work and must have had experience of advocacy in magistrates' courts throughout the previous eighteen months. They must also present themselves for interview if required to do so.[24]

In September 1986 the Education and Training Committee referred to the fact that until very recently the training of solicitors had been generalist; the same subjects were taught to everyone. It commented that, as society was getting more complex and the intricacies of the legal system more refined, it was no longer possible for lawyers to pretend to be omni-competent. Solicitors were now permitted to identify the areas of work in which they had experience, but so far they had not been permitted to claim expert or special skills. Experience was a matter of fact; skill was a matter of judgment. But specialisation was also a matter of fact, and the question was whether the Law Society should now promote recognition of the fact. The trend was clear. There were the recent *ad hoc* panels for Mental Health Review Tribunal work, for child care cases and for duty solicitor schemes. Under the Insolvency Act 1985 the profession was required to establish a scheme for the licensing of practitioners to undertake certain activities under the Act. Consumer agencies had told the Committee that a formal specialisation scheme backed by the Law Society would assist in the search for the right solicitor for a client's problem, which at present tended to be a hit or miss affair. In the US there were now fourteen states with specialisation schemes,[25] and schemes were in operation in both Canada and Australia.

The Committee proposed[26] that the Law Society should establish a Specialisation Board consisting of senior members of the profession, which would identify areas of practice to be recognised as a specialty (such as Landlord and Tenant Law,

Employment Law, Welfare Law and, possibly, Personal Injury Litigation etc.). Specialists would have to have had three years general experience as a solicitor, with sufficient experience in the field in question, and should take an examination — though for a limited period existing experts should have the right to be approved without an examination, on the basis of two independent references, evidence of participation in continuing legal education, and an interview. (Firms would be permitted to advertise the fact that they had a specialist but not that the firm itself was a specialist.)

Somewhat against the current trend, however, the Committee's proposals ran into serious opposition. Consultation with Local Law Societies about the proposals showed that, although two-thirds (53 out of 81) agreed broadly that specialisation was in principle a good idea, a clear majority (48 against 20) had rejected the Committee's proposals. The main objection had been a revolt on behalf of the general practitioner — the feeling that the proliferation of specialist qualifications would divide the profession and weaken the standing of the generalist.[27] In view of this negative response, the Committee decided to recommend to the Council that it should develop a policy of accreditation in the one new area of legal aid work, but that it should not otherwise work to stimulate further specialisation in the profession. The recommendation was debated at the July 1987 meeting of the Council which eventually decided that 'the whole issue should be given further careful consideration and that the Committee would report further in due course'. It was not clear whether this would in practice mean the death of the whole concept or whether it might still be resurrected at a later date.[28]

The profession is clearly worried about the trend toward formal specialisation but at the Law Society's management level there is equally considerable concern in promoting the concept. The White Paper on legal aid published in March 1987 said that the Government accepted that it was 'desirable in principle that solicitors doing legal aid work should have special skills in the area concerned' and was attracted 'by the idea that legal aid should be done by panels of solicitors with specialist experience in each category'. It would be discussing the problem with the Law Society.[29] The idea of panels of specialist lawyers in the personal injury field is also squarely on the table through the proposals of the Civil Justice Review (p. 145 below). The Law Society's new scheme for providing advice to personal injury victims (ALAS, p. 50 above) equally provides the embryonic basis for a system of accreditation in that field. Whilst it may be that the Committee's actual proposals will now be shelved, it therefore seems likely that the profession's reluctance to take specialisation further will gradually be eroded by pressure from a combination of consumer interests, the Government and the leadership from the Law Society.

COMPLAINTS AGAINST LAWYERS AND DISCIPLINARY PROCEDURES

One of the disciplines to which a professional person is subject is that his livelihood is ultimately dependent on his reputation. The advocate is particularly exposed in this regard, since his work is carried out in public where it may be the subject not merely of private comment by those present but of public criticism by a judge. Failures of behaviour or of standards of work by advocates occasionally result also in criticisms being passed by a judge to the head of chambers or Leader of a Circuit for informal handling. In the case of work done in the relative privacy of chambers or a solicitor's office, the pressure to do good work is less obvious but hardly less real. A solicitor knows from his first day as an articled clerk that progress in the firm will depend on what his fellow professionals and especially his superiors think of him. Even after he has become a partner he remains subject to the impact of their disapproval and, in extreme cases, their rejection. In his relations with clients he is to an extent protected by the reputation of his firm, but every solicitor is aware that if his work is below par even the most loyal client may ultimately take his custom elsewhere. The barrister is even less protected from the consequences of his own incompetence than the solicitor. Other things being equal, he will have the benefit of the reputation of his chambers but if his own skills are seen by solicitors as being below the necessary minimum level they will try to ensure that he does not get their instructions. Members of both branches of the profession will also be conscious of the fact that the competence or otherwise of the work they do will have a direct bearing on the insurance premiums that they, their firms or chambers have to pay.*

Standards of conduct and performance are also protected by

---

* In 1986, London Insurance Brokers, the then insurers of the solicitors' profession, produced a booklet (*Maintaining Professional Standards — the Claims Experience*) summarising the profession's claims experience and the lessons that could be learnt from it. A solicitor employed by the insurers wrote a series of articles in the *Law Society's Gazette* describing some of the mistakes which commonly led to claims under the profession's master policy and indicating ways in which they could be avoided. (See *Law Society's Gazette*, 29 May 1985, p. 1559; 29 January 1986, p. 263; and 24 September 1986, p. 2814.)

the widely shared sense amongst professional persons that the very notion of professionalism connotes both competence and devotion to the client's interests. It may be fashionable to sneer at such traditional values (and there is no doubt that on occasion members of the legal as much as of other professions show scant regard for the values themselves). But the basic ethic of the professional man's notion of service to his client is undoubtedly a significant factor in the maintenance of standards.

Obviously, however, more formal controls are also needed to keep the professional man up to the mark and to deal with the problem of deviations from the norm. The more formal processes include a variety of systems, some imposed from without, others developed by the profession itself.

The most stringent controls relate to safeguards for client moneys. Solicitors are subject to severe and strictly enforced rules to ensure that they do not mingle client money with their own. Failures in regard to these rules are the single most common reason for disciplinary action against solicitors. Even minor and innocent errors in the way that the accounts and client moneys are handled may be visited by disciplinary penalties. Since 1942 the Law Society has maintained a Compensation Fund to reimburse clients who have suffered from misuse of their money by a solicitor, and it told the Royal Commission on Legal Services that since the start of the fund it had paid every such claim in full. The fund is financed by an annual contribution imposed on all solicitors who take out a practising certificate.

Both sides of the profession now require practitioners to carry insurance against liability for negligence. Until 1966 the legal position in regard to negligence liability was that barristers were wholly immune whilst solicitors were wholly liable. In *Rondel* v. *Worsley*[30] in that year the House of Lords held that the immunity attached not, as had previously been thought, to barristers as such, but rather to advocacy, including preparation of trial, by solicitors and barristers alike. This decision was refined by the House of Lords in 1978 in *Saif Ali* v. *Mitchell*,[31] which established that a barrister could be sued for advisory work even in the context of possible or pending litigation. Solicitors in private practice have been required to have indemnity insurance since 1976; for the year commencing in August 1987 the minimum level of such insurance is £500,000 per claim. Barristers have been required to insure since 1982; the minimum level in 1987 was £250,000 per claim. But about one third of all solicitors' firms and many sets of barristers

chambers carry far more than the minimum of insurance.
Chambers with a substantial civil practice have cover for claims
of £1, 2, 5 or even 10 million; solicitors carry even higher levels
of cover. The cost of premiums is now becoming a matter of great
anxiety to the profession. (It was reported in May 1987, for
instance, that a set of chambers with 29 members were paying
£28,000 for cover up to £5 million and that a 37-partner City
firm with a good claims record was paying £400,000 for cover up
to £40 million.[32])

Premiums are fixed by reference to gross fees in the light of
claims experience. A rate at around two to three per cent of
gross fees is the norm, but those against whom claims are made
find a significant jump in their premiums. (The same study in
May 1987 stated that a small set of chambers doing 'good
quality' civil work with a couple of claims totalling £140,000 had
been asked for a premium equal to 15 per cent of their gross
fees.) The number and level of claims is rising rapidly and in the
coming years we shall undoubtedly hear much more about the
growing strain for the profession of carrying adequate insurance
cover and about the need for some means of limiting liability.

Each side of the profession also, of course, has a system for
dealing with complaints from clients and for disciplining its
members. The basic rules of professional conduct are laid down
by the professional bodies. Those that regulate the conduct of
solicitors have tended to emphasise unfair competition as
between members of the profession with rules against advertising, touting, and undercutting of fees, but these rules are now in
the process of modification in the light of the new approach to
advertising. The rules against splitting of fees with non-lawyers,
against acting for both sides or where there is a conflict of
interest, and requiring supervision of a solicitor's office by staff
of an appropriate level, are more obviously designed for the
benefit of the client. In the case of barristers most of the rules
concern the niceties and proprieties of relationships with
solicitors, prohibitions on engaging in other unworthy or
incompatible occupations, and rules against advertising and
touting and conflict of interest.

Until recently neither side of the profession gave sufficient
attention to the problem of the client with a grievance about the
work done for him by his lawyers. As regards fees, in the case of
the solicitors' branch the client is assisted most significantly by
the remuneration certificate procedure under which he can
complain about the level of the bill to the Law Society. A senior
solicitor is then asked to look at the bill and the file and to

express a view as to whether he has been overcharged. The service is free and can never result in the bill being increased. It is therefore of substantial value to the general body of clients — though probably few know of its existence, and it does not apply to cases involving litigation (contentious matters).

The client can always refer his own solicitor's bill to the court for a review called 'taxation'. The court taxation applies even where solicitor and client have agreed on the fee; the client still has the right to object later that the fee is too high. The system for complaining about one's own solicitor's bill is very rarely used, partly no doubt because unless the bill is reduced by more than one sixth the client has to pay the costs of the taxation, which may be considerable. But in principle it is plainly right and proper that such a system should exist. There is no equivalent for fees charged by barristers. The client has no way of complaining that the barrister's fee is too high. This seems entirely wrong, the more so since there is so much evidence that barristers' clerks exploit the position to charge fees that are outrageously high. The argument that the fee is reasonable because it has been agreed is manifestly unsatisfactory. The fact that it does not apply to fees charged by solicitors makes it clear that the Bar is being treated as a case apart.

If the client's complaint concerned allegedly shoddy or incompetent work, however, his position was less happy. If the work was done so badly as to amount to negligence, the Law Society would tell the client to seek his remedy by starting proceedings against the solicitor. This would rarely be what the client wanted. Having just had a bad experience with one solicitor he was being invited to start with another — and, to add insult to injury, he would commonly find that the first solicitor would insist on being paid before releasing the papers in the case. (A solicitor has a lien over the papers which legally entitles him to hold them until he has been paid. He may, however, be satisfied with an undertaking from the second firm regarding the costs.) Moreover, there often appeared to be difficulties in getting one solicitor to act in a case against another.

Incompetence of a serious character might amount to professional misconduct — a concept that normally connotes moral turpitude, a criminal conviction for a serious offence, theft, misuse of money or something similar. In exceptional circumstances it was also held to include bad professional work. But generally both sides of the profession did not tackle poor work as part of the disciplinary process. The Law Society, for instance, told the Royal Commission in oral evidence that when complaints were made which involved a possible claim in the courts, any question of professional responsibility was seldom investigated.[33] In fact, the Law Society only investigated a small proportion of the complaints made to it. According to the Royal Commission, of the 5,000 complaints received in 1978 the Law Society investigated only the 30 per cent or so which appeared to relate to professional misconduct. The remaining 70 per cent were not investigated — and the Law Society was unable to say what proportion concerned bad professional work.[34] The Royal Commission recommended that the Law Society should change its policy to deal with allegations of bad professional work, including incompetence or inefficiency, regardless of whether this might give rise to a possible negligence action.[35] It also urged that the Law Society should investigate all complaints other than those that were clearly misconceived or frivolous.[36]

Since the Royal Commission's report in 1979 significant developments have occurred. One is the establishment throughout the country of a panel of solicitors skilled in negligence actions who have indicated their willingness to take on cases of alleged professional negligence. A client who has difficulty in finding a solicitor to take his case can ask the Law Society or the Local Law Society to find an appropriate solicitor to act for him. This no longer seems to be a bone of contention. Secondly, following the recommendation of the Royal Commission's report, the Administration of Justice Act 1985 specifically empowered the Law Society to give the client a remedy for poor professional work.

Under section 1 of the Act the solicitor can be required by the Law Society to rectify any error, omission or other deficiency, to take other action to put the matter right, and to refund, remit or waive costs wholly or in part in respect of the matter complained of. The power exists if in the view of the Law Society the work done was not, in any respect, of the quality that could reasonably have been expected of a solicitor (whatever that means). The Act also gives the Law Society the power to call for the solicitor's file to see how the matter has been handled. The Law Society therefore has full power to deal with the problem of shoddy work. It has also set up a new system for helping clients to put their complaints into coherent form, by organising a team of (often retired) solicitors to make themselves available free of charge to help with this problem. In 1987 there were 18 such 'interview panel' solicitors and the Law Society hoped eventually to have some 200.

In a different approach to the same problem the Law Society announced in June 1986 that clients with negligence claims against solicitors could in future pursue them through a new cheap arbitration scheme, run by the Chartered Institute of Arbitrators. Taking a case through the courts is expensive and could take a long time. It might be worthwhile in the larger case, but for small claims it is often not what is needed. The arbitration system would operate without an oral hearing — on the basis of written submissions and documentary evidence. Neither side could be forced to use the new scheme but, if they agreed, the arbitrator's award would be legally binding on both sides and it would be regarded as a disciplinary matter for a solicitor not to comply with an award against him. There was to be a modest registration fee to cover costs but the arbitrator would have the power to award any part of that fee to the winner. The Law Society would bear the balance of the costs of the scheme.[37]

The Law Society has also drastically altered its machinery for handling complaints. The main thrust of the change was to deflect the criticism, noted already by the Royal Commission, that the complaints machinery was too inward looking. (The Royal Commission said that it had evidence 'of a general feeling of unease about the Law Society's handling of complaints, a feeling that "lawyers look after their own"'.[38]) The Commission recommended that the investigation process and the adjudication process should be separated within the Law Society. The Professional Purposes Department which carried out the investigation of complaints was responsible to the Professional Purposes Committee, the body which adjudicated on complaints not disposed of by the department; in the view of the Commission, the processes were too closely associated. There was also a lack of any active lay element in the bodies and procedures dealing with complaints. The Royal Commission was of the opinion that lay persons should sit in on both the investigation stage and the adjudication stage.[39]

The impetus to reform received a powerful stimulus a few years later through the disaster (for the Law Society) of the Glanville Davies case. Mr Davies, a respected and senior member of the Council of the Law Society and chairman of the Legal Aid Committee from 1971 to 1975, acted in the 1970s for a Mr Leslie Parsons in a series of matters relating to a machine patented by Mr Parsons. The relationship eventually turned sour and from 1976 Mr Parsons changed his solicitors. He then made a series of complaints to the Law Society about Mr Davies,

which were forcefully put and presented with reams of documen-
tation. The main complaint was that he had been grossly
overcharged. But the Law Society did nothing about the
allegations — or nothing appropriate. Mr Parsons, a formidable
character, was not deterred, however, and pursued the matter
relentlessly over the succeeding years. He applied to have the
solicitors' bill reviewed by the court, he launched further
repeated complaints to the Law Society and eventually he asked
the High Court to have Mr Glanville Davies struck off the Rolls.
In the end he succeeded in each of these objectives. The bill was
reduced by the court from £193,000 to £67,000. Mr Davies was
shown to have grossly inflated and even fabricated many items
of the bill, and he did not even contest the application that he
should be struck off.

The Law Society, to its acute discomfiture, was found to have
rejected the complaints as unfounded and to have told the
solicitor acting on the complaint for Mr Parsons: 'In the
circumstances no further correspondence can be entertained
from you or your client in this matter'. When all of this came to
light — and it was followed with a mass of publicity from the
media — the Law Society, to its credit, set up an inquiry by a
committee of its own members. Their verdict minced no words.
In a 22-page indictment of the handling of the case, the
committee of three said that the treatment of the lay client 'fell
far short of that which he was entitled to expect and he had been
seriously wronged over the handling of the complaints'. The
complaints, the report said, were many and recurring.[40]

> Whilst we found nothing which casts doubt on the integrity of
> those concerned with the handling of the complaints we have
> found administrative failures, mistakes, wrong decisions,
> errors of judgment, failures in communication, high-
> handedness and insensitivity on a scale that must have done
> great harm to the Law Society. The whole episode is a
> disgrace to the Law Society.

In the end Mr Parsons actually sued the Law Society for
incompetence in its handling of the case. The Law Society
denied that it had failed in its statutory duty to investigate his
allegations — but it eventually settled the case out of court by
paying him the sum of £50,000 plus costs of £15,000.[41]

The fall-out from this unfortunate affair was considerable —
not least in terms of the devastating blow to the self-esteem of
solicitors both in the Law Society and throughout the country.
One of the results, however, was a request to management

consultants Coopers and Lybrand to examine the structure of the complaints machinery. Initially in July 1985, Coopers and Lybrand recommended that the Law Society hive off its entire complaints machinery to a new statutorily independent Complaints Board funded by the profession, with five solicitor members elected by the profession, five lay members appointed by the appropriate Minister and a solicitor chairman appointed by the Master of the Rolls.[42] This, however, was thought by the profession to go too far — though the Young Solicitors approved the concept.[43] But a second draft of a plan produced by Coopers and Lybrand provided for an adaptation of the concept originally proposed by the Royal Commission, with separate investigation and adjudication branches and a strong lay element.[44] The scheme which was adopted by the Law Society and which went into operation as from September 1986 also removed the whole complaints system from the Law Society headquarters in Chancery Lane to a new address in Victoria.

There are two levels of committee, an eleven-person Investigation Committee, with a lay chairman and a majority of lay members, responsible for overseeing the crucial sifting stage, and an 18-person Adjudication Committee with a solicitor chairman and a majority of solicitor members. The Investigation Commitee is supposed to refer complaints which it thinks have merit to the Adjudication Committee but the reality is that a high proportion of complaints never reach the Investigation Committee. They are dealt with instead at a lower level by staff known as investigation officers.

The complaints made by clients tend to fall into certain patterns. Typically, they relate to delay, inaction, apparent lack of interest in the client and his problem, mistakes in presenting the facts, failure to communicate, excessive costs, papers which have gone missing and time limits that have been missed. Sometimes, of course, it turns out on investigation that the solicitor is not actually at fault. Some clients have no understanding of how long even well conducted cases take, or what may seem to the client to be an excessive bill proves on independent scrutiny to be perfectly reasonable.

The first inquiry into how the system was working, published in July 1987,[45] said that the vast majority of complaints are disposed of at the investigation officer level. They usually send a copy of the complaint to the solicitor concerned for his comments, which are then sent to the complainant. If the complainant does not reply within three months, unless the case is clearly serious, it is taken off the active list — though the complainant does not know this. (The National Consumer Council has suggested that the complainant should at least be told.)

Where there is evidence of 'shoddy work' the officer calls for the solicitor's file, on which a report is written and sent to the solicitor, though not to the complainant. If action is needed, it is taken by the Adjudication Committee. The aim is not so much to order payment of compensation but rather to try to put the complainant into the position he would have been in if the work had been done properly.

The Investigation Committee does not actually investigate complaints. Its function is to monitor the handling of complaints, and to look at files going to the Adjudication Committee. This has 12 solicitor members (six of whom are non-Council members) and six lay members. The sanctions it has available include a rebuke, a severe rebuke, and placing conditions on the practising certificate. But the imposition of heavy sanctions such as suspension from practice, payment of a penalty or of a contribution to costs requires a decision by the Solicitors' Disciplinary Tribunal.

The Solicitors' Disciplinary Tribunal hears only the most serious cases. It sits with two solicitors and one lay member. In 1986 a total of 32 solicitors were struck off by the Tribunal out of a total of 150 cases heard, while 14 were suspended, 55 fined and 16 reprimanded. Anything involving dishonesty and most criminal convictions other than minor motoring cases lead to more or less automatic striking off. Most other charges end with a fine. Usually such cases involve faulty accounting procedures. Once a person has been struck off the Rolls it is a long and usually difficult process to get reinstated.

The Bar too has its equivalent complaints and disciplinary machinery. Complaints against barristers come not only from lay clients but just as often from judges, from other barristers or from solicitors. (A significant proportion of complaints against solicitors too are brought by other solicitors.) They cover a wide range including allegations of misleading the court, late return of briefs, failure to comply with the rules regulating the relations between the two branches of the profession, discourtesy to the court etc. Each complaint is investigated by the Professional Conduct Committee of the Bar (PCC) which considers a written report from one of its own number who has been charged by it with the responsibility of inquiring into the matter. If the PCC comes to the conclusion that the barrister has committed an act of professional misconduct, it will prosecute him before the disciplinary tribunal. There are lay representatives on both the disciplinary tribunal and the PCC. No complaint is dismissed unless the lay representatives on the PCC agree. The Bar has recently been at pains to deny the suggestion that it will not deal with delay, inefficiency and incompetence. According to the Chairman of the PCC, 'recent cases of breach of professional standards which the PCC have found proved have included unreasonable delay by counsel in dealing with his instructions'.[46] In another case a barrister was disbarred for professional incompetence in 'failing properly to prepare and master the brief in relation to the defendant's antecedent history'.[47]

As we have seen, both sides of the profession have lay persons involved in the investigation stage of the complaints machinery and in the adjudication stage. But only the solicitors' branch is subject to the additional scrutiny of the statutory Lay Observer who was established by Parliament in 1974 under the Solicitors' Act of that year. His function is to inquire into any complaints brought to him regarding the Law Society's handling of a complaint against a solicitor and to make an annual report which is published. The Lay Observer, whose services are free, has his office in the Royal Courts of Justice in the Strand. The number who complain to the Lay Observer is very small — typically 200 to 300 a year. It is actually rare for the Lay Observer to criticise the Law Society in more than a handful of cases each year. The first two incumbents of the office were respectively a former admiral and a former general. Their tone was decidedly mild. The third Lay Observer, Mr Lionel Lightman, appointed in 1986, came from the Office of Fair Trading and seems to be made of sterner stuff. His first report in July 1987 contained a robuster style of criticism both of the Law Society and of solicitors. But plainly the Lay Observer is only a marginal factor in the network of systems concerning complaints. It seems improbable that he could be capable of having much effect on standards.

In fact, it is somewhat questionable altogether as to what is the real significance of complaints and disciplinary procedures in the struggle to maintain adequate standards. Several million legal transactions are handled each year by solicitors and barristers; only a tiny fraction result in any formal complaint. Mr Philip Ely, Chairman of the Adjudication Committee, stated at a conference in June 1987 that complaints were running at an average of 1,500 to 2,000 a month, (18,000 to 24,000 a year, compared with some 5,000 a decade earlier and 9,000 in 1985), and the signs were that the numbers were increasing. So, for whatever reason, the new complaints system seems to have generated a considerably greater number of complaints, or people seem more prone to complain.

Research, including peer review on anonymous random samples of work done by lawyers in different categories of case, might possibly do more to reveal defects in working standards than any number of complaints, which depend on clients recognising the problem and having the energy to take up the matter. Certainly, it would be a better way of testing the standards of the profession generally.[48] But at present no mechanism exists to conduct such research, and it would not be easy to persuade the profession to permit access to the files to enable it to be done. Perhaps the Law Society should have the power to permit access to solicitors' files for the purpose of anonymous and reputable research on quality of work, and not simply as now to investigate allegations of negligence or breaches of the ethical rules in individual cases. Or perhaps the Lay Observer might be given a research capacity to inquire more generally into the standards of work done by solicitors. This would be a good deal more useful than his present labour of delving into a couple of hundred, probably untypical, cases per year.

Another approach to the problem of ensuring adequate standards is that they be prescribed by edict of the professional organisations. The Royal Commission on Legal Services recommended that the profession should promulgate written standards as an authoritative indication of good practice, and the Law Society has now implemented this proposal. The first standards published in June 1985[49] dealt with Communication with the Client, Responsibility for the Client's Case and Information on Costs for the Individual Client. The guidelines suggested that at the first interview the client should be told how the solicitor intended to deal with the problem. He should be given an explanatory leaflet about the firm's methods of charging. He should be kept informed of the progress of the matter and of reasons for any serious delay. This might often be assisted by sending the client copies of the correspondence.

The standards state that the client must be told the name of the partner responsible for the conduct of the matter and the name of any other person in the firm involved in the day-to-day conduct of the case. If the case is transferred to someone else, the client should be so informed and some explanation should be given. The client paying his own bill should be told that he may, if he wishes, set a limit to charges that will be incurred without further reference to him. Whether or not he has set such a limit, he should be informed at least every six months of the approximate amount of costs to date and in appropriate cases an interim bill should be sent.

Not to be outdone, the Bar too has now decided to concentrate on professional standards. The chairman of the Bar Council's Professional Standards Committee which began work in January 1987 described the committee as 'a new venture for the Bar'. The Committee would be concerned with a wide range of activities all dealing with maintaining and improving the quality of the service provided by the Bar — including recruitment, education, pupillage, post-entry training, complaints and the Code of Conduct.[50]

It seems that the Bar is also moving in the same direction as the Law Society in improving the system for dealing with shoddy work. *The Times* of 15 June 1987 reported that the Professional Standards Committee of the Bar Council was about to consider a report recommending that the Bar should have a small claims arbitration procedure to settle minor disputes where a member of the public had a claim for compensation against a barrister. (Such claims would relate only to out-of-court work, since, as has been seen, a barrister cannot be made liable for incompetence in the field of advocacy or the preparation of advocacy.) The draft report also made proposals for improving the system for dealing with allegations of incompetence and discourtesy by barristers. The Professional Standards Committee of the Bar also has in hand the redrafting of the Bar's Code of Conduct.

The trend of professional standards is to involve the client more in the matter. If, for instance, a lawyer is to send his client copies of the correspondence there is an obvious possibility that the client may then start badgering him with views and opinions. But research has shown that clients who take an active part in their case do significantly better in terms of the final result than the normal passive clients.[51] Douglas Rosenthal studied a sample of sixty personal injury cases in New York. He found that most lawyers decided without consulting their clients when to issue a writ, whether it was worthwhile to sue, whether to sue in the higher or the lower courts, in what venue and how to conduct the negotiations. They decided at what point to pitch the initial demand, and at what point to make the first approach for settlement talks and with what degree of belligerence. These were all regarded by the lawyers as technical matters on which the client would have nothing of value to contribute. Lay clients were 'assumed to be virtually helpless in coping with complex personal problems, to be nuisances when they try to involve themselves in the experts' province, and to be incapable of accepting effective decision making responsibility'.[52] But, contrary to these assumptions, the few who tried to help their lawyers with the case did much better. Three-quarters of the active clients, compared with 41 per cent of the passive clients, got what the independent panel of experts thought was a good result. Rosenthal urged that active participation of the client should become the norm.

Clients might possibly be the best means of all for keeping the professional man on his toes. It would go against the grain for most lay people to have to take up an active stance. But since no one knows more about the facts of his own case than the lay client himself and no one cares more about the outcome than he, perhaps it is not wholly unreasonable to think that he has a sufficient stake in the matter to want to take a hand himself to influence the course of events. If clients could be persuaded of this elementary notion, lawyers could find themselves under real pressure to provide better legal services.

4

The Judges

The judiciary are very much the dignified part of the English legal system. They enjoy high status as incorruptible, austere, remote. Opinion may vary as to whether their personal views intrude on their decision-making or whether they favour particular interests, or whether they are as forward-looking as they might be. But when it comes to determining the facts of a case, handling a trial, summing up to a jury or simply looking the part, there is widespread agreement that the English judges do it as well as any, and better than most.

But what powers do they exercise, how are they appointed, who are they, how do they perform their functions, can they be dismissed, do they receive any training, how much should they be heard outside the court room, what is the relation between the judicial and the political process? All of these are questions that intrigue and mystify the ordinary citizen.

Judges do perform important functions outside the judicial forum by conducting inquiries into events such as Bloody Sunday in Londonderry, the Brixton riots or the Zeebrugge ferry disaster. But the power of the judge lies principally in his duty to decide the cases that come before him. Deciding a case involves a decision as to the facts, an application of the law to those facts and a final conclusion as to the consequences of the finding on fact and law. So in a criminal case the court has to decide whether the accused is guilty and, if so, what is the appropriate penalty. In a civil case the question is rather which of the parties wins the case and, if the plaintiff, what damages or other remedy he should have.

In the crown court, the higher criminal court, the judge is

relieved of the burden of deciding the facts because this is done by the jury — though if he wants to try to influence the jury he has some opportunity to do so by the way he chooses to sum up the facts. Obviously he has to be careful not to provide the basis for a successful appeal on the ground that he has gone too far in seeking to persuade the jury to his point of view. But normally a judge can make his summing up 'appeal-proof', whilst at the same time indicating his true opinion of the facts through a combination of tone of voice, raised eyebrows, pauses for effect and other forms of 'body language'. The danger that a judge may be tempted to lead the jury in this way is aggravated in criminal cases by the fact that he knows, whilst the jury does not, whether the accused has a criminal record. The possibility that the judge will exert undue influence on the jury is avoided in the United States by a rule that he should sum up only on the law, not on the facts. There are occasional examples of cases where one feels that the English judge does abuse his position of trust and power to cajole the jury into taking his view of the case.* But given the temptation, it is striking how relatively rare it is for this form of judge power to become a source of criticism. Most judges seem to play it fairly straight and not to abuse their power.

In magistrates' courts, lay justices are relieved of the burden of deciding the law because they are told the law by their clerk who is supposed to have a professional qualification — though in fact many do not.⁺ But with these two exceptions, all other decisions in court cases are made from the bench. It is the court that decides all aspects of the case both in the county court (save for the annual handful of jury cases) and in the High Court. It is the court that decides on sentence in all criminal cases even when there is a jury and, apart again from the handful of civil jury cases, the court also decides on damages. Finally, judges also have a major role in fashioning the law — both through the

---

* For an example when the judge appeared to go too far see press reports on 24 July 1987 of Mr Justice Caulfield's summing up in the libel action brought by Mr Jeffrey Archer against *The Star* newspaper. The judge summed up strongly for Mr Archer and the jury proceeded to give him a record £500,000 damages.

⁺ A survey carried out by the Justices' Clerks Society in 1982 showed that out of 310 deputy clerks to justices only 79 (25 per cent) were qualified as barristers or solicitors. 92 (30 per cent) had a Court Clerk Diploma and there were 139 others. Out of 1,194 court clerks, 27 per cent were barristers or solicitors, 48 per cent had the Diploma and there were 303 others. The results show that the lay magistrates are mainly advised by court clerks who themselves have a less than satisfactory training. ('Professional Qualification of Court Clerks in the Magistrates' Courts', Justices' Clerks Society, September 1985.)

interpretation of statutes and in developing the common law when there is no relevant statute. The judges have traditionally played down this function by asserting that they 'find' or 'declare' the law rather than 'making' it. But the reality is that the judges have considerable power of decision over what law they find or declare.[1]

The power wielded by the judge is therefore very great — and unlike the position on the Continent of Europe where trial judges usually sit three together, in England the trial judge usually sits alone. The chief exception is in the magistrates' courts where lay magistrates must sit with at least one other and usually sit with two others. A professional magistrate ('stipendiary') sits alone just like a judge.

THE JUDICIAL HIERARCHY

So who are the judges who exercise all this power? They come in different ranks and degrees. The highest in the land are the nine law lords (officially known as Lords of Appeal in Ordinary) who sit in the House of Lords in its appellate capacity. Proceedings in the House of Lords take place in upstairs committee rooms in the Palace of Westminster, though the actual judgment is delivered in the House of Lords chamber. The case load is light — a mere fifty or so appeals a year, though the same judges also serve in the Judicial Committee of the Privy Council which still has a small number of cases a year as the final court of appeal for miscellaneous surviving colonial and Commonwealth jurisdictions. The law lords almost to a man (there are no women) are judges who have worked their way to the top from the High Court bench, via the Court of Appeal. They will normally have served five to ten years in the High Court and five or so years in the Court of Appeal before being elevated to the highest judicial tier. It is typically British that in the rarefied atmosphere of the House of Lords the pomp and circumstance normally attending the law should be less rather than more. The law lords wear neither wigs nor robes. They turn up simply in ordinary lounge suits — though counsel are fully wigged and robed.

Below them are the twenty or so Court of Appeal judges, the Lords Justices of Appeal. Where the House of Lords sit with five and the trial courts sit normally with one judge, the Court of Appeal sits with three. The Master of the Rolls is the chief judge in the Civil Division and the Lord Chief Justice in the Criminal Division. Both play an important part in determining which cases are heard by what judges. Usually they ensure that they are themselves sitting for all the most significant cases. The identity of the judges in the case may be crucial. Lawyers sometimes cheer, or, as the case may be, groan, when they learn who is to sit in the case. The power to allocate the judge to the case is therefore of some significance.

The next tier down are the eighty or so High Court judges. The High Court has from time immemorial been broken into specialised divisions, though the details of the divisions have varied from time to time. Currently they are the Queen's Bench Division (which deals mainly with debt, contract claims, actions for personal injuries and libel actions), the Chancery Division (companies, partnerships, bankruptcies, trusts, mortgages etc.), and the Family Division (all aspects of family law and especially breakdown of marriage and the resulting problems relating to children and property). These historic divisions may still make sense as a way of expediting the business of the courts — though whether it is sensible that they should each have so different a procedure is another matter. But the judges on appointment are assigned by the Lord Chancellor to one or other division and tend then to stay there for the duration. Queen's Bench Division Judges, and to some extent Family Division judges, also hear criminal cases in the crown court. Judges assigned to the Chancery Division are exempt from taking criminal cases.

The tier below the High Court judges are the Circuit judges who sit in the crown court conducting criminal cases and in the county court where they hear civil cases. Currently there are close to 400 circuit judges. Curiously, there is virtually no promotion from the ranks of circuit judge to the High Court bench. Once the mysterious processes of selection in the Lord Chancellor's Department have determined that an individual is of circuit judge rather than High Court judge calibre, it is almost impossible to demonstrate that this assessment was wrong. (Current exceptions include Reginald Payne, Robert Mais, Ralph Kilner-Brown and Hilary Talbot.)· But acceptance of a circuit judgeship usually means the end of ambitions to rise to greater eminence, whereas every High Court judge may aspire to move up the judicial ladder toward the House of Lords. For appointments below the level of High Court judges one can indicate to the Lord Chancellor's Department that one is prepared to be considered, whereas such immodesty would be thought a major *faux pas* for those hoping to be appointed to the higher judiciary.

The ranks of full-time judges also include pre-trial judges in the High Court called Masters and their equivalent outside

London, Registrars and County Court and District Registrars.
There are in all something over 200 of these. The registrar in
the county court not only runs the court as chief administrator
but has important judicial functions in sitting as the judge in
small claims cases involving sums of up to £500.

The English system, however, also uses part-time judges on a
massive scale, especially in the crown courts where the volume
of business always threatens to engulf the judicial manpower.
The normal progression is to start as an Assistant Recorder for a
few years sitting *ad hoc* as and when asked to do so, and then as
Recorder. Those who are being considered for appointment to the
High Court bench will then progress to part-time Deputy High
Court judges. There are currently some 500 Recorders, about the
same number of Assistant Recorders and some 50 Deputy High
Court judges. The great advantage of using part-time judges is
not simply that it adds to the available pool of manpower but
that it gives the Lord Chancellor's Department the chance to
test the mettle of the judge to see whether he is fit to appoint to
the full-time bench. It also incidentally gives the individual the
opportunity of seeing whether he cares for the judicial life, both
on and off the bench.

One striking difference between the British system and that
on the Continent is that judges there have a career which starts
in the mid-twenties straight from law school, whereas in
Britain, as in the rest of the common law world, judges are
chosen from the ranks of successful practitioners. There has
never been any serious discussion in the common law world of
whether the Continental system has sufficient merit to suggest
emulation. It has always been simply assumed that the common
law way is best — as indeed it seems to be, not least because it
results in a judiciary that has higher general stature and
authority. The judges are usually people of demonstrated
capacity before ever being appointed.

CATCHING YOUR JUDGE

Can the Lord Chancellor's Department get the recruits they
want for the bench? This depends on the balance between the
financial remuneration on offer, the would-be recruit's current
and future earning capacity and an overall appreciation of the
comparison between the judicial and the practitioner's life-style.
The salaries of judges are based on the recommendation of the
Top Salaries Review Body. In making its recommendations it
always makes reference to the relationship between earnings at

the Bar and those offered to judges. In its report for 1984-5[2] the Review Body said 'information on earnings at the Bar is of great importance to our work, but is notoriously difficult to obtain'. From time to time it had conducted its own survey, most recently for the 1980-81 review. It had conducted a fresh survey for the current inquiry based on a 25 per cent sample of the practising Bar and information from those newly appointed as High Court and Circuit judges. However, the survey of practitioners had resulted in a disappointing response. Only half of those approached had replied, which meant that the results had to be treated 'with considerable caution' and could give at best only a broad indication of the earnings opportunities available at the Bar to those who might be considered for a judicial appointment. There was also a poor response to the request for information from newly appointed judges. And there was no information at all regarding the earnings of solicitors. Subject to these caveats, the Review Body said that the average net receipts at the Bar for those appointed to the High Court bench between 1980 and 1984 in April 1984 terms were £91,500 (median £73,480). The comparable figures for those appointed to the circuit bench were on average £49,180 and median £48,620. The Review Body stated:[3]

> We have been told that recruitment to most judicial appointments including the High Court Bench is now broadly satisfactory, but that there is particular difficulty in obtaining sufficient good recruits to the Circuit Bench.

The general field for appoinment to the circuit bench was that of leading junior barristers and to some extent also Queen's Counsel, though mainly those with earnings in the lower quartile of QCs. Broadly the range of income for these categories as at April 1985 was in the range £37,000 to £46,000 and, on this basis, the Review Body recommended that the appropriate salary for circuit judges should be £40,000, as compared with £60,000 for High Court judges.[4]

As from April 1987 the salary of the different levels of judges was £81,000 for the Lord Chief Justice (the same as an Admiral of the Fleet, Field-Marshal or Marshal of the Royal Air Force); £74,750 for law lords, judges of the Court of Appeal and the Master of the Rolls (almost the same as the Secretary to the Cabinet); £65,000 for High Court judges (the same as the 24 Permanent Secretaries of Government Departments and the 21 plain Admirals, Generals and Air Marshals); and £43,500 for Circuit judges (the same as a Grade 2 Deputy Secretary on appointment — though Senior Circuit judges earned £48,250).

Some Queen's Counsel are currently earnings hundreds of thousands of pounds a year. (The rumour that Mr Robert Alexander QC was the first barrister to earn over £1 million a year was denied.) The leaders of the Bar are certainly over the half-million figure — compared with something like £350,000 for the leading City solicitors.* But most even of these top earners are sooner or later tempted by a High Court judgeship. This is because there is a good deal more to the office of being a judge than the annual take-home pay. For one thing, there is the fact that a judge gets a pension — two-thirds of his final salary after fifteen years on the bench. This is no mean consideration, since so many barristers have made woefully inadequate provision for their own retirement. For those offered a High Court judgeship there is an automatic knighthood, great status, and the possibility of further judicial preferment. For a judge at any level there is almost certainly a less crushing burden of work than for the busy practitioner. There is also the feeling amongst those who reach the top of the profession that a judicial appointment is an opportunity not merely for private advantage but also for public service.

THE APPOINTMENT PROCESS

Once a judge has been appointed to the full-time bench he is in practice virtually irremovable. Certainly, neither incompetence nor a basic lack of judicial qualities would justify his dismissal. It is therefore important that mistakes not be made. There have been notorious examples of outstanding advocates who made poor judges. So, how does the system of appointment work? Technically, almost all the judges are appointed by the Sovereign acting normally on the advice of the Lord Chancellor or, in the case of the most senior judges, of the Prime Minister. But it is the Lord Chancellor and his senior officials who actually decide. Obviously the Lord Chancellor is too busy to do all the leg-work himself. The task of identifying the right people falls principally on the Permanent Secretary (currently Sir Derek Oulton, KCB, QC) and the Deputy Secretary also known

---

* Information about the highest incomes amongst solicitors is as scarce as that regarding leading barristers. In late 1985 it was said that 'while a junior salaried partner may earn "as little as £40,000 a year", middle ranking partners in the larger firms expect to draw between £150,000 and £200,000 a year'. (See Ole Hansen, *New Law Journal*, 4 October 1985). See also p. 34 above and *Law Society's Gazette*, 22 January 1986, p. 169 and 4 February 1987, p. 317.

as the Deputy Clerk to the Crown (currently Mr Tom Legg). The main task of producing names actually falls on the Deputy Secretary who goes about the country talking with judges, senior circuit administrators and leaders of the practising Bar trying to identify that elusive quality which makes someone a potentially good or at least adequate judge.

Until recently little was known about the process which led to the appointment of judges. In May 1986, however, a pamphlet issued by the Lord Chancellor's Office set out some basic information about the system of judicial appointment and the policies pursued.[5] According to this, the basic principle is that no single person's view about the suitability of a particular candidate should be decisive. Every name is exhaustively considered through an elaborate process of consultation with senior judges, Leaders of the Circuit Bars and other senior members of the profession. In particular, the Presiding Judges of the six circuits are regularly consulted about candidates who practise on their circuits, and the four Heads of Division (the Lord Chief Justice, the Master of the Rolls, the President of the Family Division and the Vice Chancellor of the Chancery Division) are also involved. Candidates who are now known to the senior officials in the Department are interviewed. The final decision is formally taken by the Lord Chancellor (who will himself see those to be appointed as High Court judges to offer them the job), but when he considers names they have already gone through a very careful sifting process. Moreover, if they are being considered for full-time appointment, they will nowadays already have a track record over several years in a part-time judicial post. The pamphlet said that 'as far as possible, candidates should be appointed to permanent judicial posts only when they have successfully prepared and proved themselves by experience in a part-time capacity'.

The pamphlet also touched on the sensitivity of the information collected about potential candidates. Insofar as this consists of facts, they would normally be available to the candidate on request 'in the form of a summary sheet so that in case of any doubts he can ensure that they are correct'. But in the case of opinions given in confidence about his professional and personal suitability, neither the records nor the comments or advice given to the Lord Chancellor can be revealed 'because otherwise the Lord Chancellor would not get the frank advice that he must have in the public interest'.

A rare glimpse of what these files contain was given in a feature article by Alan Rusbridger in *The Guardian* of 28 June

1986, based on an interview with a barrister, John Parris, who managed to get a friendly secretary in the Lord Chancellor's Office to smuggle out his file. He was so shocked by what he saw that he decided there was little point in staying on at the Bar.[6]

There were sheaves of cuttings from the trials I had done. There were press cuttings from the *Evening Standard* about an actress I had been to a first night with. There was even an advertisement in *The Times* offering charter of a yacht I had in the Mediterra¬ean. But what really finished me off were getting on for a hundred scrappy notes addressed to the Lord Chancellor, many of them from one particular judge I had crossed swords with. Some of them were downright bloody lies. The most damning one was from this judge saying: 'Sleeps with his divorce clients'! It was totally untrue.

The chief objection to the present system of selection is that it is handled secretly by a small group of civil servants who, although they consult widely with judges and senior barristers, nevertheless wield great powers of patronage. The JUSTICE report on the Judiciary in 1972 recommended that the Lord Chancellor should have a small advisory committee to assist him, which could comprise representatives of the Bar, the Law Society, academic lawyers, the judiciary and possibly some lay members, for instance, with skills in personnel matters and selection procedures. Interested bodies could propose names to the committee and individuals wishing to be considered could put their own names forward. The Lord Chancellor himself could likewise put names to the committee, but he would not be permitted to make appointments without having first secured the committee's view. The JUSTICE committee's proposal landed with an extremely dull thud. No-one at that time paid any attention.

Recently, however, the proposal has attracted some notice in the context of mounting criticism of the way the selection procedure operates. Thus in April 1986, the then Vice Chairman of the Bar, Mr Peter Scott, QC (who a few months later became Chairman) suggested that it was time to go even further than JUSTICE had recommended and to hand the power of making the actual appointments to a broadly based Judicial Appointments Board. The Board members would include judges, barristers, solicitors and laymen. The chairman would be the Lord Chancellor or perhaps the Attorney General.

Mr Scott acknowledged that the quality of the judiciary was generally high and that one should be slow to change a system that was working well. But there were some disturbing elements in the present system, notably the concentration of so much power in the hands of the Lord Chancellor and his senior officials. Candidates for judicial office never knew why they had not been chosen and had no opportunity to challenge damning things said about them. The system seemed 'in some ways designed to reduce rather than encourage the availability of the best candidates'. Increasingly, Mr Scott suggested, barristers were 'beginning to question both the advantages of judicial appointments and the way that they are made'.[7]

The new pamphlet on judicial appointments was issued by the Lord Chancellor's Department a few weeks after the interview with Mr Scott was published in the Bar's new house journal, *Counsel*. Launching the pamphlet at the end of May 1986 the then Lord Chancellor, Lord Hailsham, said he was firmly against the idea of a Judicial Appointments Board making decisions or even having an advisory committee to assist the Lord Chancellor in his task. Speaking on Radio 4, Lord Hailsham said 'It would not be subject to parliamentary accountability; it would be a permanent mafia of the judges appointing one another or the Bar appointing themselves to higher office. I don't think that the public would approve of that.' Lord Hailsham said that he had three principal considerations: to retain parliamentary responsibility and accountability through the use of a Minister; to remove judicial appointment from the arena of party politics; and to preserve the impartiality and integrity of the judiciary. The idea of a judicial appointments board he thought would destroy parliamentary accountability, and there would be constitutional problems in relation to its composition. A board consisting of judges or practising lawyers would be open to accusations of partiality and corruption; and a board composed of the Great and the Good would, in his opinion, be ignorant of the essential criteria.

Commenting on the pamphlet and Lord Hailsham's remarks, the *New Law Journal* said that, for all the sincerity of the Lord Chancellor's views, they were unlikely to satisfy the critics. They were concerned that the Lord Chancellor should be so dependent on what he was told by his senior officials; that barristers wishing to become High Court judges were not permitted to apply (whereas for lesser appointments they can); that those not chosen would never know the reason; that those who did apply were unable to get any proper assessment of their prospects; and that candidates were unable to refute damning untruths about them on their files.[8] All these points were rejected by Lord Hailsham who claimed that candidates were always free to consult his officials and that those who had been rejected could ask why.

It seems objectionable that the whole process of appointment to the bench should be so secretive and so much in the hands of unaccountable officials. The suggestion that the Lord Chancellor is accountable through Parliament for his appointments is pure theory. In reality the process of appointments is completely outside the system of accountability. But whether, if it were otherwise, different people would be appointed as judges is another question. It is not obvious that there are significant numbers of persons who seem eligible for appointment who are not offered judicial positions. The pool of available manpower at least at the Bar is after all not so great. It might almost be said that the Lord Chancellor's Department is already scratching around to find enough judges. There is little evidence that there are many people of talent and sufficient experience who are overlooked, or that a more open and accountable system of appointment would provide very different results.

WHAT SORT OF PEOPLE BECOME JUDGES?

A common gibe is that judges are elderly. If this was true in former times, it seems no longer to be the case today. For one thing, there has for over a quarter of a century been a retiring age — of 75 for senior judges and 72 for circuit judges and recorders. (By contrast, there is no retirement age in the United States.) The only judge in recent years to soldier on well beyond retirement age was the indestructible Lord Denning, who was not affected by compulsory retirement because he was already a judge in 1959 when it came into effect. (In his late seventies and early eighties Lord Denning used to joke that he had all the Christian virtues save that of resignation. He finally went at the venerable age of 83.)

Nevertheless many have the impression that judges tend to be in their dotage. An ATV programme 'Scales of Justice' in November 1986 stated that 'judges are overwhelmingly male and often very old'. Stung by the rebuke, the Lord Chancellor's Department retorted that the average age of Circuit judges, High Court judges, Court of Appeal judges and law lords was only 60 years 9 months. (The average age for the circuit and the High Court bench was nearly 61, for the Court of Appeal 65, and for the House of Lords 66 and a half.) Full-time judges are commonly appointed these days in their early or mid-fifties and occasionally earlier. Nicholas Browne-Wilkinson, Gordon Slynn, Robert Goff, Elizabeth Butler-Sloss, Margaret Booth are all examples of High Court judges appointed in their forties. Part-time judges are typically appointed in their late thirties to early or mid-forties. A series of parliamentary replies from the Attorney General Sir Patrick Mayhew at the end of July 1987 revealed, however, that retired judges were being used to a significant extent to overcome an acute shortage of judges. In 1986 retired Lords Justices, High Court judges and circuit judges had sat for more than a total of 2,000 judge days, as against nearly 90,000 days sat by such judges in active service. A retired Lord Justice was paid £324 a day, a High Court judge £294 and a circuit judge £151 for such work.

The allegation that the judges tend to be male certainly is true. In May 1986 of the 114 most senior judges (law lords, Lords Justices of Appeal and High Court judges) only three were women. All three were High Court judges attached to the Family Division. No woman has as yet been appointed to the Court of Appeal or the House of Lords. Lower down the judicial hierarchy the position is substantially the same. Of the 343 circuit judges in 1987, only 16 were women; of the 534 recorders, only 22 were women.

The women's movement would not be alone in expressing concern over this apparent evidence of sex discrimination. The fact is, however, that until now there have been few women eligible for appointment to the bench simply because there are few women at that level of seniority in the profession. It is only in very recent years that women have started to come into the profession in any significant number. In 1955 there were only 64 women in practice at the Bar (3 per cent of the total). In 1986 there were 744 (14 per cent). The rapid build-up of women in the profession can be seen in the figures of those called to the Bar. In 1975, there were 166 (21 per cent); in 1980, the comparable figure was 240 (or 26 per cent), and in 1985 303 (or 32 per cent). The number of women QCs still remains very small, however. Until 1986 only 18 out of 797 QCs were women. In the three years prior to 1986 there were a mere three women in a total of 120 new silks. In 1984 there was no woman in a list of 43 names. In 1986, however, there were five women appointed out of a total of 58 and in 1987 there were two out of 53. It can be said therefore that there is no sign of any form of positive discrimination to redress the current imbalance. But the issue of sex discrimination in regard to judicial appointment will not really be put to the test until the next generation. For the moment the choice of eligible women is obviously very restricted.

If there are few women among the judges, there are even fewer persons who are non-white. Mota Singh, a circuit judge, is the only Asian person who sits on the bench as a full-time judge and there are no blacks at all. In July 1987 not one of the recorders was non-white but there were two non-white assistant recorders — out of just over 400. There is no doubt that racial discrimination is a significant problem in the legal profession; both sides of the profession have now set up committees to tackle the issue directly. But at the level of judicial appointments the more obvious reason why there are so few non-white judges, as in the case of women, is the tiny number of senior non-white practitioners who would be eligible for such appointments. (In 1987 there was only one black Queen's Counsel out of over 550.) In a few years time, when more have reached the appropriate age, the issue of racial discrimination in judicial appointments may be more of a live one than it is at present. The fact that at the Bar many black barristers have been (or have felt) forced to join 'ghetto' chambers where all, or virtually all, members are drawn from the same ethnic background is bound to aggravate the problem — if only because such candidates for judicial office may not easily get the support of the judicial and practitioner community for which the Lord Chancellor's Department looks when making appointments.

Judges appointed as High Court judges or above must all have been former barristers. Solicitors are not yet eligible, though this is likely to change sometime in the not too distant future as part of the changing balance of power between the two branches of the profession. (Sir John Donaldson, Master of the Rolls, lent his considerable authority to this campaign in an interview in the Bar's new journal *Counsel* in July 1986.) Circuit judges, recorders and assistant recorders can be either barristers or solicitors — though about 90 per cent of each category are still barristers. A report issued in 1972 by JUSTICE proposed that the pool from which judges are selected should include solicitors and academic lawyers.[9] At that time solicitors were not even eligible to be appointed circuit judges and the Courts Act 1971, which gave solicitors for the first time the right to be appointed as recorders, had only just been passed. By 1987 solicitor judges had been functioning for nearly fifteen years and well over a hundred had been appointed. (In July 1987 the total of full-time and part-time solicitor judges as circuit judges (40), recorders (31) and assistant recorders (67) numbered 138 — out of 1,422.)

The argument as to whether solicitors should be eligible for the bench originally turned principally on whether they had the necessary experience, especially in advocacy. This issue is now dead. For well over a decade solicitors have been judges in the crown courts, even though they have no right to appear in the court as advocates in a jury trial! There has been no serious suggestion that solicitor judges have failed to perform their job competently. It follows that, sooner or later, the argument for them to be eligible to be appointed as High Court, and in due course Court of Appeal, judges will also be accepted. It is only a matter of time. Nothing except the self-interest of the barrister branch can be said to be against it. The case for academic appointments to the bench likewise seems unanswerable especially at the appeal court level. There are many examples of outstanding judges in other common law jurisdictions who came to the bench from the university law school — including Oliver Wendell Holmes, Benjamin Cardozo, William O. Douglas and Felix Frankfurter in the United States and Chief Justice Bora Laskin in Canada. To prevent the ablest academic lawyers from making a contribution as judges is not simply to diminish the academic branch of the legal profession but to deprive the community of the widest range of selection for judicial office.

THE BACKGROUND OF JUDGES

If most judges are male, middle-aged and white, what of their social background? The evidence of all the studies shows that English judges are generally drawn from a relatively narrow social class. The great majority have been to Oxbridge and before that to public schools. A study by K. Goldstein Jackson published in *New Society* of 14 May 1970, for instance, looked at the backgrounds of 359 judges, including not only the higher judiciary but also county court judges (now called circuit judges) and metropolitan magistrates. This found that 81 per cent had been to public schools and 76 per cent had been to Oxford or Cambridge. In how many countries in the world would the schooling of the judges be an issue? England must be the paradigm case of the hierarchical society where this topic excites such interest.

All the surveys that have been done reveal similar results.[10] But these figures have to be seen in perspective. Entrants to the legal profession in England, as in most other countries, have always been, and certainly remain, overwhelmingly middle-class. The class background of barristers, and the preponderance of public school backgrounds, has in the past probably been somewhat higher than that of solicitors, though in recent years this difference has probably been decreasing. But entrants to all faculties in the universities have also remained middle-class, in spite of the elaborate system of mandatory grants for those successful in obtaining places at the universities and poly-technics.* The proportion of working-class entrants to univers-ities generally is about the same today as it was pre-war — a depressing statistic for those who believe in the potential scope for social engineering. Even when one removes the financial barrier to education, the working class is grossly under-represented in the university student population. If not only practising lawyers but the general body of university students are predominantly middle-class, it is hardly surprising that the profile of the judges should be upper middle-class.

THE APPOINTMENT PROCESS AND POLITICS

Since the Lord Chancellor is a political appointment and a member of the executive by virtue of his membership of the Cabinet, how far does politics intrude into the business of appointing judges? In former times the appointment of judges was decidedly prone to party political influence. Professor Harold Laski, for instance, produced statistics to show that out of 339 judges appointed between 1822 and 1906, 80 were Members of Parliament at the time of nomination and another 11 had been candidates; and that out of 83 judges appointed who left Parliament for the bench, 63 were appointed by their party while in office. It has been calculated that in 1956, 23 per cent of the High Court, Court of Appeal or House of Lords judges had been either MPs or candidates — 11 per cent Conservative, 10 per cent Liberal, and 2 per cent Labour.[12] But for the past two or more decades it has been broadly accepted that the Lord

---

* The Robbins Report on Higher Education found that the proportion of students with fathers in manual occupations remained virtually static in the more than 30 years from 1928 to 1961. The Royal Commission on Legal Services showed that children of fathers in professional or managerial occupations were 21 per cent of all children aged 16-19; 50 per cent of those aged 20-24 in full-time education; 54 per cent of those studying law at university; and 76 per cent of those admitted to Middle Temple and Gray's Inn. A study done at the College of Law for the Royal Commission showed that 54 per cent of Bar students and 35 per cent of solicitor students had attended public schools. (For the references and other statistics available at the time, see Michael Zander, *The State of Knowledge about the English Legal Profession* (Barry Rose, London, 1980) pp. 22-3.)

Chancellor does not allow party political considerations to influence his choice of judges. During that period it has become very rare for anyone to be appointed to the bench direct from Parliament, and it is equally rare for the issue of party politics to be brought up in criticism of the Lord Chancellor's appointments. It is true that a person with markedly radical political views, either of the Right or the Left, would be unlikely to be appointed to the bench. But affiliation with any of the main political parties would these days be regarded as an irrelevant factor. The sceptic might suggest that the kind of 'safe' lawyers who make it to the bench are conservative with a small 'c', and it is therefore largely irrelevant whether they happen to be official Tories. This issue is considered further below, but it can at least be counted a mercy that party politics in the narrow sense is not a contentious issue in the appointment of judges.

Curiously, for magistrates the question of political appointment is dealt with in a totally different way. Magistrates are not technically called judges. But in fact they act as judges in handling 98 per cent of all the criminal cases in the country with the help of their clerks who guide them on the law.

There are more than 27,500 lay magistrates, unpaid and only slightly trained. Their power to sentence is limited to a term of six months imprisonment (or two consecutive terms of six months) or a fine of up to £1,000 (from 1988, £2,000). In London and a few large conurbations the work of magistrates is handled also by professional magistrates called stipendiaries ('stipes') of whom there are currently 62 — 48 in London and 14 in provincial cities. The chief advantage of stipendiaries is that they get through their work faster partly through expertise, partly no doubt because they sit alone.

Nominations come from 96 local Advisory Committees whose membership in almost all cases is secret.[13] There are close to 2,000 members of these committees which range in size from five to thirty. Most have around ten members. They are appointed by the Lord Chancellor. Appointment is normally for six years but this is renewable for a further period of six years; twelve years is supposed to be the maximum. Most committee members are themselves justices, so that in practice there is a real danger that the particular complexion of the bench will to an extent reproduce itself.* But the final decision is for the Lord Chancellor. For reasons which are somewhat unsatisfactory, conventional wisdom in recent decades has been that the Lord Chancellor should take the politics of candidates for appointment into account. Indeed, the form of recommendation for appointment to the bench actually requires that the proposer states the party political affiliation, if any, of the candidate. A candidate for appointment who has not declared his party affiliation will be asked to reveal it when he is interviewed. Many prospective JPs understandably find this offensive. When submitting names for new appointments, the local committee which advises the Lord Chancellor on appointments is required to specify the numbers of votes cast locally for the main parties. Also the annual confidential report made by such committees is supposed to state the number of magistrates with affiliations with each of the main parties. The attention given to political persuasion stems directly from the opinion of the Royal Commission of 1909-10 on the Magistrates that 'It is not in the public interest that there be an undue preponderance of justices drawn from one political party' and that 'appointments influenced by considerations of political service and interests are highly detrimental to public interest'. The 1948 Royal Commission on Justices of the Peace thought likewise that appointments should not be made for political service. But there is no doubt that service in local politics has been and remains one of the main, or possibly even *the* main, background for appointment to the bench.

Every study that has been done in modern times about the background of magistrates shows that involvement in local politics plays a key part in the processes which lead to the selection of a high proportion of those chosen as justices. It equally plays a critical part in the choice of those who serve on the advisory committees, which in turn determines who gets appointed. Advisory committees are composed mainly of senior magistrates in post. The conclusion of Elizabeth Burney, author of a recent study of the magistracy, was:[14]

Politics emerges as only one of the many overlapping social networks from which magistrates are drawn but they have a unique importance not only because of the undue emphasis

---

* A study of the composition of the bench in Rochdale, Lancashire, revealed that 49 per cent of magistrates were members of the Rotary Club or its women's equivalent, the 'Inner Wheel', and that at least 28 per cent were freemasons. Moreover, 27 per cent of the Rotary Club members had connections with local law, including the justices' clerk, a police superintendent, a chief constable, a probation officer and three solicitors. Also the magistrates overlapped considerably with other public bodies, notably the local Health Executive Council and Hospital Management Committee (D. Bartlett and J. Walker, *New Society*, 19 April 1973 and 25 December 1975).

laid on them by central government but because of the influence which can be wielded by quite a small group of politically organised magistrates. Not only do active politicians often dominate the advisory committees, but when it comes to internal bench elections for posts such as chairman of the bench ... then quite disproportionate power can be wielded by a political caucus.

On the other hand, she reported that in the whole of her investigation she never came across any suggestion that political affiliation implied partial justice in cases tried by the courts.

The whole rationale for attempting to achieve a political balance in the composition of the magistrates' bench must be seen as somewhat suspect. Lord Dilhorne, when Lord Chancellor, spoke in 1963 of the necessity 'to distinguish between the individual magistrate, whose politics were irrelevant, and the need to keep a political balance on the bench and avoid the predominance of one political colour or the other'. It is by no means obvious that having a political balance on the bench has anything whatever to do with justice being done. At most, it might be related to justice being seen to be done, on the ground that too many justices of a particular political persuasion may at least create an apprehension of potential bias.

Much the same is true of the view that justices should not be drawn from too narrow a social class. Recent Lord Chancellors have made considerable efforts to try to increase the number and proportion of working-class magistrates, though without signal success. The Royal Commission in 1948 found that only 15 per cent of male JPs were wage-earners, but by 1966 a sample found that this had risen to only 15.9 per cent. Another study in 1971/2 found only 13 per cent of the sample in this category, and Elizabeth Burney in her 1979 study had 12 per cent of wage-earners.[15] (Wage-earner is, of course, by no means the same as working-class — so that the proportion of working-class, as this term is normally understood, is no doubt even lower. But whether that necessarily diminishes the quality of justice in the magistrates' courts must be open to doubt.)

ARE JUDGES BASICALLY CONSERVATIVE?

Very few subscribe to the view that there is any crude relationship between judges and politics — that Ministers of the Crown or senior civil servants will, for instance, attempt to

influence judges in regard to pending cases they are trying. The
very idea is unthinkable. If a judge who was in the middle of a
trial dealing with a politically high-profile issue happened to
meet the Minister in charge of that area of policy, he would be
scandalised if the Minister even so much as raised the general
matter — let alone discussed the actual case.

But the social origins and political views of judges can, of
course, have an influence in much subtler ways — as part of the
determinants of their decision-making, where there is scope for
choice. To the Marxist it is axiomatic that a middle-class judge
will hold middle-class values. But this view is also firmly held
by many who cannot in any way be described as Marxists.
Certainly it is a fashionable opinion amongst those on the
political Left. The most serious exposition of the argument was
in Professor John Griffith's influential and provocative book,
The Politics of the Judiciary, first published in 1977. According
to Griffith, the judges interpret the public interest from the
point of view of their own class.[16]

> And the public interest, so defined, is by a natural, not an
> artificial, coincidence, the interest of others in authority,
> whether in government, in the City or in the church. It
> includes the maintenance of order, the protection of private
> property, the promotion of certain general economic aims, the
> containment of the trade union movement, and the contin-
> uance of governments which conduct their business largely in
> private and on the advice of other members of the governing
> group.

Griffith does not deny that the judges are capable of moving
with the times and of adjusting to changed circumstances. But
their function, he argues, 'is to do so belatedly'. They should not
be seen, as they so often claim, as the strong and natural
defenders of liberty or of the weak against the state. If anything,
the precise contrary is more probable. They are mainly to be
seen as the upholders of law and order, of the established
distribution of power, of the conventional view.

Lord Devlin, the distinguished former law lord, has objected
that, although Griffith argues that there are categories of cases
that the judges as a group decide unfairly, he has not
demonstrated more than that *he* would have decided such cases
differently.[17]

To my mind none of the evidence [assembled by Griffith] adds
much to the inherent probability that men and women of a

certain age will be inclined by nature to favour the status quo. Is it displeasing to the public at large that the guardians of the law should share this common tendency?

Griffith, he contends, has not so much demonstrated a major problem of our society as simply a facet of the uniform phenomenon caused by the fact that 'in any peaceful and law-abiding democratic society in which the mortality rate is constantly declining government falls into the hands of the ageing'. In Lord Devlin's telling phrase 'the oligarchs who rise to the top in a democratic society are usually mature, safe and orthodox men' — and the silent majority may see this as a very good thing.

It must also be said that Professor Griffith has perhaps not given quite enough weight to the great variations in judicial responses. It may be true that very often the judges favour the Big Battalions, the Establishment and the *status quo*. But there are so many counter examples that the thesis is not quite so impressive in its own terms as appears at first sight.[18] Those who believe that the judges are biased against the common man often say that this tendency is displayed most plainly in the field of trade union law. Yet a comprehensive survey of judicial decisions involving disputes between workers and employers from 1871 to 1966 hardly supported this belief. There were 127 decisions (including appeals) reviewed in the study. Of these, 48 (or 38 per cent) were determined in favour of the workers.[19] Certainly, more cases were decided in favour of the employers than of the workers, but the picture is not as one-sided as the proponents of the Griffith thesis might lead one to expect.

Similarly, if the Griffith view were a theory which helped to explain historical developments or patterns of decisions, one would expect it to apply to the decisions of courts determining challenges to Mrs Thatcher's Government. A more than normally conservative government ought to be particularly congenial to judges whose natural function is to uphold the *status quo*. But the fact is that in the recent past the Thatcher Government has lost case after case in the courts. Hugo Young, *The Guardian*'s respected columnist, in an article in October 1985, said that hardly a week passed without a judicial decision calling a Minister to task. Most of the early cases in administrative law, he suggested, revolved around the actions of Labour Governments when they were predictably seeking to increase state power in the post-war era. But this instinct could no longer be identified with Labour alone. 'The Thatcher

Government is living proof of that: a government deeply committed to getting the state off people's backs but unable to resist the tendency to give it more and more power.' This was probably an unstoppable trend. But the judges had responded and, according to Young, on their record 'should finally have nailed the lie that they are Tory judges'.

TRAINING FOR JUDGING

Throughout the continent of Europe it is regarded as obvious that judges need to be trained for their work. In these countries those who opt for the judicial career go to a special course after ordinary law school which typically takes two or more years (in France it is two and a half years). In England and all other common law countries the assumption is that by the time a person is appointed a judge he has knocked around the system for so long that he can be expected to know enough about it to function effectively. The theory always was that all one needed to do was to take him out of the scrum, give him the referee's whistle and tell him to get on with it.

The idea that judges might actually need training was ridiculed. Even so intellectual a figure as the former law lord Lord Devlin thought it was plainly a wrong-headed view. In an address to the annual meeting of the Howard League for Penal Reform in 1976 Lord Devlin said that the words' 'judicial training' occasioned alarm. The judge, he said, speaks for the ordinary citizen.

> Once you start training him in anything ... he loses the essential character of the English judge. He no longer speaks and reacts as the ordinary man, he sits on the bench as what would never be more or better than a half trained expert.

But this traditional attitude was swept away in the late 1970s as a result of the recommendations of an official committee chaired by Lord Bridge.[20] The Committee recommended that judges did need training especially in the complex business of sentencing, and in 1979 the Judicial Studies Board was set up under the Lord Chancellor's Department. It has proved to be an unexpected success. Training for judges is now an accepted part of the system. In 1984, for instance, the Board organised 3 three-and-a-half day residential courses for experienced crown court judges and recorders, involving some 240 participants, and 3 three-day seminars for over 100 new assistant recorders. As from October 1985 the Board has provided training also for judges involved in civil and family work, and it has now started also to supervise the training of magistrates, which was previously the concern of an Advisory Committee.* Where a few years ago the judges scoffed at the idea that training might be necessary or even desirable, today they recognise its value and appear to welcome this development, though it is only compulsory for new judges and can hardly be said to be very extensive. The content is a mixture of sentencing exercises on problems sent out in advance, lectures and seminars on aspects of evidence and procedure, probation, community service, prison overcrowding and such like. A new judge will be expected to do two or three such sessions in the first few years. The Board also publishes a journal, which is sent to all judges, containing information regarding both new developments in the law and the system and the latest relevant statistics. No doubt more could be done but, considering how new this whole enterprise is, it seems to have got off to an excellent start and to be gaining in strength. The crucial change is that the Board is in being and is expanding. The concept of judicial training is established and will undoubtedly play an increasing role.

On the other hand, it should not be thought that the judges have in other contexts suddenly become open to being taught how to do their job. In fact the Bridge Report on Judicial Training said that the word 'training' had aroused such fears and hostility that it thought it should be dropped.[21]

It is said that 'training' implies that there are trainers who can train people to be judges and that ... this must, despite all protestations to the contrary, represent a threat to judicial independence.... [I]f the use of the word training itself is so generally felt to carry objectionable overtones it had better be abandoned.

Judicial Studies was thought to be a more politic phrase than Judicial Training. A series of informal dinners given a few years ago by senior Home Office officials for selected judges had to be

---

* One of the first fruits of this new role was the issue to each Magistrates' Courts Committee in April 1987 of glossy cards to be used in training, setting out the stages of reaching a decision on verdict and sentence. In the same month the BBC were allowed to record actual magistrates' deliberations in Coventry (broadcast on Radio 4 on 15 and 17 April 1987). It seems that not everyone was impressed with the quality of the performance by the justices. The fact that the cards were issued by the Judicial Studies Board in the very same month was a coincidence. But according to at least one clerk to the justices they could prove extremely useful in raising the level. (See Robin Haynes, 'Decision-Making under the Miscroscope', *Justice of the Peace*, 8 August 1987, p. 151.)

abandoned after objections on the ground that they threatened the independence of the judiciary. Even the Lord Chief Justice has had serious difficulties in getting the judges to respond to his attempts in the past few years to bring down the tariff for sentences for certain types of offences, especially non-violent offences.

Training for magistrates has been a familiar part of the system for much longer — but the case for such training is obviously quite different, since all but a few magistrates are lay persons with no background in law. There is, in fact, a school of thought that training for lay magistrates is a misconception in that it creates the risk that they may thereby lose their 'layness', which is their main attribute. According to this view, since they cannot (and should not) be turned into mini-lawyers, it is best to leave them in their natural state, innocent of any legal knowledge. But this view has not prevailed. Training has been part of the system since 1966. Since then they have had to undertake to complete a course of instruction within a year of appointment. Responsibility for the courses rests with the local Magistrates' Courts Committee on which both bench and local council members are represented.

The training is divided into two stages. The first has to be completed before the magistrate sits on the bench. It consists of three periods of observing in court, one of which is supposed to be in a court other than his or her own. Stage One is also supposed to include some elementary instruction on the role of the magistrate, court procedure, evidence, ways of dealing with offenders and on domestic and other civil proceedings. But since these things are also dealt with in Stage Two, most courts confine themselves to the barest outline, often in a single session. New justices also receive a basic handbook sent to them by the Lord Chancellor's Office together with the Home Office booklet on available sentences and their uses. Stage Two, which is supposed to be completed within a year of appointment, consists of instruction on six listed topics — usually through weekend or evening lectures and weekend courses. During this period the new justice of the peace is required to visit a local prison and another penal institution.

A survey in 1974 by Dr John Baldwin showed that although most new justices spoke highly of their training a substantial proportion had not in fact completed the whole of it.[22] An informal check in regard to training carried out in 1977 by Miss Elizabeth Burney confirmed this impression.[23] Training, such as it is, is mainly in the hands of the clerk whose main expertise is in law and procedure. Clerks may have less experience in other important areas including the broad issues of sentencing, the business of chairing a court and what sorts of questions justices can ask. Miss Burney proposed amendments to the scheme of training,[24] but it seems clear from several studies that the chief influence on magistrates is the experience of being a member of a particular bench. Even neighbouring benches differ markedly in their approach to problems, particularly of sentencing.[25] Formal training sessions inevitably make less impact than working for years with other magistrates on a day-to-day basis. But formal training does nevertheless have a valuable, if limited, role to play. The fact that the Judicial Studies Board now oversees the national programme of training for magistrates may help to strengthen this process.

DISMISSAL

The machinery for dismissal of judges has virtually never been needed. In the case of judges of the High Court and above who hold their offices 'during good behaviour', dismissal requires an address of both Houses of Parliament — which has occurred only once, in 1830.[26] In that case Sir Jonah Barrington, a judge of the High Court of Admiralty in Ireland, was charged with appropriating to his own use sums of £682, £200 and £40. Proceedings against the judge were conducted in each House and each passed a resolution calling for his dismissal. This was presented to the King who graciously agreed.

In the intervening years there have been a number of instances when the power was invoked. In 1906 347 MPs backed a motion for inquiry into the conduct of Mr Justice Grantham, a notoriously outspoken and intemperate judge. Grantham, a Conservative who did not trouble to conceal his views, unseated a successful Liberal candidate for a corrupt electoral practice in holding a party in September 1905 which he deemed to be 'on the eve' of an election, whilst upholding the election of a Conservative who held a party in the same month on the ground that the election was not then imminent! He had also been heard to make biased remarks about a trial at a dinner party. His conduct was almost universally condemned by those who spoke in the debate in the House of Commons, but the general view was that no corrupt motive had been shown and in the absence of corruption or moral turpitude, the House should not resort to the extreme penalty of passing an address for removal.

More recently in 1973 a motion was put down for the removal

from office of Sir John Donaldson, later the Master of the Rolls but then President of the controversial National Industrial Relations Court. The court had ordered the sequestration of assets held in the 'political fund' of the Amalgamated Union of Engineering Workers, which had defied the court. The judge was criticised by trade unionists and the motion accusing him of 'political prejudice and partiality' was signd by 187 Labour MPs. The Lord Chancellor, Lord Hailsham, entered the fray with his customary vigour, strongly attacking the proponents of the motion in a public speech. He invited the public to note the names of the MPs concerned and their party, and called on them to 'strike a blow for the integrity and independence of the judges of this country'. This aroused the wrath of Labour MPs who proceeded to table a motion condemning the Lord Chancellor for improperly attempting to influence the proceedings of the House and describing his speech as 'a gross contempt of the House of Commons'. In the event, however, neither motion was debated. The Speaker did not give priority to a debate on the Lord Chancellor's speech and no time was ever found for the motion to remove Sir John Donaldson.

If really serious criticism of a judge sufficient to justify his dismissal should ever emerge, the way in which it would normally be dealt with is by the Lord Chancellor of the day putting it to the judge that he should resign. This is in fact what happened in the case of Mr Justice Hallet, who in the 1950s developed a reputation for constantly interrupting trials and who eventually resigned after yet another such case.

Circuit judges, recorders and stipendiary magistrates can be dismissed by the Lord Chancellor for 'inability or misbehaviour'. But in the years since the Courts Act 1971 this has occurred only once — Judge Bruce Campbell was sacked in 1983 after being convicted of smuggling spirits, cigarettes and tobacco into England in his yacht, for which he was fined £2,000. Curiously, the fact that he was dismissed benefitted him financially. If, as he had wished, he had resigned he could not have kept any part of his pension. The Lord Chancellor, however, refused to permit him to resign as he wanted to dismiss him. But a judge who is dismissed for conduct which does not arise out of his office can in the discretion of the Crown keep his accrued pension, which is what happened.*

---

* In an earlier incident in 1851 Judge Ramshaw, a Liverpool county court judge, was dismissed after there had been repeated complaints about him. The Chancellor of the Duchy of Lancaster inquired into the matter and found that

In addition to the power to dismiss a judge there is, of course, also the power not to re-appoint those who have been appointed for a limited period only, such as recorders. This happened in December 1984 in the case of Judge Manus Nunan whose case was subsequently taken up by the controversial Judge Pickles and the media. In interviews given to the press, and later in his book (*Straight from the Bench*, 1987), Judge Pickles contended that Nunan had been dismissed because he was Irish in the wake of the Brighton bomb when the IRA almost succeeded in killing the Prime Minister and half the Cabinet. The Lord Chancellor, Lord Hailsham, felt sufficiently outraged over this allegation to write to *The Guardian* of 14 July 1986 categorically to deny the suggestion. Nunan's appointment had not been extended, he said, on the ground that his judicial performance had been the subject of criticism.

Lay magistrates hold office at pleasure and can therefore be removed by the Lord Chancellor at any time without showing cause, but in fact it is only done for cause. Often the reason is that the justice does not comply with the duty to sit a certain minimum number of days per year. But occasionally a justice is removed because of some improper conduct. Sometimes it follows conviction for a criminal offence — though conviction for a minor motoring offence usually results in nothing more than a reprimand. Drunken driving used always to result in dismissal but in recent years it has been dealt with by suspension from sitting during any period of disqualification from driving. Unless there were aggravating circumstances a justice would be allowed to return to sit on the bench after his period of suspension had elapsed. On occasion, defiance of the law by a justice has led to dismissal, for instance in 1972 when a Welsh magistrate told the Lord Chancellor that she refused to impose penalties on people who non-violently broke laws that were unfair to the Welsh language. She had helped to pay the fine of the chairman of the Welsh Language Society who was imprisoned for refusing to pay a fine imposed for daubing paint on English road signs. In 1975 a Humberside justice who objected to rate increases was dismissed for refusing to sign distress

there were insufficient grounds for his dismissal, whereupon he laid on a public banquet in the courthouse to celebrate his non-dismissal. He made a speech threatening retribution against the press if they were rude to him. When the *Liverpool Journal* published the gist of his speech he had the editor arrested, fined and imprisoned on the ground that the publication 'discomposed his mind for the administration of justice that morning'. There was a national outcry which then resulted in his being dismissed by the Lord Chancellor.

warrants in respect of persons who failed to pay their rates. In 1985 Mrs Kathleen Cripps was dismissed by the Lord Chancellor for taking part in a CND demonstration outside the court where she normally sat in connection with a case being heard there. She applied unsuccessfully to the High Court for judicial review of the decision.[27]

The powers of the Lord Chancellor in regard to the dismissal of judges or magistrates are untrammelled save by the conventions established by practice. From time to time the suggestion has been made that the system would be improved if there were some form of fair hearing for a judge before he was dismissed and if the allegations against him were sifted by some form of tribunal or special commission. JUSTICE, in its 1972 report on the judiciary chaired by Peter Webster, QC (who later became a High Court judge), recommended that there should be a three-man judicial commission to which the Lord Chancellor should have to refer any case in which he thought there were grounds for dismissing a judge of the High Court or above. The commission should inquire into the matter and recommend whether the question should be referred to the Judicial Committee of the Privy Council, which would then advise the Queen whether the judge should be dismissed. Any other judge dismissed by the Lord Chancellor should have the right to appeal to the Judicial Committee which would appoint a judicial commission and the same procedure would then apply.

At the time this proposal attracted virtually no notice, but recently it has come into focus as a result of controversy over the judges. Surprisingly, Lord Hailsham, so determined to avoid any form of judicial commission for appointments, came out in support of the idea of such a commission in relation to proposed dismissals. In May 1986 in press and radio interviews at the time of the publication of the new official pamphlet on judicial appointments, he said that it was vital that any serious complaint against a judge should be properly investigated and that natural justice should be observed. This would rule out the Lord Chancellor acting as investigator, judge and jury. Some form of complaints board, he thought, should be established to inquire into the matter. The judge would be able to make his case to the board, which would then make recommendations to the Lord Chancellor, whose decision would then be final. Nothing, however, had been done about this proposal before Lord Hailsham ceased to be Lord Chancellor in June 1987.

The Times of 19 June 1987 reported that the Lord Chief Justice, Lord Lane, had 'vetoed' Lord Hailsham's idea of a judicial complaints board to advise the Lord Chancellor. One factor behind his thinking was said to be that judges sitting on a complaints board would be in an exposed and invidious position with their advice being open to formal challenge. It was by then unlikely that this proposal would in any event be acted upon, at least for the present. A judicial commission to hear general complaints about judges may not be a good idea, but there would be value in some form of procedure whereby a serious allegation against a judge which appeared to constitute a *prima facie* case justifying dismissal should be investigated by, say, three senior judges who would report to the Lord Chancellor. This is in fact the procedure in Scotland.

COMPLAINTS ABOUT JUDGES

Criticism of judges, however, is usually not over allegations of serious misconduct or grave impropriety but over decisions that are seen as wrong-headed. The classic instance is the case of the lenient sentence, such as the sentence imposed in the 'Vicarage rape case' in February 1987 when the entire country seemed gripped by a fever of rage over what were felt to be woefully inadequate sentences. Mr Justice Leonard, an experienced and usually rather tough judge, gave two defendants sentences of five and three years for particularly horrifying rapes and five years for aggravated burglary on the same occasion, whilst the ring-leader got ten years for the burglary alone. The disproportion between the rape and the burglary sentences created a widespread sense that the judge had got it entirely wrong. (The feeling was confirmed by the Lord Chief Justice when he considered an appeal for the co-defendant in June 1987.) The judge was severely criticised by the media for his decision. Cases of a similar kind seem to crop up every few months.

There is at present no procedure for dealing with such cases other than the possibility that the Lord Chancellor may have a private word with the judge concerned, which he is very loath to do.* Calls for the judge's dismissal are wide of the mark. A judge cannot, and should not, be at risk of dismissal for incorrect

---

* A rare example occurred in 1987. The Lord Chancellor's Department let it be known in a parliamentary answer on 21 July that Judge Michael Argyle, a senior judge at the Old Bailey, had been severely reprimanded by the Lord Chancellor, Lord Havers, for an anti-immigrant and anti-government speech made on a private occasion to students at Trent Polytechnic. The speech on 13 March 1987, had created a furore when its contents were leaked to the national press. *The Observer* reported two days later that the judge had told the

decisions. That would threaten the essence of the independent judiciary. The 1972 JUSTICE report suggested that complaints about the behaviour of a judge should be put to a complaints tribunal consisting of judges, lawyers and non-lawyers. The proceedings would be *in camera* and there should be a sifting procedure so that judges did not have to face frivolous complaints. But such a body would not deal with complaints about incorrect or foolish decisions so much as complaints about overbearing, rude or otherwise objectionable behaviour towards litigants, lawyers, witnesses or others involved in court cases. There were press reports in June 1986 that the Lord Chancellor's Department was considering spot checks on part-time judges by 'inspectors' who could be retired circuit judges or, possibly, serving judges. Their task would be to check on how recorders and assistant recorders were performing, with a view to reporting on their suitability for promotion. But nothing more has so far been heard of this suggestion.

Media criticism of individual judges is one source of accountability — though frequently the media, and especially the popular press, are themselves guilty of 'going over the top'. In Spring 1987 both the Lord Chancellor and the Master of the Rolls expressed concern about attacks on the judiciary by the media. Sir John Donaldson, speaking to a conference of solicitors in Oxford on 12 April 1987, said that media criticism of judges because of the sentences they handed down damaged public respect for the judiciary. He deprecated either adulation of or attacks on judges, which produced a kind of 'popular ratings system — a sort of judicial top ten'. This, he suggested, created a climate which made it more difficult 'for the judge to discharge a duty which is difficult enough as it is'. His concern, he said, was 'with the potential damage to the public respect for the judges and for the rule of law which seems to be inherent in the continuance of ill-informed criticism on its present scale'. Three days later, on 15 April, the Lord Chancellor chimed in to similar effect. Speaking at a banquet in the City of London given by the London Solicitors' Company, Lord Hailsham warned against the danger of trial of judges through 'irresponsible comment'. Justice, he said, was not a cloistered virtue but 'let there be

---

law students at the Polytechnic that there were five million illegal immigrants in Britain, that judges should be able to impose the death sentence on anyone convicted of an offence carrying more than a 15-year sentence and that the government had 'fallen flat on its face' with rising anarchy on the streets in Britain. Asked at the meeting what proof he had of the numbers of illegal immigrants, he replied: 'I don't have the figures, but just go to Bradford'.

some self-discipline, let criticism be well-informed, well-researched and temperately expressed'. Trial by the media could undermine the independence of the judiciary and public confidence in the judicial process.

Commenting on Sir John Donaldson's speech, *The Times* of 14 April 1987 said that if his approach were adopted there would be a silence broken only by the sound of judges. Sir John seemed not to realise that although the media were often guilty of instant comment, often of a crude and ignorant character, they always found room for later voices contradicting and correcting. The media's constant need for controversy made sure of that. The media had a role to play — for instance in showing the need to reopen doubtful cases like the 1974 Birmingham bomb case. Nor was Sir John convincing when he claimed that hostile criticism of the judges was unfair because they could not answer back.[28]

> Whenever that claim is made about anyone, all other citizens should be on their guard. It is remarkable how often the suggestion that they have no means of answering back is made on behalf of the most powerful and vocal in the land, such as Whitehall permanent secretaries and judges.

Lord Hailsham for his part was reprimanded by Louis Blom-Cooper, QC for moaning about 'intemperate criticism'. Since when, he asked in *The Guardian* of 24 March 1987, 'has it ever been justifiable to complain of intemperancy?' So long as the critic tried to be accurate and fair and did not impugn the judge's motives or scandalise the court, he could be as outspoken — even as outrageous — as he wished. No-one should know this better than the then Lord Chancellor himself for in February 1968, whilst MP and shadow Home Secretary, he had as Quintin Hogg written an article for *Punch* in which he took the Court of Appeal severely to task for its strictures on lawyers and parliamentarians. The recent judgment of the Court of Appeal, he wrote, was an example of the 'blindness which sometimes descends on the best of judges'. As a result of the article, proceedings had been brought against Mr Hogg to have him held in contempt of court, but the Court of Appeal rejected the application. Lord Denning said, 'the criticism here complained of, however wide of the mark, whether expressed in good taste or bad taste, seems to me to be within the limits of reasonable courtesy and good faith'. Lord Justice Edmund Davies said:

> Whether, despite his great learning and his distinction as a

Queen's Counsel, Mr Hogg paid proper respect to the standards of accuracy, fairness and good taste ... may unhappily be open to doubt ... inaccurate though the article is now acknowledged to be in a material respect, I have no doubt that the contempt has not been made out.

JUDGES AND THE MEDIA

Whether Lord Hailsham blushed is not recorded but this was only one in a series of unhappy episodes arising out of his concern for proper relations between the judges and the press. In recent years the media, especially radio and television, have tried to get judges to take part in public affairs by contributing articles, giving interviews or taking part in studio discussion programmes. The Lord Chancellor, for his part, had tried to control this development by insisting that judges get permission from his office before participating in such programmes. On 21 January 1986 Hugo Young devoted his *Guardian* column to the issue. Lord Hailsham, he said, was an old and brilliant man who had been a jewel of our post-war politics 'gleaming with untarnished quality beside the bankers and bootboys who have come and gone from the table he has occupied for much of his political life'. But he had become deformed by a single obsession — the independence of the judiciary. Sometimes he had been fully justified.

When Labour politicians, Michael Foot among them, launched the most unjustified attacks on the integrity of the bench under the Heath Government, Hailsham retaliated with an eloquence that vanquished their odious insinuations.

But latterly an increasingly perfervid note had crept into his utterances defending the judges. In the course of making a Radio Four programme about the Bar, Hugo Young had approached a number of judges for contributions, only to be told that the Lord Chancellor had refused permission. Not that the judges were being stopped from broadcasting. The senior official in the Lord Chancellor's Department was indignant at the idea. They were simply 'consulting' and the advice not to take part was in order that judicial independence should be preserved. In Young's eyes there was something more than slightly ironic in the theory that the independence of the judiciary could only be protected by removing the independence of individual judges to decide for themselves whether or not to take part in such programmes. (Lord Templeman and Lord Edmund Davies in fact defied the

ban and took part anyway, but it was subsequently explained
that law lords are not affected by the rules.) Judges, Young said,
should be allowed to contribute to the enlightenment of the
public, not least to improve the image of the law 'to demonstrate
the truth that many of them, far from being toffee-nosed
reactionaries, are ordinary men of the world, with matchless
experience, first class minds, judicious habits of speech and a
certain sagacity'.

Two days later *The Guardian* published a reply from Lord
Hailsham himself. Young had got his facts entirely wrong.
Judges were not prevented from media appearances by Lord
Hailsham but by the operation of the 'Kilmuir rules' laid down
by the then Lord Chancellor in 1955. The principle of the rules
was that the judges should keep out of the public eye.

> So long as a judge keeps silent his reputation for impartiality
> remains unassailable; but every utterance which he makes in
> public, except in the course of the performance of his judicial
> duties, must necessarily bring him within the focus of
> criticism. It would moreover be inappropriate for the judiciary
> to be associated with any series of talks or anything which
> could fairly be interpreted as entertainment.*

According to Lord Hailsham these rules had been reviewed in
1971, 1977, 1979 and most recently in 1985. On each occasion
the judiciary had been consulted — the higher judges through
the heads of Divisions, the circuit judges through their own
organisation. In 1985 this had been the view expressed by the
judges after questionnaires had been sent to every circuit judge,
every High Court judge and every Court of Appeal judge. On
each occasion the overwhelming consensus was in favour of
continuing the rules.

In Lord Hailsham's view there were only two alternatives.
Either every judge should be left to make up his own mind
whether to accept such invitations, or else judges must recognise
that they owed a duty to one another and to the judiciary itself
to organise a collective policy which could only be done by
channelling invitations through a collective clearing house, for
which no-one had yet suggested a better alternative to the Lord
Chancellor's Office.

A fortnight later *The Guardian* published a long piece by one
of Her Majesty's Circuit judges, the irrepressible Judge Pickles.

---

* Lord Denning, always a law unto himself, appeared on 'Desert Island Discs'
whilst Master of the Rolls.

He questioned whether the Kilmuir rules were justified merely because the judges approved of them. 'We are not running a private company. The public and what they think, matter most. What do they think about them?'. He accused the Lord Chancellor of requiring excessive conformity. Two Court of Appeal judges had commented critically in court on the Government's proposed abolition of a statutory right of appeal in certain cases. The Lord Chancellor, Pickles wrote, had required them to write him a letter of apology. One was subsequently made a law lord. Would he have been promoted, Judge Pickles asked rhetorically, if he had not been prepared to apologise?

Lord Scarman speaking in June 1979 at the annual meeting of JUSTICE had said that judges should be free to take part in the press, radio and television on major social and legal issues. Lord Scarman himself had often done so. Judges could participate, he thought, on issues such as contempt of court, the right to privacy, the Bill of Rights issue, the development of administrative law, or sentencing policy. But a fine line had to be drawn. If they were talking about trade union law they should stick to what the law could do, and not get into what the law ought to be. Judge Pickles corroborated this view.

Following this lecture the Lord Chancellor had written to all the judges on 25 January 1980 stating that, although he 'had no power to give directions to fellow judges', he hoped judges invited to take part in programmes would consult his office so that a consistent policy could be maintained.

In December 1981 Judge Pickles was asked by the BBC 'Panorama' programme to take part in a programme on prison overcrowding and sentencing policy. Permission was asked from the Lord Chancellor's Department but it was refused — though Lord Justice Lawton appeared in the programme. If he had not asked permission, there had been a breach of the rules. If he had asked, the Lord Chancellor had refused one judge and allowed another. This, Pickles suggested, was questionable. 'Might it appear that the Kilmuir rules could tempt a Lord Chancellor to prefer "safe" pro-government judges to those with new or dissenting notions?' When Radio Leeds wanted to interview Judge Pickles in April 1985 about a play he had written, both the Lord Chancellor and his Permanent Secretary, Sir Derek Oulton, had said he should not. 'That is how control is achieved. Lord Hailsham may say he is only giving advice; but having asked for it and received an answer it is hard for a judge to reject it.'

On 22 March 1985 the *Daily Telegraph* published an article by

Judge Pickles on penal policy, parole, the pressure put on judges by Ministers to shorten prison sentences and the prison system. The very same day Sir Derek Oulton wrote to the judge that the publication of the article 'appears on the face of it such a flagrant breach of the convention [that judges should refrain from taking part in current political controversy] that the Lord Chancellor must regard it as prima facie judicial mis-behaviour'. Before taking the matter further, the Lord Chancellor would like to have the judge's comments. When Pickles failed to make a prompt response he was told that unless his comments were in the hands of the Lord Chancellor by 26 April, the Lord Chancellor would 'proceed to consider your future on the circuit bench'. There ensued an acrimonious correspondence in which Pickles stood his ground, defying the Lord Chancellor to do his worst. 'I realise that you may well try to dismiss me. You are certainly ruthless enough and you may be shortsighted enough.' Lord Hailsham and his officials must have been sorely tempted to take up Judge Pickles' invitation. But they held off in spite of many further provocations in the form of newspaper articles, broadcasts, and then a book. They probably concluded that getting rid of Judge Pickles would create too much of a row and be counter-productive. Better to let him continue sounding off like a spouting whale until the media tired of him.

For Hugo Young, however, (*The Guardian*, 18 February 1986), the whole saga raised the question of judges' independence 'and the ruthless administrative control by which the Lord Chancellor in practice diminishes it'. It was one thing to decide that it would be desirable for judges to be silent. It was even acceptable that judges should be advised to consult the Lord Chancellor's Department. But what was surely intolerable 'is for the Lord Chancellor, or still worse his officials, to threaten with dismissal a judge who in the exercise of his sane discretion, chooses to make a public statement'.

Even if the rules were relaxed it would not, he thought, lead to a torrent of judicial appearances.

Most judges would in no circumstances talk to a reporter. Many are far too ambitious to risk offending by a single misplaced murmur the sensibilities of the Department that has absolute and uninvigilated control over their promotion prospects. Many also cling to the long established belief that judges will be better guardians of justice if they remain the exclusive brethren.

But some did not agree and they should not be prevented from making a contribution to public discussion of issues such as sentencing, parole, bail, delay, criminal procedure, the quality of barristers and the like. For them our apparatus of civil liberties should offer better protection than 'velvet verbiage about independence — which conceals the bullet'.

Writing a few days later, the *New Law Journal* of 28 February agreed editorially that it was time for the Kilmuir rules to be relaxed, though it was questionable in what way and by how much. There was an argument for saying that the independence of the judges was threatened not by the fact that they made their views on issues known in public but by the fact that they held such views.

> The difference is that if judges make their views known their independence may be publicly called in question. That their independence may in fact be questionable is deemed largely irrelevant so long as it is hidden from the public.

At the end of the 1980s therefore the great issues seemed to be whether the system of appointment or dismissal of judges is sufficiently open, whether judges should be more free to take part in media debates, and whether judges are over sensitive to media criticism. Seen in proper perspective none of these matters can be regarded as of capital importance. Whether there is or is not some form of commission to vet candidates for judicial office or to sift allegations justifying dismissal of judges is unlikely to make any great substantive difference, save in terms of procedural fairness. It hardly seems likely that a different selection process would produce large or even significant numbers of different appointments or that the tiny number dismissed would change. If judges were released from the straitjacket of the Kilmuir rules it does not seem probable that many would wish to take part in radio or television broadcasts. Nor is it in the least likely that the popular press could be persuaded to moderate occasional outbursts of judge-bashing.

On the much more important question of how judges and magistrates actually do their job of judging, the evidence seems on the whole encouraging. The centuries-old institution of the lay magistracy continues as strong as ever and seems to give rise to remarkably little controversy or criticism. The main issue is whether the justices are as well trained and the court clerks are as well qualified legally as they should be. The judges too seem generally to enjoy high public esteem. They are more polite and better informed than in former times. With rare and colourful exceptions, they are also less inclined than formerly to hold eccentric views. Most probably tend to conservative views on issues of social policy and law and order but most members, at least of the higher judiciary, can also on occasion be persuaded to respond to the argument that the law needs to be kept abreast of changing times. The judges are not in the van of advanced thinking — but it would be remarkable (and probably undesirable) if they were. Judged as a collective enterprise the contemporary English judiciary seems broadly to give tolerable satisfaction*.

---

* For a less sanguine view see Carol Harlow, 'Refurbishing the Judicial Service' in Carol Harlow (ed.), *Public Law and Politics* (Sweet & Maxwell, London, 1986), pp. 182-206. See also D. Pannick, *Judges* (Oxford University Press, Oxford, 1987).

5

Justice in the Civil Courts

Civil litigation is the process for the resolution of disputes which the parties have been unable to resolve for themselves. They come to the court for a decision on a point of law, or more frequently, on facts over which they cannot agree. Typically, litigation in the civil courts is a personal injuries action arising out of a factory or road accident in which the plaintiff wants damages. Each side comes with its witnesses who are examined and cross-examined. The lawyers make their opening and closing speeches and the judge decides the case, which is heard in open court.*

A civil trial is broadly similar in its basic character to a trial in the criminal courts — both following the main features of what is known as the common law 'adversary system'. On the continent of Europe the 'inquisitorial system' has the judges calling and examining the witnesses, with the lawyers for the parties playing a subsidiary role. The judges have read a full statement of the evidence before the trial in the pre-trial dossier. There are few rules of evidence, anything relevant is generally deemed to be admissible. In the common law system, by

---

* The belief that justice should be done in open court and in public is deeply rooted. But in fact an extraordinary number of cases are heard behind closed doors. *The Independent* started a major campaign in 1987 to expose the extent of this situation. Cases heard in private include small claims arbitrations in county courts, hearings in pre-trial matters in the Queens Bench Division of the High Court (though not usually of the Chancery Division), and most matters in the Family Division. In an editorial on 17 February 1987 the paper said that on the previous day no fewer than 66 cases had been dealt with in the High Court in London behind closed doors and that in the previous week the number had been over 350.

contrast, it is the parties rather than the judge who decide how to run the case. Typically the judge will have seen no papers about the case when the trial starts. He knows nothing about it. It is the parties not the judge who call and examine the witnesses. If a relevant witness is not called by either side, the judge will not regard himself as entitled to call him for the court. The judge may ask an occasional question of a witness but basically he is like the umpire in a tennis match watching the parties hitting the ball over the net, simply calling the score and the result and ensuring that the lawyers keep to the rules.

There are elaborate rules of evidence. Various kinds of relevant evidence are excluded on the ground that they might be prejudicial or unreliable. Relevant documents in the possession of each party normally have to be made available to the other side ahead of the trial through the process known as discovery. But the evidence of witnesses and even their identity does not have to be revealed before the trial ('trial by ambush') — though this has recently been changed in regard to the evidence of expert witnesses in personal injury and medical negligence cases.* Trials are heard by professional judges in the High Court or the county court.† Trial by jury, formerly common in civil as in criminal cases, is now a rarity.

A TRIAL IS A RARE EVENT

In reality, however, a trial in a civil case is a wholly exceptional event. Well over 98 per cent of all cases which even get so far as the issue of legal proceedings are resolved short of a trial, and most civil disputes do not involve the issue of a writ. It has been estimated, for instance, that there are 300,000 claims made in respect of personal injuries per year; that legal proceedings are started in only 55,000 of these (18 per cent); and that a mere 3,650 (7 per cent of the 55,000, but only one to two per cent of the original 300,000[1]) come to trial.

Moreover, even if the issue comes to court a trial is a rarity. The great majority of writs are issued to recover money for debts usually owed to shops, mail-order concerns, traders, public utilities, and for a great variety of services rendered. In 1985, for instance, in the Queen's Bench Division of the High Court, such

---

* The rule for medical negligence cases was changed in October 1987 by a new Order 38, rule 37 which provides for mutual advance disclosure unless there are special reasons to the contrary.
† The High Court has unlimited jurisdiction; the county court's jurisdiction is normally limited to cases involving less than £5,000.

claims accounted for 138,000 out of 209,000 actions (66 per cent). The single next largest category was personal injury cases which numbered 33,800 (16 per cent of the total). In the county courts the number of debt actions was no less than 1.7 million out of a total of 2.2 million (or 77 per cent).

The plaintiff in most cases in both the High Court and the county court is some form of company or institution suing to recover money from a private citizen. The normal outcome of an action for money owed by way of debt is that the defendant pays, or if he does not, judgment is given for the full amount without any form of contest. Either the defendant fails to respond to the proceedings at all and judgment is given in default of any appearance or he responds with an acceptance of the plaintiff's case and agrees to judgment being given, often subject to an arrangement for paying the debt by instalments. Sometimes judgment is given summarily on application by the plaintiff on the basis that, although the defendant has purported to defend, there is no substance in his defence. (In 1985, in the Queen's Bench Division, judgment was given without a trial in 94,870 cases. By contrast, there were only 1,835 cases decided after a trial. In the county court there were 1.3 million cases decided without a trial, compared with a mere 73,500 decided after trial — of which 44,600 were under the special procedure called 'arbitration' for small claims. Ordinary trials therefore repre- sented only 2 per cent of cases ending in a judgment in the county court and 1.8 per cent of cases ending in judgment in the High Court.)

In divorce cases *any* proceedings in open court are today highly exceptional. Divorces nowadays are virtually all dealt with under the special procedure introduced in 1973 which did away with the need for any court hearing for the actual divorce. The papers are simply presented to the judge in chambers by the registrar and, provided they are in order, the divorce is pronounced without either spouse being either present or even represented. (In 1985, there were 162,000 divorce or nullity decrees granted; in only 464 cases (0.3 per cent) was there a trial.) The reality therefore is that civil trials occur in only a tiny proportion of untypical cases — above all in personal injury cases, but even in that category most cases do not get as far as a trial.

There are many reasons why trials are so rare in civil cases. One, which applies especially in debt cases, is that there is actually no basis for contesting the case. The money is owed. But even when there are grounds for contesting the matter, a contest is far from common. One reason is fear of the courtroom. Many people dread the idea of appearing in court as witnesses. As plaintiffs they would rather settle the case and collect less in the way of damages than expose themselves to the agony of having to stand up and give evidence in a courtroom. They prefer to concede rather than having to face up to cross-examination.

Another powerful reason for settling the case is fear of the costs. This may affect both sides. Even a wealthy litigant or an insurance company normally prefers to settle the case rather than allow the costs to pile up as the issue reaches the courtroom. The trial is by far the most expensive part of the whole process since at that point everyone has to be present — the parties and the lawyers, together with all the witnesses for both sides. Under the English indemnity rule of costs, under which the loser pays the bulk of the winner's costs, there is plainly an incentive to avoid a trial if there seems to be any possibility of losing. Even a settlement at the door of the court on the morning of the trial saves a great deal of money if the case would otherwise have gone on for any length of time.

Another reason for the tendency to run away from a trial is the uncertainty of litigation. A bird in the hand in the form of an offer is frequently more attractive than the promise of one and a half or two in the bush, obtainable only if the evidence and the lawyers together succeed in persuading the court. Many are the cases that have been lost unexpectedly through a witness not performing as it was thought he would ('not coming up to proof'). But the uncertainty extends equally to the amount of damages and how long it will take to get them. The general psychological stress on individual litigants created by uncertainty often accounts for the decision to reach a compromise on an action — or even to withdraw it.

PAYMENT INTO COURT

The pressure to accept a half-way reasonable offer is spiced in the English system by the 'payment into court' rule under which the defendant pays a sum of money into court which he judges is less than the claim is worth but enough to tempt the plaintiff. The offer is that amount of damages plus costs to date. The threat behind the offer is that, if it is not accepted and the case goes to trial, the plaintiff must pay the costs of both sides from the date of payment into court unless he succeeds in getting an award greater than the amount paid in. The judge is not told how much has been paid into court, or even whether there has been a payment in. The fixing of damages is not a precise affair and estimates of what a case is worth can sometimes vary quite widely. It sometimes happens therefore that the judge awards damages that are less than the defendant or his insurers have paid into court. When this happens, the result is a catastrophe for the plaintiff. His award of damages can largely or even wholly be wiped out by the costs that he now has to pay. By contrast, if the plaintiff accepts the amount paid into court, it will be accompanied by the payment of his costs to date. Lawyers are therefore understandably chary about recommending that a payment into court be rejected. The rule is highly favourable to the defendant, who is usually backed by insurance and is therefore anyway in economically the stronger position. The defence case is essentially run by the insurance company. An insurance company does not care whether any particular case is won or lost, but for the plaintiff success is crucial. He has only that one case and he badly wants his damages. He can therefore usually be manoeuvred into accepting less than the case is worth in order to be assured of getting something.

Various ideas have been advanced for reform of the rule regarding payment into court. One proposed by the Winn Committee in September 1968 was to have separate offers on liability and the amount of damages so as to make the system less unfair where the plaintiff wins on liability which perhaps takes most of the trial but loses on the level of damages and then has to pay all the costs.[2] Another obvious improvement would be to give a reasonable margin of error — so that the defendant would still pay the costs even though the judge's award was below the offer — provided it was more than, say, 90 per cent of the amount paid into court. A third would be to permit the plaintiff as well as the defendant to make a proposal as to settlement with implications for costs — rather than giving only the defendant the chance to put pressure on the plaintiff. This method has now been introduced in Canada.[3]

PREPARATION OF THE CASE

The lay public tends to believe that cases are won and lost through the brilliance (or lack of it) of the advocates. But every lawyer knows that, although the quality of the advocate is not unimportant, the quality of the preparation of the case is much more important. By the time the advocate first rises to his feet in court the outcome of the case has usually been predetermined by the work done in preparation of the case. Patrick Hastings, one of the greatest advocates of all times, once said that 'at least ninety per cent of all cases win or lose themselves and that the ultimate result would have been the same whatever counsel the parties had chosen to represent them'. Another familiar saying is that 'of every hundred cases, ninety win themselves, three are won by advocacy, and seven are lost by advocacy'. Most lawyers would broadly agree with both statements.

A major problem in the preparation of cases is that lawyers are torn between wanting to do what is needed to get the right result and not wanting to do too much too early. If the case is going to be settled before the trial, the extent of preparation necessary in the eyes of most lawyers will be less than would be appropriate if the case were actually going to trial. In fact, in most lawyers' offices the wheels start to grind furiously only in the run-up to the trial. Until then the collection of relevant material is conducted at a much lower pitch of intensity. The trouble is that, as a result, the factual data available to the lawyers wishing to negotiate a settlement may not be as complete as ideally they should be.

The problems of discovering the facts are compounded by the fact that the claimant so often does not even take advice from lawyers until weeks after the accident. The Oxford Socio-Legal Centre's national study of personal injury cases found that more than half of all accident victims who sought legal advice waited more than a month before going for such advice[4] — whereas the defendant insurance company will normally have very early notice of the accident and will often have investigated what happened before the plaintiff has even told his lawyers about it. It is usually only just before the trial that the whole story begins to come into sharp focus. Cases settled at an earlier point have therefore often been settled on an inadequate basis of knowledge. There is no obvious solution to the problem. Lawyers cannot be compelled to prepare cases fully at an earlier stage and, if they in fact did so, the costs would rise accordingly, perhaps considerably. In an individual case this might well make a difference but whether it would be worth the time and trouble over the whole range of civil cases is less clear. Again there is no way of reaching an authoritative view as to the pros and cons of the problem without empirical research, which has not been undertaken.

Knowledge of what goes on behind solicitors' doors in the handling of litigation is sketchy and unsystematic. If one is looking for hard information as to how the system works one is mainly confined to data in regard to cases that reach the court.

The pre-trial settlement which accounts for so large a majority of cases in which a writ is issued is like the submerged bulk of an iceberg.* Court cases, the tip of the iceberg, have, however, in recent years come to be quite extensively studied.

LAUNCH OF THE CIVIL JUSTICE REVIEW

The most recent and most wide-ranging attempt to map the territory has been the Civil Justice Review begun by the Lord Chancellor in 1985. The background was the recommendation of the Benson Royal Commission on Legal Services in 1979 that there should be 'a full appraisal of procedure and of the operation in practice of our system of justice in particular in all civil courts'.[5]

In November 1983, the Government's response to the Royal Commission's Report stated that the Lord Chancellor intended to undertake a complete and systematic review of civil procedure. In September 1984 a two-day seminar organised by the Law Commission with the support of the Lord Chancellor was held at the London School of Economics. The seminar considered a plan drawn up by the Lord Chancellor's Department that a major study be undertaken by teams of management consultants working under a small advisory committee with officials from the Lord Chancellor's Department. The seminar, which was attended by virtually all the Great and the Good in the field of civil procedure, rejected this plan. Overwhelmingly it thought that the whole exercise should be conducted instead on the more independent basis of a standing advisory committee of lawyers and non-lawyers appointed by the Lord Chancellor and attached to the Law Commission.[6] But the Lord Chancellor, Lord Hailsham, rejected this advice. The only concession made to the view of the experts expressed at the seminar was considerably to broaden the membership of the advisory committee. But the basic concept remained, as it had been from the outset, a series of studies from management consultants directed by officials in the Lord Chancellor's Department — under the general supervision of the independent advisory committee.

The programme of work was announced by Lord Hailsham in February 1985. The Civil Justice Review would look in turn at each of the main classes of civil business — personal injuries, small claims, debt, housing and commercial cases. The focus

---

* But see Hazel Genn, *Hard Bargaining, A Study of the Process of Out of Court Settlement in Personal Injury Actions* (Oxford University Press, Oxford, 1987).

would be in terms of jurisdiction, procedure and court administration. The Lord Chancellor himself would direct the show,
which it was thought would run for about three years at a cost of
some half a million pounds, most of which would go to the
management consultants. The ten-man independent advisory
committee, chaired by Sir Maurice Hodgson, of British Home
Stores, included a broadly based team of lawyers and non-
lawyers, of whom only three were orthodox lawyers — a law
lord, a senior barrister and a senior solicitor.* The method would
be to start in each area with a factual study of the progress of
cases through the courts based on a lengthy brief to the
management consultants from the officials and the advisory
committee. This would be followed by a consultation paper
written by officials with the advisory committee which analysed
the findings of the factual inquiry and outlined proposals for
change. The third stage was to be Ministerial decisions followed
by legislation and implementation. At the time of the announcement, and then Lord Chancellor, Lord Hailsham, 78 years old,
had already held the office for over nine years — longer than
anyone this century. The chief credit for the project goes jointly
to the Lord Chancellor, to Sir Derek Oulton, the Permanent
Secretary, and at a less senior level to Mr Richard White, who
was then put in charge of the execution of the exercise. Lord
Hailsham gave it his whole-hearted personal support, he took a
close interest in its progress, and everyone concerned was under
no doubt that he wanted to see speedy results. The personal
injuries consultation paper issued on 19 February 1986 allowed
for consultation, for instance, only to 31 July. The small claims
paper published on 23 September 1986 allowed for consultation
only until 31 January. The same breathless pace was maintained on each of the topics under review. There seemed every
reason to suppose that the new Lord Chancellor, Lord Havers,
would keep up the momentum.

The idea of employing management consultants to produce the
raw material for the inquiry was a bold one. It ran counter to
tradition in both legal research and the production of official
statistics on the legal system. (The seminar in September 1984
had been strongly opposed to management consultants.) The
brief to each of the consultants emphasised that the purpose was

---

* The other members, in addition to the chairman, were the deputy managing
director of GEC, a senior trade unionist, a representative of the insurance
industry, an academic lawyer and representatives of the National Consumer
Council and the National Association of Citizens' Advice Bureaux.

to identify ways of cutting the cost, the delays and the complexity of civil litigation.

On personal injuries the remit specifically excluded reform of the actual law and therefore did not permit any inquiry into the desirability of replacement of the common law system based on proof of fault by some form of no-fault system. This had been the subject of the Pearson Royal Commission on Civil Liability and Compensation for Personal Injury set up in 1975 in the wake of the thalidomide tragedy. The Commission, which reported in March 1978, proposed, amongst other things, that a no-fault scheme should be established for road accidents, by way of an extension of the industrial injuries scheme, though the ordinary tort system would survive for serious cases where the potential damages exceeded those available under the no-fault scheme. It also recommended that damages for non-pecuniary loss such as pain and suffering should not be recoverable in tort where the plaintiff recovered completely within three months. The effect of these two recommendations would have been to eliminate a mass of minor cases. But the proposals did not find favour with either the Government or the public and it quickly became clear that they were not to be implemented. The whole question of reform of the system of compensation for injuries has now been shelved and there seems to be no prospect of its being officially reopened for the foreseeable future.*

The cost and delays of civil litigation have been a matter of comment for decades. In fact, there have been no less than thirty-five separate reports on civil litigation this century, two of which were recent and specifically directed to personal injury litigation — the Winn Committee inquiry published in 1968 and the Cantley Report of 1979.[8] But the net result of all this huge expenditure of man-hours in studying the problems and making proposals has not been impressive. Costs have continued to rise and delays have remained a serious problem.

The Winn Committee said that delay was 'a very great reproach', particularly in fatal accident cases. The Cantley Committee looked at delay in all High Court personal injury

---

* The British Medical Association has, however, taken up the cry for no-fault compensation as a way of meeting the ever increasing cost to doctors of defending medical negligence claims. On 23 June 1987 *The Times* reported that annual subscriptions to the Medical Defence Union and the Medical Protection Society rose by 70 per cent to £576 and Dr Wall of the MDU predicted a further rise to nearly £800 to cover rising claims. Dr Wall said that the BMA would be pressing for no-fault compensation which would avoid an individual doctor being sued and would put the burden on the state.

cases from 1974 to 1977. In the 21,018 cases studied, the average period between the accident and the final disposal of the case was over three and a half years. Delay before the writ was issued was usually not too long. In two-fifths of cases the writ was issued within a year of the accident and in 75 per cent within two years of the accident. Considering that often the victim of the accident delays for many months before he takes the problem to a solicitor, this, the Committee thought, was not too bad. 'In most cases the writ is issued within a reasonable time after the cause of action'.[9] The Cantley Committee thought that normally the delay between issue of the writ and setting the case down for trial was also not too serious. In nearly half of all cases the case was set down within a year of issue of the writ and in 80 per cent within two years.[10] But there was a minority of cases which were delayed excessively. Two per cent were set down for trial more than four years after the issue of the writ! Moreover, setting down for trial is not the same as holding the trial. There is a delay of many more months before the case is actually heard.

In evaluating these figures the Cantley Committee drew attention to certain fundamental considerations. One was that litigation was the litigation of the parties — that the court was there to assist them and to resolve the dispute if asked to do so by the parties. But 'the court does not intervene unless asked to do so by the parties'.[11] One should not, the Committee thought, 'lightly interfere with this method of conducting litigation and encourage an undue degree of court intervention if to do so would be to lose the advantages of economy and flexibility which our system brings'.[12] Secondly, the overwhelming majority of cases did not come to trial. Any reform which concentrated on speeding cases to trial but which made settlements more expensive 'might be bought at an unduly high price'.[13] So delay which allowed the parties to reach a fair settlement was not undue delay. Reforms which aimed to reduce the time before trial might result in more trials and therefore greater delays (as when a new motorway draws so much more traffic as actually to make matters worse). Also, if more steps had to be taken, and earlier, in a higher proportion of cases, it might make the cost of settling cases higher than it already was.

The whole system, Cantley thought, 'might more properly be regarded as the procedure for settlement of actions than a procedure for trials'.[14] It was impossible to identify types of cases that took longer and those that took shorter. Everything depended on the particular circumstances of the case. One factor certainly was the expertise of the firm concerned. The least efficient and the least experienced were also the slowest. But most cases, the Committee thought, were handled by firms that were experienced and had able lawyers. It should also be remembered that much of the criticism of delay came from the layman and, while some of it was justified, often it was made with insufficient understanding of the process. The layman was, for instance, unaware of the fact that the full extent of the injuries might take a considerable time to become apparent. The layman would also not be aware of how much careful work was necessary to get a case ready for litigation.

Having reviewed a number of possible options to reduce delay, the Cantley Committee concluded that there was only one which was sensible having regard to the need not to take a sledge-hammer to crack a nut. Its proposal was to focus on the cases where it was abundantly clear that there was delay. So in any case which had not been set down for trial within 18 months of the date of the issue of the writ the rules should require the plaintiff's lawyers to report to the court what stage had been reached. The court, if so minded, would then issue directions to get the case moving more speedily. Short of this, the Committee did not think that it would be right or economic to get the court to take on the task of monitoring the progress of cases. It would cost too much in terms of court staff and would run counter to the basic philosophy of the common law system, that it was for the parties to conduct their own litigation, not for the court to take over the case.

But even this modest reform was thought to be too much. It was not specifically rejected by the Lord Chancellor's Department; it was simply not implemented. The reason was not spelled out, but was probably the result of what was felt to be the likely cost implication of a new procedure requiring court action. The message from the Treasury was that all government departments had to contribute to a reduction in the level of public expenditure, and the Lord Chancellor's Department plainly felt inhibited from embarking on a new system that would require more manpower in the court staff.

A few years later, however, in 1983, the Master of the Rolls, Sir John Donaldson, indicated that the philosophy of the English system might be undergoing a transformation as a result of new computerised technology. Sir John has become famous amongst lawyers for his belief in the utility of the new technological toys. The case which provoked his remarks was one of medical negligence which came on for trial eight years after the events which it concerned. The time might be ripe, Sir John Donaldson thought, 'for procedural changes designed to enable the courts and the judiciary to play a greater part than heretofore in encouraging the parties and their advisers to speed up the process of litigation'. The advent of the computer and the word-processor now made it technically practicable for the courts to take the initiative on a semi-automatic basis. He hoped that such cases and the general desire to improve the system might 'lead to a reconsideration of the policy of inertia on the part of the courts'.[15]

PERSONAL INJURIES

In fact, this reconsideration did not have to wait long. The study of personal injuries litigation by management consultants Inbucon selected by the Lord Chancellor for the Civil Justice Review produced a consultation paper in February 1986 full of radical proposals designed, amongst other things, to reduce delays. The evidence of the survey showed that most delay occurred after the case had been taken to the lawyers. The median interval between the accident and first seeking advice was no more than three months. There was said to be a remarkably long interval between the issue of a writ and service of the next formal document — the statement of claim. In the High Court in London the median was an incredible 21 months, and outside London about a year. The overall time from the incident to a settlement varied from an average of 33 months in the county court to 70 months in the High Court in London — though the median figures were less dramatic, 22 months and 44 months respectively. The average time from incident to trial was, surprisingly, not longer — from 35 weeks in the county court to 62 weeks in the London High Court. (The median figures were 30 weeks and 46 weeks respectively.)[16] Solicitors asked to give their views as to the causes of delay instanced, in particular, waiting for the plaintiff's medical condition to stabilise, waiting to get medical reports and waiting for trial. Again surprisingly, very few cited the conduct of insurance companies as a cause of delay.[17]

The conclusion, according to the Consultation Paper, was that High Court cases took four, five or six years from accident to completion and even in the county court cases could take three or more years. Even when the case was started it took nearly two years in the High Court in London before the defendant was provided with details of the plaintiff's case. Delay, the Consultation Paper said, was objectionable in causing personal stress, anxiety and financial hardship to plaintiffs and their families. It was liable to sap their morale and determination and increased the pressure to accept a low settlement. It was also liable to reduce the availability of evidence and to erode the reliability of evidence that was available. It led to inefficient business dealing, with files opened and re-opened over months and years. Compensation was not available until long after it was needed. Delay also lowered the public's estimation of the system's ability to provide a forum for resolving disputes. In short, the system was inefficient and dilatory.[18]

The evidence of the study was equally that the cost was much too high. In High Court cases the average costs of the plaintiff alone were £6,830 in London and £2,480 outside London. In the county court they were an average of £2,540.[19] In the county court the costs were an average of 99 per cent of the plaintiff's damages recovered. In the High Court the equivalent proportion was about a quarter (26 per cent in London and 24 per cent outside London).[20] Cases that went for trial were on average about half as costly again as those that settled.[21] (The Pearson Royal Commission had found on the basis of data collected in 1972 that the total cost of operating the tort system was 87 per cent of the total damages paid out as compensation.[22])

The consultants estimated that, when the costs of both sides were taken together, costs in the county court amounted to 125 per cent of the amount of damages, whilst in the High Court they were between 50 per cent and 75 per cent.[23] Admittedly most of the burden of costs in personal injury cases fell on institutions — because normally the plaintiff wins and the costs are borne by insurance companies, trade unions or the legal aid fund — but there was no reason why those who paid insurance premiums, or trade union membership dues, or the tax-payer should have to pay costs generated by avoidable inefficiency in the legal system. Moreover, there was clear evidence (particularly, from the massive study conducted by the Socio-Legal Centre in Oxford[24]) that potential claimants were deterred by fear of the cost from initiating claims. For the majority of litigants who paid their own way and for those with legal aid who paid a contribution, high costs could produce major anxieties over a long period of time.* For them the choice might

---

* The anxiety would be considerably heightened if the Government were to implement the proposal in the 1987 White Paper ('Legal Aid in England and Wales: A New Framework') that contributions be payable not, as previously, for a maximum of twelve months but throughout the duration of the case. It seems well possible that many people who would be eligible for legal aid will refuse an offer on these terms.

be between abandoning a claim, settling for too low a figure, or raising funds by liquidating life savings or disposing of the family home.

The solution had to be something bold. There was nothing, the Consultation Paper argued, which suggested that minor adjustments might achieve the changes that were needed. 'Worthwhile improvements, if these are to be aimed for, will require radical changes in procedure, jurisdiction and forensic methods'.[25] The objectives to be aimed at were, first, early action, to get proceedings under way; secondly, for the great mass of cases, a substantial reduction in the costs incurred and the time taken to get a result; and thirdly, for the large, difficult cases, much earlier trial or settlement than now without increasing overall costs.

Ideas to bring cases on more quickly included reduction of the period within which an action could be started from three years to one year after the accident; obliging a solicitor to start the action within a fixed period after first having been consulted; and, as has been noted, requiring solicitors who handled personal injury cases to have a specialist qualification.

The Consultation Paper then considered the problem of the relatively small case. It was clear that the ordinary county court trial system was neither simple nor cheap. One possible model for reform, it suggested, was to extend the jurisdiction of the small claims procedure in the county court (known confusingly as 'arbitration'). This was introduced in 1973 as a way of encouraging more ordinary people to bring their cases to the courts. Previous research had shown that the overwhelming majority of those who brought claims in the county courts were companies and other businesses. Arbitration hearings are conducted in private; they have a simplified form of pre-trial procedure designed for use by parties without lawyers; the court is permitted to ignore the rules of evidence; the hearing is supposed to be informal; and instead of the normal rule that the loser pays the winner's costs, each side pays his own costs. The system now applies to most contested cases in the county court for amounts under £500. The Consultation Paper argued, however, that this system was not suitable unless the matters in dispute were very straightforward. It therefore rejected this model for personal injury cases (though, as will be seen, a separate Consultation Paper on small claims argued for an extension of the 'arbitration system' to a wider range of cases).

A possible different model was provided by the Criminal Injuries Compensation Board which handles applications from persons injured through criminal violence and deals with 30,000 cases a year, mainly by paper adjudications. In nine out of ten cases the applicant accepts the decision on the papers by a single board member. The remainder go to a hearing of three board members. If that model were adapted for use in ordinary litigation of small cases, the claimant would furnish the court with the statements of his witnesses and of any relevant reports. The defendant would be given a stated period in which to lodge counter-statements and other reports. The adjudicator would then decide the case without any hearing. On receipt of the decision, either party would have the right to ask for an oral hearing. The adjudicator would also have the right to switch the case to an oral hearing in cases of special difficulty. The procedure would apply compulsorily to certain categories of case — road accidents and other cases where no more than £5,000 appears likely to be in issue — and could be made available also in other cases if the parties agreed. The cost to the parties would be minimal; waiting time from completion of the file to decision could be drastically reduced, and there would normally be no need to attend a hearing. On the other hand, the adjudicator would have no chance to evaluate the witnesses in person, there would be no oral argument and the parties would not have the satisfaction of attending a hearing of their case.

For more substantial cases, involving more than £5,000, the main objective, the Consultation Paper suggested, was to eliminate unnecessary delays. The procedure should be directed toward earlier settlement or trial. The chief means to this end would be to give the court new powers and responsibilities — to set and maintain a strict timetable with penalties for delay, to review the case put by each party, and to define the issues for trial. Applications for adjournments would be refused unless signed by the litigants themselves. The two parties would be required to 'put their cards on the table' with full and early disclosure of their respective cases. Instead of the court adopting the traditional common law passive approach, there would be an active pre-trial hearing based on evidence already disclosed, at which the possibility of a settlement would be explored. If this failed, the trial would then be limited simply to issues and evidence which remained in dispute after the pre-trial hearing. Instead of the judge coming to a case without knowledge of its details, the judge for the trial would have the master file in advance with all the relevant documents, including statements of the witnesses. The lawyers would also have given the court a note of the issues in dispute and the propositions of law to be advanced. Opening speeches by counsel would be abolished and closing speeches would be limited in time. The lawyers would agree in advance the passages in the witnesses' statements that could be taken from the written version and which therefore would not have to be given in open court.

This sounded like a radical programme. Admittedly, the Consultation Paper sketched its ideas with frustrating brevity so that on many points it was not easy to see exactly what was actually proposed. Also, considering the enormous cost of the report done by the management consultants, it was surprising that it demonstrated no awareness of evidence from other jurisdictions, such as the United States, where the concept of full 'cards on the table' has been familiar for decades. That evidence is not wholly encouraging either in terms of cutting costs or in cutting delays. The danger of full pre-trial disclosure is that it may drag out the pre-trial stage and hugely increase the costs. Of all this, there was no discussion in the Inbucon report nor in the Consultation Paper. But the broad outlines of the proposals were tolerably clear. Reaction, however, proved to be mixed.

A preliminary point taken by several commentators was that the management consultants' study was misleading in that it dealt only with the small minority of cases in which proceedings are issued, which represent only an estimated 15 per cent of personal injury claims. To make a great issue over the costs and delays of so small a proportion of the total number of claims, it was suggested, was to get the problem seriously out of focus. In the great majority of cases, settlements were reached within a reasonable time and at reasonable costs — mainly borne by defendant insurance companies. There were also objections that for the cases in which proceedings are started the delays reported in the study were unrepresentative. The Masters of the Queen's Bench Division, for instance, produced figures based on a much larger sample showing that the delay figures in the Inbucon study may have been considerably higher than was normal. The most startling difference was in regard to the time it took for solicitors to serve a statement of claim after issue of a writ. According to the Review's study (based on only 22 cases) the median in London was 21 months; the QB Masters' study (based on 655 cases) gave a median of one month! The time between the start of proceedings and the case being set down for trial also showed a remarkable discrepancy. The Review figure (based on 19 cases) was 19 months in the High Court in London compared with six and a half months for the QB Masters' study. But the median figures for the time between the accident and the ultimate trial were not widely divergent. In the Review study it was a median of 46 months, compared with 39 months in the QB Masters' study.

When the responses to the Consultation Paper were analysed it was found, however, that the overwhelming majority agreed that neither the duration nor the cost of personal injury cases was felt to be acceptable. The majority of responses also agreed that steps should be taken to encourage more victims of accidents to make claims for damages — through information in leaflets issued by the DHSS, leaflets in doctors' waiting rooms and in hospitals, advertising and a variety of other means. Nearly all respondents agreed with the proposition that the general principle in personal injuries litigation should be that of 'cards on the table', or early disclosure by each side to the other of its case, and that the material should also be provided to the judge before the trial. These were, however, certain qualifications. The Law Society, which favoured the principle in general terms, wanted to limit it to all material other than the statements of witnesses — which would be to exclude the most important category of material. One reason given by the Law Society was the probability that it would tend to lead to delays in settlements as solicitors would advise waiting for the exchange of witness statements before entering into serious negotiations. But this point could be met, at least partially, by setting an early date for (simultaneous) exchange of witness statements. The London Common Law Bar Association took the same line as the Law Society, but the Bar Council, the Association of County Court and District Court Registrars and JUSTICE all thought that each side should provide full details, including witness statements.

The great mass of respondents, including the Bar, the Law Society, circuit judges and registrars, favoured the idea that the court should at the outset fix the date by which each side was to have its case in order. Most who responded also agreed that court control of progress of a case should be enforced by requiring strict adherence to the timetable, subject to automatic penalties for delay. Neither the Bar nor the Law Society, however, expressed an opinion on the matter. This is significant, since the penalties would presumably have to be on the lawyers rather than the litigants, or else the parties would be punished for the dilatoriness of their lawyers. At present, there are time limits for every stage of an action but they are totally disregarded by all — lawyers give each other extensions of time more or less automatically and the courts exert no pressure whatever for time limits to be kept. It would require a revolution in the approach of all concerned if a proposal for enforcement of strict penalties for failure to keep to time limits were to have any impact.

Opinion was divided as to whether opening speeches by counsel should be abolished. Neither the judges, registrars, the Bar nor the Law Society thought they should. But they all agreed with the majority who said that the time for such speeches should be limited. All but the Law Society also agreed that the time allowed for closing speeches should be controlled by the court.

In regard to three important matters there was a clear majority who thought that the Consultation Paper had got it wrong. One was that the time within which an action must be brought should be reduced from three years to one year, subject to exceptions for special cases. Those who opposed this proposal included not only the Law Society but the TUC, the National Consumer Council (NCC), the National Association of Citizens' Advice Bureaux (NACAB), and JUSTICE, though the judges and the registrars supported the proposal.

A second point, on which more or less everyone of consequence opposed what was proposed, was the suggestion that small cases involving sums of under £5,000 which did not go to the county court's so-called arbitration system should be dealt with by some form of adjudication simply on the papers. Those who opposed this included the judges, the Bar, the Law Society, the NCC, the TUC, and NACAB. The NCC said that a paper adjudication would give an advantage to those who could afford skilled professional help in preparing the papers. Even ordinary solicitors might find themselves consulting barristers to draft the adjudication papers, with resulting costs. NACAB said that 'parties want an opportunity to explain their case orally and would feel dissatisfied with arbitration on paper'. Oral evidence with the possibility of questioning witnesses was essential, it thought, to the quality of judgments. The Law Society thought that paper adjudications would tend to give the defence the advantage. At present, if a defendant was being unreasonable, the plaintiff's remedy was to go to court. But that threat, such as it was, would cease if all such cases had to go first to a paper adjudication. It would encourage defendants to hold out rather than to settle.

The great majority of respondents were also opposed to the proposed rule that any solicitor wishing to undertake personal injury work should first have to qualify as a specialist. Some, however, including the London Common Law Bar Association, the Law Society, the NCC and NACAB, favoured the idea of a voluntary specialist qualification with the right to advertise the fact. In relation to each of these three issues the weight of opposition seemed likely to swamp the proposal. All three were headed for the dustbin.

There was a divided reaction to several other proposals put forward in the Consultation Paper. One was that the small claims system in county courts, now limited to cases involving amounts of under £500, should be extended to a wider range of cases. There was a good deal of support for this idea, notably from the Law Society, the TUC, NACAB and JUSTICE. On the other hand, it was opposed by an even larger number, including the registrars, the Bar and the Association of British Insurers. There was a considerable difference of opinion on the proposal that there should be a pre-trial hearing at which a judicial officer should have all the evidence and other documents of each side and should explore with them the prospects for a settlement. Those in favour of this idea included registrars, the Law Society, the Association of British Insurers, NACAB and JUSTICE. But those opposed were equally numerous and included the circuit judges, the Bar and the London Common Law Bar Association.

The idea that litigants should personally have to sign or counter-sign applications for adjournments was another topic on which views were divided. The majority thought it would not be a worthwhile idea, at least partly because it would not achieve its purpose since litigants would normally do as they were requested or advised by their lawyers. But the registrars, the insurance industry and JUSTICE were amongst those who thought it worth a try. The other topic on which there was a serious division of opinion was whether pre-trial written statements of witnesses should be treated by the court as their evidence, subject to oral cross-examination by the opposing party. Some respondents, including the registrars and JUSTICE, thought this would be valuable. More, however, including the circuit judges, the London Common Law Bar, the Law Society and the insurance industry disagreed, on the ground that oral evidence was essential for disputed issues, to establish the credibility of witnesses and to put them at their ease. Moreover, it was suggested, oral evidence did not always accord with prior written statements.

SMALL CLAIMS

The Civil Justice Review process followed the Consultation
Paper on Personal Injuries with another in September 1986 on
Small Claims based on work done by management consultants,
Messrs Touche Ross. This was, however, different in the result
in that it expressed itself as broadly satisfied with the existing
arbitration system in county courts. This system is now used in
the majority of contested cases in county courts, with the
registrar rather than the judge normally acting as judge. (In
1985 44,700 cases were heard by registrars under the small
claims procedure, while 28,900, excluding possession and matrimonial cases, were dealt with by ordinary county court trial
before a judge. As has been seen, however, the great majority of
small claims are uncontested; in 1985 there were some 1.3
million claims under £500.)

The study by the consultants was based on a weighted (and
problematic)* sample of 876 cases set down for arbitration. The
average amount of money claimed was £216.[26] The average
award was £186.[27] Sixty-five per cent of successful plaintiffs said
that they were paid the whole or a large part of the amount
awarded; in a further 10 per cent of cases the plaintiff received a
half or less.[28] In about a quarter of the cases, the total costs and
expenses awarded by the court were greater than the amount
claimed on the summons in respect of court fee and costs.[29] Two-
thirds of litigants said they had had to take time off to attend
the court and over half said that they had lost earnings in doing
so.[30]

Perhaps surprisingly, the outcome of cases varied little as
between those who were and those who were not represented by
lawyers. The overall success rate for all plaintiffs was 67 per

---

* The instructions to the consultants specified that at least three-quarters of the
sample should be cases brought by individuals or small businesses. This is a
much larger proportion than is typical either of cases brought or cases heard by
arbitration, and the sample was therefore skewed. Also since most cases started
do not get as far as being set down for arbitration, the sample was untypical in
that sense too. The consultants interviewed a small number of plaintiffs (247)
and a smaller proportion of defendants (161) in the same cases. They also spoke
to potential litigants who had sought advice from CABx about specified types of
complaints, but the number (50) was very small. It follows that the statistical
findings of the study and suggestions for change based on such findings have to
be treated as suspect. (Detailed criticisms of the shortcomings of the sample were
presented powerfully at a seminar in London in February 1987 by Dr C. Whelan
of the University of Warwick School of Law, published in *Civil Justice Quarterly*,
July 1987, p. 237.

cent, compared with 70 per cent for plaintiffs who were represented against a defendant who was not.[31] The time taken by proceedings varied considerably. At one extreme, one court had completed three-quarters of all its cases within four months of the defence, while, at the other, four courts took nine months to a year to complete three-quarters of their cases.[32] The two chief factors that seemed to affect the duration of the case were whether there was a pre-trial hearing (which generally seemed to delay and on the whole did not greatly assist matters), and whether the date for the hearing was imposed by the court, as opposed to being requested by the parties (which again created extra delay).

Most litigants appeared to be well satisfied with the system. No less than 81 per cent of the admittedly small number of plaintiffs interviewed said that they would 'very likely' or 'quite likely' use the system again.[33] The conclusions drawn in the Consultation Paper were that[34]

> The small claims procedure emerges as substantially sound in that it is able to produce results, without major delay and cost, which satisfy a large number of those who use it. It is workable in that it produces those results by a process which many litigants are able to operate without undue difficulty. However, litigants may be prejudiced by the lack of a uniform procedure and the current diversity of approach.

The suggestions for change were accordingly modest in scope. One was that courts should not normally have a pre-trial hearing but should aim to dispose of small claims at a single hearing. This might mean having to spend a few extra minutes at the hearing sorting out the issues in dispute, but this would be a small price to pay for the major advantage to the parties of having to come to court — and taking time off work or disrupting other activities — only once. Parties should be given clear pre-trial directions and advice as to how to prepare their case. The court should fix the dates for hearings rather than waiting for the parties to indicate their readiness. Courts should be instructed that it was the registrar's function to assist an unrepresented party by questioning both him and the other party, and that represented parties should only be permitted to put questions through the registrar. The paper suggested that litigants should have the right to bring any kind of represent-ative instead of being limited to having a lawyer. This worked in most tribunals and appeared to give rise to no particular problems. The paper also raised for consideration whether the limit for the special procedure should be raised from £500 to a much higher level of, say, £5,000. Finally, it proposed that the style 'small claims court' should replace 'county court arbitration'. The public use of that expression was so general that it should now be adopted.

The National Association of Citizens' Advice Bureaux (NACAB) thought that the Small Claims Consultation Paper was too complacent. It considered that overall the small claims machinery was too slow and cumbersome. There were great variations in the approach of registrars. Some were informal; some not. Some allowed lay representatives to speak for litigants; others did not. There were similar variations in respect to the use of preliminary hearings, the swearing in of witnesses, rulings on costs, cross-examination and other matters. The training of registrars was inadequate. More might be done to get in arbitrators from outside the judicial system. In Manchester the local authority Fair Trading Officers had been trained and used very successfully as arbitrators. There should be unrestricted rights of audience so that anyone could be heard in a small claims arbitration. Contrary to what the Review found, it thought that costs were a severe deterrent to many would-be litigants.

The National Consumer Council (NCC), in its comments on the Consultation Paper, said that the great majority of consumers with unresolved disputes did not make use of the system; county courts had an unapproachable and forbidding image and too often used jargon. The procedure was not as informal or simple to use as it should be. Previously the NCC had thought that the pre-trial review should be strengthened, but it had been persuaded by the argument that it would be better to abolish it. Previously also it had thought that, in order to promote the simplest approach, legal representation should normally be banned. But it had now come to the same conclusion as NACAB — that it was better to have access for any representative, lawyer or non-lawyer. It was of the opinion that there should be a new free-standing arbitration code, written in plain English, which would set out all the procedural rules, and the forms should be re-drafted to make them simpler.

COMMERCIAL CASES

The third paper in the series produced by the Civil Justice Review was that published in November 1986 on the commercial court, prepared by Coopers and Lybrand Associates. This showed that the specialised skills of the commercial court judges were much in demand. (The number of writs issued in 1986 up to November was over 2,000, compared with 913 in 1979.) A common preconception about commercial cases was that they were procedurally complex with voluminous pleadings and lengthy trials. The findings showed that this was to some extent a myth. Although some of the cases were long and complex, 90 per cent of the cases studied in depth had pleadings of less than 22 pages, and in four-fifths the trial was under 11 days. Nor was it true that these cases involved large numbers of legal personnel, parties or witnesses. Nearly half (43 per cent) of the cases studied in depth had only junior counsel in attendance. There was wide variation in the amount of damages claimed, ranging from £345 to over £9 million. The median amount was £68,000. One proposal was to remove the smaller cases from the commercial court list by a restriction on cases involving sums of less than, say, £50,000, unless the issue justified a hearing before a specialised judge. Alternatively, there might be a rule requiring special permission to have a case in the commercial list in all cases.

Case management would be assisted by an automatic time-table of six months in which pleadings would have to be exchanged and disclosure of evidence take place. This would be followed by a pre-trial hearing at which the issues for trial would be identified. The court would monitor the progress of cases to ensure that the timetable was adhered to. Especially complex cases would be assigned to one judge who would handle all aspects of the case.

DEBT ENFORCEMENT

The fourth report issued by the Civil Justice Review in January 1987 was that on debt enforcement, which is by far the largest single item of civil court business. (As has been seen, the great majority of the two million or so claims brought each year in the civil courts are for unpaid debts arising out of the supply of goods, services and credit.) On the whole, the management consultants Touche Ross found that the system was working tolerably well. The average size of debt cases in the High Court was found to be about £5,000, compared with just over £200 in the county court. The paper recommended that all debt cases should in future start in the county court. Substantial cases would be transferred to the High Court if they became contested, and debts over £3,000 would be enforced by the High Court

Sheriff rather than by the county court bailiffs. The study conducted by the management consultants showed that more than 60 per cent of creditors were able to recover at least part of the debt, but a year after judgment half the claims in the sample were still wholly or partly unpaid. The study showed that, contrary to conventional wisdom, the county court bailiffs were no less effective in recovery than the sheriffs in the High Court.

The Consultation Paper suggested that a new form be used to invite settlement of claims by debtors without the need for recourse to legal proceedings at all. But the idea that the court should take over the task of stage-managing the process of enforcement through an Enforcement Office, as proposed by the Payne Committee in 1969, was rejected on the ground that it would involve greater cost and delay without necessarily any real improvement in the success rate.

HOUSING CASES

The last of the five specific Consultation Papers, also issued in January 1987, was on housing cases. The data were based on a study conducted not by management consultants but by the School for Advanced Urban Studies of the University of Bristol. They found an enormous crush of possession cases — in 1985 there were over 138,000 such cases in county courts in England and Wales, often at the rate of 40 to 50 such cases in a morning. The heavy caseload prevented courts from concentraitng on the difficult cases. Also such actions imposed a heavy burden on landlords who were supposed to attend, and since most of the cases resulted simply from arrears of rent the tenant was put under a threat of eviction at far too early a stage. Instead, it was suggested that there should be a new form of arrears action where judgment could be given without any hearing — like an ordinary debt case. Only if the tenant then failed to keep up the payments ordered would there have to be a hearing to decide whether eviction was appropriate. The paper also proposed that there should be a new form of small claims procedure, informal and quicker and cheaper than the present system, to cover disputes about repairs, improvements, service charges and tenants' rights. Appeals against decisions on rent by rent officers should be dealt with by rent assessment committees on the papers without a hearing.

The paper was greeted critically by the Law Centres Federation and *Law Centres News* which said it would have the effect of increasing homelessness. The proposals would mean 'fewer rights for tenants, the homeless and mortgagors'. Considerable numbers of private landlords would be able to evict tenants in an informal hearing before a registrar without representation being available to the tenant. More private tenants would face speedy eviction and homelessness. The proposed new second hearing in the arrears action at which eviction was the sole issue, and removal of the present power to suspend eviction on condition that the tenant pays the debt by instalments, would also result in more evictions and the forcing of families into bed and breakfast accommodation. The new 'housing action' would give the landlord an advantage because legal aid would be available only in complex cases — as determined by the registrar. Most cases would be treated like small claims and in most of such cases only the landlord would be represented.

The Housing Consultation Paper was even more severely criticised by the Law Society in a fifty-page response which comprehensively demolished the whole argument on which the paper was based, and all its main proposals. It found the data unconvincing, the analysis of problems faulty and the prescribed remedies ill-adapted to the needs of the parties to housing cases. It thought the proposed new arrears action, for instance, would actually increase delays and costs and could lead to more evictions. The new informal arbitration procedure would be liable to lead to rough justice in a class of case which had extremely serious consequences for both landlord and tenant. The weight of the Law Society's criticisms seemed sufficiently great to sink the Consultation Paper.

THE GENERAL ISSUES PAPER

The final tranche of the Civil Justice consultation process was launched at the end of March 1987 with the publication of a 112-page paper entitled *General Issues* which canvassed options on a wide front in the whole field of civil litigation.

On delay, it thought that this was not a serious problem in the fields of debt cases, housing cases or small claims, which between them formed the bulk of all civil business in the courts. According to the debt study the formal process of obtaining an undefended judgment took on average 47 days in the High Court and 55 days in the county court. Uncontested county court enforcement warrants took an average of 35 days, whilst in the High Court the equivalent period was 84 days. In housing cases for possession the average time from summons to hearing was

7.2 weeks. For small claims the average time from summons to hearing was between 24 and 36 weeks, though there were considerable variations between courts.

Personal injury actions showed much greater delays. In the county court, the median time from start of proceedings to the stage of asking for trial ('setting the case down') was 13 months; in the High Court the comparable period was 19 months. In commercial cases the median time from start of proceedings to pre-trial hearing was almost 16 months.

Time taken from the issue of proceedings until the case is set down for trial is largely in the hands of the parties. Time taken from setting down to the hearing is largely the responsibility of the court. The Review teams each carried out a survey of waiting times for trial. The average for county court personal injury actions was about two months. In the High Court outside London it varied from circuit to circuit. The worst was 12 months; the best, three months. The average was five months. In London, however, the delays were appalling. The general list in the Queen's Bench Division had a delay of 20 months on average from the setting down of the case to trial. In the Commercial Court it was two years for a hearing of 4 or more days and three years for a hearing due to last more than 6 weeks. By contrast, in the Chancery Division — a by-word for delay in former times — long cases were now having to wait only 8 to 9 months and shorter witness actions were being listed a mere 6 to 8 weeks ahead. In the Patents Court cases only had to wait some five months and in the Family Division delay for cases due to last over two days had been reduced from five months to 14 weeks.

So far as the cost of civil litigation was concerned, total expenditure in 1985-6 was £149 million. Non-judicial costs amounted to £125 million, of which staff costs were £72 million and accommodation costs £27 million. Judicial salaries were £23 million. Court fees paid by the public are supposed to cover the outgoings of the system other than judicial salaries. In 1985-6 they amounted to £126 million, so that apart from judicial salaries and legal aid the cost to the state of conducting civil business was virtually nil. (The net cost of civil legal aid in the same year was £95 million.)

Civil justice is currently dispensed through a bewildering array of different jurisdictions. According to the Review, these various courts, Divisions of the High Court and special jurisdictions 'may be regarded as a collection of parts or at best a federation of separate activities'. It was doubtful 'whether the sum of the separate parts is now well suited to meet the sum of the needs arising'. It therefore had to be asked 'whether the present degree of fragmentation is sustainable or whether it impedes the overall effectiveness of the system'. The objectives of quality of justice, efficiency and effectiveness, the Consultation Paper suggested, would be better met if instead the system became a single unit able to offer rational allocation of judicial skills and time, accommodation, support staff, finance and administrative arrangements, including clear overall management information and early identification of malfunction or shortages with early action to rectify them. Either the High Court and the county court should be amalgamated into a single civil court or they should remain formally separate but be much more closely integrated. There should, however, remain two distinct levels of civil court and two tiers of judges (High Court and circuit judges). Also the specialist divisions of the High Court (Queen's Bench Division, Family Division and Chancery Division) should be retained but the judges should be flexibly deployed wherever they were needed. Some High Court judges, it was even suggested, might be primarily located in the provinces on circuit — a suggestion that provoked immediate dismay amongst the judges, who clearly did not fancy the idea of being asked to leave the London area to be stationed for prolonged periods out in the Styx. The judges also were understandably less than enthusiastic about the proposal that the two-month High Court Long Vacation and three other vacations taking up a further twenty working days should be abolished or that the court day (which at present runs from 10.00 a.m. to 1 p.m. and 2 p.m. to 4 p.m.) should be extended by an hour. Judges should, of course, have proper holidays but the Review considered that the system of vacations, which it said plainly held up the progress of business and was wasteful of staff and accommodation, could no longer be justified.

Most types of cases, it was suggested, should start in the county court which would become a court of general unlimited jurisdiction. Cases would be transferred to the High Court only if they needed greater expertise than was available in the county court. There would be a single system of costs with a higher and a lower rate which would be awarded on the basis of the nature of the work and the need for a higher or lower fee-earner — no longer by reference to the court in which the work was done. There would be a single procedural code for all civil cases. The present great variety of ways of starting an action should be reduced to two — one for cases involving evidence, the other for all other cases.

On the question of pre-trial procedure, the Review came down firmly in favour of early and complete disclosure by each party of its case — even if this had the effect of increasing the overall cost of civil cases.

To some extent, the increased cost would probably be offset by earlier settlement but, if there were an actual increase in the cost of disposing of civil cases, this might have to be accepted 'as the price for speedier resolution and more informed settlements'. The conclusion of the paper was that 'if necessary, the price of earlier disposal should be paid'. This was so especially in areas of work like personal injury litigation where the costs were in practice borne largely by insurance companies and where most plaintiffs either had legal aid or were supported by trade unions or insurance.

The objective of requiring the parties to put their cards on the table could be served by various changes. One would be to make the parties state more precisely the nature of their cases in the pleadings, including an indication of how allegations would be proved. Another would be to require each party to state certain facts (e.g. relating to speed, direction of travel or other basic facts) without sight of the other side's documents. Witness statements should be exchanged as a matter of course. Some of those who had commented on the proposal to this effect in the Personal Injury Consultation Paper had said that it would not work well. But this view was probably over gloomy. It worked in personal injury cases in regard to experts' reports, and since October 1986 the court had had the power to order the exchange of witness statements in the Chancery Division, the Commercial Court, the Admiralty Court and before the Official Referee. It was also routine already in matrimonial proceedings. Parties would have to disclose their evidence pre-trial if they wished to rely on it at trial. If matters emerged at the trial which had not been revealed pre-trial, it would reflect on the credibility of the witness (and possibly on the probity of the lawyers). The change might lead to some increase in cost but it did not seem reasonable to expect a great increase in statement-taking in cases that were now well run. In so far as cases were now not run well, some increase in cost might, on balance, be an acceptable price to pay for better preparation.

The Review also addressed the notorious weakness of pre-trial procedure. Procedures for ensuring disclosure of information and for defining issues within a given timescale had long been seen as a weak spot in the system. Procedural reformers had struggled in vain for decades to make the system effective. The reasons were clear. The parties had no desire to collaborate with each other and the professional ethos of lawyers encouraged them to make maximum use of technical rules. There was no stigma attached to non-compliance with the rules. Secondly, although the rules provided for stages and time-limits (to which no one paid attention), there was no overall timetable for a case. The third reason was the lack of sanctions and their ineffectiveness where they were applied. Exhortation to do better was virtually useless.

The method for introducing discipline to the civil process, the Review suggested, was to set an overall timetable and to put the court in charge of the minority of cases which did not conform. The Review rejected the traditional view, expressed most recently by the Cantley Committee, that litigation was basically a private matter between the parties which could be delayed to suit their convenience. Delay had an impact on the quality of justice. The memory of witnesses faded, or they died or became otherwise unavailable. Disputes festered. The law and the system were brought into disrepute. Control of the time taken by civil proceedings 'should now be accepted as a function proper to the court acting where appropriate of its own motion'.[35] The defendant should be required to notify the court of an intention to defend and there should then be an automatic rule that the case had to be set down as ready for trial within a specified period which would be prescribed for different types of case. (For personal injury cases, for instance, it might be 12 months.) Variation of the basic timetable could be applied for in individual cases. The court would then monitor performance by reference to the overall timetable. In any instance where the case had not been set down within the prescribed period the court would send out a request for information to the plaintiff's solicitor. (If no reply were received within 14 days, a reminder would be sent — with copy to the client!) If this still produced no result, or the reply indicated a need for court involvement, the matter would be referred to a hearing before a Master or registrar at which either a summons could be issued requiring information from the lawyers for one or other side or the action could be ordered to be set down or, in extreme cases, an order be made that it would be struck out unless certain steps were taken within a specified time.

Save when requested by one of the parties, the pre-trial or preparatory hearing should normally be dispensed with for all but the heavier cases — those likely to last for three or more days. In really heavy cases the pre-trial hearing should be taken by the trial judge himself. The cost of such a hearing might be considerable but the potential savings achieved at the trial itself would more than offset such costs. It was objected by the lawyers that this would require them to change their working habits by preparing cases earlier, but the Review argued that, from a different perspective, such changes might be considered advantages rather than the reverse. (The Review did not, however, address itself to the critical question as to how with the divided profession one ensures that the barrister who attends at the pre-trial hearing is also available several weeks later at the trial. The system has always proceeded on the premise that adjournments are not normally granted simply because of the unavailability of counsel of one's choice. If this continued, the prospects for success of the pre-trial preparatory hearing would be somewhat qualified.)

So far as the trial itself is concerned, the General Issues Paper confirmed the recommendation in the Personal Injury Consultation Paper that statements exchanged in advance of the hearing should be taken as evidence of the witness, subject to cross-examination. The judge would read the material in advance. In fact, the judge would be able to make a preliminary assessment of the case before the hearing and would be able to indicate to the lawyers at the outset what help he required from them at the trial. In a crucial passage the Review said:[36]

> Notwithstanding the objection of some lawyers, it has now to be clearly recognised, as many lawyers already do, that the present form of trial has become outdated. The concept of the oral trial as a single, continuous event at which all the issues are tested and decided had its original justification in the difficulty of recalling a jury once dispersed and refreshing their memories. Except for the purposes of defamation cases the civil jury finally vanished during the Second World War but the trial hearing is still shaped as though to accommodate its non-existent presence.

The English view, for instance, that the spontaneous oral recollections of a witness are the surest way of testing the reliability of evidence was a matter of tradition and habit. It should now be adjusted to take account of the fact that there must be doubt about the reliability of recollections months or years after the event and as to which the witness's memory had been refreshed by reference to an earlier statement.[37]

Also the unnerving effect of the courtroom atmosphere and the impact of skilful cross-examination might do more to discomfort the witness than to test the probability of his statements. It was not suggested that oral testimony should be dispensed with — merely that there should be less reluctance to use evidence on paper. The Review acknowledged, however, that insofar as trials relied on information not made public at the trial some way would have to be found to permit the press and the public to have access to it. Also the rules of evidence should be altered to allow hearsay evidence to be admitted without restriction. Judges, unlike juries, did not need to be protected against doubtful sources of evidence. A judge was trained to be able to evaluate the weight to be given to evidence. Abolition of the rule against hearsay evidence would simplify pre-trial procedure and eliminate arguments at the trial about the admissibility of evidence. It should also not be necessary to take the judge through the whole story since he could read it up for himself beforehand. The trial could then get more speedily to the crucial matters in issue. There was a modern tendency (aggravated by the photocopier) for the lawyers to agree huge bundles of documents to place before the court. Judges should feel able to penalise the lawyers personally in costs when this practice was abused by the inclusion of masses of unnecessary documents.

The Review also proposed that the civil justice system should be reformed so as to maximise efficiency. Thus judges should be encouraged to report pressure points to the Presiding Judge in the circuit. Courts should have stated objectives by way of performance indicators to speed the through-put of cases; basic statistical information should be produced, analysed and disseminated to management and judges so as to stimulate action. The Lord Chancellor's Department was giving high priority to computerising the system for handling county court debt cases, and for installation of desk computers. Computerisation must be a long-term objective for the entire court system.

The Civil Justice Review's five detailed reports together with the General Issues Paper unquestionably represent the most radical official programme of reform on the subject ever produced in this country. The process reflected a distinctively Thatcherite approach to law reform. Instead of the traditional inquiry independent of government, the relevant government department was deeply involved at every stage — formulating the issues, guiding the collection of data and preparing the consultation papers. The department was exposed throughout to the detailed scrutiny and review of the independent advisory committee. The timetable was distressingly tight. (Five major

studies completed and published with accompanying analysis
and proposals in under two years, with the General Issues paper
completed only a few weeks later and the whole consultation
completed in under two and a half years, was an impressive
achievement.) The cost at just over half a million pounds was
high — management consultants do not come cheap. Nor can it
be said that the work they produced was always very
sophisticated. But considering the track record for inquiries into
aspects of the legal system this one looks as if it may prove to
have been worthwhile if only in stirring up debate and moving it
along.

The contrast with the deeply conservative reports issued by
the Evershed Committee in 1953 and the Winn Committee in
1968 is startling. All previous attempts to reform the civil
justice system have essentially failed. Will this attempt also run
into the sand? The cynic is bound to be sceptical about the
prospects. The legal profession, the judges and court staffs have
hitherto all been extremely resistant to change. The historical
record shows that exhortation is not sufficient. But there are
some reasons to think that the present situation may be
different and that the prospects for reform could be better than
in the past. First, the Lord Chancellor's Department seems now
to have the bit between its teeth. Having driven the Civil
Justice Review along so firmly since its inception in 1985, it
would be surprising if the Department now allowed the pressure
to slacken. Lord Hailsham's successor as Lord Chancellor, Lord
Havers, is therefore likely to find himself promoting the same
broad policy as that supported so vigorously by his predecessor.

Secondly, the lawyers and the judges are in a somewhat more
constructive frame of mind than ever before — slightly less
prone than hitherto to advance footling and self-interested
objections to reform proposals. This is, of course, not to say that
they will easily be brought to accept changes which threaten
their perceived interests. No doubt entrenched vested interests
and the sheer native conservatism of the lawyers will play a
major role in impeding progress. (There was clear evidence of
this in the storm that blew up in the summer of 1987 in the
opposition of the judges to the Civil Justice Review notion that
High Court judges be sent to live in the provinces and that the
county court and the High Court might be amalgamated, with
the result amongst other things that the status of the High
Court judges might be affected and solicitors' rights of audience
might be extended.) But the new element in the situation is that
efficiency, reduction of cost and delay, and proper management

of the system are now recognised as proper and important objectives. (The willingness of the lawyers to concern themselves with increased efficiency is distinctly enhanced by the new notion that increases in remuneration out of public funds are conditional on such co-operativeness.)

Whether in fact the proposed reforms will have the desired effect is, of course, a different question. Mr Richard White, the official in the Lord Chancellor's Department perhaps most responsible for the Civil Justice Review, was candid enough to admit at the Law Society's annual conference in October 1986 that the changes would probably not have the effect of reducing costs. He had initially thought that they would do so but he had changed his mind. They should, he thought, have the effect of reducing delays, however.[38] The sceptic will perhaps ask to see the evidence before he accepts even this limited prediction. The main problems of civil litigation — cost, complexity and delay — are in a sense endemic. It is difficult to imagine that they will ever be eliminated.

Some argue that the solution is for the state to provide alternative dispute resolution systems which will avoid the costs and delays of the ordinary courts. Various forms of arbitration, compulsory and non-compulsory, with hearings and without hearings, binding and non-binding, or conciliation procedures, are increasingly mooted. But the signs are not encouraging. Either they turn out to be just about as costly and as liable to delays as the court system, or they provide a solution which is, for one or another reason, not acceptable — either because they are too expensive for the state, or too crude and brusque to be satisfactory to the parties. Private sector systems for which the parties can be charged the going rate may to some extent be viable but there is no sign that a system has been devised which would allow the state to provide a better method of adjudication through some form of alternative dispute resolution process.[39] It seems that we are stuck with the system we have got and the chances of improving it dramatically are not good.

6

The Criminal Justice System

Everyone has opinions about the problems of the criminal justice system. Questions of crime and punishment are permanently fascinating. The media devote endless space to reporting and discussing the issues. There are frequent parliamentary debates and politicians of all persuasions deliver themselves of strongly held views as to what should be done. Interest groups such as the police, the civil libertarians, the lawyers, magistrates, justices' clerks, and organisations such as JUSTICE, are continually producing reports and memoranda to forward the process of debate by suggestions for improvements in the system. For the broad mass of the general public, the main concern is probably that villains should not 'get away with it' and that they should receive appropriately heavy sentences from the courts. The police naturally share the same basic attitude. Civil libertarians are concerned more with the position of the accused and tend to emphasise the ways in which the system is tipped in favour of the state and the danger of miscarriages of justice. For them the criminal justice process seems to bear heavily on the individual and to give him little chance.

CRIMINAL LAW REVISION COMMITTEE REPORT

Almost every aspect of the criminal justice system is a subject of controversy — from class bias in arrest and prosecution policy*

---

* A powerful case has been made in recent research for instance that class bias arises in the way in which the police prosecute, whereas other enforcement systems do not. The police prosecute most detected offences. Agencies which to whether we should continue to use the dock for defendants rather than have them sit with their lawyers as in the United States. But certain issues have emerged as the mainstream concerns about the system and it is to these that this chapter is mainly directed. Controversy as to whether major changes are needed in the criminal justice system has been raging fiercely in England especially since the 1960s. In 1964 the then Home Secretary, Mr Henry Brooke, asked his standing advisory committee, the Criminal Law Revision Committee, to consider what reforms were needed to the rules of evidence in criminal cases.

The Committee produced its report — the notorious Eleventh Report[1] — eight years later in 1972, in which it proposed a major recasting of the rules of the process. The criminal justice system, it said, had got badly out of balance. Far from being, as some thought, tipped toward the state, it had become too favourable to the accused. In former times the scales had been loaded against the defence in ways which it was difficult now to remember. Trials were often conducted with indecent haste. (The Old Bailey Sessions Papers for the period 1670 to 1730 show that a jury typically heard twelve to twenty cases in a day!). The accused would normally have been legally unrepresented and, even when he had a lawyer, until 1836 the defending barrister could do little more than urge points of law and advise the accused what questions to ask witnesses. The defendant was rarely competent to perform the task of cross-examining witnesses effectively. Until as late as 1898 an accused person in a criminal trial, as well as his spouse, had no right to give sworn evidence. During the previous sixty or so years the judges had allowed the defendant to make an unsworn statement from the dock but the disadvantage was that he could not be questioned by the prosecution and the statement was likely therefore to carry less weight with the jury. Rights of appeal were virtually non-existent. The Court of Criminal Appeal was not set up until 1907. Before then a conviction could only be queried on narrow legal grounds, and then only with the active involvement of the trial judge. The penal system was harsh. There was capital punishment for scores of offences and transportation and flogging were everyday penalties. It was little wonder that the judges had sought to mitigate the

---

enforce safety, pollution, fraud and tax laws prosecute very rarely. Consequently working-class crime is prosecuted frequently, while middle-class crime is not. (See Andrew Sanders, 'Class Bias in Prosecutions', *The Howard Journal*, 1985, p. 176.)

harshness of the system by rules of evidence which favoured the defendant.

In the view of the Committee, however, the balance had tipped too far toward the defence. There were now few complaints that trials were too short. Accused persons who appeared in the higher courts were normally legally represented. The accused and his or her spouse could give sworn evidence. There were full rights of appeal against both conviction and sentence and the Court of Appeal was not allowed to increase a sentence — only to reduce it. The quality of juries and lay magistrates had greatly improved as a result of better education and, in the case of magistrates, of training. Moreover, criminals today were a good deal more sophisticated than in former times. Petty criminals might be only a little less ignorant and feckless about defending themselves, but there was now 'a large and increasing class of sophisticated professional criminals who are not only highly skilful in organising their crimes and in the steps they take to avoid detection but are well aware of their legal rights and use every possible means to avoid conviction if caught'.[2] These included refusal to answer questions put by the police and elaborate manufacture of false evidence.

Whereas the rules of evidence designed to protect the accused might have been necessary 'in order to give accused persons some protection, however inadequate, against injustice', there was also, the Committee thought, 'a good deal of feeling in the Committee and elsewhere that the law of evidence should now be less tender to criminals generally'.[3] (This statement of the Committee was widely criticised since it seemed to treat defendants as criminals prior to conviction.) The Committee was therefore of the opinion that the time had come to be less protective of the accused, if for no other reason than that 'It is as much in the public interest that a guilty person should be convicted as it is that an innocent person should be acquitted' — a dramatic re-writing of the traditional belief that it is better that ten guilty men go free than that one innocent one be convicted.*

The Committee made a long series of recommendations, nearly all of which were designed to assist the prosecution. The most important and the most controversial was that the suspect's right of silence in the police station should be

---

* The question whether juries acquit too many guilty defendants, espoused especially by Sir Robert Mark, Commissioner of the Metropolitan Police at the same period, is considered at p. 230 below.

abolished. Instead of being cautioned in the time-honoured formula 'You do not have to say anything unless you want to do so, but anything you say will be taken down and may be used in evidence', the suspect would be warned that, if he failed to speak at that stage, adverse inferences might be drawn at his trial. The prosecution and the judge would both be entitled to invite the jury to draw such inferences if the evidence warranted it. The right of silence in the police station, the Committee said, seemed 'contrary to common sense and, without helping the innocent, [gave] an unnecessary advantage to the guilty'.[4] Hardened criminals often took advantage of the right of silence to refuse to answer questions which might hamper the police and could even bring their investigation to a halt. The abolition of the rule 'would help justice'.*

This proposal was greeted with a chorus of protest not simply from the civil libertarians but from a broad community of interest groups including Members of both Houses of Parliament, the legal profession and even the judges.[5] It was widely condemned as threatening the fundamental principle that it was for the prosecution to prove its case. There could be many legitimate reasons why an innocent person might be silent — for instance to protect someone else, as a result of confusion or lack of intellectual capacity, from surprise or indignation at the accusation. The Committee had clearly misjudged the mood of the times and paid a great price, for the whole of its report on which it had laboured for so many years went down the drain. Neither Conservative nor Labour Governments felt able to implement a report which had drawn so much criticism.

ROYAL COMMISSION ON CRIMINAL PROCEDURE

Five years later, however, the Callaghan Labour Government set up a Royal Commission to look at the same general area with a remit that was both broader and narrower. It was broader in that it covered not simply the rules of evidence but also practice and procedure. It was narrower in being focussed on pre-trial matters and especially police powers, and the system for prosecution of offences. The most important difference between the Criminal Law Revision Committee (CLRC) and the Royal Commission on Criminal Procedure, however, was their

---

* The Committee also proposed that the defendant's right not to give evidence should be changed. He should be invited to give evidence and refusal to do so could then result in comment by both prosecution and the judge.

respective composition and methods of work. The CLRC consisted entirely of Establishment judges and lawyers, but with no-one recognisably representing the interests of either the accused or the police. The Royal Commission, by contrast, had a lay chairman and a majority of lay members and its members included two senior police officers and at least one lawyer who had substantial experience representing the defence. The CLRC worked behind closed doors and neither took evidence nor conducted any research. The Royal Commission solicited and received mountains of evidence, it travelled widely both in England and Wales and abroad, and it commissioned a considerable volume of research.

The Commission's report[6] published in January 1981 was largely unanimous. Where there were dissents, only one or two members out of fifteen disagreed with the majority of their colleagues. Given the fierce passions that run on these matters, this substantial measure of agreement was a considerable feat of chairmanship by Sir Cyril Philips, oriental historian and former head of the School of Oriental and African Studies at London University. The reception of the report, however, was far from unanimous. The political Left and the civil libertarians (the National Council for Civil Liberties, the Legal Action Group, the Haldane Society et al.) denounced it as too favourable to the police and the prosecution. But this time the rest of the relevant interest groups — the legal profession, the police, the magistrates, justices' clerks and judges — broadly approved the main recommendations. The Government plainly felt that it had a sufficient measure of agreement on which to proceed to legislate. It introduced its first Police and Criminal Evidence Bill in the autumn of 1982 but had to start afresh when Mrs Thatcher called a General Election in May 1983. The second Bill received the Royal Assent in the autumn of 1984. The Bill proved highly controversial as it was going through Parliament, and it was much amended. (Over a thousand amendments were made to the two versions of the Bill before it became law!). But the final product was, in the main, recognisably what the Government wanted, though on many relatively minor matters, and a few major ones, it had been persuaded to accept alterations. The Act, which went into force on 1 January 1986, amounted to a major recasting of the whole law on the powers of the police. It also included some of the recommendations from the much criticised 1972 report of the CLRC.

The main theme of the Royal Commission and of the Government in steering the Police and Criminal Evidence Bill through Parliament was to strike a fair balance between, on the one hand, the rights of the citizen and the suspect, and on the other, the police and the state. This balance must be judged both from the details of each part of the process and its overall impact.

One mistake not made by the Royal Commission or the Government was to follow the CLRC in recommending the abolition of the suspect's right of silence. The right of silence was in fact not merely preserved but strengthened — by requiring that the caution be administered at an earlier point (at the moment when a police officer first suspects the person of having committed an offence, rather than, as before, when he has admissible evidence of guilt), and that it be communicated not merely orally as before but also in writing. The Royal Commission was persuaded to recommend the preservation of the right of silence partly because a majority of its members may actually have concluded that the CLRC had been wrong in principle. But the Commission also had the advantage of empirical data which showed that surprisingly few suspects in the police station actually have the strength of will to remain silent.

Research has shown that most suspects talk — and usually without any great pressure from the police to get them to do so.[7] Two researchers from the Policy Studies Institute who observed police work in the London Metropolitan area for a two-year period and saw many interviews with suspects, said: 'In the course of our research we never saw anyone remain silent under questioning'.[8] Some suspects deny the offence, most admit it usually more or less immediately or within a few hours, and only a tiny proportion keep silent thoughout. A study by the present writer of cases tried at the Old Bailey showed that, according to the police statements, in just over one-third of the cases (35 per cent) the suspect made self-incriminating admissions immediately and in 38 per cent admissions were made within the first two hours.[9] In a study of over 1,300 cases in Sheffield it was found that some 70 per cent of those pleading guilty said they had told the police right from the start that they had committed the offence and 19 per cent of these had volunteered the information unprompted.[10] The cynics would argue therefore that in this context one can 'have one's cake and eat it'. The right of silence, with its symbolic reverberations in terms of the fundamentals of the system, is preserved, but so few seemingly rely on it that little harm is in fact done to the progress of police investigations.

The right of silence in fact never surfaced as an issue during the debates on the Royal Commission's Report or the Government's legislation and seemed to be a dead duck. It was very surprising therefore that the Home Secretary, Mr Douglas Hurd, giving the annual Police Foundation lecture on 30 July 1987 indicated that he might be willing to reopen the whole question. 'Is it really in the interests of justice', he asked, 'that experienced criminals should be able to refuse to answer all police questions secure in the knowledge that a jury will never hear of it? Does the present law really protect the innocent whose interests will generally lie in answering questions frankly? Is it really unthinkable that the jury should be allowed to know about the defendant's silence and be able to draw its own conclusions?' He did not answer his own question but invited informed opinion to consider the matter over the coming weeks.

The Law Society responded immediately in a statement by one of its senior officials Mr Walter Merricks, who had himself been a member of the Royal Commission. He reminded the Home Secretary that the Commission's proposals had been a carefully balanced package and that if this part were to be reopened, the new arrest and interrogation procedures would need rewriting.

At first the Home Secretary's kite seemed unlikely to fly — not least because it was based on a false premise. The jury *does* already know about the defendant's silence and can (and no doubt often does) draw its own conclusions. The right of silence only prevents the prosecution and the judge from suggesting that silence is evidence of guilt. This presents little difficulty for the police. Most suspects talk — and even when they do not, the majority are convicted anyway, often after pleading guilty. But the fact that the issue had been opened by the Home Secretary meant that it was suddenly back on the political agenda. In September 1987 the Lord Chief Justice supported police arguments that the right of silence should be abolished (*The Times*, 26 September 1987).

THE POLICE AND CRIMINAL EVIDENCE ACT 1984

Police powers for the investigation of crime have been significantly increased by the new Act.[11] The police were, for instance, given a new power to stop and search persons in the street for offensive weapons, house-breaking implements and anything that can be used for taking a motor vehicle. The power to stop and search for stolen goods, previously available only to the police in London, was extended nationwide. New general powers were given to the police to get a search warrant to look for evidence of serious offences. Virtually anything found during the course of a lawful search may now be seized by the police and used in evidence — whether or not it was what they were looking for. The power of arrest was extended to cover a variety of new situations, notably where the police officer regards an arrest as necessary to ascertain the apparent offender's name and address or to stop him causing injury to persons, damage to property, an obstruction of the highway or an offence against public decency. A suspect can be held without charges for questioning for up to 96 hours. The police can take fingerprints for criminal investigation purposes (rather than having to get authority from the justices for them to be taken).

At the same time, the new powers were qualified by a variety of restrictions and qualifications. Thus before exercising the power of stop and search the police officer must identify himself and the station from which he comes; he must tell the person searched the grounds and the reason for the search; he must have reasonable suspicion genuinely related to the individual at the time (as opposed to a stereotype impression because he is young, scruffy, black, a person with previous convictions etc.);* he must also normally make a record of the event and inform the person concerned of his right to a copy of the record. Unless the power existed under the old law, the new right to get a search warrant does not normally apply to certain types of exempt material — such as the records of doctors, Citizens' Advice Bureaux, and other advisory agencies, school authorities, social workers and probation officers, the contents of a journalist's notebook and any material held by a journalist in confidence.

If the police want access to material held as a result of a confidential relationship which is not included in the category of exempt material, they must ask a judge rather than the magistrates. Unless he is in some way implicated in the crime, the person holding such material must be given an opportunity of being there to contest the application. If the judge grants the police access to the material, it will be by way of an order to produce rather than a search warrant. Where the police enter premises with the householder's consent (which is much more common than after obtaining a search warrant), they must now tell the citizen that he is not obliged to give consent and, if he

---

* This requirement is not in the Act but in the Code of Practice on Stop and Search, which is one of the four Codes accompanying the Act.

does agree, such consent must be in writing.

All persons in custody in a police station are now the specific responsibility of a custody officer whose functions include seeing that the suspect is informed about his rights both orally and in writing. He must be told of his right of silence, of his right of access to a solicitor, of his right to have someone outside the station informed of his whereabouts, and to have a copy of the custody record form on which all the details of what transpires in the police station are recorded. The custody officer must also ensure that this record is in fact maintained and he is personally responsible for the well-being of the prisoner. No-one may be detained without charges for longer than 24 hours, unless it is a serious offence and unless an officer of the rank of superintendent has approved. No-one can be held for longer than 36 hours unless a magistrates' court has approved and then only after a hearing at which the suspect and, if he wishes, his lawyer must be present. The lawyer in such hearings is provided free of charge regardless of means. The lawyer who comes to advise an arrested person in the police station will normally also be available free of charge without regard to means — but access to a lawyer can be delayed for up to 36 hours if the offence is serious and if a superintendent reasonably believes that bringing in the lawyer may lead to criminal associates being alerted or the destruction of evidence or concealment of the proceeds of the crime. At each stage there is therefore a tension between the new powers and the restrictions or safeguards.

One vital aspect of the new regime is the system of Codes of Practice accompanying the 1984 Act — on Stop and Search, Search of Premises, Questioning of Suspects in the Police Station and Identification. (When tape recording is introduced generally, there will be a fifth code on that subject.) It is true that, technically, the Codes are not law and a breach of the Codes therefore cannot in itself give rise either to a criminal prosecution of a police officer or a civil action for damages against the police. Some argue that this makes the Codes virtually useless as a control of the police. But a breach of the Codes does automatically constitute an offence against police discipline — and although one does not expect many such proceedings, police officers plainly regard the threat as a real one. More important than the theoretical threat of disciplinary proceedings is the fact that the police are treating the Codes as the Bible — to be followed basically to the letter. Every police officer had extended training over several days on the new Act; each has his own copy of the Codes, which are extremely detailed and lengthy. The fact that they are so detailed may help to establish their authority and importance in the mind of the police officer, who tends by nature to be rule-oriented. Certainly it has been made abundantly clear by senior and middle-aged police management that officers are expected to play it according to the book and, if anything, in the early stages the problem may have been a tendency on the part of officers to stick slavishly to the rules, even to the point of absurdity, rather than the opposite problem of ignoring them too readily, as in the bad old days of the Judges' Rules prior to the 1984 Act.

The police were at first euphoric about the proposals in the Royal Commission's report. By the time it came to implementation of the new Act, however, they viewed them with considerably less enthusiasm. Satisfaction at the extension of their powers was tempered by anxiety about the requirements of record keeping, greater information to be given to suspects, better access to lawyers, controls on the length of detention and other new protections for the suspect. The civil libertarians, for their part, were not hugely impressed by the new controls and safeguards, believing that many would turn out to be on paper only.

HOW IS PACE WORKING?

The debate about the Act started long before it was even a gleam in the eye of the draftsman, with the publication of the Royal Commission's Report. It continued furiously throughout the passage of the Mark I and the Mark II Bill through Parliament and the lead period of more than a year before the Act came into force. Now that the Act is actually in force the debate rages on — though how it is working is a matter of controversy. The police view that the Act is creating serious problems for the service was given some support in an article published in March 1987 in *Policing* by Ian McKenzie, a former police officer working with the Director of the Police Foundation, and Barrie Irving on research into how interrogation techniques have been affected by the new Act. Barrie Irving had conducted research on interrogation in Brighton for the Royal Commission; now he had gone back to study the impact of the Act. The first report by his co-worker, Mr McKenzie, focussed on the effect of the new requirement in the Code of Practice that officers make a contemporaneous note of the exchanges in the interrogation process. Mr McKenzie reported that this requirement was making it more difficult for police to break down a suspect's story. Suspects, he suggested, had plenty of time to weigh their answers and could stop the process of note-taking by demanding to have a note read back to them. A CID officer was quoted as saying 'The flow is gone. You can't test what people say because all the time they're one step ahead of you. With the determined criminal, the one who has really got something to hide, you'll never get near him.'[12]

Ian McKenzie's report suggested that the whole style of questioning of suspects by the police had changed. Officers, for instance, no longer had a short preliminary meeting with the suspect to have a first look at him to size up the best way of handling him. Intensive questioning under pressure and close observation had given way to the tediously long-winded questioning required by the obligation to keep a full note, which meant that the suspect was in a better position to study the officers than they him. Almost half of every interview was silence, whilst the officer was writing. It was the officer rather than the suspect who was likely to display signs of stress such as heavy sighing or rubbing of the hand he was writing with. The scope of interviews was tighter and the information sought and obtained more restricted. Officers, for instance, hardly went beyond the narrow confines of the offence under investigation. 'The checking of TICs — further offences of a similar nature which may be taken into consideration by the courts — is no longer a prevalent feature of the interrogation sequence.'[13] Mr McKenzie admitted that all this might change when tape recorders were introduced in police stations, but in the meanwhile the police might have lost their skill in interrogation.

However, a different and much less gloomy picture of the impact of the new Act was given in January 1987 by Pat Johnson who, as Deputy Secretary of the Police Federation, was heavily involved in preparing its evidence to the Police Commission and then with its response to the Commission's report and to the two versions of the Bill and the Codes of Practice. Mr Johnson returned to ordinary police duties with the West Yorkshire force in August 1986. Writing in the *Police Review* under the heading 'The Bogy that Wasn't',[14] he said that PACE 'was seen as the death knell of policing as we had known it and signalling the end of a balanced approach to crime and wrongdoers which would tip the scales too much in favour of the accused'. The catalogue of fears expressed by the police service before the Act came into force was so great that the Federation had almost been convinced that the Bill 'was a criminal's charter and that there was no hope for the poor, hard-pressed police'. But now that he was 'up to his elbows in the daily operation of the Act', his impression was that in fact little had changed. Arrested persons were not generally asking for copies of the Codes. Efficient handling avoided the charge desk being clogged up. Meal breaks and other breaks appeared to present no more problems than they ever did. Handing over at the end of a shift was accomplished with a minimum of fuss or delay. The periodic reviews of the need for detention reminded officers that suspects should not be left to languish in the cells. It could not be denied that there was a greater demand for meticulous attention to detail and to the rights of the prisoner, but he had yet to 'find real evidence of that being a great handicap to his colleagues'. What he had observed was that the custody officer who was in charge of the well-being of all prisoners 'at last wields some real influence in an area of policing where, previously, while he might have held that responsibility, decisions were often made by others'. Now everyone entering the charge area was aware of the custody officer's authority.

Naturally, there had been 'touchy moments' but the Codes had served 'to spell out most clearly not only where responsibility lies but also the consequences of ignoring the safeguards'. In fact, the Codes had proved more than useful in settling arguments. It seemed to Mr Johnson that 'one by-product of the Act has been to increase efficiency and effectiveness amongst rank and file officers'. They were all too aware of the constraints on time and in consequence planned their use of time in much better fashion. Even the contemporaneous notes issue seemed to be 'dying a death'.

The Home Office produces regular statistics on a quarterly basis regarding certain police powers under the Act. These show that in 1986 the police recorded 109,800 stops and searches of persons and vehicles.* Of these, 44 per cent were in regard to stolen goods, 29 per cent for drugs, 9 per cent for going equipped to commit burglary or housebreaking, and 10 per cent for miscellaneous other categories. Stops and searches for offensive weapons — which gave rise to most of the fuss both in the deliberations of the Royal Commission itself and in the debates that led up to the enactment of the legislation — accounted for only 6 per cent of the total. (The figures relate only to stops and searches, not to stops for the purpose of questioning. Most forces

---

* The level of searches was highest in the first quarter (34,500) and was lower in each of the succeeding quarters (26,500, 23,900, 24,900).

used to record stops for questioning, but no longer do so because it is not required by the Act. The difference is enormous. Thus the Metropolitan Force recorded 607,000 stops in 1984, but between April and December 1985 when the force adopted the procedures required under PACE there were only 24,600 recorded stops and searches.)

The 'hit rate' in the form of arrests for an offence following a stop and search varied from 15 per cent in the case of stolen goods and going equipped to 19 per cent for drugs and offensive weapons. Overall it was 17 per cent. This was slightly better than the comparable figures for arrests following use of stop and search powers before the Act — which ran at a rate of a little over 10 per cent.

There were 377 recorded road blocks under the Act in 1986 involving the blocking of some 1,280 roads and the stopping of an estimated 61,100 or so vehicles. The result was a total of 34 arrests arising out of the road blocks and 30 arrests for completely different matters.

The statistics also deal (very confusingly) with the problem of detention for questioning. Under the Act the police have to get permission from a magistrates' court to hold a suspect for questioning beyond 36 hours. The figures show that in 1986 there were only 696 persons in respect of whom an application for a warrant of further detention was made — and that the application succeeded in all but 12 cases. (About three-quarters of those so held were ultimately charged.) But many of these were cases where in the event the suspect was not in the end held for more than 36 hours. The Act unfortunately does not require that the numbers of arrests be recorded nor that records be kept of the numbers held for up to 24 hours or up to 36 hours. These highly important statistics are therefore not available. Moreover, the data regarding length of detention under warrants of detention are meaningless, because police forces interpret the start of the period in different ways. But the statistics do show that 1,008 persons held for under 36 hours were released without charges, and there were another 179 cases of persons released without charges in respect of whom a warrant of further detention had been obtained.

The much discussed and much criticised power to conduct an intimate search of body orifices was used in relation to 104 persons during 1986. In only three of these cases was the search conducted by a police officer. Sixty of the searches were for drugs — and drugs were found in seven instances; 45 intimate searches were for weapons and in five cases a weapon was found.

There are also some (rather poor) statistics on the use made by suspects of the right to see a solicitor, over which the police expressed great anxiety before, during and after the enactment of the new legislation. The Act requires that all suspects be informed of the right to see a solicitor, though access can be delayed in certain circumstances where the offence is a serious one. The solicitor is free of charge regardless of means. Figures published by the Law Society showed that in the period January to November 1986 over 130,000 suspects were assisted under the scheme, and that projections suggested that this figure would be over 200,000 annually once the scheme had become properly established. Unfortunately, again the statistics are less helpful than they should be because there is no record of the proportion of cases in which the scheme is used. But it is safe to assert that the numbers receiving the help of solicitors under the Act is distinctly higher than before it was passed, so that it has had *some* impact.

The debate about the merits or otherwise of the new system introduced by the Police and Criminal Justice Act and the Codes of Practice will obviously continue for many years. The system was the product of about as careful a process of debate as can be expected in a modern democracy. A Royal Commission investigated the problems over several years. It commissioned its own research and received a mass of evidence from all interested parties. Its Report was commented on extensively. The legislation, which broadly put into effect the ideas of the Royal Commission, was exhaustively debated in Parliament and the Codes were drafted and re-drafted in the light of comments from all quarters. The final product seemed, to the present writer at least, a conscientious attempt to hold the balance fairly between the different interests. No doubt some details might have been dealt with more satisfactorily in a different way, but broadly the Act appears to reflect a tolerable approximation to the highest common denominator of reasonable informed opinion in the late 1980s. Research on the impact of the Act will gradually emerge, and meanwhile we shall no doubt have the reactions of the various interested constituencies such as the police and the civil libertarians. The process of tinkering with the system in the form of further legislation to deal with problems as they gradually surface will clearly continue.

The first official assessment of the overall impact of the new Act by the Home Secretary suggested, however, that amending legislation would do no more than tinker. In his Police Foundation lecture in July 1987, Mr Hurd said that increased familiarity with the new powers seemed to be stimulating a recovery in the numbers of crimes cleared up, after a fall during the early months of 1986. The figures for 1987 were better. Earlier in the year the Home Office had carried out a trawl of police and other organisations to identify where the shoe was still pinching. The response to this study 'suggested that while some minor changes of practice [might] be needed there [was] no need to question the fundamental balance struck in the Act'.

WILL PACE AFFECT DETECTION OF CRIME?

It is, of course, an open question whether all the new powers under PACE have much to do with reducing the level of crime, or catching or even convicting more criminals. Curiously, alterations in police powers do not necessarily enable the police to make any more 'good arrests'. This is because, contrary to what is widely supposed, the police are only rarely in a position to make progress in a criminal investigation through use of the powers bestowed by the law. In the overwhelming majority of instances where someone is arrested for a criminal offence it is because the crime has been reported to the police by a member of the public and the report of the crime includes sufficient information to enable the police also to identify the culprit. A study of how crimes come to be detected conducted for the Royal Commission on Criminal Procedure showed that out of a random sample of nearly 1,000 cases, 82 per cent were reported to the police — mostly by the victim. In an additional sample of 174 serious cases the proportion reported to the police, again usually by the victim, was 94 per cent.[15] The author's conclusion was that police officers play only a small role in discovery of offences, and certainly a much smaller part than the sociological tradition of the police in the discovery of crime might appear to suggest.[16] In the same study the author concluded that 'more often than not crimes are detected because the identity of the suspect is relatively clear from the outset'.[17] Unless the police get assistance in cracking the case they rarely have enough leads to discover the culprit. In real life the kind of sleuthing engaged in by mythical heroes from Sherlock Holmes to Kojak is relatively rare. Whether police powers are somewhat greater or somewhat less may therefore not make as much difference to the capacity of the police to catch criminals as one might think.

For one thing, the great majority of crimes are not reported at all. The British Crime Survey conducted by the Home Office and published in 1983 showed, for instance, that at most only one half of all burglaries, a quarter of sexual offences and a very small proportion of vandalism cases are reported to the police.[18] The second British Crime Survey published in 1985 produced broadly similar data. Overall, 62 per cent of all crimes were not reported. Only thefts of cars were almost always reported.[19] Of those crimes that are reported, an arrest is normally only possible if the citizen can identify the criminal or at least provide the basis for such an identification. The whole paraphernalia of police powers is somewhat marginal to this process. In a few situations it will be of great practical relevance but in the majority of cases it will make little, if any, difference one way or the other. David Steer in his study for the Royal Commission on Criminal Procedure on how crimes are detected concluded that 'there [were] no obvious powers which police might be given that would greatly enhance their effectiveness in the detection of crime'.[20]

Moreover, the precise extent of police powers does not necessarily indicate what the police will actually do in practice on the ground. For instance, changing the rules about search warrants makes only a marginal impact if most searches of premises are made without a search warrant.* Also the police may behave illegally — and when they do and evidence results, the traditional approach of the English courts is normally to admit even illegally obtained evidence. (Under the English rule the judges distinguished traditionally between confessions, which were inadmissible if they followed a threat or promise made by a person in authority such as a police officer, and other evidence which was only inadmissible in the discretion of the court. But in recent years, the courts narrowed the situation in which a confession would be held inadmissible and the extent of the discretion to exclude other evidence illegally or improperly obtained. In the United States by contrast the courts have always taken a much stronger line in excluding the 'fruit from the poisoned tree'.) The Police and Criminal Evidence Act gives the judge discretion to exclude evidence obtained by improper

---

* There is some conflict in the empirical data. According to a survey done by the police for the Royal Commission on Criminal Procedure, 43 per cent of all searches were under warrant — 61 per cent in London, 24 per cent in the provinces. (*The Investigation and Prosecution of Criminal Offences in England and Wales: The Law and Procedure*, Cmnd. 8092-1, 1981, pp. 126-9.) But a survey conducted by K. W. Lidstone of Sheffield University showed that out of 201 entries on premises for the purposes of a search, only 34 (17 per cent) were backed by a warrant. ('Magistrates, Police and Search Warrants' [1984] *Criminal Law Review*, 449.) But both showed searches without a warrant to be a clear majority.

means if in his view admission of the evidence would render the proceedings unfair[21] — but it is highly probable that the basic philosophy of English judges will continue to be that relevant evidence should generally be admitted even if it has been obtained by reprehensible methods. The discretion to exclude the evidence will probably be reserved only for the worst cases of police misconduct — though the rules on the admissibility of confessions remain stricter than for other evidence.

This is not to say that the drawing and re-drawing of the extent of police powers is unimportant, only that it makes less difference to the success of the police in criminal investigation than is generally supposed and that to some extent its importance may be mainly symbolic. It is important to get the balance in the structure of police powers right, because it is plainly unsatisfactory if it is felt to be wrong. The balance should so far as possible be fair as between the interests of the suspect and the interests of the police. But one should not be lulled into a false sense that by re-ordering the rules regarding police powers one has necessarily made any great contribution to improving, let alone solving, the problem of crime. It is right to do it for its own sake and because here and there it will actually make a difference on the ground. But re-shaping the rules probably does little that results in more, or for that matter fewer, criminals being brought to justice.

WHY DO SO MANY DEFENDANTS PLEAD GUILTY?

When it comes to the trial the most striking feature of the system is that, in spite of all the rhetoric about the prosecution having to prove its case beyond a reasonable doubt, in the great majority of cases the defendant pleads guilty. This happens in well over 90 per cent of cases in the magistrates' courts and in more than 60 per cent of cases in the crown court. There are many reasons for this phenomenon. The most common is probably that the defendant is guilty, and he knows, or believes, that the police have the evidence to prove the fact — often in the form of his own confession. Police stations will shortly all be wired for tape-recording of the questioning of suspects. The police, who were originally strongly opposed to tape-recording in the police station, are now strongly in favour of it, as they have discovered that it has no adverse impact on the frequency of defendants' admissions and confessions and that, once the admission is on tape, it makes the prosecution's position much stronger. The defendant is more prone to plead guilty and, if he pleads not guilty, less prone to challenge the confession. (Tape-recording also eases the police burden of keeping a full and accurate contemporaneous note.) The Government announced on 2 April 1987 that, after an experiment involving some 9,000 interviews, the scheme had been declared successful and would be applied throughout the country. It was hoped that the programme for providing the necessary facilities would be complete by 1991.

Defendants may also be tempted to plead guilty by the belief that the case will be dealt with more quickly, possibly with less publicity — and with a lower sentence. The Court of Appeal has for years allowed that a person who pleads guilty should normally be given a lesser sentence. Informed estimates of the discount for a guilty plea suggest that it may amount to as much as a quarter, or even a third, off.[22] Many defendants who come to court intending to plead not guilty are persuaded by their barrister on the day that pleading guilty may be the better part of valour. In fact, research has shown that barristers have significantly different rates of guilty pleas — suggesting that some like a fight more than others.[23] The annual statistics also show that the rate of guilty pleas in the North and the North East is consistently and dramatically higher than in the South.* This phenomenon has not yet been examined by research. Assuming it is not simply the result of differences in recording pleas, it may be an expression of the blunt, no-nonsense approach of the Northerner, resulting in more robust advice to clients to plead guilty. (Though the Court of Appeal ruled in 1986 that a last minute change of plea may not bring as high a discount as one that comes in better time — no doubt because it does not save resources to the same extent as the early guilty plea. But even so, there will still be some benefit.) Obviously the possibility of a significantly lower sentence acts as a powerful incentive to plead guilty.

But by far the most frequent reason for a guilty plea is not the influence of a lower sentence, whether appreciated later or earlier, but rather the exchanges in the police station. By the time the suspect has made a statement in the station it is normally too late for him to retract it or to allege successfully that it has been extracted from him by unfair means. (In a study of almost 1,500 cases in the crown court in Birmingham and

---

* In 1985, for instance, the proportion of defendants pleading guilty on the North Eastern circuit was 81 per cent compared with 45 per cent in London. In 1984 the comparable figures were 79 per cent and 43 per cent.

London no less than 88 per cent of those confessing to the police in Birmingham and about two-thirds in London, pleaded guilty.[24]) Until 1986 the police had to tread extremely warily for fear of falling foul of the rule that a confession obtained as a result of a threat or promise was inadmissible as not being 'voluntary'. But under the Police and Criminal Evidence Act this rule has been somewhat changed. A confession is automatically inadmissible now only if it was obtained through oppression or in circumstances likely to make it unreliable. This may legitimate the typical give and take in the police station which is apt to lead the defendant to make a confession ('If you make a statement we may be able to drop the more serious charges, or put in a good word for you, or allow you home on police bail. . . .').

PRE-TRIAL CUSTODY

Another factor that may influence the plea is whether the defendant is in pre-trial custody or out on bail. It seems that, other things being equal, those remanded in custody pre-trial are more likely to plead guilty than those on bail, perhaps because they are infected with a greater sense of hopelessness or because they are less likely to have access to legal advice. The circumstances of those remanded in custody is notoriously unsatisfactory. They are commonly locked up in their cells with nothing to do for 23 hours of the day, unable to associate with convicted prisoners, and not permitted to work or to take part in the normal periods of prison recreation. Also the periods for which they are held can be very considerable. Defendants in custody are supposed to be a priority for trial but the average delays are serious, especially in the London area.*

Pre-trial custody appears to be in conflict with the principle that a man is presumed innocent until proven guilty. If he is innocent, why is he in custody? This question relates most obviously to the two thousand or so persons each year who are acquitted after having been detained in custody. In some

---

* The average time between committal and trial for custody cases in 1986 was 10.4 weeks, and in London 18.2 weeks. For defendants on bail the comparable figures in 1986 were 15.2 weeks and 26.7 in London. Even proceedings in the magistrates' courts involve considerable and increasing delays. The average time from first listing date to completion of the case in the magistrates' court was just over 4 weeks (30 days) in October 1986. But for indictable offences the period was just over 7 weeks (50 days), compared with a little over 5 weeks (39 days) in June 1985.

countries they would at least be entitled to apply for compensation, but this possibility does not exist in English law. Under the Bail Act 1974 there is a presumption that the defendant should get bail unless the court is satisfied that there are substantial grounds for believing that, if released on bail, he would fail to turn up for his trial, commit an offence or obstruct justice.

The court is permitted to take into account the strength of the evidence against him, the nature and seriousness of the charge and the character and antecedents of the accused.[25] He may also be detained if there are further inquiries to be made. Since the great majority of those who come before the courts are in fact eventually found guilty it would be absurd to pretend that the probability is that any particular defendant will be found not guilty. The reality is that the presumption of innocence is set aside for the purposes of the question as to whether the defendant should be kept in custody pending trial. Technically, the court expresses no opinion as to whether the defendant will be found guilty, but in a sense it deals with the problem almost as if he were guilty. This is most obviously the case where he is remanded in order to prevent him committing offences. The implication is that this means *other* offences. Normally the concept of preventive detention is not known in English law. But in this context a person is locked up on the basis that if he were guilty of the offence with which he is charged (on which the court says nothing), it would be right to stop him committing other similar offences. From a layman's perspective it seems a strange way to apply the presumption of innocence. The explanation is that the presumption is not applicable to all situations. Its chief function is to lay upon the prosecution the duty of proving its case beyond a reasonable doubt. But it is not allowed to override the felt necessity to be able to keep some defendants in custody pre-trial. Scrupulous application of the presumption of innocence gives way to the demands of security, protection of the public and the integrity of the administration of justice.

There has over the past twenty years been great concern over the size of the remand population. By European standards the English rate per 100,000 of the population is relatively good — in marked contrast to the proportion we imprison, where our rate is the worst in Europe. Nevertheless, the numbers are high and growing. During the 1970s, as a result of efforts culminating in the Bail Act 1976, the number and the proportion of remand prisoners in custody were decreasing. The proportion remanded on bail went from 66 per cent in 1967 to 89 per cent in

1976. Since then the proportion has remained at around that very high level. But the *numbers* in custody on remand and the proportion of the prison population they represent have been growing remorselessly. In 1974 the average daily population of prisoners on remand was 5,081 (14 per cent of the prison population). At the end of January 1987 it was 10,539 (22 per cent of the prison population). Between 1972 and 1982 the average daily male population of untried prisoners rose by 88 per cent, compared with an increase of only 8 per cent in numbers of convicted and sentenced prisoners over the same period. The main reason for the increase appears to be not only a growth in the numbers being remanded but, even more, lengthening delays in bringing prisoners to trial. The problem of the remand population is serious and getting worse. The Lord Chancellor's Department has for years been struggling to keep abreast of the rising tide of cases but the task now seems beyond it.*

CROWN COURT OR MAGISTRATES' COURT

If a case does get to trial the nature of the trial will depend very much on whether it takes place in the magistrates' court or the crown court; the overwhelming proportion of cases are heard by the magistrates. In 1985 magistrates dealt with 2.15 million defendants and the crown courts with some 98,000 — plus a further 7,700 who were tried in the magistrates' court but sentenced in the crown court. Theoretically, they operate under the same basic rules and principles but the reality is vastly different. In the magistrates' court the proceedings are normally conducted at bewildering speed. The defendant is commonly unrepresented (although the proportion who have a lawyer is now much greater than it was formerly). The proceedings in

---

* The average time spent in custody by male prisoners facing trial in magistrates' courts and crown courts was 55 days compared with 36 days in 1980. In 1986 the Home Office started an experiment in certain areas with time limits in order to speed cases. Periods of time are set for the different stages of the case. If the requisite stage has not been reached in that time a defendant in custody has to be released on bail. Ultimately, the Home Office also has powers to provide by rule that if the stages of the case are not completed in time in regard to a defendant on bail he will be free altogether. But this power has not yet been utilised. For the moment the experiment is confined to time limits for defendants in custody which would result only in releasing them on bail. But it seems doubtful whether this will have much impact. The experimental time limits are drawn so generously that they do not provide much of a spur to action and inevitably exceptions are allowed so that there is always a loophole. The American experience with time limits has not so far been very encouraging.[26]

magistrates' courts are stage-managed by the clerk — especially when the court consists, as it normally does, of lay justices. The rules of evidence are not always carefully observed. The procedure tends to be somewhat rough and ready. The description 'summary' justice is apt.

In the crown court, by contrast, the whole process is more formal, lengthier and more dignified. The judge sits in full robes and wig with a jury. He is in command — the court clerk plays little role. The pace is deliberate, even ponderous. The defendant is virtually always represented by one or more barristers. English barristers do not jump up and down taking points by way of objection à la Perry Mason, but the rules of evidence are normally observed much more carefully than in the magistrates' courts. Where in the magistrates' court the decision is that of the bench, sometimes after a retirement, with or without the clerk, in the crown court the decision as to guilt is that of the jury whilst sentence is imposed by the judge.

THE ENGLISH COMPARED WITH A CONTINENTAL CRIMINAL TRIAL SYSTEM

In both the magistrates' and the crown court the procedure is mainly oral. Witnesses come to give their evidence in open court and can be cross-examined by the opposing party. In the magistrates' court when the defendant is unrepresented, cross-examination is usually a non-event. The defendant has no idea how to cross-examine and the court, though theoretically willing to assist him, cannot in practice do so to any useful extent. Cross-examination in the crown court is often said to be one of the glories of the common law system. In the Continental system cross-examination in this sense is virtually unknown. There the witnesses are examined mainly by the presiding judge on the basis of the dossier drawn up by a pre-trial judge who will have seen them and will have taken down a full account of their evidence. The trial judge reads the dossier containing the evidence beforehand. There is therefore little chance of surprises and relatively little for the lawyers to do. They play a minor role, asking only supplementary questions after the court has finished the questioning of the defendant and the witnesses.

In crown court trials the prosecution must give the defence advance copies of the evidence it intends to call. (This system has now also been extended to trials in magistrates' courts for offences that could have been dealt with at the higher level where the accused asks for advance disclosure — though the

prosecution can choose whether to supply full witness statements or only police summaries.) The triers of fact (the jury in
the crown court and the bench in the magistrates' court) do not
have access to these pre-trial statements. The evidence unfolds
for them essentially from the mouths of the witnesses. Cross-
examination, however, only rarely has the devastating impact so
frequently given to it in fictional trials. The destruction of the
witness by the implacable questioning of opposing counsel does
sometimes happen and when it occurs it has a dramatic effect.
But normally cross-examination is a fairly wooden affair.
Counsel puts it to the witness that he is lying or has been
mistaken. The witness denies the suggestion and they move on
to repeat the same process on the next point. The effectiveness of
cross-examination usually depends on the extent to which the
barrister in the case is supplied by his instructing solicitors with
ammunition in the form of information showing that the
witness's evidence is less than the truth. Normally such
material is simply not available. If the barrister has no means of
demonstrating that the witness is lying other than by suggesting it, he is not likely to make much impact.

Another significant difference between the English and the
Continental system is the approach to evidence that has to be
excluded. All systems exclude evidence that is not relevant and
evidence which is wholly unreliable — such as that of very
young children or of persons suffering from mental disability.
But the particular feature of the English system has been the
exclusion of relevant evidence of persons who might normally be
thought to be perfectly credible witnesses. The reason was the
historical existence of the jury, inexperienced and often largely
illiterate. The judges decided early on that there were some
categories of relevant evidence that were not fit for the jury to
hear. A classic example is evidence showing the defendant to be
a person with a prior record. If this information were available
to the jury there is obviously the danger that its members would
too readily jump to the conclusion that the defendant was guilty
— even if the evidence on the current charge was not wholly
convincing. In the Continental system, by contrast, the defendant's whole history, including any previous convictions, is
known to the court from the outset. (In fact, in an English trial
the judge himself, and in the magistrates' court, the clerk, does
know about the defendant's record, but the jury, and the
magistrates, do not — until after a verdict of guilty.)

There are a few exceptions to the general rule. One, for
instance, is when the accused claims to be of good character. The

prosecution can obviously then show the jury that the defendant's claim is false. Another is if the facts of the present case and of the case in which he was previously convicted are remarkably similar and where there is some peculiar identifying factor which makes it virtually certain that the offences were committed by the same person so that the danger of coincidence is effectively eliminated. A third, more problematic, exception occurs when the defendant casts aspersions on the character of any of the prosecution witnesses. The theory of this so called 'tit-for-tat' rule is that the jury should know that the defendant who is attacking the character of prosecution witnesses is himself not a blameless character. The rule severely hampers the defence of someone with prior convictions where the imputations are a central part of his case — where for instance he wants to allege that the police planted the incriminating evidence on him. If that is his story, the effect of the 'tit-for-tat' rule is that he can only introduce it at the risk of having his previous convictions made known to the jury. The Criminal Law Revision Committee recommended in its 1972 Eleventh Report that in such a situation the rule should not apply since it unfairly handicaps the defendant in putting his defence, but this recommendation, regrettably, has not been implemented.

The Committee in the same report also proposed that there should be a further exception — where the defendant admits the basic facts (the *actus reus*) but denies that he had the necessary knowledge or intent (*mens rea*). (He agrees that the police did find stolen goods in his garage but says that he did not know they were stolen.) The jury would then be told that he has previous convictions for handling stolen goods. This recommendation was widely condemned when the Committee reported in 1972 and it has not been implemented. It is thought to run too much against the deep-seated belief that to admit previous convictions is unfair. Continental jurists would regard this as pure sentimentality. The jury is trying to assess the probability of the defendant being guilty of handling stolen goods. He does not deny that he had them. In terms of probabilities, if he has a record it makes his defence considerably less credible. There is plainly force in the point and, since seven out of ten defendants do in fact have prior convictions and most not guilty pleas are based on a denial of the criminal knowledge or intent, it would be likely to have some effect on the level of acquittals. Would the extra convictions mainly be of the guilty or the innocent? It seems probable that although some would be innocent, many more would be guilty. Yet there is not the slightest prospect of the proposal being implemented. At no time since 1972 has there been any significant level of support for the idea — even the police have apparently felt it was not worth promoting.

By contrast, the other main traditional peculiarity of the English rules of evidence, the hearsay rule, is in the process of substantial modification. The rule prohibits the witness from testifying about what someone else told him. So witness A cannot give evidence of what B said to him and even less of what B said to C. The reason for the rule is that, by definition, the author of the statement is not there to be cross-examined about the alleged statement and the credibility of the evidence therefore cannot be tested. It applies also to documents. So a document cannot normally be admitted in evidence unless its author is in the witness box to explain its provenance. In Continental systems the rule is unknown. Hearsay evidence is allowed in for what it is worth. Its weight is assessed by the court. In civil cases the rule has been drastically reformed and may soon even be abolished, but in criminal cases it has so far been adhered to rather strictly.

There are some exceptions to the rule, the most important of which is for confessions or admissions, which are allowed in even though they are hearsay, on the somewhat unconvincing ground that a statement made to one's disadvantage is likely to be true. The actual reason is that the criminal justice system would grind to a halt if confessions could not be utilised by the prosecution. But unless the case comes within one of the recognised exceptions to the rule, it is applied rather rigorously. So in a 1965 case the prosecution foundered where its evidence was that the defendants had conspired to sell cars with log books from other cars that had been wrecked. The prosecution wanted to call an officer in charge of the records of the manufacturers of the stolen cars to produce microfilms of the cards filled in by workmen, showing the numbers of the cylinder blocks which coincided with the numbers of the cylinder blocks of the cars sold by the defendants. The House of Lords held that the admission of the records would be a breach of the rule against hearsay evidence because the witness could not assert that he personally knew about the particular cylinder block numbers.[27] The actual problem created by the decision was immediately rectified by legislation permitting introduction of evidence of business or trade records,[28] and this was extended in 1984 to other records made under some form of duty such as that of an employee.[29] But this left a host of documents still inadmissible.

The Roskill Committee in its report in 1986 recommended

that, at least for fraud trials, the hearsay rule should be considerably relaxed.[30] The Government decided to accept this recommendation and to apply it more broadly to all criminal cases. The Criminal Justice Bill introduced in 1986 and reintroduced in July 1987 after the General Election would allow first-hand documentary hearsay evidence to be admissible, together with business records containing information supplied by a person with personal knowledge of the matter, and the reports of experts. The Bill also permitted live video links from abroad to enable a witness to give evidence in an English case by satellite, and live video links for the evidence of children in sex cases so as to spare the child the distress created by the trauma of the courtroom.* These amount to significant alterations in the traditional rules.

Generally, however, the process of trial runs according to the traditional rules. The judge in the English system sits relatively passive as an umpire, whilst the case is conducted by the parties through their lawyers — if they have any. Sometimes this 'adversary' system has the unfortunate result that relevant witnesses are not called by either side and important questions that could be answered are not put because the lawyers do not want to prejudice their own party's case. But most English lawyers and judges seem convinced that this is nevertheless better than the Continental 'inquisitorial' model of trial where the court calls the witnesses and asks the questions, with the lawyers for the parties playing only a subsidiary role. The advantage of the Continental system is that it may sometimes produce a closer approximation to the truth. The principal disadvantage is that it does not give the same appearance of being fair, because the court is so heavily involved in the process of questioning the witnesses. Also the Continental system requires a massive establishment of pre-trial judges to collect, sift and sort the evidence. The fact that the acquittal rate in Continental cases is very low may be attributable to the

---

* At the time this book went to press, the Government had just announced that it would not go further by allowing the evidence of the child in such cases to be presented simply on video made before the trial with the question put by one interviewer. It had been suggested that if the suspect had already been identified at the time of the interview, he and his lawyers could observe the questioning through a one-way mirror and feed questions to the interviewer who would be wearing a miniature earphone. If he was only identified later, there would have to be a second interview of the child. (See for debate on this issue, *New Law Journal*, 30 January 1987, p. 108; 6 March 1987, p. 216; 10 April 1987, p. 351. See also Patricia Wynn Davies, 'How children should be seen and heard', *Law Magazine*, 24 July 1987, p. 20.)

intensity of this pre-trial sifting. When a case goes to trial it is likely to end in a guilty verdict, not perhaps so much because the court is biassed by its reading of the pre-trial dossier but because the pre-trial process has weeded out the weak cases which in the English system do often go to trial.

THE CROWN PROSECUTION SERVICE AND DIRECTED ACQUITTALS

In England almost half of all jury acquittals are directed by the judge. One of the chief arguments for the introduction of the new Crown Prosecution Service (CPS) which took the handling of prosecutions from the police and gave it instead to prosecution lawyers was that it might help to reduce the rate of these directed acquittals which seem, almost by definition, to be weak cases. The campaign to ensure that prosecutions are handled by lawyers independent of the police was launched by JUSTICE in 1970, largely on the ground that it was wrong that the police should both investigate and prosecute criminal cases. In most countries in the world, including Scotland, these two functions are distinct. The Royal Commission on Criminal Procedure agreed and the Thatcher Government implemented the policy, even though it involved the significant extra cost of employing several hundred more lawyers and would therefore result in an equivalent increase in the number of civil servants. It was widely predicted that the establishment of the CPS would result in the weeding out of many weak cases which previously would have been pursued by the police to the point where either the judge or the jury threw the case out.

But it is far from certain that this will happen. For one thing, the CPS has been established with such grave shortage of resources that the quality of its entire operation was threatened from the outset. The service began in London in April 1986 and in the rest of the country the following October, with loud (and well-founded) cries of woe and lamentation as to the inadequacy of Treasury provision. When it started in October 1986 the service was several hundred lawyers short of its proper complement and this condition has continued, especially in the London area. (A Written Parliamentary reply by the Attorney General to Mr Peter Bruinvels on 11 March 1987 stated that there was a staff shortfall of 22 per cent. In Inner London there were only 75 lawyers in post, out of a complement of 152.) Use has had to be made on a massive scale of barristers and solicitors in private practice working *ad hoc* on a fee-for-case basis with little or no supervision. Because of the shortage of staff, those in post were working excessive hours and many were in any event inexperienced and not by any means as well qualified as they should have been.

A survey of the staff of the CPS by their civil service union published in April 1987 showed that three out of five crown prosecutors were actively looking for other employment — only months after the service had been launched! The First Division Association sent questionnaires to 1,020 of its members. The response rate was 72 per cent. It was clear that morale in the new service was at rock bottom. Only 32 lawyers out of 739 expressed confidence in the service's senior management. The press verdict was that the service was close to collapse. The message penetrated to the Treasury and the Attorney General announced on 11 March that there would be both higher pay and a 13 per cent increase in staff complement — though it had proved impossible previously to fill even the smaller number of jobs.

However, even in the unlikely event that the manpower problem can be solved with recruits of sufficient ability and experience, it does not follow that the number of directed acquittals will fall significantly. One problem is that the new service, in order to establish its credibility with the police on whom it relies for its information, will not in practice feel able to be as independent as it should. The police were generally not enthusiastic about having their prosecution powers taken away and have not necessarily been as co-operative toward the new service as would have been desirable. Any such tendency might understandably be aggravated if the police feel that their views as to the need for a prosecution are too readily being set aside by over-independent prosecution lawyers.

But in any event directed acquittals occur in cases where the prosecution has been in the past, and will in the future be run by barristers. The barrister has always been independent of the police and his situation has not been affected by the establishment of the new service. If the 'independent' barrister did not spot the weakness in the prosecution's case before, why will he do so now? Moreover, in Scotland, where the prosecutor (the procurator fiscal) is unquestionably independent of the police, he nevertheless tends to follow the police view of the case in the great majority of cases. Research has shown that the fiscals prosecuted in 92 per cent of cases referred to them by the police. Although they have the power to ask for further information, they do so rather infrequently — in the study in only 6 per cent

of cases. The fiscals normally act solely on the information
supplied by the police with little or no further inquiry. (In 63 per
cent of cases in the study the decision as to whether to go ahead
was taken on the same day that the fiscal received the papers.[31])
For all these reasons it must be doubtful therefore whether the
advent of the new Crown Prosecution Service will significntly
reduce the high proportion of directed acquittals.

This prediction received confirmation from the first annual
figures for acquittals since the establishment of the Crown
Prosecution Service which were published in July 1987. These
showed that, far from going down, the proportion of directed
acquittals in 1986 had risen to 52 per cent as compared with 48
per cent in 1985. This was hardly comforting for those who
established the CPS with high hopes that it would reduce the
proportion of directed acquittals — especially since it has proved
vastly more costly than was originally forecast.

CRIMINAL APPEALS

After a criminal case has been concluded there is, of course, still
the possibility of an appeal but the appeal system is highly
restrictive, and remarkably small numbers of convicted persons
do in fact appeal. The basic underlying philosophy is that the
defendant has had his day in court and only exceptional
circumstances justify an appeal. It was not until 1907 that the
system even granted a right of appeal in criminal cases tried at
the higher level, and even then only with leave of the trial judge
or the appeal court. If the Court of Appeal thinks that an
application for leave to appeal is frivolous it can penalise the
would-be applicant by adding up to three months to his sentence
— a considerable and rather harsh disincentive.* If the appeal is
based on alleged new evidence, the Court of Appeal will consider
it only if it was not available at the trial. The fact that it was
not produced at the trial because of a tactical decision by the
lawyers or even their negligence would not be sufficient ground.
This can be extremely hard on the accused.

A classic illustration was Luke Dougherty's case. The defen-

---

* In March 1987 in the case of *Monnell* and *Morris*, the European Court of
Human Justice ruled that the power was not contrary to the European
Convention on Human Rights. The court was told that although there were no
precise figures it seemed that the power was exercised in only some 60 to 65
cases a year (out of well over 6,000) and that the loss of time ordered ranged
from 7 days to 64 days. In three-quarters of the cases the loss of time ordered
was 28 days.

dant was charged in 1972 with shoplifting at a time when he
was actually on a bus outing with some twenty others, many of
whom knew him. His apparently cast-iron alibi did not stand up
in court, however. The solicitor called only two witnesses — one
was Dougherty's girl friend and the other happened to have
previous convictions. The jury disbelieved them. Dougherty was
convicted and sent to prision. An application for legal aid for the
appeal so that statements could be obtained from the other
passengers on the bus was refused on the ground that the
evidence had been available at the trial and could not therefore
be called on the appeal. Had it not been for the intervention of a
former Lord Chancellor, Lord Gardiner, who took up the case
and eventually got Dougherty released by the Home Office, a
grotesque miscarriage of justice would have been perpetuated.

An appeal against conviction can be based on the contention
that the jury came to the wrong result — that its decision was
against the weight of the evidence. But the prospects for such an
appeal are dim. Until the mid-1960s the Court of Appeal took
the view that if there was any evidence on which a reasonable
jury could have convicted, the verdict of guilty must stand. In
1966 the court was given a new statutory formula to interpret
(whether it regarded the verdict as 'unsafe and unsatisfactory'[32])
and since then it has slightly relaxed the test. There are even a
few cases in which the court has been prepared to quash a
conviction on the ground that it had a 'lurking doubt' about the
jury's decision.[33] But generally the court is very slow to
interfere with the jury's verdict. Appeal courts anyway tend to
have a bias in favour of the decision of the trial court — partly
because they do not want to encourage too many appeals; partly
because the trial court did after all see the witnesses and have
the chance of observing their demeanour. But where the decision
was by a jury this tendency is even greater because of the
special aura of sanctity that surrounds jury decisions. Judges
feel that they would almost be subverting the constitution if
they frequently differed from a jury. This feeling seems
considerably exaggerated. It would be perfectly sensible to have
a principle for cases tried in the crown court that a convicted
person should first have to be found guilty by a jury of twelve
ordinary citizens and that that verdict must then be upheld by
the professional judges in the Court of Appeal. The additional
level of judicial screening would then be seen as a fail-safe
mechanism to avoid miscarriages of justices rather than, as now,
appropriate only for exceptional cases.

When the Court of Appeal does allow an appeal it has the

option of either quashing the conviction or of applying the proviso to section 2 of the Criminal Appeal Act on the basis that, although the defendant had a valid ground of appeal, there was no overall miscarriage of justice. If the defect in the trial was a major one, the court is supposed to quash the conviction even though the defendant was rightly convicted — on the ground that the system should not allow a conviction to stand where the trial was vitiated by some egregious error. On the other hand, the court is understandably reluctant to release a villain back on to the streets simply because there has been a technical error during the trial.

An option not previously available save in one situation is the intermediate solution of ordering a retrial. The reason is simple and curious — the English system has only permitted a retrial where the appeal is allowed on the ground of fresh evidence. Even then virtually no use has been made of the power. The average number of retrials ordered is usually less than half a dozen per year. There is no rational explanation for the traditional refusal of the English system to contemplate retrials. The explanation normally given has been that it would be unfair to the accused to put him through the ordeal of a second trial. But this manifestly does not justify the policy since where the court decides to apply the proviso to section 2, most defendants would presumably prefer to take their chances with a second trial rather than go straight back to prison. At all events, a change in the rule was foreshadowed in March 1987 when the Home Office circulated a discussion paper in which it said that it had come to the conclusion that the Court of Appeal should be given a general power to order a retrial but that before implementing the idea it sought views. No resolution of the issue had been determined by the time the Criminal Justice Bill was reintroduced in July 1987 after the General Election, but the signs were that this ancient anomaly in English law was shortly to be dealt with.

In 1985 there were some 98,200 persons dealt with in the crown courts. In the same year in relation to persons dealt with in the crown court, there were a mere 1,066 appeals against conviction, 6,282 appeals against sentence and 669 appeals against both conviction and sentence. (Obviously the appeals were not all in relation to matters dealt with in 1985 — some would have related to trials held in 1984.) Most were refused leave or abandoned their appeal. Only 181 had their convictions quashed.

MISCARRIAGES OF JUSTICE

If the chances of succeeding on an appeal are slight, they are a good deal worse for someone who, after losing his appeal, tries to persuade the Home Office that he has been the victim of a miscarriage of justice. Miscarriages of justices are a blot on every legal system. There is none that can escape the problem. Usually they seem to result from honest error by witnesses who wrongly identify the accused person. Sometimes they are the result of mistakes by the police who build a case out of circumstantial evidence which happens to be misleading. Occasionally the mistake is due to wilful and knowing distortion of the truth by the witnesses for the prosecution or the police themselves, or conscious suppression of evidence that would have helped the defence. Sometimes an innocent accused person finds himself convicted because he is caught up as a co-defendant with guilty friends or associates. Sometimes the fault lies with inadequate work by the defence lawyers or imprecision in the tests done by forensic experts. Sometimes the jury believes the wrong witnesses.

When someone has been convicted and has exhausted his rights of appeal, the system operates on the basis that only the most cogent evidence will be sufficient to disturb the result. There is naturally, and properly, a considerable reluctance to have the executive overturn decisions reached by the judicial process. Yet there remains the mechanism of a petition to the Home Secretary to re-open a concluded case — and thousands each year are launched in hope from prisoners.

The Home Secretary has the power to recommend a Free Pardon but this is done only in the extremely rare case where it is shown beyond a reasonable doubt that the defendant did not commit the offence — normally as the result of fresh evidence. To say that he is then pardoned for something that he did not do is odd. In fact, it is even odder than appears at first sight since a Free Pardon does not even cause the conviction to be expunged. It merely relieves the person concerned from its pains and penalties. The conviction itself stands until it is quashed by the Court of Appeal. This bizarre situation became apparent in 1984 after Barry Foster appealed against conviction for rape of a ten-year-old child when another man confessed and was sentenced for the crime. Foster was given a Free Pardon but the Court of Appeal said that in order to have the conviction quashed he had also to bring an appeal. Alternatives open to the Home Office other than a Free Pardon are to remit the balance of the sentence or to refer the case back to the Court of Appeal, in which case it will then be dealt with exactly like any other appeal.

The Devlin Committee on Identification Evidence in its report in 1976 said that in considering allegations of miscarriages of justice the Home Office adopted too severe an approach. It also thought that the Home Office should consider the establishment of some form of independent review tribunal to which cases that were not suitable to be referred back to the Court of Appeal could be sent.[34] In 1982 the House of Commons Home Affairs Select Committee agreed that there should be an independent element in the decision whether to grant a Free Pardon or to remit the sentence. It was unreasonable, it thought, 'that the Home Secretary should be expected to decide whether to grant a free pardon or remit a sentence on the advice of his officials alone'.[35] There should, it said, be some form of independent review body with wide powers to decide how to investigate cases. The review body should not be prevented from considering the testimony of someone who was available at the trial but was not called then; it thought the traditional rule about fresh evidence was 'unduly restrictive'.[36] It also wanted to see the Home Office adopt a less severe standard of proof before being prepared to recommend a pardon. The royal prerogative should be exercised if the Home Office thought the original verdict was 'unsafe and unsatisfactory' just like the court. But the Government, predictably, rejected the plea for a new independent body to assist the Home Office to decide whether a petition from a prisoner had merit.[37] Commenting editorially, the *Criminal Law Review* said that unless there was some legal or procedural irregularity in the trial the conviction was unlikely to be upset.[38]

> Where the judge has summed up faultlessly and the trial was properly conducted, and it is the jury which has allegedly gone against the weight of the evidence, the appeal mechanism has virtually no effect. So sacrosanct is the verdict of a jury held to be that it is exceedingly rare for the Court of Appeal to overturn one.

A more radical approach to the problem of miscarriages of justice is that of the well-known author and campaigner Ludovic Kennedy who has himself investigated many such cases. In June 1986 he told the first ever annual conference held by the Bar that, in his view, the great majority of such cases came about 'as a result of CID officers manipulating the evidence'. The police,

he thought, did not do this knowingly to frame the innocent —
'rather to ensure the conviction of those who, lacking corrobor-
ative evidence and often under pressure to get results, they have
deluded themselves into thinking are guilty'.[39] According to
Mr Kennedy the police practised a variety of ploys including
false confessions, planting of evidence, suppression of evidence
favourable to the accused and persuading witnesses to change
their minds. He concluded that the only answer was to go over to
the Continental and in particular the French system, under
which in serious cases the pre-trial judge assumes responsibility
for the investigation, directing the police inquiries and himself
questioning the witnesses, including the suspect himself. The
search for the truth in the Continental trial system was also
likely to be more effective than the equivalent processes in
England. For a start, the defendant was a compellable witness
— though as a safeguard the prosecution had to prove him
guilty. Under our system, by contrast, he could shelter behind
the (very rarely exercised) right not to give evidence and if he
chose to plead guilty the court did not inquire into the matter
but accepted the plea without any evidence. The Continental
court called and questioned the witnesses, which ensured both
that relevant witnesses would be called and that the right
questions were put.

But even if Mr Kennedy were right in thinking that most
miscarriages of justice are due to police manipulation of
evidence, it is clear that there is little support for his view that
we should go over to the Continental method of pre-trial
investigation supervised by a judge. It would require an
enormous expansion in the numbers of judges and would run
counter to the traditional legal culture in which the inquiry is
handled by the police.* Moreover, there is no evidence that the
Continental system which Mr Kennedy favours results in fewer
miscarriages of justice.

Even if more were exposed in our system, it would not prove
that this was because there were more. It might merely be the
result of a more efficient system for revealing such cases — or
more and better investigative journalists. For every such case

---

* Also, it is far from certain that Mr Kennedy's description of the operation of
the Continental system gives the real picture. There is some empirical work
which suggests that the investigating magistrate, who notionally supervises the
police, in practice usually does not figure in the inquiry at all, and when he does,
generally follows the leads supplied to him by the police. (See A. Goldstein and
M. Marcus, 'The Myth of Judicial Supervision in Three Inquisitorial Systems:
France, Italy and Germany', *Yale Law Journal* (1977), pp. 240-83).

that is exposed, there are bound to be more that have not been sufficiently documented or proved but which nevertheless are in truth miscarriages of justice. There is therefore no way in which the numbers of such occurrences could ever be successfully quantified. All one can say with complete confidence is that such cases do occur in every system. It is therefore almost certainly a mistake to think that by adopting the radically different approach of a different legal culture one will make significant progress in reducing the incidence of such cases. Much better is to tighten up the procedures in one's own system and to construct a large safety net for the cases that appear to merit investigation. The single greatest lack in the English system, identified by both the Devlin Committee and the House of Commons Home Affairs Committee, is the absence of machinery independent of the Home Office with its own investigators that could be used to inquire further into cases that raise serious doubts. At present, if the Home Office wants further inquiries to be made it normally asks the police force that carried out the original investigation, or sometimes a different force, to look at the case again. It might occasionally be better if the further inquiry could be handled from outside the normal police service, even if the actual investigators were serving police officers seconded to the special unit. One can understand the reluctance of government to establish such a unit but it might make a real contribution to ensuring appropriate inquiry into some unusually difficult and troublesome cases.

Recently, for instance, there have been a number of *causes célèbres* in which it is argued powerfully that a miscarriage of justice has occurred. Three concerned IRA terrorism cases — the six men convicted of bombing two Birmingham public houses in 1974 which resulted in 21 deaths and 162 persons injured, four people serving life sentences for the Guildford pub bombings of the same year which killed five, and the seven members of the Maguire family jailed in the aftermath for handling explosives.

On 6 January 1987 the Home Secretary saw an all-party delegation of MPs and peers, including former Home Secretary, Mr Merlyn Rees, in connection with all three cases. Needless to say, a campaign suggesting that convicted IRA bombers have been wrongly convicted is about the last that politicians or the media would support. But two days later *The Times* (no less) in an unusually strong editorial, and after rehearsing the doubts about all three cases, actually called for a Free Pardon for all 17 defendants. Instead, Mr Hurd announced that he would refer the case of the six Birmingham bombers back to the Court of Appeal on the grounds of fresh forensic evidence and the testimony of a police officer who claimed that he had seen five of the six defendants with signs of injuries inflicted by the police. But in the other two cases, though in the view of reputable observers the doubts are no less grave, he refused to intervene. The excuse given was that there was nothing new in the two cases to justify their being reopened.* But even if there were no new evidence in the technical sense (on which there is dispute), there was undoubtedly something new in the form of increased doubt about the verdicts — generated largely by the efforts of investigative journalists and the media.

In fact, almost all cases which have been reopened have resulted from the efforts of authors and journalists such as Paul Foot, Ludovic Kennedy, Robert Kee, Chris Mullin, or the work of the BBC TV series 'Rough Justice' based on the files of the organisation JUSTICE and its former secretary Tom Sargant. Yet, the work of the investigative journalist in this area is not well regarded by either the Home Office or the courts.† The Lord Chief Justice, Lord Lane, was, for instance, savagely critical in December 1986 of the BBC's 'Out of Court' programme which raised doubts about the conviction for murder of Margaret Livesey who had been accused of killing her 14-year-old son. The programme was an entirely sober and careful account of the reasons for doubts about the case and the general issue of miscarriages of justice. But in the view of the Lord Chief Justice it amounted to a 'deliberate attack on the integrity and reliabilty of the system of criminal justice in this country'. *The Guardian* carried a report of the outburst under the heading 'Law Lord lashes BBC deceit'. The attitude of the Lord Chief Justice was probably typical of that of many judges — based on a feeling that the proper role of journalists is limited to accurate

---

* See the remarkable correspondence in *The Guardian* of 23, 24, 27 and 30 January 1987, involving the junior Home Office Minister, Mr David Mellor, and his predecessor Mr Alex Lyon. Mr Lyon revealed the extraordinary fact that until he put a stop to the practice, the Home Office had been in the habit of asking the Lord Chief Justice for his view as to whether a case should be referred back to the Court of Appeal and of not reopening it if he thought it should not be. See also the Home Secretary's letter to *The Times* of 30 July 1987 in which he said that a case should only be referred to the Court of Appeal when there was new and substantial matter which had not been before the court. However on 14 August 1987 Mr Hurd announced that, in view of new material in a Yorkshire TV programme 'First Tuesday', he had asked the police to re-examine the Guildford pub case.
† A rare exception was when the Home Secretary announced that he would refer the Birmingham bombers case back to the Court of Appeal and alluded expressly to two 'World in Action' TV programmes and the book about the case by Mr Chris Mullin.

reporting of the deliberations of the judges. 'Justinian' of *The Financial Times* writing on 12 January 1987 said that there was a 'growing feeling among the judges and the legal profession as a whole' that investigation of specific cases and general aspects of the machinery of justice is 'irrelevant, impertinent and counter productive'. Any suggestion that the courts may have got it wrong or, worse, that there are systemic faults, verges on *lèse majesté*.

JUSTICE, the highly respected British section of the International Commission of Jurists, estimates that there may be as many as 200 to 300 miscarriages of justice a year in the English system and that few of these are corrected. Even if the true number is far lower, there is serious reason to believe that they are by no means uncommon. It would be better if the system were more open to this reality, and more appreciative of the efforts of those such as JUSTICE, individual researchers, journalists and the media generally who devote themselves to painstaking inquiries into whether a miscarriage of justice has occurred. Nothing brings a legal system into disrepute so much as seeming indifference to what appears to be a case of someone serving a prison sentence for an offence he did not commit. All reasonable steps should be taken to ensure that such cases are properly investigated in a way that inspires confidence.

For the tiny number who do succeed in getting their conviction set aside by a pardon there is no *right* to compensation but it is possible to ask for an *ex gratia* payment. Until 1982 the record amount paid was £79,000 paid to John Preece who spent eight years in prison for murder, after vital prosecution evidence given by the Home Office pathologist, Dr Alan Clift, had been discredited. In 1985 the sum of £121,000 was paid to Geoffrey Davis who had also been convicted on the evidence of Dr Clift. The amount of compensation is determined by an outside assessor — the chairman of the Criminal Injuries Compensation Board. The Home Secretary announced in November 1985 that he would in future regard himself as bound to follow the assessor's view. But it is easier to pass through the proverbial eye of the needle than to get compensation for a miscarriage of justice. In the nine years between 1972 and 1981, there were only 47 cases in which such payments were made — an average of just over five cases per year.[40]

7

The Jury

There is no institution that more expresses the philosophy of the English justice system than the jury. Its roots lie deep in history. It is based on the participation of the ordinary citizen and it has complete ultimate power over the final result. The jury seems to be regarded with affection by most who participate in the justice system as professionals and by the overwhelming majority of the public at large. It has been copied in many other countries. Yet the very idea is at one level improbable. Citizens who mostly have no experience of legal procedures, or of the law or of listening to cases in court, or of concentrating on evidence and retaining facts over what may be many hours, days or even weeks are expected to understand and remember enough of what they have heard to do justice to a fellow citizen. It is extraordinary that it works at all — let alone that it has given reasonable satisfaction over hundreds of years.

When the jury system was first imported to Britain by the Normans after the Conquest its function was administrative rather than judicial. Jurors were local citizens summoned to report on oath (hence the origin of the word) on matters within their knowledge. Domesday Book, for instance, was compiled by such inquiries. It was Henry II who appreciated the use that could be made of the same device in the context of court cases. Originally the role of the jury was the same — to state what they knew rather than to deliberate on evidence produced by the parties. But gradually over the centuries this changed until gradually it came to be accepted that a juror should know as little as possible about the facts of the case before the trial.

USE OF THE JURY

Until relatively recently, jury trial was normal in civil as well
as criminal cases. In fact, until the middle of the nineteenth
century jury trial was the only form of trial in the common law
courts. A small breach was made in that year when trial by
judge alone was permitted with the consent of both parties. In
1873 in matters 'requiring prolonged examination of documents
or accounts or any scientific or local investigation' the court was
given power to remit the case to an official Referee, and ten
years later a further change provided that, save in six
exceptional types of case, trial by jury had to be specially asked
for. Only in cases of libel, slander, malicious prosecution, false
imprisonment, seduction and breach of promise of marriage,[1]
and the later addition of fraud, was there an absolute right of
trial by jury. Until the First World War, trial by jury still
occurred in the majority of cases. In 1913, 55 per cent of High
Court cases were heard by juries. Between the wars the number
fluctuated — 36 per cent in 1918, around 10 per cent in the
years from 1920 to 1922, 36 per cent in 1926 and down to 12 per
cent in 1935. After the Second World War it declined even
further. In the early 1950s it was only 2 to 3 per cent.

In January 1965 the Court of Appeal in *Ward* v. *James* held
that in personal injury litigation juries should be permitted only
in exceptional circumstances. Lord Denning, giving judgment
for a unanimous court of five (instead of the usual three) judges,
said that parties rarely asked for juries any more. Solicitors
tended to advise their clients to go for the relative security of a
decision by a judge sitting alone, rather than the unpredictabil-
ity of a jury decision. As Lord Denning put it[2]:

> If I were you, I should not ask for a jury. I should have a judge
> alone. You know where you stand with a judge, and if he goes
> wrong, you can always go to the Court of Appeal. But as for a
> jury, you never know what they will do, and if they go wrong,
> there is no putting them right. The Court of Appeal hardly
> ever interferes with the verdict of a jury.

Judges, Lord Denning said, broadly knew the tariff for damages
and could fit the particular case into the pattern of decisions
arrived at by the courts in cases with comparable injuries.
Juries, by contrast, had no knowledge of the precedents, and
their damages awards, as a result, were wildly unpredictable.
The award of damages was a figure based not on some abstract

justice but on an amalgam of dozens or hundreds of decisions in similar cases. The jury was not informed about previous similar cases, nor about awards in previous cases. Only the judge was in a position to fit the present case into the appropriate category of damages.

The Court of Appeal's decision in *Ward* v. *James* provoked uproar. The media joined in roundly condemning Lord Denning and his brethren for, in effect, abolishing the Englishman's sacred right of trial by jury. In response, the court took the earliest opportunity to defuse public fury. In a case only a few weeks later, it held that it had by no means intended to abolish the right to trial by jury nor to take away the court's statutory discretion to authorise a jury trial.[3] It had only wanted to give guidance for the ordinary case. But in exceptional cases, the court said, it could still be desirable to have a jury. The decision was a wholly illogical sop to public opinion. If the jury is not suitable for ordinary cases because it cannot be expected to have any idea of the current conventional level of damages, it must equally be unsuitable for the unusual case. But in practice it did not matter. The row provoked by the decision was based on the totally false impression that the court was abolishing a living institution, whereas in fact the civil jury had already almost died a natural death. In 1963, two years before the decision, the number of jury trials in London in the Queen's Bench Division was 27 out of a total of 962 (or 2.8 per cent). Since *Ward* v. *James* the number has normally been two dozen or so a year.*

The great majority of civil jury trials are in libel and slander cases. In 1974 the Faulks Committee[4] recommended that juries should no longer be available as of right in such cases. The rule for libel and slander it thought should be the same as in other cases, namely it should be for the court to decide whether in the particular circumstances a jury was appropriate. There were many situations in which a jury would not be best. Libel actions often turned on 'barbed subtleties, specialist jargon and group attitudes of warring academics, men of letters, theatrical personalities or financiers',[5] where the jury was not likely to have any relevant insight or knowledge. It was not true, as was

---

* In the United States by contrast, civil jury trials are still the norm. Curiously, in Northern Ireland too, civil jury trials have remained very common. But in May 1987 the UK Government laid regulations before Parliament abolishing the right to trial by jury in civil cases in Northern Ireland. The move provoked a strong reaction from the Northern Ireland Bar. It said that between 90 and 95 per cent of cases for which jury trial was appropriate under the Judicature Act were set down for trial by jury.

so often supposed, that judges were remote from the life of the community. They were, the Committee said, well in touch with the emotions, conventions, language and way of life of the rest of the community.

> The idea that judges live in an ivory tower is wholly outdated. They go by train and bus, they look at television, and they hear, in matrimonial, criminal, accident and other cases, every kind of expression which the ordinary man uses, and they have learnt how he lives.[6]

It was often more satisfactory to have a reasoned judgment from a judge than the verdict of the jury which gave no reasons. Juries were unpredictable, more expensive for the parties and they often had trouble with complex or long cases. The Committee did not, however, think it right to take away the right of jury trial altogether. There were some situations where jury trial was right.

> We recognise it to be undesirable that a judge sitting alone should be embroiled in a matter of political, religious or moral controversy... Broadly, where the issue is one that raises strong feelings among the general public so that a judge alone might be suspected, however mistakenly, of prejudice, conscious or unconscious, we should expect that trial by jury be awarded ... but that in cases which did not involve such controversial questions a judge alone would be more likely to be selected.[7]

The Faulks Committee also addressed itself to the question of the role of the jury in fixing damages. It accepted the basic case against this practice which had led the Court of Appeal in *Ward* v. *James* to rule that in personal injury cases juries were not normally appropriate. It proposed as a compromise solution that the jury should fix the type of damages (normal, nominal, contemptuous, or exemplary) and that the judge should then determine the actual amount. This would get round the problem of the jury not having the necessary knowledge to determine the level of damages.*

---

* The extent to which jury damages awards can be bizarre was illustrated by the £450,000 ordered to be paid in June 1987 to a retired naval officer Martin Packard in respect of a serious libel in an Athens newspaper, in Greek, of which a mere 50 or so copies are distributed in this country. This record was broken only a month later by the half million pounds awarded to Mr Jeffrey Archer for a libel that was far less serious but much more widely published. A person who received such damages for a physical injury would have to show that he and his prospects had been shattered.

But neither of these recommendations of the Faulks Committee has been implemented. There is still a right of either party to demand a jury trial in libel and slander cases and the jury still fixes the amount of damages. The only change that was introduced is a new rule in the Supreme Court Act 1981 that, even in cases when there is normally a right to have a jury trial, it can be denied where the court is of opinion 'that the trial requires any prolonged examination of documents or accounts or any scientific or local investigation which cannot conveniently be made with a jury'.[8]

Nevertheless, subject to the odd case, mainly of libel or slander, the civil jury is now as dead as the dodo and there is no one arguing for its return. In criminal cases, by contrast, the argument is not whether the jury trial be retained but to what cases it should apply. There is a deep, almost mystical, attachment to the idea of the jury which is shared by the ordinary citizen as well as most of those who participate professionally in the criminal justice system as judges or lawyers — though, significantly, not by the police. The depth of this feeling has been tested in recent years by the increasing pressure created directly or indirectly by the Treasury which has been looking for financial economies through a reduction in the cases going to the crown court. (Crown court cases cost on average about three times as much as those in the magistrates' courts.)

Since 1977 criminal cases have been divided into three types. The most serious are those triable only on indictment of the crown court; the least serious are those triable only summarily in the magistrates' court. In between are those triable either way. In the case of either way offences the defendant always has the right to ask for trial at the higher level, though, if he opts for summary trial, the prosecution can ask the court to require trial in the crown court. The James Committee[9] in 1975 recommended that various offences, including most driving offences, small theft cases and cases involving small amounts of criminal damage, should be transferred to the summary only category. The objections of the motorists' lobby over the proposals for driving offences were swept aside by the Government and the proposals were implemented in 1977. But the recommendation in regard to small theft cases and criminal damage ran into major opposition from a variety of quarters. It was pointed out that an accusation of theft, even of a small amount, could ruin a person's career and that it was wrong not to allow the defendant to put his case to a jury of his peers. (In

Scotland, such cases have for long been triable only summarily. The court there consists not of lay magistrates but of sheriffs who are professional judges.)

The Labour Government in fact included the change in its Criminal Law Bill in 1977 but, when it became clear that the proposal would be defeated in the House of Lords, it withdrew the clause before the issue was even tested by a vote. The trial of small criminal damage cases was subsequently transferred to the summary only category in 1980. No one made much fuss and, emboldened by this success, Mrs Thatcher's Government came forward in a consultation paper in 1986 with a variant of the James Committee proposal regarding small thefts.[10]

A survey in London had shown that cases of theft and handling of goods worth less than £50 constituted 10 per cent of all crown court cases. The Government proposed that such cases would be triable only summarily save where special circumstances made the offence particularly grave — for instance, thefts from the person or multiple offences. It accepted that it would not be right to give the magistrates a discretion to decide whether the effect of a conviction would be especially serious for the particular defendant. That would be widely regarded as inviting invidious distinctions which would often be based on social class, though there might be a case for allowing a right to elect trial by jury for defendants with no previous conviction for an offence of dishonesty. However, when the Government published its Criminal Justice Bill in November 1986 there was no mention of small theft cases in the category of offences for which the right of trial by jury would no longer be available. It was clear that the Conservative Government, like its Labour predecessor, had decided not to risk getting involved in this emotive issue. The Bill did, however, propose to increase the summary only criminal damage threshold from £400 to £2,000 and added driving while disqualified, taking a motor vehicle without authority, and common assault and battery to the list of summary only offences. When the Bill was reintroduced after the 1987 General Election these provisions were again included.

Considering the fuss made over the preservation of the right to trial by jury, it might be assumed that most defendants charged with offences that can be tried either in the magistrates' court or the crown court opt for trial at the higher level so as to get the advantage of a jury trial. This is not the case, however. The overwhelming majority, amounting to just under 80 per cent, prefer to be tried by the magistrates. Research conducted for the James Committee in 1976 showed that people choose

summary trial because they want to get it over as quickly as
possible and to get the lightest sentence. The majority intend to
plead guilty, whereas the majority of those who opt for crown
court trial intend to plead not guilty — even though in the event
many actually end by pleading guilty. Those who prefer crown
court trial usually do so because there is a jury to try the case
and the acquittal rate is thought to be higher.[11] (In 1986, Home
Office research supported the widespread belief that the rate of
acquittal in the crown court is significantly higher. Two
matched samples of cases in which the defendant pleaded not
guilty showed that in the magistrates' courts the acquittal rate
was 30 per cent as against 57 per cent in the crown court.[12])

JURY SERVICE

Most of the public rows arising from the problem of trial by jury
relate nowadays, however, in one way or another to the
processes of selecting jurymen. Until recently most of the
population was excluded from jury service. Eligibility was
founded on a property qualification (based on liability to pay
rates) dating from the eighteenth century. The Morris Committee in 1965 estimated that 78 per cent of the names on the
electoral register did not qualify — either because they had no
property or because they were wives or other relatives of the
person in whose name the property was held.[13] Since 1974 the
qualification for jury service is being on the electoral register,
being between the ages of 16 and 65, and having been resident
in the United Kingdom for at least five years since the age of
13.[14] The Government's Criminal Justice Bill published in
November 1986 included a provision extending eligibility for
jury service to anyone between the ages of 65 and 70, subject to
an automatic right of excusal. (The clause was reintroduced
when the Bill was restored after the 1987 General Election.)
This will permit utilisation of mature persons with time on their
hands, subject to a right for them to avoid jury service if they
feel it would be burdensome.

But some people are disqualified, ineligible or excused. The
rules about disqualification arising out of previous convictions
were tightened up in 1984 as a result of a Private Member's Bill
piloted through Parliament by Mr John Watson MP and Lord
Renton. Anyone who has served any period of imprisonment
during the previous ten years, or has had a suspended prison
sentence or a community service order in that period is
disqualified, as is also anybody placed on probation during the

previous five years.[15] Prison sentences of five or more years disqualify one from jury service for life. The notice summoning one for jury services states the disqualified categories and asks whether the person is in these categories. Serving on a jury while knowing oneself to be disqualified is a criminal offence punishable with a fine of £400. But checks are very rare and considerable numbers of disqualified persons probably do serve on juries.

Anyone whose profession involves them in the administration of justice (as judge, lawyer, police officer, prison officer, court clerk or usher etc.) is ineligible, because it is feared they might exert undue influence on other members of the jury. The same reason explains the ineligibility of ministers of religion. The mentally ill or mentally handicapped are also ineligible. Then there are persons who can claim to be excused because they are deemed to have more pressing business elsewhere — MPs, members of the armed services, doctors, dentists, nurses and midwives. In addition, a person can ask to be excused because he has some particular reason why it would be inconvenient to serve on a jury at that time. Court staff are instructed to deal with such *ad hoc* requests for excusal as sympathetically as possible. Illness, having to care for very young children, a holiday already booked or an examination to be taken would be typical cases. At the discretion of the jury summoning officer, others may also be excused on grounds such as illness, disability, illiteracy or insufficient mastery of English.

Being summoned for jury service is a civic duty that is statistically unlikely to come round more than once in a lifetime — though there is no actual guarantee of this unless the judge excuses jurymen in a long case from future jury service. Once selected for a jury, one is obviously required to continue to serve until the case is concluded, which in exceptional instances may be weeks or even months later. Normally jury service is for two weeks, though there is no assurance that one will necessarily be working as a juryman on each day. In fact, people called for jury service often complain that they are kept waiting around with nothing to do for several of the days in their fortnight. There is financial compensation for travel expenses, a modest subsistence allowance for expenses and a loss of earnings allowance (limited as at January 1987 to a maximum of only £25.40 per day). About six weeks notice is usually given for jury service, so there is normally time to make the necessary arrangements.

Prior to 1981 the actual method of selecting names for the jury panel was left to each summoning officer. Every court had its own method and many were far from random. It was said that in some areas the clerk took names in order from particular districts — with the result that when the street happened to be one favoured by the criminal fraternity, large numbers of people wth previous convictions found themselves on the panel at the same time. All this has now been stopped since a new system, devised for the Lord Chancellor's Department by the Royal Statistical Society, came into effect in February 1981. The method is now random in a sense accepted by statisticians.

The names of those who are left after any disqualified, ineligible or excused persons have been removed are then put on to cards. The jury bailiff takes a number of cards from the batch of the jury panel and, having shuffled the cards, he calls out the names for the particular cases. When a name is called and the person comes forward both sides have the opportunity to challenge. The defence have until now had three peremptory challenges without giving any reason. (The number was reduced from twenty to seven in 1949 and from seven to three in 1977.) The defence also have the right to an unlimited number of challenges for cause. The prosecution have no right to peremptory challenges. Instead, they can ask a juryman to 'stand by' which means he will not be needed unless there are not enough members of the panel to select a jury of twelve, in which case they will be called again and asked to serve unless challenged for cause. The prosecution, like the defence, have an unlimited number of challenges for cause.

PEREMPTORY CHALLENGE

The defence right to peremptory challenge has recently proved controversial. Correspondence in *The Times* in 1985 suggested that a pin-striped suit, an old school tie, a prominently displayed copy of a serious newspaper were all liable to result in the juryman being excluded.[16] In an editorial *The Times* of 13 June 1985 argued that, especially at the Old Bailey and other courts in London and the South East, the practice of challenge which had previously been virtually obsolete was now a regular occurrence. The peremptory challenge, it was suggested, was used by the defence 'in an endeavour to achieve as far as possible a jury composed of people believed by the defence to be likely to be hostile to the prosecution and sympathetic to the defendant. Race, class, age, sex and education all seem to play a part in this selection process.' There was, it was said, 'a discernible tendency' to favour those 'who seem to be young, unskilled and relatively uneducated'. The right, urged the Thunderer, was being abused and should be abolished. Tory backbench MPs, led by Mr Toby Jessell, took up the cry* and in November 1985 the Home Secretary, Mr Douglas Hurd, announced that the Attorney General would be asking the new Crown Prosecution Service when it was set up in Spring 1986 to conduct research into the alleged abuse of the system.

Then in January 1986 the Roskill Committee on Fraud Trials said that its evidence showed that 'the public, the press and many legal practitioners now believe that this ancient right (of peremptory challenge) is abused cynically and systematically to manipulate cases towards a desired result'.[17] The current situation it thought 'bids fair to bring the whole system of jury trial into public disrepute'. This was wholly unacceptable. The Committee had sympathy with the objective of using challenges to try to secure a better racial or sexual balance on a jury, but it had none with the objective of eliminating jurors who could understand the evidence or were biassed in favour of the prosecution and replacing them by others who could not or were likely to be biassed in favour of the defence. At least for fraud trials, it thought the practice should be abolished, together with the prosecution's right to stand by for the Crown.

But the Committee was not unanimous. In a powerful dissent Mr Walter Merricks, a former defence solicitor and legal journalist, who later became a senior official of the Law Society, argued that it would be 'unwise, impracticable and unrealistic to legislate for fraud cases' before the Crown Prosecution Service had completed the research commissioned by the Government.[18] The Roskill Committee had said that it had sympathy with challenges to achieve a better racial or sexual balance on the

---

* Mr Jessell subsequently scored something of a coup when he got hold of a confidential note apparently made by one of the lawyers in the 'Cyprus Secrets' case regarding a meeting of counsel in the case on the subject of their attitude to the selection of the jury: 'Robin Simpson's point was that we wanted a young, working-class jury. Michael Hill made the comment that he really wanted an anti-establishment jury and that we were better off to have a young middle-age middle-class jury. Robert Harman pointed out that there was a dichotomy of views that we will just take what we get. John Alliot's view was that we couldn't improve on fate. Gilbert Gray indicated that if the jury is not too well educated and if of too low an intelligence, they may take more note of the Judge and therefore we ought to go for people who were young, not unsmart but no women. Victor Durand chimed in by saying that if the jury were young they may be unpatriotic. John Alliott indicated that we ought to pool resources as far as any challenges were concerned and Michael Hill pointed out that we ought to challenge one, two, three, by one counsel, and so on with another counsel until we achieved a joint policy'. (House of Commons Hansard, 31 March 1987, col. 991).

jury but its proposal would in effect make that impossible since challenges for cause could not be used in that way. If the grounds for challenge for cause were to be extended to cover such issues it would require the judge to get involved in the process of jury selection and this would be dangerous. Peremptory challenge might be difficult to defend logically but it was 'but one feature of a complex and not wholly logical system in which the checks and balances have evolved over a long period, and which should be disturbed only after a wide-ranging examination of the consequences'.[19]

But rather than wait for the research, the Government decided instead to rush ahead with action. In a White Paper published in March 1986,[20] the Home Office said that peremptory challenge was sometimes used for entirely proper reasons — such as to save time or possibly embarrassment to someone who would otherwise be challenged for cause, or to adjust the age, sex, or race balance on the jury, or to remove someone suspected of being biassed against the accused. But it was contrary to the interests of justice that persons should be removed because they were thought to have insight or respect for the law which was inimical to the defence. The problem was most acute in cases involving several defendants, if they pooled their challenges. The Government had no wish to interfere unnecessarily with a long-standing right that could be used in ways that were consistent with justice. But as far as practicable, and providing it did not seriously prejudice a defendant's right to a fair trial, juries should be composed of a random selection of those who were neither ineligible nor disqualified. The question was whether that could be achieved without either leaving defendants with an understandable sense of grievance or opening up challenge for cause to an unseemly and disturbing degree.[21]

One possibility, the White Paper said, would be to require the *prosecution* to use the power of stand-by to redress any apparent distortion in the jury resulting from excessive use of peremptory challenges. But this would open the prosecution to charges that it was abusing the system just as the defence was now accused. Another possibility would be simply to abolish peremptory challenges as recommended by the majority of the Roskill Committee. Possibly jurors' occupations could again be stated, as was the case before 1973, to assist challenge for cause. (At present the only information available to the defence is the juror's name and address.) A different alternative would be to reduce the number of peremptory challenges from three to two, or one, per defendant or to impose a special limit for multi-defendant cases. The Government said that it invited views and that in the meanwhile the proposed study by the Crown Prosecution Service would go ahead.

The Law Society opposed any change in the system, at least without hard evidence of any significant level of abuse.[22] It approved Mr Merricks' dissent from the report of the Roskill Committee. It thought that extensions of the right of challenge for cause would in practice cause insurmountable difficulties. The Vice Chairman of the Criminal Bar Association, Mr David Cocks QC, agreed. Peremptory challenge, he said, was needed to act as a check on the danger of jury rigging by the authorities.

> Lest this sound far fetched it is certainly within the recent memory of many members of the Bar that juries at one particular London court would be summarily dismissed if they acquitted, with a muttered comment from the judge such as that he hoped the defendant broke into some of their houses, whilst convicting juries would be kept together throughout the session.

Also it gave the defendant at least some say, however slight, in the make-up of the jury which might remove more obvious sources of grievance. Moreover, the defence's right of peremptory challenge and the prosecution's right of stand-by gave the system a rough working balance. If peremptory challenges were abolished it would lead to much greater use of challenges for cause which could involve 'a minute and time wasting examination of jurors' personalities and antecedents'.[23] He pointed to the American experience (see p. 222) and suggested that it was not one which we would wish to imitate here.

The first solid data about the frequency of peremptory challenge came with the informal release in February 1987 of the interim results of the study carried out by the Crown Prosecution Service. The study was based on 192 cases prosecuted between December 1985 and October 1986 by the Director of Public Prosecutions and 2,594 cases prosecuted by the Crown Prosecution Service in 1986. The rate of use of peremptory challenge was greatest in multi-defendant trials in Inner London. In DPP cases there were peremptory challenges in 75 per cent of multi-defendant trials in Inner London compared with 55 per cent in single-defendant trials in Inner London and 39 per cent of multi-defendant trials and 19 per cent of single-defendant trials in other parts of the country.

For non-DPP cases the rate of challenge was equally highest

in Inner London. One or more challenges were used in 37 per cent of single-defendant and 39 per cent of multi-defendant trials. Outside Inner London, by contrast, the proportion was 10 per cent for single-defendant and 17 per cent for multi-defendant trials. Defendants who used peremptory challenges used one, two or three challenges equally often.

The evidence did not, however, show any indication that use of peremptory challenge was associated with a greater likelihood of an acquittal. Just under half (45 per cent) of DPP trials in which one or more peremptory challenges were issued ended with one or more convictions. This was virtually identical to the conviction rate of 46 per cent in DPP trials in which there had been no challenges. In non-DPP cases the relative proportions were 53 per cent as against 51 per cent. The study therefore did not support the suggestion that peremptory challenge was an abuse of the system which resulted in acquittals.

Since this was the sole ground for abolition of the right of peremptory challenge one might have thought that this evidence would cause the Government to drop the proposal. But the Government was unimpressed. Its Criminal Justice Bill in November 1986 included a clause simply to abolish the defence right of peremptory challenge with no compensating mention of the prosecution's right to stand-by for the crown. This was to remain, so that the prosecution would apparently retain a virtually unlimited right to alter the composition of the jury. In practice this right is rarely used but its availability when the defence have lost even the limited right of removing up to three jurors per defendant is demonstrably unfair, a point the Government did in the end accept.* Although the abolition of the right of peremptory challenge generated fierce controversy during the passage of the first version of the Bill through

---

* In Spring 1987, during the passage of the first version of the Criminal Justice Bill through the Commons, the Home Secretary Mr Douglas Hurd wrote to his Labour Shadow Mr Gerald Kaufman, sending him the text of a proposed draft of guidelines that would be issued to the Crown Prosecution Service if the abolition of the peremptory challenge went through. These stated that it was customary that the right of stand-by should be used 'only sparingly and in exceptional circumstances' and it was generally accepted, not in order 'to influence the overall composition of a jury or with a view to tactical advantage'. The removal of the right of peremptory challenge made it appropriate that the Crown should only assert the right of stand-by 'on the basis of clearly defined and restrictive criteria'. It should only be done where it was essential, not merely to serve the direct interests of the prosecution. The two grounds for the exercise of the power were if jury vetting (see below) revealed grounds for excluding someone and where he seemed manifestly unfitted for jury service by reason, for instance, of illiteracy.

Parliament, the Thatcher Government stuck doggedly to its guns and reintroduced the clause in the Mark II version of the Bill after the General Election of June 1987.

CHALLENGE FOR CAUSE

In regard to challenge for cause, prosecution and defence are, by contrast, on the same footing. The process of challenge for cause in England and the United States differs in one significant detail. In England it is not normally permissible to ask questions to try to establish cause, whereas in the US such questions are allowed. The result is that challenges for cause are rare in this country. Since defence counsel normally have nothing to go on other than the name, address, physical appearance of the juror and some intuitive sense of what sort of person he or she may be, there is no basis for any challenge. In the US, by contrast, defence lawyers can ask a virtually endless number of questions to try to establish some possible grounds for showing the potential bias of the person concerned. Where in England the jury is usually selected in a matter of minutes, in the US it can sometimes take as many days.

Selecting the jury for the trial of John De Lorean in April 1984 on charges of trafficking some $24m. worth of cocaine, took an unprecedented five weeks. De Lorean's counsel subjected nearly 130 would-be jurors to rigorous questioning. Since De Lorean was eventually acquitted, he probably felt that the cost of this protracted process was money well spent. Defence lawyers in the US often use experts to advise on the psychological profile of jurors who would be suitable or unsuitable for the particular cause. Whether such advice has any scientific basis is a matter of opinion. In the Watergate trial of former Attorney General John Mitchell and a senior Republican figure Mr Maurice Stans, the psychologist's profile suggested that middle-class, educated persons should be kept off the jury. After both defendants had been acquitted, the *New York Times* reported, however, that the crucial juror had been a bank manager who got on to the jury at the last minute owing to the illness of one of those who had previously been selected. According to the story, the rest of the jury were ready to convict but it was the bank manager, as it were, playing the role of Henry Fonda in *Twelve Angry Men*, who persuaded the others to acquit.

There is a broad consensus that nothing comparable to the laborious American practice of questioning jurors should be permitted on this side of the Atlantic. The general rule inhibiting questions was confirmed in a Practice Note issued by the Lord Chief Justice in 1973. In 1972, in the widely publicised trial of members of the 'Angry Brigade' accused of bombing the homes of various prominent politicians, the judge had agreed to the defence lawyer's suggestion that he should ask jurors to exclude themselves for a variety of reasons — for instance, if they were subscribing members of the Conservative Party, if they had relatives in the police force or were serving in the armed services in Northern Ireland, or if they were constituents of any of the politicians whose homes were alleged to have been the target for actual or planned bombings. Thirty-nine people were removed from the panel as a result of challenges and another nineteen admitted they fell into one or other of the judge's categories.[24]

Lord Widgery, the then Lord Chief Justice, clearly disapproved of this and he used the case as an opportunity to state the basic rule. The Practice Note said that a juror should be excused if he is personally concerned in the facts of the particular case. He could also be excused at the discretion of the judge on grounds of personal hardship or conscientious objection to jury service. But it was 'contrary to established practice for jurors to be excluded on more general grounds such as race, religion or political beliefs or occupation'.[25] Apart from saving time and cost, the strength of this approach is that it takes seriously the principle that a jury consists of twelve individuals chosen at random from the electoral register, with all their prejudices. The resulting verdict can be seen as more solidly based than the verdict of a 'neutered' American jury consisting of those who have survived the process of questioning by lawyers for the parties. The negative side is that if the parties cannot ask questions to establish bias, egregious bias or other grounds for elimination which in fact exist may not emerge. That the British system does not carry its principles all the way may be seen from the fact that in Northern Ireland juries were abolished in cases involving terrorism because of the special problems allegedly created by IRA intimidation and equally by the alleged prosecution practice of eliminating Catholics from the jury by use of a combination of stand-by and challenge. An inquiry by Lord Diplock in 1972 led to the introduction in the following year of 'Diplock courts', with a single judge and no jury to try such cases.*

---

* The Irish Government in 1986 urged the British Government to change these to three-judge courts but although the point was pressed hard, the British Government did not seem ready to agree and it remains a contentious issue between the two governments.

There are occasional individual exceptions to the basic English rule. In 1981 at the trial of Newton Rose, a black man accused of murder, the judge advised potential jurors to disqualify themselves if they had strong views against black people or supported either the extreme Right or the extreme Left ('like the Socialist Workers Party or the Anti-Nazi League').[26] In the 1982 case of the 'Bradford Twelve', Asians charged with making petrol bombs in self-defence, the judge asked the jurors selected for the case questions such as whether they, or any close family member, were associated with or sympathetic to the National Front, the British Movement or any other group which had expressed suspicion of non-whites, or were in the police force or had suffered any loss in the riots in 1981 in Leeds or Bradford. (The defendants were ultimately acquitted by the jury.)

In October 1984 a judge refused a defence application on behalf of four Asians accused of assaulting a police officer at a National Front demonstration to move the trial from Maidstone where few Asians lived.[27] The judge, Mr Justice Woolf, as he then was, said, however, that he accepted the basic point of trying to get a number of Asians on to the jury and ordered that the jury panel should be drawn from Gravesend, an area with a large Asian population. (It is doubtful, however, whether a judge has any power to direct how a jury is to be summoned. The duty to summon the jury rests with court officials acting on behalf of the Lord Chancellor.) In another case with racial overtones arising out of disturbances in the St Paul's district of Bristol in April 1980, the judge, Mr Justice Stocker, said that he had a discretion himself to stand jurors by until a reasonable racial balance was achieved — though in the event it did not prove necessary to use it since a racially mixed jury was empanelled without any use of the stand-by procedure.[28] (The use of peremptory challenges by the defence resulted in three West Indians and an Asian being on the jury.)

But judicial views on this difficult problem have not been consistent. In another case in 1982 a black defendant charged with rape wanted a substantial number of blacks on the jury. There was no black on the entire jury panel. The Recorder at Nottingham Crown Court ruled that there was no requirement in law that the panel include any black.[29] In 1986, Judge Mander sitting in Stoke-on-Trent took a similar view. A black youth claimed that at least two members of a jury for conspiracy to rob should be black. Only blacks, he argued, could fully appreciate the way blacks were treated by the police, which was an integral part of his case. The judge, differing from Mr Justice Woolf, said that he had no power to manipulate the jury panel in order to achieve a racial balance. It would be quite improper for the panel to be artificially enlarged to include some blacks. It would equally be wholly wrong for officers of the court or the judge to take steps to interfere with randomness of selection of jurors. Even if the judge did so, the prosecution could nullify his decision by asking black jurors to stand by — though that would be an act of racial discrimination in itself. But the most fundamental point of principle, Judge Mander said, was that defendants could not be allowed to specify what kind of jury was to try them. Otherwise there would be no limit. Minority groups such as homosexuals, Freemasons, militant feminists, alcoholics, members of extreme political groups, even criminals, could argue in similar fashion that they should be distinguished from the general mass on the electoral rolls. If this was to be contemplated it should be done by legislation, not by the courts. It would be a fundamental change in the method of selecting juries.[30]

Of the two positions, Judge Mander's view seems the more consistent with the underlying philosophy of the English system. The basic principle is random selection. Exceptions are reasonably allowed for those with previous convictions, and for those who, because of their occupation, might exert undue influence in the jury room or who have more important business elsewhere. The right of peremptory challenge is a valuable safety valve to give the defendant some minor role in eliminating those felt for any reason to be unsuitable. The Government's decision to abolish this ancient right seems wholly misconceived. In the end it will probably create more problems than it solves.

The judge has a limited discretion to stand a juror by even though there has been no challenge — for instance, when it appears that a juror in taking the oath has difficulty in reading the words from the card, or in understanding English. The judge also has a discretion to move the venue of a trial if that seems the right thing to do because of the danger of local prejudice. The system would be entering upon dangerous ground if it permitted manipulation of the process by the court to achieve a particular racial, sex or age balance at the instance of the accused. On the other hand, there is plainly force in the view that some discretion be left to the court to stand jurors by to achieve a jury that seems fair in the light of the particular problems posed by the case. This is most likely to be because of the race of the accused. Any official recognition of an exception to the general rule of random selection is unwelcome — but the existence of serious racial tensions in contemporary Britain cannot be wished away. In a particularly sensitive case discreet informal steps could be taken by the court staff to ensure that there are some members of the appropriate ethnic minority in the group of persons to be called for the case, but any such tampering with the ordinary process is plainly fraught with difficulty. Hitherto the racial problem has been ignored by the Court of Appeal. But with the right of peremptory challenge abolished, this issue is bound now to be a real one. The best probably is to recognise the reality of the difficulty and to give the judge the right to attempt to achieve what he feels to be a fair balance on the jury by a use of the stand-by procedure.

The evidence, however, is that these variations in jury composition probably do not make as much difference to the result as one might imagine. It has already been seen that the use of the right of peremptory challenge seems to make no observable impact on the result of cases. The Home Office monitored the apparent impact of the changes in the composition of the jury resulting from the Juries Act 1974, which significantly brought down the average age of juries and introduced many more women. The study compared the overall acquittal rate nationally for three months before the 1974 Act came into force with the figures for the three months after. No significant differences emerged. A study by two experienced researchers from the Institute of Judicial Administration in Birmingham, Dr John Baldwin and Dr Michael McConville, showed likewise that jury verdicts in a sample of 326 jury cases in Birmingham could not be correlated with the age, sex, race, or occupation of jurors, nor even with the numbers of times they had sat on a jury. They found that 'however one regarded the material no consistent patterns were apparent. The presence of women, younger or working class jurors appeared to make no difference to jury results'. They concluded:[31]

> We can confidently state that no single social factor (nor, so far as we can detect, any group of factors operating in combination) produced any significant variations in the verdicts returned. . . . The truth of the matter is that most juries in Birmingham were extremely mixed, and it is to be expected that the amalgam of personal and social attributes that make up a jury will produce verdicts that reflect the unique social mix rather than the broad social characteristics of the individuals concerned.

JURY VETTING

The most controversial area of tampering with jury selection is undoubtedly the vetting process available to the prosecution in especially sensitive cases. This first came to public notice in 1978 during the 'ABC' trial of a soldier and two journalists under the Official Secrets Act. On the first day of the trial counsel for one of the defendants learned from the clerk of the court that prosecution counsel had a list of the potential jurors. 'Anyone who is known to be disloyal would obviously be disqualified', said Mr John Leonard, QC for the prosecution. (In fact no one was removed on this ground.) It later emerged from a television programme that the foreman of the jury in the case had been a member of the elite SAS (Special Air Service Regiment). When this came to light, the whole jury was discharged.

However, as a result of the political storm that surrounded these events the Labour Attorney General, Mr Sam Silkin, published for the first time the guidelines for vetting of jury panels which he had established three years earlier. These provided that in certain exceptional cases jurors might be kept off by use of the prosecution's right to stand by on the grounds of their extreme views or undesirable associations. The approval of the Director of Public Prosecutions was needed for vetting to take place. The types of cases in the original guidelines were serious offences where strong political motives were involved, such as IRA and other terrorist cases, cases under the Official Secrets Act and serious offences alleged to have been committed by members of a gang of professional criminals. In the previous three years there had been a total of 25 cases in which vetting had occurred. Subsequently, in 1980, these guidelines were tightened up to require the consent of the Attorney General himself. Also such checks were no longer to be allowed in cases involving strong political motives, save in terrorism cases. Vetting in cases involving security checks would only be authorised when national security was involved and where it was anticipated that the court would sit *in camera*. Gang trials would no longer qualify.

The checks are made in criminal records, Special Branch and CID records and in terrorist and Official Secrets Act cases by the security services. They are not supposed to go further, though there is reason to suspect that this aspect of the rules is not always scrupulously observed by the authorities. Both the judge and the defence are supposed to be informed when checks of the jury have been authorised. Jury vetting is a further invasion of the principle of random selection, though one used in only a handful of cases a year. Each time that it comes to light so much public controversy has been generated[32] that it is likely that the Attorney General's office knows not to risk provoking such a political fuss unless it feels it to be essential. Some strongly object to vetting on principle, but, if peremptory challenge and challenge for bias are accepted, it does not seem unreasonable that in the tiny number of cases involving terrorism and national security the authorities should be able to see whether in fact any member of the jury panel is a security risk or has associations which would indicate a serious bias in favour of the defence. The defendant cannot be said to have a right that any particular person serve on a jury and his civil liberties can therefore hardly be said to be imperilled if a potential security risk is removed from the trial. Considering all the other exceptions to the principle of random selection, this seems a relatively minor one.

HOW THE JURY PERFORMS

The most critical question about the jury is not, however, how its members get chosen but how they perform in action. Historically, the weight of impressionistic opinion has been very favourable to the jury. Judges and lawyers have spoken on countless occasion of the virtues and blessings of the system in variations in Blackstone's view that it is 'the glory of English law' and that 'The liberties of England cannot but subsist so long as this palladium remains sacred and inviolate'. It has been variously described as the safeguard of liberty, an essential check on unpopular laws and the best means for establishing the truth. The general public too seems to have been mainly convinced of the value of the system. The only real dissentient voice has been from the police who in recent years, starting in the 1960s, have expressed the view that juries acquit far too many guilty persons. This was, in particular, the well publicised opinion of Sir Robert Mark, former Commissioner of the Metropolitan Police. But one week after Sir Robert Mark's 1973 Dimbleby Lecture on BBC Television in which he made his celebrated attack on jury trial, a *Sunday Times* poll showed that 78 per cent of the public preferred jury trial to the system of trial by judge alone.

The scientific evidence, such as it is, tends also to support the system of jury trial. There are no studies based on observation of live juries in actual cases. The fear has always been that such research might in some way affect the administration of justice and there has been extreme reluctance even to contemplate it. Any hope that there might be some attempt to conduct such research has now been dashed by the enactment of section 8 of the Contempt of Court Act 1981 which made it contempt of court to 'obtain, disclose or solicit any particulars of statements made, opinions expressed, arguments advanced or votes cast by members of a jury in the course of their deliberations in any legal proceedings'. The clause was introduced by lawyer members of the House of Lords and was passed against the advice of the Government.* Ironically one of those most involved was Lord Roskill who later, as chairman of the Committee on Fraud Trials, found himself hoist with his own petard — unable, because of it, to conduct research which the committee might otherwise have wished to pursue.

The available research has therefore been based either on mock juries (where the jury listens to a tape or video recording of a trial transcript) or shadow juries (where a duplicate research jury listens to a real trial and when the actual jury retires, so does the shadow jury). The mock or shadow jury is then monitored by the researchers. There have also been studies in which lawyers and judges have been asked for their evaluation of the jury's decisions.

The broad impression of almost all such research on both sides of the Atlantic has been that juries do a surprisingly good job. They seem to listen to the evidence, and to understand it, and the conclusion they arrive at is usually explicable in terms of the evidence. Occasionally, of course, they go wrong and give a decision which is wholly against the weight of the evidence and there is no sensible explanation as to how this happened. But the research evidence suggests that this is rare.[33] In a study conducted by the present writer, for instance, barristers who had appeared for the prosecution agreed with barristers who had represented the defence that most of the acquittals in the sample were understandable in the light of the trial and the evidence.[34]

But the study conducted by Baldwin and McConville in the

---

* The clause followed a surprising decision of the Divisional Court, holding that it was not contempt of court for a member of the jury in the Jeremy Thorpe case in which he described what happened in the jury room in the much publicised trial of the former Liberal leader on an attempted murder charge. (*Attorney-General* v. *New Statesman and Nation Publishing Co. Ltd.* [1980] 1 All E.R. 644.)

Birmingham crown court reached a somewhat contrary view. They asked the trial judge, the police, and solicitors for the prosecution and the defence what they thought of the result of the case in 370 contested trials. Of these, 114 had ended in acquittal. The acquittal was seen as doubtful or highly questionable by the judge and at least one other respondent in 41 of these acquittal cases. (There were also some cases, though a smaller number, where convictions were thought to be doubtful or highly questionable.) The researchers concluded that in general[35]

> the performance of the jury did not always appear to accord with the principle underlying the trial system in England that it is better to acquit those who are probably guilty than to convict any who are possibly innocent. On the contrary, the jury appeared on occasion to be over-ready to acquit those who were probably guilty and insufficiently prepared to protect the possibly innocent.

The latest piece of evidence on the matter is the Home Office research conducted by Julie Vennard based on a sample of 320 contested crown court cases in different courts. Miss Vennard (who compared the outcome of these cases with a sample of contested cases in magistrates' courts) said that, on the whole, jury acquittals 'corresponded with identifiable weaknesses in the prosecution case or an explanation from the defendant which was not manifestly discredited'.[36] Acquittals which were not explicable in those terms were in the minority. The research evidence on this important question, though conflicting, is nevertheless substantially favourable to the jury system.

The view expressed by Sir Robert Mark that juries acquit too many guilty persons was based to a large extent on the statistic that about one in every two jury cases end in acquittal. In his 1973 BBC Dimbleby Lecture 'Minority Verdict', the former Commissioner of the Metropolitan Police said that obviously the police could not expect to get a conviction in every case and sometimes they would launch a prosecution against someone who was innocent. But in his opinion 'a failure rate of one in two is far too high ... the proportion of those acquittals relating to those whom experienced police officers believe to be guilty is too high to be acceptable'. The statistic quoted by Sir Robert was technically right, though it was presented in such a way as to make it highly misleading. Between 1973 and 1976 the acquittal rate rose from 42 per cent to 47 per cent. In 1979 it rose to 50 per cent and it has been around that level ever since. At first sight this seems an alarmingly high 'failure' rate; but in fact the figures are considerably less disturbing. To start with, they are for contested trials and leave out of account the fact that more than 60 per cent of crown court cases end with guilty pleas. Secondly, they conceal the fact that each year almost half of all acquittals are directed by the judge and therefore cannot be said to be based on jury decisions at all. In 1985, for instance, there were 16,641 defendants who were acquitted in crown court cases. Of these, no less than 7,932 (or 48 per cent) were acquittals directed by the judge. This proportion has hardly varied during the past decade. Many believe that the proportion of directed acquittals will decline from 1986 since the new Crown Prosecution Service may succeed in screening out some of the weak prosecution cases that previously were allowed to go forward. But this is an assumption that remains to be proved (see pp. 198-200), and, even if true, it is unlikely to eliminate this as a major cause of acquittals.

When guilty pleas, directed acquittals and convictions are added, the proportion of *jury* acquittals turns out to be only around 10 per cent of crown court cases. This is hardly a sensationally high figure. Indeed, it could hardly be less in a system that takes seriously the universally accepted principle that it is for the prosecution to prove its case beyond a reasonable doubt. Some defendants are, of course, wholly innocent. But where proof of guilt must be beyond a reasonable doubt it follows that some guilty persons will be entitled to an acquittal simply because the prosecution cannot produce sufficient evidence. A jury acquittal rate of about one in ten does not appear therefore to justify any great anxiety about the jury system. Moreover, the available research has completely discredited the theory that professional criminals 'get away with it' more than others. If anything, rather the contrary. They plead guilty as often; they are convicted as often and, when they go down they go down harder in that their sentences are, naturally, longer.[37]

But can the jury really cope with long, complicated cases such as fraud trials which go on for weeks and months? This question was put to the Roskill Committee which was set up in 1983. For more than two decades it had been repeatedly said that this was the exceptional category of case which should be treated differently. The Roskill Committee (whose report started by quoting the Psalmist 'For one day in Thy courts is better than a thousand') concluded that there was merit in this point. The available research did not help very much, since researchers for obvious reasons have used short rather than long trials. Even the small amount of research commissioned by the Roskill Committee suffered in this way. In one study done for it by the Medical Research Council's Applied Psychology Unit in Cambridge volunteers were asked to listen to the judge's one and a half hour summing up in a fraud case and were then asked questions to test their comprehension and recall of the material. The memory questionnaire consisted of 38 multiple choice questions on important details of the trial. Performance varied from 18 per cent to 65 per cent correct, with a mean of 43 per cent. This the researchers said was 'not an impressive score, bearing in mind that a score of 27 per cent could be obtained purely by guessing'.[38] Comprehension was measured by asking people to summarise the main points of the trial. Few people showed an adequate understanding of the charges or of the circumstances which surrounded them.

Obviously the experiment made no attempt to replicate the conditions of a trial. It lacked the repetition of material that is a feature of a trial (opening speeches by both counsel, examination and cross-examination of witnesses, closing speeches by counsel and summing up by the judge). Equally the drama and impact of the trial itself were absent. Nor did the subjects in the experiment have the opportunity to pool their collective memories as juries do, with the result that the weaker brethren may be assisted by those with better memories. On the other hand, the summing up was relatively brief and still comprehension and recall were poor.

On the basis of this evidence and its other impressions the Committee concluded that long fraud trials were so complex that it was not reasonable to expect jurors to be able to cope. There were often multiple defendants and many charges.

> The background against which frauds are alleged to have been committed — the sophisticated world of high finance and international trading — is probably a mystery to most or all of the jurors, its customs and practices a closed book.[39]

The language of accountancy would be unfamiliar. The evidence often ran into hundreds or even thousands of documents. The MRC research supported 'the view of experienced observers and the promptings of commonsense, that the most complex of fraud cases will exceed the limits of comprehension of members of a jury.'[40] Many jurors were simply out of their depth in such cases.

But the Committee did not go so far as to recommend replacing the jury for all fraud cases. Only in the most complex cases (which it estimated might be some two dozen a year) should there be a different system. This it suggested should be a special tribunal consisting of a judge and two lay members selected from a panel of persons chosen by the Lord Chancellor, with expertise in complex business transactions. Either prosecution or defence should be allowed to apply to a High Court judge for the special tribunal.

Again, however, Mr Walter Merricks dissented. In a powerful statement he effectively demolished the Committee's reasoning. First he pointed to the weight of expert evidence received by the Committee which was 'overwhelmingly in favour of retaining the jury'.[41] The vast majority of the solicitors' profession (from both prosecution and defence), the magistrates, the Bar and even the police had opposed the removal of jury trial. The judges had been divided but many judges had grave reservations about removing the right to trial by jury. Both the Society of Conservative Lawyers and the Society of Labour Lawyers had been 'emphatic in insisting on the retention of jury trial'. The submissions from the Bar were almost unanimous. Those who were against the jury came mainly from the financial and accountancy world and when pressed in oral evidence 'it became clear that most of them based their views on generalised impressions'.[42] The Committee thought there were cases that were not prosecuted because of the difficulty of presenting very complex cases to the jury. But analysis by the DPP of all his fraud cases in 1983 showed that there was only one out of 71 not prosecuted in which the decision not to prosecute was caused by the complexity of the evidence.

It had, Mr Merricks suggested, become a convention of the unwritten constitution that citizens should not be subjected to more than a short period of imprisonment otherwise than on a jury's verdict. Parliament should not be invited to abrogate this constitutional right without evidence that jury trial had broken down in serious fraud cases *and* that all possible procedural improvements had been considered and found inadequate. 'A mere hunch, unsupported by tested evidence, that the system might at some time in the future prove inadequate should not be enough.'[43] The burden was on those who proposed to change the system. There was no hard evidence as to the extent of jury incomprehension. But the anecdotal evidence received by the Committee had not clearly supported the view that juries were unable to follow the evidence in these cases. 'Most judges and lawyers who made submissions to us thought that juries mostly reached the right result, or at least an understandable result.'[44]

There was a danger that if a special expert tribunal were set up the trial would become simply an exchange between lawyers and the tribunal in impenetrable jargon. The function of a trial as a publicly comprehensible exposition of the case would be threatened. Moreover, the fundamental issue in most fraud trials was one of dishonesty. It would be dangerous to entrust this judgment to experts. The legal standard of dishonesty was the standard of the ordinary man and experts were not ordinary men. It would also be difficult to define the cases in which the special tribunal would be appropriate.

Mr Merricks' dissent attracted much notice and support in comments on the Roskill Committee Report. Clearly he had had the better of the argument. The Government gave the report a warm welcome generally but its proposal on this particular issue was clearly too controversial and, after hesitating for a period, it announced that it would not be implemented.

In its statement on 2 October 1986 the Government said that the Home Secretary did not for the time being intend to pursue the recommendation for a special tribunal to replace juries in serious fraud cases, though the proposal might be re-examined in the future. Nevertheless other measures proposed by the Roskill Committee to make it easier for juries to understand the evidence in complex cases would be implemented. There would, for instance, be changes in the rules of evidence to permit the introduction of schedules and charts which summarised evidence and presented it more clearly. The judge would be able to hold a pre-trial preparatory hearing in open court at which he could make orders designed to simplify the presentation of evidence to the jury.* But the case for replacement of the jury even in these exceptionally difficult cases had not been made out.

Nothing could more powerfully have demonstrated the strength of feeling about the importance of jury trial in criminal cases. That feeling had been clearly shown in the public reaction to the jury acquittal in February 1985 of Clive Ponting, the civil servant who leaked confidential documents to Labour MP Mr Tam Dalyell concerning the sinking in the Falklands war of the *General Belgrano*. The jury was widely recognised to have ignored the judge's direction on the law in order to acquit a responsible public servant who it was felt was honestly blowing

---

* The 1986 Criminal Justice Bill included in clause 20 provision for rules to be made 'for the purpose of helping juries to understand complicated issues of fact or technical terms' in regard to the furnishing of evidence in any form and glossaries. This was repeated in clause 29 of the second version of the Bill after the 1987 General Election.

the whistle on his Minister. A few months later, in October 1985, a jury had acquitted all eight defendants accused in the 'Cyprus Secrets' case of leaking top secret material to Russian agents. Most of the evidence was heard *in camera* but there was a widespread public impression that the jury had acquitted because the service interrogators had mistreated the accused whilst investigating the alleged offences. Both cases represented the jury at its archetypal best — refusing to knuckle under to fierce pressure from the executive branch even in an area as sensitive as national security. The Government's rejection of the Roskill Committee's proposal for the replacement of jury trial in long complex fraud cases was the culmination of this period in which the jury was confirmed as an essential and valued part of the justice system.

The jury system is strong because it has so many different virtues. The fact that it has existed for hundreds of years is obviously part of this strength. Judges like the jury because it relieves them of the dilemma of having to decide the facts and which witnesses are to be believed. The brief decision Guilty or Not Guilty is also a way of reducing anxiety about the result of cases. It may be right or wrong but it inspires confidence in a way that a reasoned decision given by a judge cannot. There is safety in the mere fact that the decision is that of a goodly number. Also the fact that the members of the jury are anonymous and cannot therefore be identified as hailing from any particular background or having particular prejudices gives the decision more weight than if it were instead by identifiable judges. But above all other considerations, there is the fact that the jury consists of ordinary citizens rather than lawyers. Over the centuries the jury has played a significant role in mitigating the harshness of the law and the system by its own form of equity and mercy.* Even governments that were discomfited by this jury independence tolerated it. The jury has not merely survived; it is probably as strong today as ever in the past.

---

* For the history of the role of the jury in defying the authorities, see a fascinating recent study, T.A. Green, *Verdict According to Conscience, 1200-1800* (University of Chicago Press, 1985). Green shows in particular that, although in modern times jury intervention is seen mainly as a matter of occasional resistance to the authorities in political cases, in earlier times it was an integral and routine feature of the administration of criminal justice in the refusal to convict defendants who faced the death penalty.

8

Who are the Real Legislators?

For most people legislation is what happens in Parliament. Probably few know much about the mechanics of the process — how bills get drafted, when a bill starts in the House of Commons and when in the House of Lords, the differences between the 'Second Reading', the 'Committee and Report stage' or 'Third Reading' and what happens when one House amends a bill coming from the other House. But any educated person knows that under our system the supreme law-giver is 'the Queen in Parliament' and that to receive 'Royal Assent' and thereby become law a statute must pass through both Houses of Parliament. It is widely known too that the Queen exercises no choice as to whether to give her Assent — she must act on the advice of her Ministers. The effective power in Parliament lies with the Government and the process of passing legislation seemingly consists of the debates between Members of both Houses of Parliament representing respectively the Government and the Opposition. Bills that pass are usually proposed by the Government — presumably on the basis of the manifesto offered to the electorate at the previous General Election.

In one sense much of this does represent reality. All legislation *does* have to pass through both Houses of Parliament, most statutes *are* proposed by the Government, and the monarch's assent *is* a formality. But these bare facts conceal as much as they reveal about the process. In particular they obscure the fact that the parliamentary process is actually only the tip of the iceberg of statutory law-making — and that the real action takes place elsewhere.

THE ORIGINS OF LEGISLATION

The origins of legislation vary greatly. Some does derive directly from the election manifesto of the Party in power. Cynics are apt to dismiss the manifesto as mere window dressing ignored by the politicians when they come to power; but research has shown that in fact a surprisingly high proportion of what parties say they intend to do they actually do carry into effect. Professor Richard Rose of Strathclyde University investigated the fate of manifesto promises made in the 1970 and the two 1974 General Election campaigns. In 1970 the Conservative Party offered 96 specific pledges and in the two 1974 elections 126. The Labour Party gave 83 such pledges in 1970 and 104 in 1974. To carry out its manifesto over a five-year term a party would need to act on 20 to 25 pledges per session of Parliament — less than half the number of bills actually enacted in a session. (In the five-year period 1980-1984 there was an average of 64 Public Acts.) Some pledges can be implemented without legislation merely by administrative action, so the actual number of bills required for this purpose is in fact less than twenty or so per session. According to Professor Rose, both Conservative and Labour Governments faithfully carried out most of their election promises. The 1970-74 Government of Mr Edward Heath fulfilled at least 80 per cent of its manifesto pledges and showed some evidence of action in another 10 per cent of cases. Labour Governments of 1974-79 faced a difficult parliamentary situation in which they were never sure of having a majority. Nevertheless they acted clearly on 54 per cent of manifesto commitments and gave some evidence of action on another 19 per cent.[1]

But although over a five-year parliament governments enact a considerable proportion of their election commitments, the resulting legislation constitutes only a small fraction of all the bills that become law in the same period. Rose estimated that in the period of Conservative Government from 1970 to 1974 only 8 per cent of government bills came from election commitments, and in the period of Labour administration from 1974 to 1979 the proportion was only a little higher at 13 per cent.[2] The great majority of bills originate within government departments. Each department of state in Whitehall is responsible for its own area of the law and from time to time it will have the opportunity to bring forward legislation. Departments have to take their turn — only the Treasury with the Finance Act to implement the

Chancellor of the Exchequer's budget can expect to have a turn every year. The mass of departmental business will throw up projects for adjustments to the law which then have to wait for a convenient opportunity to be included in the next departmental bill. The periodic Administration of Justice Bill introduced by the Lord Chancellor's Department, or the Criminal Justice Bill brought in by the Home Office, or Housing Bill emanating from the Department of the Environment, are typical instances of portmanteau pieces of legislation into which the department puts a miscellaneous rag-bag of items, some of which may have been gathering dust in Whitehall pigeon-holes for a considerable period.

A surprisingly high proportion of government bills owe their origins to the recommendations of some advisory body independent of government. Dr Helen Beynon of the Law Department of Reading University studied all the public bills to receive Royal Assent between 1951 and 1975 — a total of 1,712 statutes. Her object was to investigate the role of *ad hoc* bodies such as Royal Commissions, departmental and inter-departmental committees, and standing bodies such as the Lord Chancellor's Law Reform Committee on civil law, the Home Secretary's Criminal Law Revision Committee or the Law Commission which makes proposals on reform of both civil and criminal law. Over the twenty-five years of the study an average of 22 per cent of all statutes were preceded by some such report. But to get a more accurate picture, Beynon then excluded 377 bills which obviously could not have been the result of such an advisory body — such as the annual Appropriation Act which authorises the bulk of annual expenditure, or legislation concerning the Civil List which pays for the monarchy, or legislation rushed through to deal with some unexpected emergency (such as the Drought Act 1976 to deal with an acute water shortage), or statutes passed to give effect to treaties or to restate the previous statute law in more accessible form ('consolidating statutes') or to repeal obsolete laws ('statute law revision'). Analysis then showed that no less than 28 per cent of these 1,335 statutes had been preceded by a report of an independent advisory committee or commission.[3] This shows the remarkable extent to which Government relies on the work of persons who are neither Ministers nor MPs nor civil servants to formulate policy. (Governments vary, however. Mrs Thatcher was the first Prime Minister of modern times, at least in her first two terms of office, not to have set up any Royal Commission. Even so major a constitutional issue as the proposal to abolish the

Greater London Council and the six Metropolitan counties was put in hand by the Government without the backing of a Royal Commission's findings.)

Needless to say, the fact that the Government bases its legislation on the report of an advisory body does not mean that its proposals will necessarily be adopted wholesale. It is a common occurrence for the Government to state that a bill is designed to implement the recommendations of a committee or commission, but when the bill is published it becomes clear that the carefully constructed package put together by the committee whose work is the basis of the legislation has been unstitched and a new and different package has been constructed.

This happened, for instance, with the 1981 Report of the Royal Commission on Criminal Procedure (the Philips Commission) which then became the basis for the controversial Police and Criminal Evidence Act 1984. The Royal Commission heard evidence from a wide range of interest groups and individuals. It travelled abroad to study the situation in other countries and it commissioned research. Most important of all, the members of the Commission itself — who between them included both laymen and different kinds of experts in the criminal justice system — worked for months to settle their proposals. But once their report was issued in January 1981 they ceased to exist as a group and thereafter neither the members nor even the chairman of the Royal Commission had any function in helping the Government to sort out its policy. Once it has reported, an *ad hoc* official committee such as a Royal Commission or Departmental Committee never meets again. (In lawyer's jargon it is *functus officio*.) It fades away and its members play no part in the subsequent history of the legislation. In the event, the Conservative Government accepted much of the Royal Commission's thinking and a considerable proportion of the Police and Criminal Evidence Act directly implements the Commission's proposals. But on some issues the Government decided to modify or in some cases completely to alter the Royal Commission's proposals. In other words, any government reserves the right to govern, even when it has apparently given up its direct function of taking the difficult decisions by referring the issue to an advisory committee in the first place.

Sometimes the Government decides to test the political temperature by issuing a Green or a White Paper. This is in effect an invitation for those interested to make their views known to it before the final decisions are taken. A Green Paper is supposedly 'softer' than a White Paper. Its policy proposals are less firm; the Government indicates a willingness to be persuaded to adopt a different course, whereas with a White Paper its policy is basically set, though it has not yet been cast in concrete. But sometimes a policy announced in a White Paper is abandoned in the light of the adverse reactions. So even a White Paper does not mean that the Government has a closed mind. The mere fact that it is prepared to consult through the White or the Green Paper machinery usually indicates some willingness to listen to the views of others outside the Whitehall machine.

MINISTERS AND CIVIL SERVANTS

Conventional wisdom suggests that the process of decision-making in Whitehall is dominated by Ministers, with civil servants more or less faithfully carrying out the wishes of Departmental Ministers and the Cabinet. Cabinet control over the content of legislation is exercised at various stages. The first point at which the Cabinet becomes involved is through establishing the priorities for bills to be introduced. The opening of a new session of an existing Parliament takes place normally in October or November. Some six to eight weeks earlier the Cabinet Office asks Departments to send in lists of bills likely to be wanted in the session due to start a year later, together with observations as to the urgency of the proposed bill, an estimate of its size and a forecast of the date on which it may be ready for drafting by Parliamentary Counsel. These proposals from departments are then collated by the Cabinet Office and are put to a Cabinet Committee known as the Future Legislation Committee, which always includes the Leaders of both Houses and the Chief Whip, since the drawing up of the legislative programme has to be closely related to the arrangement of parliamentary business. The meeting with Ministers from the departments concerned may take place early in the New Year. A provisional list of bills for the session due to begin in the autumn is prepared with regard to the amount of time likely to be available for legislation and to the fact that time must always be left for emergency measures the need for which has not yet arisen and for annual legislation such as the Finance Bill. The Future Legislation Committee will also try to set priorities. But the list must then be approved by the full Cabinet.

During the rest of the session, while the bill is being prepared, the Future Legislation Committee has general charge of the matter. Between Easter and the summer recess the Committee reviews the progress of the bills decided upon and considers any further proposals for additions to the programme. At some point after the summer recess the Committee presents to the full Cabinet a complete outline of the items on the agenda for the forthcoming session to be mentioned in the Queen's Speech at the opening of Parliament.

When the new session has been opened, usually in early November, control of the programme passes from the Cabinet Future Legislation Committee to its Legislation Committee, which performs the function of monitoring the progress of bills both before they are introduced and whilst they wend their way through the various parliamentary stages. Before a bill is ready for presentation to Parliament it must be submitted in draft to the Legislation Committee which is normally presided over by a senior Cabinet Minister and whose membership includes the Leaders of both Houses, the Lord Chancellor, the Attorney and the Solicitor General and the Chief Whip. Ministers with bills on the agenda attend, commonly accompanied both by the draftsmen and by senior officials. If the bill is approved by the Legislation Committee, it will be given an approximate date of presentation and the Committee decides in which House the measure is to be introduced. The choice is often simply a matter of convenience and of the state of parliamentary business in each House. But the tradition is that bills involving significant expenditure should start in the Commons — though most such bills can now technically start in the Lords as well.

This description of the role of the Cabinet only gives the formal position, however. It says nothing of the degree of Cabinet scrutiny of proposals for legislation. There is no doubt that the Cabinet is genuinely in charge of the decision to authorise legislation on a particular subject. It will also approve the broad policy of a bill both when the proposal first comes forward for consideration and later when the final draft of the bill is offered for approval before presentation to Parliament. But most of the detail is inevitably left to the Minister concerned. It is his responsibility to sort out the contents of his own bill with his officials. Cabinet Ministers from other departments will only have a limited amount of time to become involved in his legislative project. They will normally have neither the inclination nor the expertise to subject his bill to informed detailed inquiry. Little is known about this aspect of the workings of government, but what can be gleaned from sources such as Richard Crossman's *Diaries of a Cabinet*

Minister suggests that neither the Cabinet itself nor Cabinet Committees actually exercise much genuine control over the content, let alone the form, of bills. Ministers are too busy and their meetings usually too brief to permit much in the way of detailed scrutiny.

It follows that a great deal of real power therefore lies in the Departmental Minister. How is this power wielded and in particular, what is the true relationship between the Minister and his officials? Obviously there are many different variations on this theme. At one extreme there is the bill that forms a central part of the Government's programme, that was fully debated in the election manifesto and during the election campaign. Such a bill is one to which the Government naturally attaches high political importance and the Minister will find himself heavily involved in directing the work of his civil servants. If he is himself an expert on the subject, he may actually have been partly responsible for the development of the policy in the first place. Even if he does not claim any special competence in the field, as the Minister in charge of the responsible department he will probably play a dominant role. The greater his abilities, the greater his dominance. But his involvement in the debates and discussions in his own department is inevitably affected by a variety of other factors. How busy is he at that particular time? The punishing work-load of Ministers was analysed in a study of the working week of fifty ministers — covering the 1964-1970 Wilson administration and the 1970-74 Heath administration. The study showed that Ministers spent a minimum of sixty hours per week (excluding weekends) working. Of this at least forty-five hours were spent in Cabinet and Cabinet Committees, Parliament, interviews and discussions with people outside the department, formal receptions and lunches, official visits and constituency responsibilities.[4] In other words, a Minister has a full-time job as a politician and as ambassador for his department before he even starts on the job of running it. It is also relevant that, because of the hours that Parliament keeps, he is apt to be distinctly short of sleep. In the 1975-6 session of Parliament, only 3 per cent of Commons sittings ended by 10 p.m. — 53 per cent went on until between 10 p.m. and midnight, 26 per cent until between midnight and 2 a.m. and no less than 17 per cent until after 2 a.m.[5]

To add to the Minister's difficulties there is the fact that he rarely stays long in the same job. Lord Crowther-Hunt wrote in 1980, for instance, that there had been no less than twenty

Ministers of Education since 1944 — an average of less than two years each. He himself had been Minister of State in that department and stayed fifteen months, which he said was just about par for the course. His immediate predecessor had been in the job only six months, and his four predecessors in the Wilson Government of 1964-70 had lasted an average of seventeen months each. Given this, where, he asked rhetorically, 'can you really expect the balance of power between ministers and their officials to lie — particularly when at the time I left, the Permanent Secretary had been there for six years and like the Deputy Secretaries, had spent the major part of his career in the department'?[6] (In short, the reality of the relationship between Ministers and civil servants is not unlike that between Sir Humphrey Appleby and Jim Hacker portrayed in 'Yes Minister'.) Also, how competent and committed to the policy does he feel his officials to be? If he regards them as incompetent or as potential saboteurs, he will feel it necessary to watch their every movement, whereas if he feels them to be basically in sympathy with the policy he will be more able to leave them to get on with it.

At the other end of the spectrum there is the bill which is pure departmental business with little or no political content, where the Minister has neither the knowledge, the inclination nor the time to involve himself. All the ideas come from the officials and the Minister simply rubber stamps their work.

Most bills will fall somewhere along the continuum between these two extremes. But there is some reason to suppose that the majority lie somewhere towards the Minister-inactive rather than the Minister-hyper-active end of the spectrum. One can deduce this from the fact that the majority of bills provoke very much less controversy than the traditional adversary model of parliamentary affairs would suggest. In popular mythology Government and Opposition are locked in a permanent Punch-and-Judy state of combat. The reality is quite different. Again, Professor Richard Rose's study in instructive. Whereas two-thirds of bills based on the party manifesto caused major divisions in the House of Commons, five-sixths of bills derived from the Whitehall process of departmental business were consensual, as witness the fact that they were enacted without any division on the second or the third reading in the House of Commons. There was no difference in the proportion of consensual legislation generated by the Whitehall process in the Conservative Government of 1970-74 and that during the Labour Government in 1974 to 1979.[7] In each case, it was five-sixths.

Another study making the same point is that by Professor John Griffith of the London School of Economics who investigated the process of legislation during three sessions of Parliament, 1967-8, 1968-9 and 1970-1. The average length of time occupied by all the various parliamentary stages of the 183 bills in the study was just over 19 hours. However, no fewer than 74 of the 183 bills (40 per cent) were dealt with in less than five hours! On the other hand, in each available session there were seven bills that absorbed over half the available time. These 21 bills averaged 96 hours of debating time.[8] The picture that emerges is clear. Most bills go through almost on the nod, whilst a few attract an immense amount of time and attention. The bills that go through with little or no fuss are likely to be ones in which the officials have played a dominant or at least a major role in the period of gestation.

THE DRAFTING PROCESS

When the Minister and his officials are satisfied that they have sorted out the outline and details of their proposed piece of legislation, the bill is sent off for drafting. The drafting of government legislation is done not in-house in the respective government departments but by the small band of Parliamentary Counsel. The office of Parliamentary Counsel dates back to 1869. (Prior to that the drafting was done by barristers in private practice.) Draftsmen typically start in the career in their late twenties shortly after qualification. Most are barristers. (Until recently they in fact had to be barristers, but in recent years solicitors have also been permitted to apply.) There are currently twenty-eight members of the office, but eight are on permanent attachment to the Law Commission. Their work-load is phenomenal. In the five years from 1980 to 1984 they added a total of 11,700 pages to the statute book. Annually the total has averaged over 2,000 pages. The members of the office regard themselves, and are regarded, as an elite. A former head of the office, Sir Granville Ram, said once:[9]

> I should be misleading you if I allowed any false modesty to prevent me from saying that only men and women of first class ability can do the work. Among past and present members of the office there have been a few who have not taken their university degrees with first class honours, but the great majority have done so, and I may say that my three immediate predecessors as First Parliamentary Counsel all had the distinction of being Fellows of All Souls.

Parliamentary Counsel receive their instructions from the department, in a document normally prepared by the department's legal staff. The department is not expected to attempt a first draft of the bill — this verges on *lèse majesté*. A chastened official recounted in 1980 what happened when she and her colleagues in the Customs and Excise Department decided to try to help Parliamentary Counsel by attempting the first draft of a bill on VAT. The draft ran to 60 clauses with a note on each. The early versions had been widely circulated within the department for comments and suggestions and later versions were debated line by line in long meetings attended by all the relevant members of the VAT planning team. But in spite of all this hard work the final product was not appreciated by the draftsman and the departmental efforts were described by the author as 'distinctly clumsy' by comparison with Parliamentary Counsel's product. She did not recommend others to repeat the exercise.[10] By a curious Whitehall convention the Minister is usually not shown the instructions to the draftsmen. They pass from the officials to Parliamentary Counsel with no intervening scrutiny by their political masters, as if this was a purely technical matter with no policy content.

Draftsmen work on bills in pairs assigned by First Parliamentary Counsel. If the two draftsmen feel the need for a preliminary conference with the department they will suggest a meeting. If the instructions seem clear enough, they will proceed to prepare their first draft which is then sent to the department. In Granville Ram's words: 'There then ensues a series of conferences, telephone calls, and letters, which often call for much hard thought, many late hours, and a great deal of work on the part of all concerned'.[11] Eventually, 'probably after many further drafts have been prepared, criticised and revised, the time comes when the draft bill is in a fit state to be shown to the Minister'. If he interests himself in the details, he will convene meetings with his own officials and the draftsmen. Occasionally a point of substance will come up which requires reference back to the Cabinet or a Cabinet sub-committee. But this is rare.

The work is almost invariably done under intense pressure of time. The draftsmen will be working on more than one piece of legislation at a time. Commonly they will not have received their instructions for the bills for the session starting in October before the previous Spring, and while scrambling on the new bill, they will also very likely be engaged on one or more bills before Parliament in the current session. The process of drafting and re-drafting normally takes many weeks and often months,

and even then there is usually a feeling that time was too short.
Bills must be ready to slot into the Government's legislative
timetable. The number of days available for legislation is
surprisingly small. In a normal session the House of Commons
only sits for some 170 days per year. Over half of the time is
spent on business other than legislation. Nearly a quarter of the
80 or so days actually available for legislation is taken up with
the Budget, and the Finance and Consolidated Fund Bills, which
leaves a mere 60 days for the entire programme of other
legislation. In an average session a government typically
introduces some 50 to 70 bills. For so many bills to pass
successfully in the session in the 60 or so days available is no
small achievement. But it requires a tight timetable and careful
planning by the Government Whips and business managers.

CRITICISM OF ENGLISH DRAFTING

The drafting of legislation is a difficult art and the draftsman is
used to receiving more brickbats than praise. One reason is that
public debate as to the merits of drafting usually takes place in
the context of litigation when, by definition, there is a conflict
between opposing factions. Where the drafting is so good that no
dispute ever arises as to the meaning of the test, its quality will
never receive a judge's encomium. The greatest tribute to a
draftsman is therefore if his text never becomes the subject of
scrutiny in a courtroom.

But where a court is struggling to discover the meaning of the
text, it is not surprisng that judges sometimes yield to the
temptation to express their exasperation in acid terms. The
problem of the quality of drafting of documents has recently
come under general scrutiny by the National Consumer
Council[12] and by the Prime Minister's adviser, Sir Derek
Rayner of Marks and Spencer. Sir Derek looked into government
forms, more than 2,000 million of which are issued annually. In
a scathing report to the Prime Minister in 1982 he said that the
language used in forms was often legalistic, lengthy and
intimidating.[13] Forms were so different that often they were not
understood by the officials who administered them. Officials
often doubted whether it was either right or necessary to
communicate with the public in simple language. Sir Derek's
report led to the White Paper 'Administrative forms in
government') which promised an aggressive commitment to a
complete overhaul of government forms.[14]

But the Plain English campaign has not made great progress

as yet with Parliamentary Counsel nor, it must be said, with the general run of English lawyers. The quality of the drafting of English statutes has come into question not simply from irascible judges but increasingly also from experts who contrast the English product unfavourably with that from other countries. It has been suggested that English statutes are more prolix, more complicated and more obscure than they need to be.* Sentences are said to be too long, with innumerable sub-clauses, provisos and qualifications. Language is said too often to be stilted and old-fashioned. There is little attempt to set out the principles of the legislation; everything is reduced to the level of minute particularity.[15]

By contrast, it is said, on the continent of Europe and notably in France, drafting, including the drafting of statutes, is lucid and succinct. The statute is apt to be drafted in language that can be understood by the layman. There are statements of principle and less clutter of detail. Sentences are short and the sequence is logical and orderly. The Continental draftsman, unlike his English counterpart, rarely finds it necessary to have definition clauses in which the meaning of words or phrases is given a technical expression. The meaning emerges from the clear use of language. Critics of the English system often attribute at least some of the defects of the method to the specialisation of function in Parliamentary Counsel's Office. On the Continent drafting is done instead within government departments — as is indeed the case in this country too for delegated legislation.

One of the chief critics has been Sir William Dale, formerly chief legal adviser to the Ministry of Education. In 1985 he published the latest in a series of comparative studies of the styles of drafting in different countries. The hallmark of the English statute, he suggested, was 'sections a page long or more, subsections of a single sentence often running to 130 words or more, some much more, and elaborate construction'.[16] By way of example, he contrasted a recent English statute, the Data Protection Act 1984, with the equivalent French law of 1978 and

---

* For a choice example see, for instance, section 38(4) of the Criminal Justice Act 1982: 'An enactment in which section 31(6) and (7) of the Criminal Law Act 1977 (pre 1949 enactments) produced the same fine or maximum fine for different convictions shall be treated for the purposes of this section as if there were omitted from it so much of it as before 29 July 1977 had the effect that a person guilty of an offence under it was liable on summary conviction to a fine or maximum fine less than the highest fine or maximum fine to which he would have been liable if his conviction had satisfied the conditions required for the imposition of the highest maximum fine.'

the German law of 1977. In the English Act most of the sections were a page long, 18 of them divided into six or more subsections. In the French law the sections had one, two or three paragraphs, and hardly ever exceeded 90 words. A paragraph usually consisted of one sentence, though the German law had three sections extending to over a page. The most economical arrangement of ideas was in the French statute. The most confused was the English. There were eight definitions in section 1, more in the body of the Act and no less than a further fourteen at the end. Section 2 was called 'The data protection principles' but it actually contained no principles. It referred instead to the First Schedule. (Sir William Dale suggests that it was an abuse of scheduling to relegate to a schedule the basic principles of protection of the privacy of citizens from infringement.) The German law was half the length of the English, and the French law was little more than one-fifth as long.[17]

A similar analysis published in the autumn of 1986, comparing English and French Nationality Law, again gave the wooden spoon to the English draftsmen. The British Act was four times as long with 53 sections and nine schedules, against 161 articles and no schedules in the French Code. The sections of the British Act averaged 40 lines as against an average of 4 to 5 lines for the articles of the Code. Working out a problem under the British Act was three to four times as laborious because of the complexity of the structure and style with more frequent reference to other texts, more complex syntax, greater use of technical terms and longer sentences.[18]

Criticisms of the statute book have come not simply from private scholars but also from an official committee (the Renton Committee on the Preparation of Legislation, which reported in 1975). The Renton Committee made it clear where the emphasis of reform should be placed. 'In principle the interests of the ultimate users should always have priority over those of the legislators.' After sifting all the criticisms and suggestions, the Committee said that it had no wish to reflect upon the skill and dedication of the parliamentary draftsmen. They had to work under pressure and constraints which made it difficult for them with the best will in the world to produce simple and clear legislation. They were inadequately staffed and often had to work against impossible deadlines. But, with masterly understatement, it concluded, 'nevertheless after making all due allowance, there remains cause for concern that difficulty is being encountered by the ultimate users of statutes'.[19] (The Committee cited as an example a 1946 provision: 'For the purposes of this Part of the Schedule a person over pensionable age, not being an insured person, shall be treated as an employed person if he would be an insured person were he under pensionable age and would be an employed person were he an insured person.' What was remarkable was not merely that this sentence had been enacted once but that it was repeatedly re-enacted.)

No doubt there are some topics on which legislation cannot be drafted so simply as to be understood by the complete layman. Even the Archangel Gabriel might have difficulties in reducing tax, copyright or property law to simple phrases intelligible to the ordinary citizen. The concepts themselves are unfamiliar and complex. Also, it is probably fairly rare that ordinary citizens want to consult the actual text of statutes. Even well-drafted statutes tend to be couched in language that for most citizens is forbiddingly formal and remote. Probably most readers of statutes are in some category of expert or semi-expert — lawyers, accountants and other professional advisers, or laymen whose job requires them to work with legislation, such as social workers, rent officers, tax officials, policemen, architects, businessmen and the like. But the draftsman can never know who is to be the ultimate user of the statute and his task must always be to reduce the drafting to the simplest possible level. Even an expert benefits from good and simple drafting. Unnecessarily complex drafting can never be justified on the ground that the likely user will normally be familiar with the subject matter. For one thing, if legislation were easier to use non-expert citizens might try to use it more often. Moreover, even judged by the test of whether the statute is readily understood by the expert, English drafting does not by any means always pass muster.

The view that Continental drafting is usually better is, of course, not accepted by all the experts. Insofar as the Continental style states general principles, it is open to the objection that it leaves too much scope for judicial interpretation and thereby creates uncertainty. According to Sir William Dale, the Continental systems manage to combine a balance between general principle and a sufficient degree of particularity. The point was supported by a comparative analysis of the nationality laws of Britain and France. The French Code was precise and detailed and dealt with borderline cases, special cases and exceptional cases, just like the statute. But it did so more briefly and more clearly. This opinion is rejected, however, by the English draftsmen and their defenders who deride the continentals for their open-ended, vague and woolly phrases which leave it to the judges to decide what the legislature intended. English statutes are drafted with elaborate and tedious pro-lixity according to the draftsmen, in order to make them clear and 'judge-proof'.

The draftsman's distaste for general principle was dramatic-ally demonstrated in the Child Abduction and Custody Act 1985 which was introduced to enable this country to ratify two international Conventions. The Articles of the Convention were set out in Schedules. But one of the Articles was omitted. This states: 'The return of the child . . . may be refused if this would not be permitted by the fundamental principles of the requested state relating to the protection of human rights and funda-mental freedoms'. Asked about this omission, the Lord Chancellor explained: '. . . its omission does not mean that we are not bound by it or cannot use it. The reason why it was left out is simply that it states a general principle which cannot easily be accommodated in a United Kingdom legal text'.[20] Lord Simon of Glaisdale, a law lord, commented on this explana-tion:[21]

> What could be more ridiculous? There is a legislative provision by which we are bound, but it cannot be included even in a Schedule which sets out the Convention because to do so would stand in contrast with the style of drafting that is insisted on contrary to the recommendations of the Renton Report.

Lord Simon's view was that there was not the least likelihood of improvement until the Office of Parliamentary Counsel was brought under a Minister capable of concern with legislative technique, namely the Lord Chancellor. The constitutional theory was that each minister was responsible for the drafting of his own piece of legislation but in practice he would bow to the authority of the expert, the draftsman.

Whatever the truth of the matter, it is far from easy to get the English draftsman to concede that his methods leave something to be desired. The Office of Parliamentary Counsel is not noted for intellectual humility or receptivity to criticism. The Statute Law Society, a learned society with a journal the *Statute Law Review*, appeared for years to be beating its head against a wall of indifference or even hostility from the draftsmen in making comments and suggestions about the condition of the statute book. In the past few years, though, it seems that the beginnings of a dialogue may have started. Some suggestions made by the critics have even been adopted. The bad old method of 'non-textual' amendments of statutes, for instance, has given way to the much handier textual method. Previously amendments would be written in a narrative form so that the reader had to compare the old text with the new text and work out for himself how the two should be read together. Under the textual technique of amendment the draftsman states unambiguously what words are being deleted and what new words are substituted so that by using scissors and paste it is a simple matter to establish what the new text is. This change came about principally through criticisms from individual experts, the Statute Law Society and the Report of the Renton Committee. But it took many years, and was a rare instance of criticisms of Parliamentary Counsel not simply hitting the mark but of implicit acknowledgement from the targets of the criticism that the point was taken.

It has not proved possible, however, to persuade the draftsman of the merit of such elementary suggestions as that definitions should all be collected in one part of a statute, or that words or phrases with a technical meaning should be italicised so that they stand out and the reader of the statute is alerted to the fact when he comes across them. For the English draftsman the old way of doing his work is normally the best way. Commenting on the fate of the Renton Committee's report in 1985, Lord Simon of Glaisdale said that the response of the Government to the report had been 'pretty tepid'. The House of Lords, he said, was well soundproofed, but 'through the mellifluous tones and felicitous compliments of the Lord Chancellor an experienced ear could detect the familiar thud of entrenching tools in Whitehall'.[22]

The Renton Committee suggested that there should be a method of continuous monitoring of the condition of the statute book by asking the official Statute Law Committee to keep it under review. But this seemingly innocuous proposal was sabotaged by Parliamentary Counsel themselves. Lord Renton has related how, after the report of his Committee had been debated in both Houses of Parliament in 1975, the Labour Lord Chancellor, Lord Elwyn-Jones, called a private meeting of the Statute Law Committee. The Committee, which has existed since 1868, is appointed by the Lord Chancellor. Normally it meets once a year. It consists of some two dozen members including MPs, Parliamentary Counsel, judges, and senior civil servants. It made proposals for implementation of the Renton Committee's proposal that it should 'keep the structure and language of the statutes under continuous review' and should issue reports every two or three years.[23] It seemed as if the proposal would go through with the support of the Lord Chancellor. But a skilful campaign behind the scenes by Parliamentary Counsel led to the Cabinet rejecting the idea. Although he had personally appeared to be in favour of the idea, the Lord Chancellor subsequently stated in a written Parliamentary Answer given in March 1978,[24]

> After very careful consideration of these recommendations the Government were not satisfied that the Statute Law Committee was an appropriate body to discharge the functions proposed for it by the Renton Committee, or that the proposal to keep the statute book under continuous review was likely to lead to any worthwhile improvement in the drafting of legislation.

In France the quality of the drafting is subjected to ante-natal scrutiny by the prestigious Conseil d'Etat whch is sent all draft legislation by initiating departments. If the department is not prepared to accept changes proposed by the Conseil d'Etat, the question is sent to the Council of Ministers for resolution. Sir William Dale proposed that there should be a Law Council to advise the British Government on draft bills.

> Its duty would be to examine [draft bills] from the point of view of coherent and orderly presentation, clarity, conciseness, soundness of legal principle, and suitability for attaining the Government's objective.[25]

But this idea has not received much support. Even the Renton Committee rejected it. It thought that the idea of compulsory prior scrutiny of bills was not desirable. It was for government departments themselves to decide whether and from whom to seek advice.[26] This seems a feeble solution, guaranteed to fail.

CODIFICATION

One basic Continental technique of writing the law has hardly been attempted in the UK — namely codification. This is in spite of the fact that the 1965 Act of Parliament which established the Law Commission as the chief law reform agency set it the task of codification as one of its principal tasks. (The Law Commissions Act said that it was the duty of the English and the Scottish Law Commissions each to 'take and keep under review all the law . . . with a view to its systematic development and reform, including in particular the codification of such law'.)

Lord Scarman, the first Chairman of the English Law Commission, went about in those heady days proclaiming that the duty to codify heralded the beginnings of a new dawn for English law. Codification, he thought, would bring together the law as it was to be found in scattered statutes and even more scattered judicial decisions and would present it in an orderly and up-to-date fashion, making it both easier to find and to use.

The Law Commission in fact started an ambitious programme of codification projects in its early years. In 1965 it announced its intention to begin codifying the law of contract, the law of landlord and tenant, family law and the law of evidence. But each in turn was abandoned — family law in 1970, contract law in 1973 and landlord and tenant law in 1978. The codification of the law of evidence was never even begun.

The main reason for the evaporation of the codification dream seems to have been a mixture of conservatism and a realisation on the part of draftsmen, legislators and even judges that it simply did not fit the basic style of English law-making. The draftsmen did not take kindly to the notion that codes had to be drafted in a broader manner than was normal for traditional statutes with statements of general principle. Legislators looked askance at the concept of a huge omnibus bill which would attempt to state the law in a vast area such as landlord and tenant. The judges objected to Lord Scarman's concept of the code coming down like an iron curtain making all pre-code law irrelevant. This they thought would be to throw the baby out with the bathwater — losing the priceless heritage of the past and wasting the fruits of legislation and litigation on innumerable points which would still be relevant to interpret the new code. Instead of comprehensive codification, the Law Commission undertook the piecemeal reform of the law through the traditional route of statutes on particular, more limited, topics — though in the field of family law it produced so much new law in the form of a whole patchwork quilt of new legislation that this area of the law at least was significantly reformed. But it remained a jumble of disconnected statutes rather than a spanking new code.

The single codification project to get anywhere was that on criminal law. This was announced in 1968. Between 1968 and 1974 the Law Commission published a number of Working Papers on the topic, the first of which in 1968 discussed the matters to be included in what it called the General Part. In its report for 1968/9 it said that it would continue working on this project but in fact no more was heard of it for the next ten years.

Then in 1979/80 it announced that its limited resources had prevented it from making further progress. But in 1980 the Law Commission asked for help from the Society of Public Teachers of Law which set up a four-man committee of distinguished academic lawyers headed by Professor J.C. Smith of Nottingham University. By 1985 they had produced a 246-page report on the General Part, including a partial draft bill. There seemed at least a possibility that this might in the end result in something recognisably like a code along Continental lines.[27] The advantage, according to the report, would be greater comprehensiveness, accessibility, comprehensibility, consistency and certainty.

But there are many who dispute that codification is likely to work any great miracles. Scepticism has been expressed about whether the code will in practice be either more certain than the previous law, or more accessible. There have been so many instances over the years where courts gave interpretations of statutory provisions that seemed contrary to what Parliament probably intended that the critics of codification doubt whether in practice it would really make a significant contribution to the predictability of the law. In the unlikely event that either the code or the judges were to deny access to pre-code statutes and cases, it would appear to make the code more accessible. But the problem of discovering the meaning of the code would still exist and would probably generate much litigation.

Continental lawyers who are familiar with the techniques of discovering the law in the common law system usually claim that codes make it quicker and therefore cheaper for the lawyer to advise his client. If this is correct, it would seem worth the effort to get experts to prepare codes and to try to see whether they can be pushed through the British parliamentary system. The criminal law code, if it eventually comes to fruition, will be a practical test of this issue. But with this single possible exception, the thrust toward codification, which started as part of the original enthusiasm of the Harold Wilson era, has now collapsed.

THE PARLIAMENTARY STAGES OF LEGISLATION

When the drafting process is complete and a bill has been approved in its final form by the Cabinet sub-committee, it is ready to be introduced in Parliament. This is the aspect of legislation of which everyone is aware and which for most people is the critical stage. As has been seen, most bills may be introduced in either House. The procedure is broadly similar in each House. A Bill must be given 'three readings' in each House before it can be sent for Royal Assent. The First Reading is a pure formality. Nothing happens save that the Clerk of the House reads the title from a dummy bill and a day is named for the Second Reading. Until this point the Bill is not even printed. The order to the Government Printer is only sent after the formal First Reading has taken place.

The Second Reading is the occasion for a debate on the general principles of the Bill. The Minister whose Bill it is opens by explaining its purpose and the effect of its separate clauses. A frontbench Opposition spokesman typically then explains why the Opposition regards it as unwelcome or defective (or both). Debate then ensues. The Bill cannot be amended on the Second Reading debate. But the Opposition can move the rejection of the Bill as a whole. If, as normally happens, this attempt to stop the Bill dead in its tracks fails, it moves into Committee. In the House of Commons the Committee generally consists of anything from 16 to 50 MPs chosen by the Select Committee of Selection on the basis of their interests and expertise, their other commitments, and the process of balancing a myriad of political considerations.

Its overall composition reflects the strength of the parties in the House. Some bills in the House of Commons are taken in a committee of the whole House. In the House of Lords this is invariably the case. The effect is that a vote in the Committee stage in the Lords is often unpredictable since no-one can know in advance which peers will turn up on the day and then stay until the division. In the Commons, by contrast, party discipline ensures that MPs are normally only absent if they have arranged to 'pair' with a member from an opposing party. The outcome of the vote is therefore normally predictable.

The task of the Committee is to consider the Bill in detail, line by line. Amendments are proffered by the Opposition, often on advice received from interest groups which shower suggestions on the members of every standing committee. The Ministerial response to amendments will vary. Sometimes, though rarely, the Minister says that he accepts the amendment and it will then be incorporated in the Bill without a formal vote. Sometimes he states that he accepts the gist of the amendment but not its drafting and that he will bring forward his own amendment at a later stage. On this assurance the amendment is withdrawn. Or he may only be prepared to go so far as to say that he will consider the point raised and come back with the Government's view later. Again, this normally leads to the amendment being withdrawn. It is only if he says that he cannot accept the amendment that the Opposition parties normally press the matter to a vote.

Government amendments are drafted by Parliamentary Counsel — normally the same as have been responsible for the original draft of the Bill itself. Parliamentary Counsel are not available to Opposition members or even to government backbenchers. They therefore have to find some other means of getting competent help with the drafting. Lawyer-MPs and lawyers working for lobbying groups or for other interested parties find themselves pressed into service to assist with the drafting of Opposition amendments. The Clerks in the Public Bill Office of each House also give guidance, and sometimes help, in the preparation of amendments. Where, as is often the case, there is a variety of amendments on the same issue, it is the task of the chairman to select the amendments to be considered. The chair in Committee is taken by a member selected by the Speaker from a panel of chairmen, usually of the Opposition party. The tradition is that they preserve the same principle of impartiality between the parties as Mr Speaker himself.

The atmosphere in the Committee stage is generally less adversarial than when the House is engaged on other stages of the Bill. The fact that the numbers are small and that, at least in the Commons, they are normally using one of the small upstairs committee rooms tends to make for a degree of informality verging on camaraderie which is not possible in the same way on the floor of the House. Sometimes, however, the full intensity of party passion is reflected in the Committee stage. In this situation the Opposition commonly will be trying its best to disrupt the Government's timetable by dragging out the debates. Eventually the Government may respond by 'moving the guillotine' so that debate is abbreviated according to a timetable which it lays down. Sometimes this results in parts of the Bill not being debated at all. But use of the guillotine is relatively rare. Normally the Opposition, even when it seeks to oppose, plays its hand carefully and judges rather nicely how far it can go in delaying the Bill without incurring the risposte of a guillotine motion.

After the Committee stage is concluded the Bill goes to the full House for the Report stage. It is then that the Government commonly comes forward with amendments to which it agreed during the course of the Committee hearings. The Opposition too can introduce amendments, whether new or ones that merely repeat issues that have previously been canvassed at an earlier stage. Often the debate on the Report stage is dominated by precisely the same individuals who took part in the Committee stage. They know the Bill in detail. They may have come to feel strongly about the principles it raises. Other members are busy about their own affairs. Generally they have little inclination to master the complexities of legislation with which they have had no previous contact. They take the line of least resistance and leave it to the experts. The same is even more true at the Third Reading. By this time the fight has normally gone out of the affair and debate is generally brief. But amendments of substance may still be passed at that late stage — especially if the Government has had insufficient time earlier to cope with all the amendments it wanted to see passed.

The largest portion of time during the parliamentary process is absorbed by the Committee stage. Professor John Griffith's study showed that on average the Second Reading took 15 per cent of the total time, the Committee stage 65 per cent, the Report stage 15 per cent, the Third Reading 2 per cent, and the remaining 3 per cent was taken with one House considering amendments passed in the other.[28] After the Third Reading, there are the final ritualistic stages. The Bill is tied up with green ribbon and is endorsed *soit baillé aux seigneurs* (let it be sent to the Lords), before being sent to the 'other place' for the Lords' concurrence. If the Bill comes from the Lords, the ribbon is red and the Norman French formula is *soit baillé aux Communes*. The procedure for passing a bill from one House to the other, harmlessly and rather pleasingly, still retains its medieval style. If the Bill is coming from Lords to Commons a Lords Clerk wearing wig and gown carries the Bill, bearing its Message informing the Commons that 'the Lords have passed the Bill to which they desire the agreement of the Commons', to the Bar of the House of Commons. He bows to the Speaker, hands the Bill and the Message to the Sergeant-at-arms, bows again and retires. In the reverse case, where the Bill comes from the Commons the procedure is similar. Rules of procedure for passage of legislation in the House of Lords are somewhat more relaxed. But basically the process is the same — apart from the major difference that, as has been seen, any peer can turn up to participate in the Committee stage.

After a Commons Bill has been through the Lords it is returned with Lords Amendments which must then be considered by MPs. The two Houses must eventually agree on amendments if the Bill is to get through all the stages before the end of the session. In theory, when one House does not agree amendments it can go back and forth several times but this is very rare. Normally the Lords concede. In the rare case where the Lords do not agree, but the Commons insist, the Parliament Acts of 1911 and 1949 ensure that the Commons prevail on a non-money Bill after the delay of one year. The Bill has to be re-introduced a second time in the next parliamentary session. It then becomes law even though the Lords again refuse to approve it. A money Bill (one that imposes a charge on public funds or tax) if rejected by the Lords does not have to be re-presented the following session. It can be sent for Royal Assent one month later.

PRIVATE MEMBERS' LEGISLATION

Most legislation is the product of the government machine, but some owes its existence to backbench Members of Parliament, and individual peers. Such legislation cannot involve much in the way of expenditure since Standing Orders forbid government expenditure other than on the recommendation of the Crown. But if the amounts involved are small the Minister may be prepared to move a resolution approving the expenditure.

A ballot takes place each session for private members wishing to introduce a bill. Normally twelve Fridays are allotted in each session for private members' legislation. Most backbenchers enter the ballot. Normally twenty bills are put forward by backbenchers under this procedure but only about half of these are in fact enacted. (In 1983/4 the number was nine; in 1984/5 it was eleven.)

Members who are successful in the ballot present their bills in dummy form on the fifth Wednesday of the session. Between the date of the announcement of the results of the ballot and presentation they have to decide what topic to address in their bill. They are deluged with suggestions from pressure groups anxious to enlist support for their own pet ideas — and willing to do the vital leg-work, drafting, lobbying and support work. Sometimes the successful MP decides instead to take on some minor item of official legislation for which the Government itself has not been able to find time in its own programme, or a bill prepared by the Law Commission. In such cases the member will have official help in drafting the bill. The promoter of the bill cannot normally call on the drafting services of Parliamentary Counsel, though members who draw one of the first ten places in the ballot are able to claim a small allowance to help pay for drafting assistance for their bills. But normally the drafting is done either by the organisation or pressure group behind the bill or by lawyer friends or associates of the MP whose bill it is. The process is somewhat haphazard and if the sponsor of the bill lacks the means to mobilise the necessary assistance, it works badly.

Private Members' bills face a variety of hurdles which make their survival highly problematic. The main one is lack of time. If bills higher in the ballot order are opposed, they will be debated at length and bills lower in the order will not be reached. Sometimes opponents of a bill will obstruct it by ensuring that other prior uncontroversial bills are delayed by extended debate. If the Government favours the bill, it can make extra time available and this occasionally happens. But, failing government help of that kind, opponents of Private Members' legislation can often manage to stop it through the weapon of time-wasting. There is also the problem of mobilising enough support to keep the House in session. Unless the House takes a decision on the bill it will be 'talked out' and it is unlikely that more time will be found for it on another day. To get a decision on the bill on the Second Reading 100 Members must be present to support the closure if it is to proceed. Even a clear majority on the Second Reading does not suffice if fewer than 100 Members are there to support it. (In February 1987 Sir Edward Gardner's attempt to get the European Convention on Human Rights incorporated into UK law failed because he was six persons short in the chamber on the Second Reading debate. By contrast, the Bill introduced in 1983 by Mr Austin Mitchell to abolish the solicitors' conveyancing monopoly only survived when there proved to be exactly 100 MPs present in the chamber to support the closure. On so slender a thread hung the future of the legal profession.) Any division other than the closure requires at least forty Members taking part. If there are not that number, the House passes to the next item of business.

Successful Private Members' bills are usually on minor problems, but some concern highly contentious issues on which the Government prefers not to take too open a position, or on which it seems more appropriate to allow parliamentarians to make up their own minds without the usual discipline imposed by the party Whips. During the 1966-70 Parliament, Private Members' legislation became a major feature and new laws were passed by this method on contraception, divorce, homosexuality, abortion, and theatre censorship. But this was unusual; normally the topics are less spicy.

ROYAL ASSENT

Royal Assent is constitutionally a formality. The monarch has no power to refuse to agree to any piece of legislation that has passed through all its stages in both Houses. Prior to 1541 it was necessary for the monarch to signify his assent to Parliament in person. The last time this was done was by Queen Victoria on 12 August 1854. The Royal Assent by Commissions Act 1541 permitted assent to be given by Letters Patent signed by the monarch personally and sealed on behalf of the Lord Chancellor by the Clerk of the Crown in Chancery (an office always held by the Permanent Secretary to the Lord Chancellor). The seal used is the Wafer Great Seal — a wafer impressed with the same device as the Great Seal of the United Kingdom, which has been used in place of the Great Seal since 1877. From 1541 to 1967 Royal Assent was given by Commission. Three or more Commissioners named in Letters Patent sat on a form placed between the throne and the Woolsack in the House of Lords. They commanded the Usher of the Black Rod to go to the Commons chamber and tell the members of that House that their attendance was desired. Mr Speaker, accompanied by some MPs, then walked to the Bar of the Lords. The Letters Patent were read out by the Clerk of the Crown. It was followed by the assent formula in Norman French, *La Reyne le Veult* (the Queen wills it).

In modern times, however, this interruption to Commons business was felt to be increasingly irksome and in 1967 the system was changed to permit Royal Assent to be given by Notification. The Royal Assent Act 1967 states that the fact that Her Majesty has signified assent may be 'notified to each House of Parliament, sitting separately, by the Speaker of that House or in the case of his absence by the person acting as such Speaker'. The former system of Assent by Commission is, however, still used once each year when Parliament is prorogued at the end of the session. Since the Commons are in any event required to attend in the Lords for the prorogation ceremony, no one objects to this ancient piece of flummery. It is a remarkable feature of the Royal Assent process that the Queen does not have the text or even the long title of the statutes to which she is giving her approval. The only information about the text given to her is the short title![29] This would seem to be verging on mockery of the monarch.

TIME TAKEN BY LEGISLATION

Major bills often take six months or more to pass. (The Police and Criminal Evidence Act, for instance, started in the Commons on 7 November 1983, and received the Royal Assent almost a year later on 31 October 1984.) But when the need arises the Mother of Parliament can move with dazzling speed. Occasionally, in some great crisis a bill has been rushed through all its stages in a day or two. The Commonwealth Immigrants Bill started in the Commons at 4 p.m. on 27 February 1968 and passed all its stages in both Commons and Lords on the same day. The Royal Assent was notified on 1 March. The Northern Ireland Bill had its Second Reading in the House of Commons at 10 p.m. on 23 February 1972 and the Royal Assent only hours later, on 24 February at 2.11 a.m. The Imprisonment (Temporary Provisions) Act 1980 passed through all its stages in 13 hours 20 minutes. The Official Secrets Act 1911 which is still law today and has given rise to endless controversy passed all its stages in a single day in August of that year. Twenty years later the junior minister who piloted the Bill through the House of Commons described the event:[30]

> I got up and proposed that the Bill be read a second time, explaining, in two sentences only, that it was considered desirable in the public interest that the measure should be passed. Hardly a word was said and the Bill was read a second time; the Speaker left the Chair. I then moved the Bill in Committee. This was the first critical moment; two men got up to speak, but both were forcibly pulled down by their neighbours after they had uttered a few sentences, and the committee stage was passed. The Speaker walked back to his chair and said: 'The question is, that I report this Bill without amendment to the House.' Again two or three people stood up; again they were pulled down by their neighbours, and the report stage was through. The Speaker turned to me and said: 'The third reading, what day?' 'Now, sir,' I replied. My heart beat fast as the Speaker said: 'The question is that this Bill be read a third time.' It was open to anyone of all the members in the House of Commons to get up and say that no bill had ever yet passed through all its stages in one day without a word of explanation from the minister in charge. . . . But to the eternal honour of those members, to whom I now offer, on behalf of that and all succeeding governments, my most

grateful thanks, not one man seriously opposed, and in a little more time than it has taken to write these words that formidable piece of legislation was passed.

WHO CAN AMEND A BILL?

When a piece of legislation is driven through Parliament pell-mell as in such cases, the control of the process by the Government of the day is obvious. But the reality is that, save in exceptional circumstances, the Government does in fact normally have effective control of the whole process of legislation. This is clear from the fact that nearly all amendments to legislation that are adopted are moved by the Minister whose bill it is. The overwhelming majority of amendments put down are of course moved by the Opposition. Professor Griffith's study of legislation over three parliamentary sessions showed that, out of a total of 4,417 amendments moved, 3,074 (or 70 per cent) were moved by the Opposition, 907 (or one-fifth) were moved by Ministers and 436 (or 10 per cent) by government backbenchers. But whereas 100 per cent of those moved by Ministers were adopted, only 4 per cent of those moved by the Opposition were adopted and only 9 per cent of those moved by government backbenchers. Moreover, of those moved by the Opposition and government backbenchers nearly all were adopted without a division which indicates that they were of a minor drafting or clarifying nature. On Report, 56 per cent of all amendments were moved by Ministers and again all but one of these 865 amendments passed. The Opposition moved 39 per cent of the amendments, but only 29 out of 599 (5 per cent) were adopted. Government backbenchers were responsible for 6 per cent of all amendments and only 10 out of 89 (11 per cent) were successful. Again one may deduce that both government backbenchers and the Opposition are only successful with minor points from the fact that 37 of their 39 amendments approved were agreed to without a division. In summary, 94 per cent of all amendments moved successfully in Committee and 96 per cent of those moved successfully on Report were moved by the Minister, and almost all those moved successfully by backbenchers or the Opposition concerned very small points.[31]

This again confirms the main theme of this chapter — that legislation is largely the work of the executive rather than of Parliament. A Minister is unlikely to move an amendment to his own Bill unless either he is persuaded that it is desirable or he believes that politically he has no choice. The latter case is very rare. The former will normally involve only points of detail, clarification, tidying up — in short, minor improvements. It is true that not a few government amendments owe their existence to points raised in the first place by the Opposition. (Professor Griffith identified 365 such cases during the three sessions he studied, of which about one-third he thought were important.) But although in a few cases the Government was forced to make concessions here and there, as Professor Griffith said,[32]

[A]gainst these achievements, must be set the long debates, the hundreds of aborted attempts at amendments, the scores of bills, including some of greatest importance, which remained effectively unchanged despite the efforts of Opposition Members and, to a lesser extent, of Government backbenchers. . . . [W]e are left with some sense of great effort making for little result and yet with a sense also that some slipshod thinking by Ministers, civil servants and draftsmen has been removed or clarified and that some bills look much better on third reading than they did on second, and that a few famous victories have been won. Whether this great effort is justified by those improvements is another matter.

The position in the House of Lords is marginally different in that the success rate of amendments moved by government backbenchers and Opposition Members is somewhat higher. In Griffith's study together they carried the day in Committee in 12 per cent of cases (as against 6 per cent in the Commons) and on Report in 19 per cent (compared with 5 per cent in the Commons).[33] Professor Griffith ascribed the difference to the less partisan atmosphere in the Lords which tended to make Ministers there more amenable to suggestion.

But whatever one thinks of the importance of the parliamentary stage it is at most merely marginal. The really important work on legislation goes on in Whitehall with civil servants playing a major, and often the dominant, role. At first blush this may seem objectionable. The faceless man in Whitehall does not have a good popular image. The fact that he is felt to be unaccountable and that his crucial role is so little understood combine to make it seem constitutionally improper for him to be wielding so much power. But this is to ignore the realities of the system and of the way it works. It cannot seriously be suggested that the work done by civil servants in the gestation process of bills could be done by Ministers, let alone by Members of Parliament who are not Ministers. Notionally officials are under the control of their Ministers but the day is too short and the items of business too numerous for the Minister really to know about and to be in charge of everything that is done in his name. He has to delegate. There is no alternative.

DELEGATED LEGISLATION

The importance of the faceless man in Whitehall, so crucial for ordinary legislation, is even more dominant for the mass of delegated legislation which pours from departments in a continuing stream. For the sixty to seventy annual statutes there are likely to be over two thousand statutory instruments. They are drafted in departments by the lawyers and administrators. Unlike statutes, they are sometimes shown to interested parties for comment in draft. Also unlike statutes, they are effectively beyond parliamentary amendment. They are put before Parliament under one of two basic procedures. The more usual is where the statutory instrument becomes law unless within 40 days it has been negatived by resolution of either House of Parliament. The less common is where it requires an affirmative resolution in order to become law — normally within 28 days of being laid before the House. But in either case, even if there is a debate on the text, it cannot be amended; it can only be rejected or approved as a whole. It is rare indeed for a statutory instrument not to be approved. This therefore is legislation by Whitehall in all but name.

QUASI LAW-MAKING

Even more striking as examples of law-making by Whitehall are the techniques of governing by code of practice, guidance note, circular, approved code, outline scheme, statement of advice or departmental circular — the list is long and seems constantly to be growing. A recent valuable comment on this trend by two academic writers, Dr Robert Baldwin and Mr John Houghton, suggested that it represents 'a discernible retreat from primary legislation in favour of government by informal rules'.[34] Each time government confronts a difficult regulatory task, 'it seems to come up with a new device'. One view of such rules was that they offered a useful structuring of discretion; another was that they were often used cynically so as to make law without resort to Parliament, to instruct judges on the meaning of statutes, and to insulate bureaucracies from review. Thus, for instance, the rules on picketing were contained in a code not an Act; the rules on police stop and search, detention and questioning were set out in lengthy codes of practice; parole policy had been drastically altered by ministerial pronouncement; and in fields such as planning, housing, matrimonial proceedings and health and safety at work there had been a distinct movement towards regulation by informal rules. In other areas such as prisons, immigration and criminal injuries compensation, the status and force of important rules was unclear. The authors argued:[35]

> For bureaucrats, the attractions of informality are plain. Such rules inexpensively and swiftly routinise the exercise of discretion; they provide easy justifications for statutory powers; they 'get the job done' whilst offering something to critics (irregular police questioning leads to disciplinary action, not exclusion of evidence); they give a flexibility that primary legislation does not offer; and they are largely immune from judicial review.

Their concern was that informal rules were 'too free from control by Parliament, executive, judiciary or any other source and that this freedom is increasingly open to exploitation'. Often there was little indication from any statute as to whether the rule was authorised and, if so, what was its effect or scope. Judges therefore had considerable latitude in deciding whether to give the rules legal effect. Often they were published haphazardly or not at all. There was little opportunity for consultation or public input in such rule-making, and lobbying might be limited to certain favoured interest groups.

It was true, of course, that informal rules had some virtues. They encouraged consistency in bureaucratic decision-making; they simplified complex issues and notified the public as to how it was being treated; they were flexible and could be issued quickly; they were less liable than formal rules to get snared in litigation; they allowed control of official action where legislation was inappropriate or politically undesirable.

The point made by the two authors, therefore, is not that informal rule-making is necessarily wrong, but that more should be done by legislators to clarify the status of rules and that the judiciary should be more prepared than it is to hold the makers of such rules to account. Thus there should be a duty normally to publish the rules so as to make them available to the persons affected. In some instances the courts might be able to construe a duty to consult with interested parties at the rule-making stages and to apply the tests of fairness and reasonableness to the rules created. The science of informal rule-making is still in its infancy. The first stage is a recognition of a problem and the mapping of its contours. The next stage, of developing a coherent approach to its solutions, is for the future. In the meanwhile, government by Whitehall continues and grows apace.

9

Bolder Perspectives for Reform

Throughout this book there has been reference to proposals for reform — some that have been implemented, some that are likely to be implemented, and some that have been urged which at present show little prospect of being implemented. The common feature of these items on the agenda is that they will leave the system essentially unchanged. If delays and costs of legal proceedings are reduced, it is not that these curses will be eliminated. If laws are made simpler, it is not that they will be simple. Whatever improvements are made in legal education, there will always be room for further improvements. Whether the defence have a right of peremptory challenge in jury selection is an important issue but, even were it abolished, the right of trial by jury remains intact. If the methods for selecting judges are altered, it does not follow that the judiciary would be transformed. In all probability, just about the same individuals as now would still be appointed. Whether police powers are increased or decreased has remarkably little effect on the numbers who commit crime — or even on the numbers arrested and successfully prosecuted. If the laws of England were to be codified, the process of finding and interpreting the law might be eased but it would not be radically transformed. However much access to justice is broadened and the legal system made accessible to the ordinary citizen, the problem of unmet need for help with legal problems will continue. Even implementation of so apparently major a change as the proposal to unify the two branches of the legal profession is unlikely in practice to work any great transformation. In all probability the two branches of the profession would continue mainly separately — with only a minority of individuals taking advantage of 'fusion'.

In other words, the reforms generally contemplated at present — however desirable and useful — would not alter the basic structure of the system. There are, however, three issues currently under debate where the changes proposed (to adopt a metaphor used in a different sphere) would 'break the mould'. These are that the United Kingdom should have its own Bill of Rights, that a Ministry of Justice be established, and that government decide to adopt the only solution to the problem of prison overcrowding which has any hope of working. None of the three proposals show any present sign of being adopted. But in a book that attempts to chart prospects for the future it seems right to address also changes that will require a leap of imagination beyond what is now seen as practicable.

A BILL OF RIGHTS FOR THE UK?

The question whether Britain should have a Bill of Rights has now been under active discussion since December 1974 when Lord Scarman put the issue on the political map by suggesting that the existence of such a device might have prevented the eruption of IRA violence in Northern Ireland on behalf of the Catholic minority.[1] If the Catholics had had the possibility of securing remedies for their grievances through the courts, maybe they would not have felt the necessity to turn to the gun. Lord Scarman's thesis was taken up by the media and became a major talking point. In the course of the succeeding years a large number of significant political figures associated themselves with Lord Scarman's campaign. From the Conservative Party these included Lord Hailsham, the then Lord Chancellor, Sir Michael Havers, the then Attorney General, Sir Edward Gardner, former Solicitor General, Mr Leon Brittan, former Home Secretary, Mr Geoffrey Rippon, and Sir Keith Joseph. From the Centre and Left of politics those who supported Lord Scarman included Mr Roy Jenkins, Mrs Shirley Williams, Lord (Sam) Silkin, former Labour Attorney General, Mr Peter Archer, former Labour Solicitor General, and Lord Gardiner, former Labour Chancellor. The Liberal-SPD Alliance has nailed its colours firmly to the mast of a Bill of Rights for the UK and the campaign was also supported in 1978 by a House of Lords Select Committee (which narrowly approved the idea by 6 votes to 5[2]) and on several occasions by a majority of the House of Lords.[3]

But neither the Conservative nor the Labour Party has

supported the idea. In the absence of support from the Government of the day, the idea obviously lacks political credibility. The nearest the campaign has so far come to any form of real political success was on Friday, 7 February 1987 when the House of Commons voted on Sir Edward Gardner's Private Member's Bill to incorporate the European Convention on Human Rights into UK law. Incorporation of the Convention is seen by everyone concerned as the only way in which Britain can in practice adopt a Bill of Rights. (The House of Lords Select Committee, for instance, which was split down the middle as to whether a Bill of Rights for the UK was a good idea, was unanimous that, if it were to be done, it should be through adoption and incorporation of the European Convention.) Sir Edward's Bill was opposed on the floor of the House of Commons by Sir Patrick Mayhew, the then Solicitor General, speaking for the Government and by Mr Nicholas Brown, Labour Opposition spokesman on legal affairs. As we noted in Chapter 8, under House of Commons procedural rules if the closure is moved on Private Members' Bills the Bill can only proceed if more than 100 MPs vote in favour of the motion. Sir Edward Gardner was only able to muster 94. His majority of 94 to 16 therefore went for naught. The Government did not mobilise opposition to the Bill but it discouraged support and no member of the Government voted with Sir Edward. On the Labour side only three junior frontbench spokesmen backed him. Even if the magic number of 100 MPs had been achieved, the political signs were clearly therefore that the Government would have found ways to stop the Bill making progress. For the time being at least this is a reform whose time has not yet come.

The UK was the first State to ratify the European Convention on Human Rights in 1951. Since 1965 the UK has allowed individual petitions to be brought against it in Strasbourg and each time this right of individual petition has come up for renewal it has been continued. It is now virtually unthinkable that any British Government would fail to renew the right of individual petition. The argument over whether Britain should have a Bill of Rights is therefore in reality over whether the Bill of Rights should be available as a remedy in the UK courts rather than solely in Strasbourg where the European Commission and Court of Human Rights have their seat.

The difference is not trivial. A remedy available only in Strasbourg is far less accessible in every sense. To have to take legal proceedings in Strasbourg is more costly, involves far greater delays, and above all is psychologically more distant than a remedy that can be sought in any English court. It is true that the right of individual petition has been increasingly used against the British Government, but the procedure is slow and cumbersome. Petititions are first considered by the Commission for admissibility. Only a very small number of cases are held to be admissible — typically around 3 per cent. Most applications fail either because they raise an issue not covered by the Convention, or the complainant has not exhausted the remedies available to him in the country where the act occurred or the complaint is held to be 'manifestly ill-founded'. Many also fail because they have been brought after the expiry of the severe time-limit, which is six months from the incident.

The minority of complaints that are held to be admissible are then substantively considered by the Commission. If it finds that there has been a breach of the Convention, an attempt is made at friendly settlement. If this fails, the matter can go either to the Committee of Ministers of Member States or to the European Court of Human Rights. By 1987 20 cases against the UK had reached the Court — of which the Government had won 13 and lost 7. (The Government lost nine of the first ten cases. But recently it has hit something of a winning streak — in the view of some experts because the Court has become notably more conservative.) The remedy in Strasbourg is certainly therefore used. But if a remedy under the Convention could be sought in the UK courts it would be used a good deal more. For one thing, the processes in the Strasbourg machinery are so much longer. A case in Strasbourg from start to finish takes many years — five or six is quite normal. The English litigation process would normally be much speedier.

To permit an action to be brought in the UK courts would also sometimes avoid the embarrassment of 'washing dirty linen' abroad. The Home Office, which has tended to be the defendant department in a high proportion of the actions brought against Britain, is said to be increasingly conscious of the unfortunate effect on this country's international reputation resulting from these well-publicised proceedings. The effect is compounded by the fact that the number of actions brought against Britain is relatively high. In fact the UK leads the other twenty members of the Council of Europe in the number of complaints laid against it in Strasbourg* and in the number of occasions on

---

* In 1982, there were 190 applications concerning the UK; the next largest number was in respect of West Germany (98) and France (93). In 1983 the comparable figures for the three countries were 152, 93 and 45; and 1984, 128, 115 and 59.

which the European Court of Human Rights has judged it guilty of a breach of the Convention. This is sometimes interpreted as evidence of the fact that human rights are less well protected in Britain than in the other member states, but it is much more likely to be the result rather of the fact that alone amongst European member countries the UK has no Bill of Rights under which such complaints can be brought before the internal courts. (It may also have something to do with the fact that Britain has the liveliest, most inventive and most effective civil liberties lawyers and civil liberties organisations, such as the National Council for Civil Liberties, MIND, and JUSTICE, of any country in Europe.)

However that may be, incorporation of the Convention into UK law would make it possible for complaints that are now brought to Strasbourg to be ventilated first in Britain's own courts. Unless Britain were then to withdraw from the European system, Strasbourg would remain as long-stop, available to a complainant who was dissatisfied with the result obtained in the courts in this country. But the complainant who *won* in the internal courts could not find himself in Strasbourg, since the Government has no right of appeal. The right of individual petition is not available to governments.

The argument therefore is not really whether we should have a Bill of Rights. The European Convention *is* a Bill of Rights. The question rather is whether the Bill of Rights should be available for use in the UK courts. At one level this seems like a relatively minor matter which turns on the difference in the cost and the delays of cases brought in Strasbourg against the comparable cost and delays if such complaints could be brought internally. But the issue in fact goes much deeper. Those who oppose incorporation of the European Convention do so not because they doubt that proceedings brought in England are likely to be quicker and cheaper than those brought in Strasbourg but because they fear the impact that an incorporated Convention would have on our system. The argument in other words is between those who want a Bill of Rights and those who do not — on the merits. The fact that we already have one in the form of the Convention in Strasbourg is regarded by both sides as marginal.

The chief argument in favour of a Bill of Rights is that it gives significant additional power to the citizen who believes that he has a grievance against the state, or any of its manifestations. He can bring an action in the courts and require the state to respond. If it does not do so effectively, so as to persuade the court, the citizen wins his case. Normally, even in the most liberal and responsive democracy, the government can choose to ignore the citizen with a grievance. But if he comes armed with a writ, he cannot be ignored. Even if in the end the government wins the case, the citizen has at least had his day in court and the satisfaction of forcing the government to explain and justify itself. Sometimes, having lost at first instance he may win on appeal. Even if he loses on appeal, he may have attracted sufficient public and political support to persuade the government to change its mind.

Without a Bill of Rights the citizen with a grievance is limited to the range of means available to protest about injustice — letters to the editor, complaint to one's MP or the Ombudsman, stirring up a group of like-minded citizens to campaign publicly for redress of the grievance and, possibly, an action in the courts based on the existing law. The difference made by a Bill of Rights is that it is not restricted by the precise state of the existing law. By presenting one's legal action as a breach of the Bill of Rights one can jump clear of the shortcomings and limitations of the present laws. The whole of the existing law is therefore in theory capable of review against the standard set by the Bill of Rights. If the present law provides a remedy for the grievance there is no need for the Bill of Rights. But if it does not, only a Bill of Rights or a change in the law can deal with the problem.

The phraseology of a Bill of Rights is broad and open-textured. So the European Convention provides protection against 'torture or inhuman or degrading treatment or punishment', and 'slavery or servitude'; it guarantees 'the right to liberty and security of the person', 'a fair and public hearing' of criminal charges, 'the right to respect for [a person's] private and family life, his home and correspondence', 'the right to freedom of thought, conscience and religion', 'the right to freedom of expression', 'the right to freedom of peaceful assembly and to freedom of association with others'. These phrases are vague and capable of a wide variety of interpretations. They are therefore open to the very reasonable objection that they will create uncertainty in that no-one can know in advance precisely how the courts will interpret them. But the other side of the same coin is that they can be used by the citizen with a grievance as a peg on which to hang the hat of his argument. So Mr Sidney Golder in Parkhurst gaol could argue that his 'right of correspondence' had been infringed when under the Prison Rules he was denied permission to consult a solicitor to see whether he had been defamed by a prison officer who accused him of taking part in a prison riot. East African Asians being 'shuttlecocked' from Britain to Belgium to prevent them coming to this country during the Idi Amin era argued that this infringed their right to 'family life'. The *Sunday Times* contended that the injunction granted to the Attorney General to stop its proposed articles accusing the Distillers Company of negligence in the thalidomide drug catastrophe was a breach of its right to 'freedom of expression'. If the broad phrase in the Bill of Rights can arguably describe the event that has occurred, the matter can be raised in the court even if the event is legitimate under the rest of the law. It is then the task of the judges to decide whether what has occurred is within the scope of the Bill of Rights or not.

In determining this issue under the text of the European Convention the courts would have to take account not simply of the broad phrases bestowing rights but of the qualifying phrases which limit virtually all the rights under the Convention. Thus, in Article 8, the right to 'private and family life, home and correspondence' is stated to be subject to the qualification that there shall be no interference with the exercise of this right

> except such as is in accordance with the law and is necessary in a democratic society in the interests of national security, public safety or the economic well-being of the country, for the prevention of disorder or crime, for the protection of health or morals, or for the protection of the rights and freedom of others.

In the view of some, the qualifying phrases emasculate the broad rights given in the opening sentence of Article 8. But this is to miss the purpose of the balance achieved by the draftsmen. The judges are invited to determine on a case-by-case basis on which side of the line a particular act or omission falls. Granted that there has been an infringement by some public authority of the right to 'private and family life, home and correspondence', can it nevertheless be justified on one of the grounds allowed as exceptions? The burden of proof lies on the government, not the citizen — a vital point since cases are often determined by the burden of proof. Moreover, the standard of proof is a high one. The government must be able to show that the exception was 'necessary'. To show that it is desirable or convenient is not enough. So the British Government lost the *Golder* case because it could not persuade the Strasbourg Court that the Prison Rule requiring consent for a prisoner to consult a solicitor was necessary for the prevention of disorder or crime. The Court held unanimously that the Rule was not necessary in a democratic society.

The vice of the open-textured phrases in a Bill of Rights therefore is the vagueness of the language and the fact that it can accordingly be used in unpredictable ways by lawyers to challenge and by judges to upset the *status quo*. The corresponding virtue is that the broad phrases can be used to address whatever may happen to be the felt grievance of the day. Since the grievances of each generation are to some extent different, it is an advantage that the scope and meaning of the Bill of Rights is flexible and thereby always capable of dealing with new circumstances as they arise.

But is it acceptable that decisions on such matters should be left to judges who in Britain, as in most countries, are appointed and are therefore unaccountable? *The Times* of 12 December 1986, in a long editorial on the problem, stated that incorporation of the Convention would bring the judges 'dangerously close to having to make decisions about what are essentially policy matters more properly in the hands of the executive'. It was true, *The Times* admitted, that the top echelons of the judges sitting as judges in the Judicial Committee of the Privy Council were constantly interpreting the written constitutions of Commonwealth countries with no apparent difficulty. Also the expansion in recent years of administrative law had obliged the judges more generally to come to terms with decisions that had political policy consequences. But a Bill of Rights would greatly expand this.

> The need to interpret the vague abstract rights embodied in it would compel judges to venture more frequently into politically dangerous territory without giving them the concrete guidance of traditional jurisprudence.

Already complaints were occasionally heard from the Left about the supposed political partiality of the judiciary. These could at present be easily dismissed. The fact that over the past few years the law had not suited the trade unions and the Left, had to do with Parliament and the electorate, not with the judiciary.

> But such complaints would have greater apparent reasonableness on both left and right, if a Bill of Rights were to enable and even compel judges to deliver judgments which could not easily be distinguished from legislative or executive decisions on a wide range of matters.

The same point was made in the 1986 Reith Lectures by the

Scottish judge, Lord McCluskey. If the application of the law be uncertain, he argued, if policy choices have to be made, the judges will inevitably and correctly be accused of making choices upon grounds other than purely legal ones 'And the courts will be dragged into politics'. Everyone agreed, he suggested, that the judges should stay out of politics. The reasons included the fact that 'judges, by reason of age, sex and background might find it difficult to appear impartial and could never hope to be representative and accountable'. That was true not simply of fields such as industrial relations but of religious and moral questions like abortion, contraception and the right to die, and socio-political questions like positive discrimination or the balance between civil rights and the investigative powers of the police. It was inevitable that such issues should come before the courts since access to the courts was a fundamental aspect of the rule of law, but 'the method of adjudication ought as far as possible to be the relatively mechanical process of applying a precise set of unambiguous rules to the facts, not a wide-ranging philosophical exercise in making policy choices'. The greater the latitude allowed to the judge, the greater was 'the risk of appearing arbitrary, capricious and biased'.

Where the law was ambiguous the judge did, of course, exercise an effective choice which he often tried to conceal by pretending that the decision had been compelled by the precedents — claiming that he had simply been the midwife rather than the parent. But this was different in degree and therefore in kind from the policy choices that judges had to make when interpreting a Bill of Rights, which Lord McCluskey described as 'a charter of super-rights, rights written in delphic words but in indelible ink on an opaque surface'. It turned judges into legislators and gave them a finality which our whole tradition had previously denied them. It asked those whose task and skill was to apply the law to become the law-makers. It required those 'whose skill it is to know what the law is, to decide what the law should be'.[4]

The Supreme Court of the United States, Lord McCluskey suggested, was a dignified cauldron in which the essentially political questions of race, civil liberties, economic regulation, abortion, contraception, freedom of expression, pornography, capital punishment and the powers of the President had been debated by lawyers and decided by lawyers. As Daniel Boorstin had said in 1955, 'The Supreme Court has become the American political conscience, a kind of secular papacy. . . . All the crises in our political history have sooner or later been stated in legal terms.' The walls between the political and the judicial systems had, in Lord McCluskey's phrase, become 'paper thin'. He did not wish to see English judges thrown into the business of fashioning rights and duties for citizens from the interplay of their subjective notions of social justice and the words of a text that accorded them a wide freedom of choice.

These arguments represent a powerful strain of opinion. They are probably shared by most English judges, lawyers and politicians. There are three main lines of response to the concern about the proper rule of courts and legislatures. First, even under the American Constitution (which seems always to be used for the purposes of comparison in this context), the Supreme Court does not necessarily have the last word. The States can if they wish overrule the Court by a constitutional amendment, though this is admittedly a cumbersome and rarely-used procedure which requires a three-quarters majority of all the States. But under the very different British constitution there would be no possibility even of that degree of entrenchment of a Bill of Rights. Under English constitutional law no parliament can bind its successors. Even if therefore the Bill of Rights Act required that any amendment or repeal of the Bill of Rights must be carried by, say, a two-thirds or three-quarters majority in both Houses of Parliament, the courts would not recognise such a requirement. A subsequent parliament would be able to amend or even repeal the Bill of Rights by a bare majority of one.

Experts seem agreed that the highest form of entrenchment achievable in the British system would be a doctrine that any repeal or amendment of the Bill of Rights must be conscious and express. So, if the courts declared a pre-Bill of Rights statute to be contrary to the provisions of the Bill of Rights, Parliament could amend the Bill of Rights by the simple expedient of passing a fresh act explicitly confirming the earlier act. This would leave the ultimate power to decide on policy matters where it should be — with the legislature. No doubt governments would be slow to amend the Bill of Rights for fear of the political odium that such an action would be likely to attract. But it is difficult to see how this limited measure of 'political entrenchment' could be offensive to those who worry that policy matters should be determined by legislatures rather than by courts. If the particular issue is sufficiently important for the legislature to cancel the decision of the courts, then it will be able to do so; if the legislature is reluctant to intervene, this, by definition, is because the politicians are content to leave the matter as it was decided by the judges. Either way, the democratic process is served.

The second point is that the judges have in reality always played a much larger role in deciding issues with a political and policy content than is generally admitted. As has already been seen, the policy role of the judges arises both in statutory interpretation and when developing the law through the operation of the doctrine of precedent. When litigants come to the courts with a disputed issue of law there is usually a real doubt about the outcome — which means that normally the judges have a genuine choice. The old view that judges do not make law, they simply declare or find or apply it, is completely discredited. Even conservative members of the legal fraternity admit that judges do make law on a considerable scale. Equally it is clear that sentencing policy, a matter of the greatest importance, has always been largely developed by the judges. Certainly, a Bill of Rights would significantly expand the scope for judicial law-making and certainly there is less guidance in the wide words of the Bill of Rights than is normally to be found in English statutes. But the difference is only one of degree.

Thirdly, if American experience is any guide, the great majority of cases coming before the courts under the Bill of Rights raise issues that are perfectly suitable for courts of law and that may indeed often be more appropriate for courts than for legislatures. A catalogue of cases that have occurred in the US shows few that raise the spectre of the courts trespassing in fields that British politicians would regard as peculiarly their domain. Cases on freedom of speech have raised issues such as the Administration's attempt to stop publication of the Pentagon Papers; the legality of a city ordinance barring armbands protesting about the Vietnam war; the right to have a pornography collection in one's private home; the lawfulness of removing 'distasteful' books from a public library; the right of the police to ban a march of American Nazis in a public park; the right to ban an anti-Vietnam war speaker at a university; the right of a State to compel students to salute the flag. Cases on freedom of religion have included decisions on the lawfulness of convictions of Jehovah's Witnesses for soliciting religious contributions without a state certificate or on the right of a State to require members of the Amish sect to comply with compulsory education laws.

Privacy issues determined by the courts include the constitutionality of abortion laws, the lawfulness of a law making the use of contraceptives by married persons illegal; whether a State could compel parents of an injured child to continue life-support systems; or the legality of a statute providing for sterilisation of persons convicted two or three times of offences of 'moral turpitude'. Cases on the right to travel included one on the right of a State to prevent poor persons from entering the State, another on the right of a State to make welfare payments dependent on a one-year residence requirement and a third on the right of the State Department to refuse to issue a passport to a Communist. There have been large numbers of decisions on the unlawfulness of rules, laws and practices which discriminate between black and white in the fields of voting, public facilities such as bars, restaurants and theatres and, above all, in education. Conditions in a variety of prisons have been held to violate the guarantee against cruel and unusual punishment.[5]

In the great majority of such cases a court is at least as sensible and competent an authority as the legislature. In some, it is plainly much more so. One can hardly expect a legislature to deal effectively with questions such as where demonstrators should be allowed to march, or what books should be available in a public library, or whether a Communist should have a passport. These are eminently the kind of issues that should be left to the appropriate public officials, subject to control by the courts. Far from there being anything objectionable in leaving the courts to regulate decision-making in such matters, it is objectionable if there is no way in which a legal challenge can be mounted where it appears that a decision was grounded on an improper invasion of a fundamental freedom.

Other things being equal, it may usually be preferable in a democracy for policy in the development of the law to be settled by the legislature as opposed to the courts. But frequently other things are not equal. Sometimes the legislature is unwilling to act; the failure of both Federal and State legislatures in the post-Second World War era to move to alleviate the plight of blacks in the United States meant that, until the courts were prepared to respond to the campaigns of the black organisations such as the NAACP, there was no succour available. Who can say that the pent-up feelings of the black minority might not otherwise in the end have spilled over into serious and sustained violence? The prisoners' rights cases were another instance of litigation which was a response to executive and legislative neglect. There are no votes in helping prisoners. To wait for the legislature to act to remedy injustices imposed on prisoners may be to wait indefinitely. In such a situation the legislative option is not in practice available. There are other situations where the legislature will not act because the matter is too minor or too low-level to warrant the sledge-hammer of a statute. A great many of the actions that are brought under the American Bill of Rights are of this character.

A Bill of Rights gives the citizen with a grievance an alternative means of attempting to get a remedy. If he can persuade the government of the day to legislate on the problem, that will often be more satisfactory. A statute can deal with an issue both in greater detail and more broadly than can a court. But sometimes the court route is the better, or possibly even the only one. History suggests that neither courts nor legislatures are the more likely to have a greater quotient of civil libertarian instincts. In some places at some times, or in regard to some issues, the solution preferred by civil libertarians will be available from parliament or the executive rather than from the judges. On other issues, or at different times and places, it will be the judges rather than the legislature who will reflect the purer civil libertarianism. A Bill of Rights is neither an open Sesame nor a Pandora's Box. It is simply an additional or alternative method for handling problems in society.

A MINISTRY OF JUSTICE?

A different kind of structural question is whether there is a case for establishing a Ministry of Justice. This is a question which has been raised from time to time for decades. The modern debate started with the Haldane Committee in 1918 which proposed that a Ministry of Justice should be established with a Minister who would perform the functions of the Home Secretary and those of the Lord Chancellor in connection with legal administration, leaving the Lord Chancellor free to devote himself to judicial work and the appointment of judges and to act as legal adviser to the Government[6]. But these proposals made no progress then and the issue has been debated in a desultory fashion ever since.

The most recent contribution to the debate was the strongly argued paper issued in 1986 by the Alliance parties ('Government, Law and Justice: The Case for a Ministry of Justice'). The chief problem identified by the Alliance paper is the bureaucratic muddle of the existing arrangements — explicable, if at all, only by the curious meanderings of historical development. At present the responsibility for the different functions of government in the justice field are divided in a chaotic manner between the Lord Chancellor, the Home Office, the Attorney

General's Department and miscellaneous other government departments. Thus the Lord Chancellor is responsible for the state of the civil law and civil procedure, whilst the Home Secretary is responsible for the criminal law and criminal procedure. The Lord Chancellor has both civil and criminal legal aid and the administration of the courts, including the appointment of the judges and magistrates — except that the Home Secretary is responsible for the magistrates' courts. The Home Secretary is also responsible for the enforcement by statutory bodies of parts of the civil law protecting individual rights such as the sex and race equality legislation. The enforcement of other parts is divided among the Lord Chancellor, the Attorney General and yet other departments.

The Department of Employment enforces health, safety and other employment law; the Department of Trade and Industry enforces commercial and consumer protection law; the Department of the Environment enforces housing law; the Foreign and Commonwealth Office is responsible for international law; and the Cabinet Office for European Community law. Tribunals come under the Lord Chancellor, who also has general responsibility for legal services. Law centres at present are funded variously by the Lord Chancellor's Department, the Department of the Environment and local authorities. No government department has actual responsibility for maintaining their financial viability nor for their general supervision or oversight. Government Bills are drafted in the Office of Parliamentary Counsel, whilst subordinate legislation is mainly drafted by the legal staffs of government departments. Parliamentary Counsel are nominally responsible to the Prime Minister but in practice they are not accountable to anyone. There is a standing Cabinet Committee on Legislation which is responsible in theory for ensuring that draft bills are fit to be presented to Parliament. But the Committee is not equipped to scrutinise the quality of the drafting of legislation nor to ensure that bills comply with the UK's obligations under treaties such as the European Convention on Human Rights. As the Alliance paper said, 'The present unintelligible and inconsistent state of our statute book is a living monument to our present system's defects in the preparation of legislation as well as to serious shortcomings in Parliamentary procedure'.

There are three government law officers: the Lord Chancellor, the Attorney General and the Solicitor General. The Lord Chancellor sits in the Cabinet and in that capacity sometimes finds himself advising the Government on legal matters, even though that is not his task and his department has no resources for the job. The job of advising the Government on legal matters falls upon the Attorney General, who is not in the Cabinet and who as a result is often in practice not asked for his view even when the matter has important constitutional or legal implications. Conduct of government litigation is the responsibility of the Treasury Solicitor, who reports not to a law officer but, oddly, to the Chancellor of the Exchequer.

In Scotland this state of confusion is matched with responsibilities for legal affairs split between the Secretary of State for Scotland and the Lord Advocate. The Lord Advocate is responsible for the prosecution of crime. He is also chief legal adviser to the Government on Scottish matters. His staff draft Scottish legislation and any parts of UK legislation that affect Scotland. He also has a variety of functions relating to the jurisdiction and procedure of civil courts, the enforcement of judgments, and procedure in inquiries and tribunals. The Secretary of State for Scotland, for his part, has responsibility for criminal justice policy and civil law, other than those parts over which the Lord Advocate is in charge. He is responsible also for the administration of courts and for recommending to the Queen appointments to the Supreme Court and the sheriff's benches.

The Alliance paper characterised these arrangements as 'archaic, incoherent and fragmentary distribution of functions'. Nor can it be said to be one of those British muddles which nevertheless works tolerably well. Anyone with inside knowledge of the affairs of government would confirm the low priority given to law reform, legal services, the quality of the statute book and legal affairs generally.

The chief author of the SDP paper, Mr Anthony Lester QC, who had been Special Adviser to Home Secretary Roy Jenkins, had argued it out more fully in the *New Law Journal* in 1984.[7] The main problem, he thought, was the inherent departmental conflict of interest. Many 'Justice' functions lay with the Home Office — the department that was also responsible for the security of the realm, immigration control, the prisons, and the police. Those 'Ministry of the Interior' functions inevitably sat uneasily with responsibility for impartial justice, the rule of law, the freedom of the individual and the rights of minorities. It was not the fault of the Home Office that it suffered from institutional schizophrenia. The protection of human rights was a residual function for the Home Office. It would be naive to expect it to count for as much in its thinking as mainline responsibilities for combating terrorism and crime, running prisons and controlling immigration. So, if the Home Office were asked to devise effective safeguards against the misuse of personal information stored in computers, it would instinctively fight to exclude its own computers and those of related departments from the proposed controls. The same was true of official secrecy and access to official information or of judicial control over police malpractice. It was natural for the Home Office to be against legal redress for citizens against the state under the European Convention on Human Rights or under English law. It was natural that officials should prefer that they, rather than judges, should decide where state power ended and personal freedom began. In France it would be inconceivable for the Ministry of the Interior to have so many of the functions which belonged to the Ministry of Justice.

The Home Office continued to be given responsibility for sex and race discrimination, even though it had no expertise in civil law and no relevant administrators in the cities where equal opportunity policies had to be put into effect. Important subjects such as privacy, with both civil and criminal law aspects, fell into the gap between the Home Office and the Lord Chancellor's Department.

The Lord Chancellor's Department (LCD) for its part now employed 10,000 civil servants but neither the LCD nor the Law Officers' Department were subject to the scrutiny of the Commons Select Committee on Home Affairs. They had successfully avoided parliamentary scrutiny with the argument that such scrutiny would threaten the independence of the judiciary. The absence of a strong and coherent Justice Department also damaged the interests of the oppressed, the victims of injustice, and of social inequality. There was no coherent policy on law centres. Proposals for the reform of administrative law were stifled at birth. The public authorities charged with the enforcement of anti-discrimination legislation were denied adequate legal services and administrative support.

The present state of the statute book, Mr Lester suggested, was an ugly monument to the defects of our system. It would not be improved so long as Parliamentary Counsel continued to work not under a Minister of Justice but in unsplendid isolation. He had painful memories of his time in Whitehall when the Home Secretary had tried to make the drafting of a particular bill fit for ordinary human use. Neither the Home Secretary nor the Attorney General had been able to change the drafting. Parliamentary Counsel were accountable only to the Prime Minister, which was the same as saying that they were accountable only to themselves.

Few able lawyers, according to Mr Lester, aspired to become law officers because they knew they would not be centrally involved in government policy. (Would Sir Geoffrey Howe have declined to become Minister of Justice?) Neither the Lord Chancellor nor the law officers were responsible for the conduct of government litigation. In the absence of a Justice Minister, no-one had 'sufficient resources, energy, or political weight to promote constitutional, institutional and substantive legal reforms'.

The Alliance paper proposed a strong and independent Department of Justice and an equivalent Department of Legal Affairs in Scotland. Both would be responsible to Parliament for the coherent and efficient performance of the functions regarding the 'state of the law', 'justice' and 'legal services'. The Department should have two of the traditional law officers: the Lord Chancellor and probably the Solicitor General. On the state of the law it would have charge of constitutional, administrative, civil and criminal law as well as compliance with international and European Community law. It would be responsible for all law reform matters, including the Law Commission, for the procedure and administration of all courts and tribunals, for the Director of Public Prosecutions and the prosecution services generally,* for the administration of civil and criminal legal aid and for relations with the legal profession.

Under this scheme legal services to government would be provided by a separate department which would provide advice to government, would conduct government litigation and would draft both primary and subordinate legislation.

One of the most intriguing proposals in the paper is that the Lord Chancellor should be able to sit in either House of Parliament — though it was suggested that preferably he should sit in the Commons. If so, it would be necessary to relieve him of his present functions of presiding in the House of Lords, sitting as a law lord and dispensing ecclesiastical patronage. The Lord Chancellor would continue to be a member of the Cabinet, and there would be a House of Commons Select Committee on the Administration of Justice to monitor the work of the new Ministry.

The only major function not allocated by this scheme was the appointment of judges. The selection of judges, the paper

---

* The paper was written before the establishment of the new Crown Prosecution Service. If the office of Attorney General survived the establishment of a Ministry of Justice, it would seem preferable that the Attorney General should retain responsibility for the CPS.

suggested, should not be in the hands of the Minister of Justice. Instead, it might be given to a statutory Judicial Services Commission chaired by a senior judge, along the lines of those that exist in several Commonwealth countries. The Commission would advise the Lord Chancellor and the Prime Minister on the appointment of the most senior judges and would itself appoint the circuit judges, stipendiary magistrates, justices of the peace, legally qualified chairmen of tribunals and Queen's Counsel. It would also be responsible for the tenure and terms and conditions of service of the entire judiciary.

This plan for the appointment of judges does not seem entirely convincing, not least because the task of appointing so many judicial personnel would be a hugely time-consuming function which would leave members of the Commission little time for their normal duties. Nor does it seem right to remove from Ministers the terms and conditions of services of the judiciary. On the other hand, it does seem desirable that the Minister of Justice should sit in the House of Commons. The best compromise might be to make the Attorney General the Minister of Justice in the Commons with a seat in the Cabinet, and to have the Lord Chancellor in the House of Lords with the principal function of appointment and control of the judiciary, possibly advised by a broadly based Judicial Commission. The role of chief legal adviser to the Government could then be played by the Solicitor General who would be in charge of advice to government departments generally, as well as government litigation. There would be no need for the Lord Chancellor to sit in the Cabinet.

The case for a Ministry of Justice turns on grounds of both efficiency and accountability. The two are of course interrelated. Accountability should have the effect of improving efficiency — and even if it does not, it at least makes it possible to require the Minister responsible to face the issue. But if a House of Commons Minister were answerable for, say, court delays, the cost of the legal system, the way that statutes are drafted, the distribution of legal services through the community, or the progress of law reform, it would increase the scope for parliamentary scrutiny and thereby would probably improve the quality of the system.

A SOLUTION TO PRISON OVERCROWDING?

The problem of what to do about prison overcrowding has in recent years come to the top of the political agenda as the issue seems increasingly both intractable and grave. The crisis in the prisons has been a running sore for more than two decades and has been officially recognised in speeches by successive Home Office Ministers, Reports from Committees of the House of Commons, warnings in the annual report of HM Chief Inspector of Prisons and guidance to the courts from the Lord Chief Justice — not to speak of countless contributions from unofficial bodies such as the Howard League for Penal Reform, NACRO, or the Prison Reform Trust.

It was in 1975 that Mr Roy Jenkins, the then Home Secretary, made his often quoted statement: 'The prison population now stands at 40,500. If it should rise to, say, 42,000 conditions in the system would approach the intolerable and drastic action to relieve the position would be inescapable.' The intolerable figure of 42,000 was reached the following year and since then it has continued to rise inexorably. In June 1987 the number in prison finally reached 50,000 and by July 1987 it had risen a further one thousand.

The amount of prison accommodation has also been rising somewhat, but the numbers in prison have for years been consistently above the level of certified accommodation. If one takes the prison system as a whole the average excess of prisoners above places available runs at about 20 per cent — there are 120 prisoners for 100 places. But in local prisons such as Leicester, Reading, Birmingham, Oxford and Leeds, where overcrowding is worst, the excess runs as high as 80 to 100 per cent. The Home Office has a substantial prison building programme currently in progress. This is supposed to produce over 13,000 places by the early 1990s and Mr Leon Brittan as Home Secretary claimed in 1983 that this would end prison overcrowding by the end of the decade. But the claim is certainly false. The Comptroller and Auditor General in a report in 1985 stated that 'the building programme will not succeed in meeting their [the Home Office's] target objective of matching total available places with aggregate prison population by the end of the decade'.[8] In fact by early 1987 even Home Office projections allowed that the overcrowding would continue well into the 1990s. Official figures suggested that the shortfall in 1995 could be in the order of 5,000 — which means that in reality it will almost certainly be much worse. Sir Brian Cubbon, Permanent Secretary, told the Public Accounts Committee in 1986 that by 1991 over ten thousand prisoners, and possibly up to twenty thousand, would still be in cells with no toilet facilities other than a chamber pot.

Reduction in the size of the prison population has been official policy of every government for many years, and a great many techniques have been unsuccessfully deployed to try to bring it about. Apart from exhortation from Ministers, they include various forms of statutory intervention — such as the introduction of suspended and partly suspended sentences (1967 and 1977) or community service orders (1972), alterations in the rules regarding parole (1983), or rules restricting those who may be sent to prison and laying down certain preconditions before a person may be sent to prison. But neither singly nor cumulatively have they had any overall impact in achieving a switch from custodial to non-custodial penalties. Parole, which was started in 1968, has enabled the executive to release significant numbers of prisoners who had served two-thirds of their sentence. But it has not proved possible to expand the scope of the parole scheme significantly. In May 1981 the Home Office published *A Review of Parole in England and Wales* in which it was argued that prisoners who had served one-third of their sentence might be released to serve the middle third of their sentence under supervision of the probation service. But this proposal was vetoed first by the judges and then by the Conservative Party Conference in October 1981, and the then Home Secretary, Mr William Whitelaw, withdrew the idea.

The Lord Chief Justice too has played a part, notably in decisions such as those in the case of *R.* v. *Bibi* in July 1980, in which the Court of Appeal held that sentences should be as short as possible. The Lord Chief Justice said:

It is no secret that our prisons are at the moment dangerously overcrowded. So much so that sentencing courts must be particularly careful to examine each case to ensure, if an immediate custodial sentence is necessary, that the sentence is as short as possible, consistent only with the duty to protect the interests of the public and to punish and deter the criminal.

A sentence of six or nine months, the Court said, could often be just as effective as eighteen months or three years. (On the other hand, the sentencing guidelines on rape cases in the case of *Billam* in February 1986 went the other way — Lord Lane held that sentences for that offence were too low.) The lead given in *Bibi* does not appear to have had any measurable impact, however. In spite of all the propaganda and exhortation, the English courts still send a higher proportion of defendants to prison than almost any other country in Europe.*

Efforts have been made over the years to reduce the numbers of prisoners held on remand prior to conviction or sentence, and fine defaulters and other categories such as the mentally ill, the homeless and the drunks. Prostitutes cannot any longer be sent to prison for soliciting, though they do find their way to prison for non-payment of fines. Since 1982 vagrants cannot be imprisoned for sleeping rough or begging. But the net result of all these efforts is again inconsequential.

The prison overcrowding crisis is not simply one affecting the morale and well-being of prisoners and prison staff. It has increasingly spilled over into demonstrations and violence. The worst to date were the events of 30 April 1979, when prisoners in eighteen prisons caused damage costing over £4 million in response to a prison officers' overtime ban. But there have been a number of disturbances of varying degrees of gravity at Albany, Dartmoor, Gartree, Hull and Wormwood Scrubs. Clearly, the danger of violent disturbances is now an ever present possibility.

The seriousness of the situation is fully appreciated by the Government but so far at least no solution to the problem has been found. In spite of everything that has been tried the prison population goes on rising. There is no shortage of current ideas as to what should be done. Thus on 24 April 1987 the Home Secretary, Mr Douglas Hurd, speaking in Oxfordshire, outlined a five-point plan to ease the crisis in crowded prisons. Full use must be made of all spare space — for instance, by repairing disused buildings. The present building programme must continue as fast as possible. Judges must recognise alternatives to custody for petty criminals. Remand prisoners awaiting trial must be dealt with more quickly, and finally the prison service must be reformed to increase prison officers' efficiency and flexibility.

All of these are no doubt worthy objectives and, if they were achieved, they might make some contribution to improve the situation. But the prospects of their being made to work at all are slim and, even if they worked, the impact they would be likely to have is negligible. The judges have been urged and exhorted to consider alternatives to custody for over a decade,

---

* A league table of imprisonment rates for the 12 EEC countries as at 1 September 1986 showed the UK at the top with 95.3 prisoners per 100,000 population, followed by Luxemburg (88.5) and West Germany (87.9). Greece had a figure of 38.8 and Holland was bottom with 34 per 100,000.

yet they have sent even higher proportions of defendants to prison. Between the 1950s and 1974 the proportionate use of imprisonment in this country fell. But since 1974 — when the crisis in the prisons was progressively getting worse — the use of prison as a sentence by the courts has risen. (In 1974 15 per cent of males over the age of 17 sentenced for indictable offences were given immediate custodial penalties. By 1978 it was 17 per cent; in 1982 it was 19 per cent, and in 1984, 20 per cent.) If more space were created in the prison system the likelihood is that the courts would react by sending even more defendants to prison. The present building programme is the largest this century. According to the National Association for the Care and Resettlement of Offenders (NACRO) in a Briefing Paper dated 20 August 1987, since early 1985 three new prisons have been built and two new prisons have opened in converted premises. Five new establishments were being built and eight were at various stages of planning. In addition, design was planned to start on two further establishments, making 20 in all. It was anticipated that in the period 1983-95 the programme would expand the capacity in the prison system by over 40 per cent. The cost was over £500,000. The Government hoped that it would greatly ease the overcrowding problem but whether this is so will depend on the reaction of the courts. If they sense a certain easing in the official pressure to avoid custodial penalties and, as a result, send more people to prison, the value of the building programme will be largely cancelled out.

In her recent book *Bricks of Shame*, Miss Vivien Stern, the Director of NACRO, argued for a new approach. A major reduction in the prison population would require first 'a change of heart and a move away from traditional views about what prison is for, what it contributes to protecting the public and reducing crime.' But any policy that requires a change of heart and attitude on the part of decision- and policy-makers is likely to fail — especially if the change of heart has already been urged unsuccessfully for many years. Miss Stern recognises that it will take a long time. She suggests that if there is to be any progress at all, 'machinery needs to be established to make things happen and develop, to find a way through the current log-jams, lack of political will and fear of hostile public or media reactions'.[9]

Again, any plan that depends on altering existing political realities and deeply-held beliefs is likely to fail — especially if it has already been tried. Miss Stern suggested that the way forward was through some new statutory mechanism 'to bring the various parts of the criminal justice process into a working relationship where they have to listen to each other, understand each other's problems and solve problems jointly'. This might be the Sentencing Council proposed by Dr Andrew Ashworth, editor of the *Criminal Law Review* and Oxford academic lawyer, to consider sentencing policy and practice, to commission research to provide systematic knowledge about the reasoning of judges and magistrates and then reformulate policy so that it is no longer excessively reliant on custodial penalties. It would be chaired by the Lord Chief Justice and would include representatives of a wide cross-section of interested groups such as judges, magistrates, the probation service, prison governors, Home Office officials and scholars.

The House of Commons Home Affairs Committee in its 1981 Report produced a similar solution in the form of a National Criminal Policy Committee to allow criminal policy to be planned. It would be at the highest level and would have expert staff. Its function would be 'to construct a comprehensive criminal policy in the light of the most modern administrative knowledge and research'.[10] But given the obstacles, it is difficult to see how the establishment of either Dr Ashworth's Sentencing Council or the Home Affairs Committee's National Criminal Policy Committee would actually have the main desired result of significantly reducing the prison population.

Dr Andrew Rutherford of Southampton University, and Chairman of the Howard League for Penal Reform, in his recent book *Prisons and the Process of Justice* urges a multi-faceted approach to the problem.[11] Thus the physical capacity of the prison system should be substantially reduced rather than increased; there should be a precise statement of minimum standards as to the physical conditions of imprisonment which are legally enforceable; and the optimal prison system staff-prisoner ratio should be determined and implemented. Certain categories of persons sentenced to imprisonment should, if space is not available, wait until called up by the prison system (this operates, for instance, in Holland where at any one time there are some 10,000 people waiting for a place!). Breach or default of non-custodial sanctions should only rarely be dealt with by imprisonment; in the English system fine defaulters represent the most rapidly growing category of prisoners, being one in four sentenced persons. The range of non-imprisonable offences should be broadened to include some categories of minor theft. Even a person who commits his tenth offence of stealing a trivial sum should not be imprisoned. The prosecution system should be used to restrict entry to the criminal justice system through the use of diversion, cautions and other alternatives to prosecution. (The recent indications from the Lord Chief Justice that the prosecution should for the first time play a role in sentence appeals may foreshadow the additional possibility of the Crown Prosecution Service playing a role in sentencing at criminal trials where by tradition it has remained silent. This could be used to attempt to influence the courts to reduce the level of sentences, as occurred in Holland — though in theory it might equally come to be used in the opposite direction to increase sentences.)

Dr Rutherford's stated objective is to achieve a drastic reduction in the size of the prison population — whereas the Home Office prediction for the early 1990s was for over 50,000 prisoners, he would like to see the numbers at the level of around 20,000! The Chief Inspector of Prisons in his 1981 report suggested that the prison system could support in reasonable circumstances a population of some 37,000. Prison governors in 1982 suggested a target of 32,000. Obviously the numbers target adopted is based on the philosophy one has toward the utility of imprisonment as well as the extent of one's sensitivity to the need for humane conditions for prisoners and one's concern about the relationship between the level of overcrowding and the likelihood of prison disturbances. But the fatal weakness of all these proposals made by both official and unofficial bodies and individuals is that they do not address the crucial issue — of what can be done if, as is all too likely, the situation in fact does not improve or actually continues to go from bad to worse. In the past there has been no shortage of seemingly good ideas which either have not been tried or have failed. There is little reason to expect that the future will be very different. In all probability we shall continue to stagger from crisis to crisis.

There is in fact only one concept which can cope with this most probable of all scenarios — early executive release for the sole purpose of reducing the prison population to an acceptable level. This is now done on a regular basis in the Republic of Ireland under the provisions of the Criminal Justice Act 1960, s.2, which gives the Minister the power to make rules providing for the temporary release of anyone serving a term of imprisonment, subject to whatever conditions may be imposed. For some years the power has been used in a significant number of cases consciously and avowedly not only as part of the normal process of acclimatising prisoners to the outside world but simply to clear the prisons. Thus the report of the Prison Service for 1981 stated that 441 prisoners were released for this reason.

In 1982 the number was 1,298 and in 1983, 1,088. Sometimes release is with supervision, sometimes without. The report for 1982 said it was 'to relieve the pressure and to provide places for new committals'. The practice of 'shedding', as it is known, had been 'accepted reluctantly as the lesser of two evils'. In 1983 the annual Report said:

> Until additional accommodation can be provided, the present practice of releasing some prisoners in advance of the normal release date to make way for committals will have to continue.... While early release because of pressure of accommodation is undesirable, it is considered to be preferable to widespread doubling up in cells designed for single occupancy.

In England over 40 per cent of prisoners currently share cells.

The advantage of early executive release is that, unlike all other approaches to the problem, it cannot fail to achieve its purpose of reducing the prison population. It only requires an annual calculation of the acceptable number that can be accommodated in the prison system, a formula for the selection of those who would be released, and, above all, the political will to carry out the policy. Once it had operated for a year or two it would probably come to be accepted as a normal part of the system — as in Ireland. The system there is not used for those serving sentences for armed robbery or serious sex offences, or for anyone regarded as a danger to the community. But there appear to be few other restrictions on use of this executive power.

In England the Home Secretary in fact already has similar powers. They were originally in emergency legislation passed in 1981 to deal with prison officers' industrial action, but the power was not then brought into effect. They are now in the Criminal Justice Act 1982, s.32, which gives the Home Secretary the power to release all but a few specified categories of prisoners up to six months early 'in order to make the best use of the places available for detention'. It was envisaged as a power to be used only in cases of exceptional emergencies such as the prison officers' dispute. What is proposed here is that it should be used instead as the normal 'regulator' to keep the prison population down.

The power has not been used at all yet, but the Home Office came close to using it in Spring 1987. *The Guardian* of 12 March 1987 carried an exclusive front-page lead story by Aileen Ballantyne that the Government had drawn up emergency

proposals to release up to 6,000 non-violent prisoners under the
1982 powers. Those most likely to benefit, it was said, were
prisoners serving sentences for burglary, shoplifting, forgery
and handling stolen goods. The Home Secretary, Mr Douglas
Hurd, and the Minister responsible for the prisons, Lord
Caithness, were due to meet the director-general of the prison
service, Mr Chris Train, that afternoon to determine the details.
Miss Ballantyne's story was true and the meeting in fact took
place — but the adverse reaction to the story, especially from
the Prime Minister herself, was sufficiently strong for them to
decide instead to drop the idea and to deny that it had been in
contemplation. A year earlier, the previous Minister responsible
for prisons, Lord Glenarthur, had told the annual conference of
Boards of Prison Visitors that even if the prison population rose
above the former record figure of 48,000 there was no question of
the Government using its executive powers of release under the
1982 Act.

> We are not prepared to impose arbitrary cuts on the prison
> population. . . . We are determined to provide the prison places
> necessary to accommodate all those whom the courts decide
> must be committed to custody. This is a central plank of our
> criminal justice policy.

Mr Hurd decided that he could not after all depart from the
traditional policy that all comers must be accommodated and
that there is no such thing as House Full in the prisons.

However, in July 1987 the situation had become so desperate
that Mr Hurd changed his mind. He told the House of Commons
on 16 July that the previous Friday the prison population stood
at 51,029, nearly 4,000 more than a year before and more than
9,300 above the certified normal accommodation. The main
reason for the increase seemed to be the growing numbers being
dealt with in the crown court and an increase in the average
length of sentences. Also the remand population had gone up by
a further 1,000 in the previous year to more than 11,000. There
were 5,000 prisoners crammed three to a cell and a further
14,000 were doubled up. In recent months, he said, the rise in
the prison population had outstripped the supply of new places
and the gap between supply and demand looked set to widen.

The Home Secretary said that he had considered but rejected
using executive release to ease the pressure on the prison
population. Rather he intended to increase the amount of
remission for good conduct for those serving sentences of up to
and including 12 months from one third to one half. This would

result in the release of some 2,500 prisoners. It was an interim measure applying only to less serious offenders. They would include some who were serving sentences for violence but the offences in question would be of the pub fight or street brawl variety.

The extent to which this is a political hot potato was shown by the reception his announcement received. The news was warmly welcomed on behalf of the Opposition by the new Shadow Home Secretary, Mr Roy Hattersley, but it was widely denounced by the Government's own backbenchers including, surprisingly, Mr Hurd's immediate predecessor Mr Leon Brittan, who said that it was 'wrong in principle and quite contrary to the rule of law and everything that we stand for, for convicted criminals to be released prematurely on whatever procedural means, not on the basis of individual consideration of their cases nor because of the application of some new or more liberal penalty, but simply because there is no room to house them'. If someone as liberal as Leon Brittan was prepared to criticise the initiative strongly, it means that it will not be easy to get the great mass of either the Tory Party or the general public to accept the basic concept of releasing prisoners to make room in the prisons. Given this, it is particularly unfortunate that the Home Secretary did not go directly to executive release as the device to achieve his objective. If there was going to be a row anyway, Mr Hurd might at least have obtained maximum advantage from it. Instead, he settled for an unsatisfactory half-way house.

Extra remission is only really relevant to those serving under 12 months, since those who are serving longer sentences can already be released early on parole. So far as the category of those serving under 12 months is concerned, it will probably prove to be merely a temporary palliative. Unless something remarkable turns up therefore, the concept of executive release will sooner or later still have to be considered. Obviously the concept is an unwelcome one. But refusal to accept it means that the government of the day will always be at the mercy of what the courts do.

The increase in the prison population in 1987 was startling. The numbers in prison increased from 46,220 on 2 January 1987 to 48,588 in February and 50,349 on 3 July. The overflow in police cells rose from 91 on 2 January to 620 on 3 July. (It was the warning from the police about crowding of police cells that finally tipped the balance and precipitated the decision to take drastic action.) If increases on such a scale can take place in a matter of a few months it is clear that nothing short of executive release will in the long run be able to cope. Short-term solutions such as that announced by Mr Hurd in July 1987 (like the increase in parole announced by Mr Brittan in 1985) will always be overtaken by events.

None of the great array of other means of dealing with the problem have any chance of working. Any of them may help, to a greater or lesser extent, but none except executive release can deal with the situation which arises when there is still gross overcrowding. Executive release is therefore the only method for actually solving the problem on a permanent basis. Obviously, if overcrowding is particularly bad one year, more have to be released. If it eases, it can be used less. Executive release is a flexible instrument that can be adapted to the actual situation.

For the moment it appears that the political will to face the facts is still lacking. It may take one or two more grave prison riots before the nettle is grasped, or possibly the issue will be forced by litigation in the European Court of Human Rights. (If the Court held that conditions in a particular prison constituted a breach of Article 3 of the Convention, which prohibits 'inhuman or degrading treatment or punishment', the Government would find itself obliged to take steps to eliminate overcrowding.) But the better course would undoubtedly be for government to adopt the policy as a conscious and willed act — because, however unpalatable, it is the right thing to do and the only way of providing a solution that will work. It has been accepted as part of the fabric of the system in Ireland. Whatever the initial row, it would be accepted just as well here.

10

Is the Legal System Heading Anywhere?

The last decade or so has seen unprecedented developments in the legal system, with events coming so thick and fast that it has been difficult to keep track of them all. But what do they all mean? Can any patterns be discerned? Where will it all lead?

It is possible to detect certain basic trends which are sufficiently well established for one to feel that they represent significant new factors. One which has emerged very clearly is a heightened commitment to accountability of the system, both internally and externally. The great number of recent official inquiries is one sign of this development. The working parts of the system have been subjected to exhaustive investigation, mostly by *ad hoc* inquiries, of the Royal Commission or Departmental Inquiry variety. It is not that such investigations were unknown in former times — they have always played some part in the process of keeping the legal system up to date. But their range, extent and number have been greater than ever before.

The same principle has been behind the recent movement to make the system for complaining against a solicitor or a police officer more independent of the professions — though some argue that the degree of independence should go even further. During the passage of the Police and Criminal Evidence Act 1984 there was the remarkable spectacle of the Police Federation tucked up in bed with the Law Society and the National Council for Civil Liberties, trying, unsuccessfully, to persuade the Government that complaints against the police should be handled by a body that was wholly independent of the police service. The principle of accountability is reflected equally in the growing tendency for the Minister steering legislation through Parliament to make available to members of the Standing Committee on the Bill his Notes on Clauses from which they can get a better sense of what the legislation is intended to achieve. Another example is the new practice of the Home Office asking the Chairman for the time being of the Criminal Injuries Compensation Board to assess the *ex gratia* payment of compensation that is now commonly made when a serious miscarriage of justice is revealed.

On the other hand, there are plenty of situations which do not reflect any new openness. The judges are still kept on a tight rein by the Lord Chancellor. The government of the day will not easily surrender powers of decision over policy matters to independent bodies. Nor is there any sign that the Lord Chancellor's Department is about to be brought under the scrutiny of the Select Committee system — a long overdue reform. The concept of research as an aspect of accountability and quality control is not yet fully accepted. The judges hate being the subject of inquiry.* Thus in 1981 the Lord Chief Justice refused permission to Dr Andrew Ashworth to carry out research on sentencing in crown courts[†] — though Dr Baldwin and Dr McConville were able to get judges to participate in their research into crown court acquittals.[1] No doubt the difference in the reaction was due to the fact that in the one case the study was focussed on decision-making by juries whereas in the other it was the judges themselves who were under the microscope. Generally it is true that the judges do not appreciate research. Lord Justice May in his concluding remarks at a two-day conference on the Crown Prosecution Service held at the London School of Economics in January 1987 went so far as to suggest that academics would be better employed in investigat-

---

* The law lords were, for instance, not best pleased when two young lecturers at the London School of Economics published a long and scholarly evaluation of the quality of their decisions — and gave them decidedly poor marks. (See W.T. Murphy and R.W. Rawlings, 'After the *ancien regime*: the writing of judgments in the House of Lords 1979/80', *Modern Law Review*, 1981, p. 617; 1982, p. 34.)
† The pilot study was authorised by the Lord Chief Justice, Lord Lane. But when the results were communicated to him he refused to authorise the project's continuation. The authors said that he gave as his reason that it would not be worth the time or the money. Many of the points raised, he said, were already known to the judges. The research found, amongst other things, that listing clerks were exercising real influence over the allocation of cases to judges according to whether they thought the case merited more or less severe sentences. The Lord Chief Justice denied that these practices were occurring — though he admitted that if they were they should not. The pilot study results are described in A. Ashworth et al., 'Sentencing in the Crown Court', Centre for Criminological Research, Occasional Paper No. 10, 1984, pp. 60-4.

ing important social issues like the reasons for crime or marital breakdown than in worrying whether the prosecution system was working properly!

Both the Bar and the Law Society made an unholy fuss about research into plea bargaining a few years ago[2] and although they would be unlikely to react quite so pig-headedly again to research results, they, like the judges, have not yet fully appreciated the value of research as a method for improving the legal system. Nor do they as yet spend any money on research themselves — in marked contrast to the American Bar Association which gives some $3 million a year to its research body, the American Bar Foundation. The Home Office has for long had a research unit which has both undertaken and commissioned research and the Lord Chancellor's Department is now also in the business of commissioning research — both in the form of instant data collected at vast expense by management consultants and through research undertaken at academic institutions. Annual statistics produced by the Home Office and the Lord Chancellor's Department are on the whole useful and better than those available in most other Western countries. A recent unfortunate exception was in the Police and Criminal Evidence Act where several errors were made in specifying the figures that were needed for proper monitoring of the effect of the legislation (see pp. 183-4 above). Nevertheless the Act is a clear example of the recent acceptance of the principle that increased information represents a gain in terms of accountability.

One type of research that is as yet not used in this country is action research of the type pioneered by the Vera Institute of Justice of New York. Vera, who since 1974 have had a small London office partly funded by the Home Office, is America's leading criminal justice research agency. For over twenty-five years it has worked to improve the system through research combined with experimentation. The research is used to modify the experiments which are then in turn monitored by research until a system that works is developed. It has proved a successful technique grounded in real knowledge of how the system operates. Vera started in 1961 with a grant from a philanthropist of $25,000; it now operates with a budget of over $6 million a year — mainly from foundations and governmental authorities. But nothing equivalent exists yet in this country.[3]

One of the dominant refrains of the past few years has, of course, been the call for increased efficiency and cost-effectiveness. It was this above all that fuelled the 1986 Legal Aid Efficiency Scrutiny and the resulting White Paper of March

1987 on Legal Aid which some see, probably rightly, as the first sign of the Treasury getting its grip on publicly funded legal services. Another manifestation of the same trend is the Standing Commission on Efficiency set up by the Lord Chancellor in September 1986 as part of the deal he struck earlier the same year with the two branches of the legal profession over increases in remuneration for criminal legal aid. The chairman is a senior official in the Lord Chancellor's Department and its members comprise senior representatives of the Bar, the Law Society, the Crown Prosecution Service and the Department itself. The first report of the Standing Commission published in March 1987 recommended that in certain defined kinds of cases Queen's Counsel should appear without a junior barrister, and that a pilot experiment be tried to reduce the length of opening and closing speeches by counsel.

The legal profession has found increasingly that the substantial expenditure of public moneys by way of remuneration of lawyers for work done in both civil and criminal cases is used by government as a catalyst to achieve reform of the profession and its ways of doing business. This is bound to continue and even accelerate. The desire to reduce costs has been behind the attempt by successive governments since the mid-1970s to transfer cases from the crown court to magistrates' courts where trials are considerably cheaper. It was also one of the main motives for the Civil Justice Review launched with fanfares by the Lord Chancellor in February 1985 (though the civil servant in charge of the Review was honest enough to admit eighteen months later that he did not in fact expect that it would have much success in this direction). The 1982 report of the Home Office Working Party on Magistrates' Courts found these courts to be run with gross inefficiency; it made a variety of proposals to remedy the problems, though many of its recommendations have not yet been implemented. The demise of the jury in civil cases can be seen principally as a reflection of the view of lawyers as to the efficiency of that method of trying cases.

The drive for efficiency and cost-cutting is also the main impetus behind the recent moves to dismantle monopolies and restrictive practices. The increase of competition in the field of conveyancing by allowing licensed conveyancers to undertake this work is a major event, with repercussions far wider than the minor fact that a hundred or so less well qualified conveyancers can now compete with solicitors for a share in the work. It led to the major relaxation of the rules in regard to advertising by solicitors and to the Law Society's campaign for the abolition of the Bar's monopoly over rights of audience in the higher courts (especially the crown court). Both are justified principally by the argument that increased competition will not only reduce costs but improve the quality of the work. (The other side of the argument is of course that costs may go up and quality down.) The question of the Bar's monopoly over rights of audience is still open — but increasingly it seems likely to be resolved ultimately in favour of the solicitors' branch, or rather in favour of the principle of client's freedom of choice and of competition.

It is not the case that the particular complexion of the government of the day makes all that much difference to the policies pursued with regard to the operation of the legal system. For the most part governments of both the main political parties seem to do remarkably similar things — even though when in Opposition each objects strenuously to what the Government is doing. Here and there, of course, there are differences of emphasis and occasionally even differences in the basic policy. Possibly the thrust toward greater efficiency and cost-effectiveness is the special hall-mark of the Thatcher Government. Maybe a Labour Lord Chancellor would not have set up the Civil Justice Review — though it was the Labour Government that established both the Royal Commission on Legal Services and that on Criminal Procedure. The Thatcher Government broadly implemented the Royal Commission on Criminal Procedure's report; possibly a Labour Government would not have done so, or not quite in the same way. Very probably a Labour Government would not have legislated to break the solicitors' conveyancing monopoly. Ironically, Labour Governments have tended to be even more solicitous of the interests of the legal profession than the Tories. A Labour Lord Chancellor would have persuaded the Prime Minister that more competition for lawyers would be bad rather than good for the general body of consumers. Lord Hailsham's argument to this effect, by contrast, was swept aside by Mrs Thatcher. Possibly, on the other hand, a Labour Government would not have established a Legal Aid Efficiency Scrutiny Team and a Labour White Paper on legal services in the late 1980s would have been couched in terms that did more to show concern for the unmet need for help with legal problems of the citizen generally and especially of the poor. But these are nuances. A Labour Government would have felt the same pressure from the Treasury to DO SOMETHING to reduce costs and, broadly, it would have reacted to most of the problems of the day in much the same way as the Conservatives.

The cause of increased efficiency has come to be supported in recent times by the advance of technology. This is one area where change is marked and visible. Lawyers, the courts, and judicial administration are all hidebound and deeply conservative. Until a few years ago a writ normally had to be served in person. The postal service seemingly was regarded as basically unsound. The court offices did not permit business to be transacted by telephone. (This is still the case, so that firms of solicitors have to send junior clerks to deal with all the minor procedural matters that are required to be handled in the course of litigation.) The pace of legal business has always been maddeningly slow. The legal culture seems to promote a lethargic style. But the advent of the new electronic technology has appeared to introduce a new note of urgency and modernity into the way that lawyers go about their work. Certainly it cannot be said to have been adopted with unusual rapidity. It was years before most firms of solicitors got used to the idea of the telex machine, and until the mid-1980s barristers' chambers were still stuck somewhere in the nineteenth century in terms of office equipment, management, and working methods. But things are definitely changing.

Many firms of solicitors use the latest gadgets and more and more are coming to use them — computers, word processors, telex and teletex, fax — though few can match the scale of the investment of the largest firms. City solicitors Linklaters and Paines placed a £6 million order in June 1987 for computer equipment to provide work-stations for 250 secretaries and 50 fee earners. The computers would be able to talk to one another, send documents in computerised form around the building and draw on the firm's computerised precedent library consisting of some eight million items. But although the scale of such operations is more grandiose in its basic features it is similar to many that are now gradually being installed in firms all over the country. Even barristers' chambers have begun to tool up for the new era of electronic communication. Many chambers have word processors and computers in the clerk's office for central management and secretarial functions, and increasingly individual barristers will have their own desk-top terminals. The legal journals are full of articles extolling the miracles and explaining the mysteries of the new technologies and their application to the work of both branches of the profession.

The new technology has even begun to influence the way the courts hear cases. The Criminal Justice Bill, for instance, introduced in 1986 and re-introduced in June 1987 after the

General Election made provision for evidence to be heard both by satellite from abroad and by live video link-up. The use of computers as a means of developing management information and of creating systems to speed up the through-put of cases in the courts is still in its infancy but its value is now beginning to be understood. The Lord Chancellor's Department has given high priority to installing a computerised system for handling the vast mass of county court debt business. It also has a programme for the installation of a large number of free-standing desk computers for court administrators. The Civil Justice Review saw these as capable of providing the support for a developing system of court control of cases. But it urged that the long-term objective had to be to develop computerised records of all cases to enable the court to identify contested cases which are not up to timetable, to institute computer-generated reminders and summonses to dilatory parties, and to improve planning of judge time, the listing of cases and the allocation of resources generally. Such developments are only a matter of time.

Another change in the system which is now well set is the increased attention given to training. The academic education of lawyers is now virtually entirely in the hands of the university law schools. The pre-war practice of going into the profession straight from school or after reading a degree other than law is now almost extinct. The overwhelming majority of practising lawyers have law degrees — and the quality of legal education in the universities, though variable and not always as good as it should be, is nevertheless markedly improving. The courses run by the professional schools in the year between leaving the university and starting life in practice are supposed to be vocational training. In fact, they are still heavily focussed on a mass of rote learning of rules of law — the teaching about the nuts and bolts of practical work is somewhat sketchy. Articles for solicitors and pupillage for barristers are again very patchy. In some instances they provide first-rate experience. But all too often the training and supervision are of little real value. When solicitors emerge fully trained they not only have to work in someone else's office for a year but must also continue their formal education for three years by attending courses. This new requirement of mandatory continuing education (the cost of which is generally met by firms rather than by the new recruits) has generated a flowering of courses all over the country run by academic institutions, local Law Societies, solicitors' firms and private organisations. This development is certain to continue.

As has been seen, even the Bar has now accepted that if it is to justify its pretension to be the specialist branch of the profession it too must be seen to engage in continuing legal education.

At the same time training for judges has become respectable. The Judicial Studies Board now runs courses and seminars for different levels of judicial personnel from assistant recorders and deputy registrars to High Court judges. Until 1985 the training was confined to criminal matters but it now deals also with civil business. This is an expanding function, which will operate through manuals as well as live instruction. The Board is now also taking on supervision of training for magistrates. The better provision for training of court clerks and justices clerks is another growth area. At every level therefore the need to provide for a more professional approach for those who operate the system has been accepted.

On the other hand, the traditional participation of untrained amateurs in the form of the jury is as strong as ever, at least in the criminal courts. And the role of the partly trained semi-amateur in the form of the lay magistrate seems equally a rock-solid part of the legal system. There is no prospect that either will be significantly altered, let alone eliminated. Both have survived already for many centuries and show every sign of continuing for many more.

The mixture of professional and lay personnel seen in the interrelationship between judge and jury in the crown court and between lay magistrate and professional (or semi-professional) court clerk in the magistrates' court is now beginning to appear also in the relationship between solicitors and lay advice agencies such as the Citizens' Advice Bureaux. The future of legal services clearly foreshadows this relationship becoming closer and more integrated as attempts are increasingly made to ensure that each area of the country has an appropriate network of advisory services. It is likely also to be reflected quite soon in the introduction of lay advocates in county court small claims cases and, if that proves a success, in other cases in the county court and possibly the magistrates' court. Most court advocacy will continue to be done by lawyers but the role of the lay advocate, which has been so successfully demonstrated in tribunals, is likely in the future to play a part also in the lower courts. The mixture of lawyer and lay personnel will continue in the processing of complaints against solicitors, in the adjudication on disciplinary charges brought against barristers and solicitors and, if it survives, in the work of the Lord Chancellor's Legal Aid Advisory Committee which would have the task of shadowing and monitoring the new Legal Aid Board. (They should be renamed 'Legal Services Board' and 'Legal Services Advisory Committee' to reflect their broad focus.) The partnership between lawyers and non-lawyers in the operation of the legal system has been one of its characteristic and fruitful features and is still expanding.

There will also be progress in the direction of finding new alternative methods of achieving the same objectives. Arbitration has for decades been a familiar alternative to court processes and seems now to be on the increase. In the criminal justice system, the caution which used to be seen mainly as a method of dealing with juveniles is increasingly being used to deal also with adults. In 1985 no less than 145,000 persons were cautioned for indictable offences, an increase of 17 per cent over 1984 and of 39 per cent over 1981. In February 1985 the Home Office issued a circular encouraging the greater use of cautioning.*

The most important duty of the new Crown Prosecution Service is to decide whether or not to continue a prosecution started by the police. It is at least a possibility that this power will come to result in the siphoning off of a significant number of cases that would previously have been prosecuted. New techniques for diverting cases from prosecution and custodial penalties are proliferating and are bound to continue to develop.

A different example of the same trend is the move toward conciliation in the field of matrimonial disputes. Whether conciliation is to be introduced as part of the official court structure is still uncertain. The Booth Committee on Procedure in Matrimonial Cases in its report (1985) recommended that conciliation should become an established part of divorce procedure. (Its remit was limited to in-court systems and therefore did not extend to pre-court and out-of-court conciliation provided by voluntary organisations, most of which are now under the umbrella of the National Family Conciliation Council.) Some two-thirds of the probation areas in England and Wales already staff in-court conciliation appointments in the divorce courts, many of which are linked to out-of-court services

---

* The circular said: 'There is no rule in law that suspected offenders must be prosecuted. It has long been recognised in the case of juveniles that there may be positive advantages for society as well as for the individual in using prosecution as a last resort. Cautioning provides an important alternative to prosecution in the case of juvenile offending; it also represents a possible course of action in the case of adults.' (See further Roy Light, 'Cautioning Adult Offenders', *Law Society's Gazette*, 3 December 1986, p. 3649.)

and this is a trend likely to develop, though in Summer 1987 it seemed unclear whether the long campaign to establish some form of Family Court would after all come to early fruition.

But while in some ways the legal system is clearly moving in new directions and responding to the pressure to bring itself up to date, in others the life of the law, of lawyers and the courts continues in essence in much the same old way. What is changing above all is the way in which the business is done. Modern technology makes a difference to the outward show, but it does not fundamentally alter the nature of the work that is done. So, in spite of all the frenetic activity, the committees of inquiry, the changes and reforms, the trends for the future may not be all that different from those of the past. Many aspects of the system are in a process of transformation. But when they have emerged from the present somewhat troubled period of gestation it may be that they will turn out to be comfortingly familiar.

It is, for instance, predictable that each year the numbers of criminal cases will rise and that the same will very probably be true of civil cases. The numbers of police officers will continue to go up, so too will the numbers of judges, barristers and solicitors. This has now been the pattern for many years and there is nothing that suggests any change. The same is true of costs. The probability must be that delays will remain more or less the same or even get worse.

The issues that have for years caused complaint about the system continue to plague us. There is no escape from them. The system will always appear too costly, the delays too great, the procedures too complex, the numbers of courts and judges insufficient, and the numbers of cases and prisoners too high. If the problems diminish at all, the improvement will tend to be marginal — whilst if they get worse, the deterioration may be significant. In the face of the constantly rising numbers of cases, the situation of those who work to improve the legal system is like that of Sisyphus.

The other troublesome problem is that the only raw material one has to work with is human nature. Those who operate any system are reluctant to change the way they do things. Even when the rules and procedures are altered they contrive to find ways of carrying on as before. The known and familiar, however wrong-headed, is more congenial than improvement designed by others. The history of the legal system is littered with improvements that made little or no difference because those concerned managed to sabotage the reform.

It is true that the mood of the present times is for change. An uncommon willingness to consider change has seized almost all the elements of the system. Historians may come to see the 1970s and 1980s as a rare moment in the history of the English legal system when the machine was taken to the pits for overhaul and replacement of worn-out parts. But to what extent it will really run much better in the future remains to be seen.

Notes

CHAPTER 1 The Legal Professional at Bay

1 The Law Society now publishes valuable statistics. See *Law Society's Gazette*, 26 September 1984, p. 2607; 16 October 1985, p. 2903; 29 October 1986, p. 3257. See also 'Where have all the young ones gone? An analysis of the Recruitment Crisis', *Law Society's Gazette*, 25 March 1987, p. 875; and 'A Crisis in Recruitment', ibid., 16 June 1987, p. 1775; *New Law Journal*, 29 May 1987, p. 487.

2 Unpublished speech given at a weekend conference of the Society of Labour Lawyers in January 1967.

3 Y. Cripps, 'The Professions: A Critical Review', *Law Society's Gazette*, 23 July 1986, p. 2297.

4 *Report of the Royal Commission on Legal Services*, 1979, Cmnd. 7648, Surveys and Studies, Table 8.31, p. 224; *Solicitors' Journal*, 3 July 1987, p. 897. A survey carried out for the Law Society in February 1986 found that 90 per cent of respondents who had used solicitors claimed to be satisfied (63 per cent very satisfied). The satisfaction level was consistent across all areas of work except criminal and motoring cases where, although 73 per cent were satisfied, 22 per cent were dissatisfied. (Research Surveys of Great Britain Limited, 'Awareness, Usage and Attitudes Towards the Professional Services and Advice Provided by Solicitors', February 1986).

5 For the Law Society's defence of its performance see *Law Society's Gazette*, 25 January 1984, p. 162.

6 *First Report of the Conveyancing Committee: Non Solicitor Conveyancers — Competence and Consumer Protection*, HMSO, September 1984 — summarised in *Law Society's Gazette*, 26 September 1984, p. 2591.

7 *Report of the Royal Commission on Legal Services*, op. cit., Table 6.1, p. 117.

8 Law Society Special Committee on Remuneration, 'Survey of the Structure and Finances of the Solicitors' Branch of the Legal Profession in Private Practice', 16 January 1986, vol. 2, Table 15.

9 The rules were set out in the *Law Society's Gazette*, 27 June 1984, p. 1803. For the Law Society's guidance on the new rules see *Law Society's Gazette*, 26 September 1984, p. 2583. See then *Gazette*, 30 October 1985, p. 3057. See also John Loosemore, 'Advertising, Property Selling and Self-regulation', *New Law Journal*, 17 May 1985, p. 482; 'Advertising — the Great Non-Debate', *New Law Journal*, 30 August 1985, p. 873; *Law Society's Gazette*, 9 July 1985, p. 2137.

10 Details of the debate in the Council were reported in the *Law Society's Gazette*, 17 December 1986, p. 3791. The Law Society's commentary on the new Publicity Code appeared in the *Gazette* of 28 January 1987, p. 235. The commentary emphasised that the Code was not just an advertising code; it applied to letterheads, nameplates, media appearances and any other form of publicity.

11 See, in particular, the excellent series of articles in the *New Law Journal*: 25 April 1986, p. 384 (Richards Butler); 25 July 1986, p. 709 (Howes Percival); 14 November 1986, p. 1095 (Hodge, Jones and Allen); 15 August 1986, p. 783 (Pannone Napier); 2 January 1987, p. 13 (Baker and McKenzie); 13 March 1987, p. 251 (Ralph Haemms and Co.); 24 April 1987, p. 377 (Clifford Chance); 12 June 1987, p. 549 (Pictons).

12 See 'Little response from Advertising: Brochures a Success', *Solicitors' Journal*, 5 June 1987, p. 760. For the impact of advertising in the United States see Alan Paterson, 'Advertising by Lawyers: the American Experience', *Journal of the Law Society of Scotland*, April 1984, p. 125.

13 See G. Bindman, 'Legal Clinics: Can we learn from the USA?', *Law Society's Gazette*, 22 September 1982, p. 1158.

14 T.J. Muris and F.S. McChesney, 'Advertising and the price and quality of legal services; the case for legal clinics', *American Bar Foundation Research Journal*, 1979, p. 179.

15 By early May 1987 the Council had issued 176 licences and expected to grant 200 by the end of May. Fewer than a hundred were expected to set up in practice right away. The next licences would be granted after the examinations in July. (*Law Society's Gazette*, 13 May 1987, p. 1374). For details of the Law Society's first ethical rules regarding the relationship between solicitors and licensed conveyancers, see *Law Society's Gazette*, 29 April 1987, pp. 1202, 1207.

16 Law Society Special Committee on Remuneration, 'Survey of Solicitors' Charges for Domestic Conveyancing', 16 December 1986, paras. 5.2.3-4.

17 See in particular its memorandum 'Conveyancing by Employed Solicitors', *Law Society's Gazette*, 30 May 1984, p. 1485.

18 Ibid.

19 *House of Commons Hansard*, 6 December 1985, col. 354; *Law Society's Gazette*, 11 December 1985, p. 3375. See also *New Law Journal*, 24 May 1985, p. 499; 14 June 1985, p. 571.

20 Section 102 states that conveyancing services, which include domestic and commercial conveyancing, both leasehold and freehold, can be carried on by building societies and other institutions. The power to authorise this is given to the Lord Chancellor under Schedule 17, which lays down criteria for permitting any group of two or more persons (including, for instance, estate agents) the power to provide legal services in the conveyancing field.

21 John Loosemore and Robert Parsons, 'A Whole New Ball Game?', *Law Society's Gazette*, 2 July 1986, pp. 2059, 2135. See also Audiam, 'The End of the Profession?', *Solicitors' Journal*, 21 February 1986, p. 135; the powerful speech by Sir David Napley, 'The Ethics of the Profession', *Law Society's Gazette*, 20 March 1985, p. 818 and reply, *New Law Journal*, 17 May 1985, p. 482.

22 Loosemore and Parsons, op. cit., p. 2135; and *Law Society's Gazette*, 5 November 1986, p. 3311.

23 W. Merricks, 'Independence for solicitors — is it under threat?', *Legal Action*, December 1986, p. 8.

24 See *Law Society's Gazette*, 17 December 1986, pp. 3790, 3799; *New Law Journal*, 19 December 1986, p. 1197.

25 The proposal was canvassed in *Law Society's Gazette*, see 7 March 1984, p. 627; 9 May 1984, p. 1261; 6 June 1984, p. 1596.

26 *Law Society's Gazette*, 4 July 1984, p. 1904.

27 *Law Society's Gazette*, 5 December 1984, p. 3404.

28 See guidelines in *Law Society's Gazette*, 30 January 1985, p. 257; *Law Society's Gazette*, 13 March 1985, p. 726; D. Bennett, 'The National Association of Solicitors Property Centres — Philosophy and Objectives', *Law Society's Gazette*, 5 November 1986, p. 3321; P. Cragg, 'The Lincoln Experience', *Law Society's Gazette*, 3 June 1987, p. 1630.

29 *Law Society's Gazette*, 19 September 1984, p. 2502; 8 May 1985, p. 1294; 19 June 1985, pp. 1757; 6 November 1985, p. 3137. See also cheap conveyancing systems *New Law Journal*, 12 July 1985, p. 672; *Law Society's Gazette*, 3 July 1985, p. 1902.

30 Law Society's Council Statement, *Law Society's Gazette*, 27 May 1987, p. 1545. The Administration of Justice Act 1985 and the Law Reform (Miscellaneous Provisions) Act 1985 provided for the Law Societies of England and Scotland to make rules under which solicitors could incorporate, subject to rules approved by the Master of the Rolls or, in Scotland, the Lord President of the Court of Session. During the debates on the English legislation the Law Society made it clear that it would not permit limited liability companies but this attitude had changed primarily as a result of great concern about the growing level of claims of negligence liability brought against solicitors. In 1987 the Law Society joined other professional bodies in asking the Government to set up an inquiry into a statutory scheme to cap liability. See *Law Society's Gazette*, 25 February 1987, p. 548. The Bar also hopes to see professional liability limited — see *Law Society's Gazette*, 29 April 1987, p. 1233.

31 For a comment see *New Law Journal*, 5 September 1986, p. 833. See also Report of the Joint Working Party of four different professional bodies: 'Inter Professional Partnerships', *Law Society's Gazette*, 8 May 1985, p. 1337.

32 *Divided we Stand: A Report on the Legal Profession*, Social Democratic Lawyers Association, 1986.

33 Note 8, above.

34 Bar Council Statement of 2 April 1984, *Law Society's Gazette*, 2 May 1987, p. 1218.

35 See *New Law Journal*, 10 August 1984, pp. 867-8, 25 January 1985, p. 71. For the Law Society's view see *Law Society's Gazette*, 31 October 1984, p. 3004.

36 *Abse* v. *Smith* [1986] 1 All E.R. 350.

37 *Practice Direction* [1986] 2 All E.R. 226.

38 *Law Society's Gazette*, 29 January 1986, p. 246.

39 Issued as an insert with the *Guardian Gazette* of 18 June 1986.

40 See *New Law Journal*, 27 June 1986, p. 597.

41 See *Law Society's Gazette*, 16 April 1986, p. 1112 and *New Law Journal*, 18 April 1986, p. 347. See also *Law Society's Gazette*, 16 October 1986, p. 3059.

42 *The Times*, 29 May 1986; *Counsel*, vol. 1, no. 2, Hilary 1986, p. 36.

43 See A.E. Bottoms and J.D. McClean, *Defendants in the Criminal Process* (Routledge & Kegan Paul, London, 1976), p. 158.

44 See further the Bar's memorandum to the Marre Committee on the Future of the Legal Profession, 2 March 1987 and the Law Society's reply, 8 April 1987.

45 *Law Society's Gazette*, 30 April 1986, p. 1300.

46 See *Law Society's Gazette*, 19 November 1986, p. 3481 and for the Bar's caustic reaction, *New Law Journal*, 14 November 1986, p. 1081.

47 See, for instance, M. Zander, *Lawyers and the Public Interest* (Weidenfeld & Nicolson, London, 1968) especially pp. 153-63, 270-332; Peter Reeves, *Are Two Legal Professions Necessary?* (Waterlow, London, 1986); Gerald Gardiner, 'Two Lawyers or One?', 23 *Current Legal Problems*, 1970, p. 1; F.A. Mann, 'Fusion of the Legal Profession', *Law Quarterly Review*, July 1977, p. 367 and evidence of the Bar, the Law Society and the Judges of the High

Court to the Royal Commission on Legal Services, *Report of the Royal Commission*, op. cit., ch. 17.

48 *Legal Aid Efficiency Scrutiny Report*, Lord Chancellor's Department, June 1986, vol. 2, s. III 3, 5 (iii).

49 See C. Chapman, 'Rights of Audience: A New Zealand Perspective', *Law Society's Gazette*, 26 March 1986, p. 954. See also N. Addison, 'Integration of the Legal Profession, An Alternative to Fusion', *Law Society's Gazette*, 17 September 1986, p. 2712.

50 The profession was fused in 1891 by statute but has remained divided. See N. Addision, 'Fusion and Division in Australia', *Law Society's Gazette*, 29 April 1987, p. 1213 and 'Fusion: Lessons Down Under', *Solicitors' Journal*, 28 November 1986, p. 878.

51 See Paul Walker, 'A New Governing Body for the Bar', *Law Society's Gazette*, 28 May 1986, p. 1628 and see also 23 July 1986, p. 2321.

52 *Counsel*, Spring 1987, p. 33.

53 The manifesto of the Campaign for the Bar was set out by Mr de Wilde in *Law Society's Gazette*, 1 May 1985, p. 1245. For the Bar Council's reply see ibid., 29 May 1985, p. 1554; and for de Wilde's reply to the reply, see ibid., 26 June 1985, p. 1845. For subsequent events, including reports of stormy annual and extraordinary general meetings of the Bar, see *Law Society's Gazette*, 28 August 1985, p. 2325; 26 February 1986, p. 611; 23 July 1986, p. 2323.

54 *Law Society's Gazette*, 25 September 1985, p. 2636.

55 *The Times*, 16 and 17 February 1984.

56 *Law Magazine*, 1 May 1987.

57 For an extended account of these proceedings see *The Times*, 21, 22, 24 and 27 March 1986. For an account of the Bar's AGM leading to the proceedings see *Law Society's Gazette*, 26 February 1986, p. 611. For a report on the outcome of the proceedings see *Law Society's Gazette*, 30 April 1986, p. 1302. For a comment on the Bar's 'victory' see *New Law Journal*, 4 April 1986, p. 297. The Bar's partial success was aided by the fact that the Law Society joined the fray with its own parallel proceedings — see *Law Society's Gazette*, 19 February 1986, p. 490; 9 April 1986, p. 1022; 23 July 1986, p. 2282.

58 *Counsel*, Hilary 1986, p. 38.

59 *Lawyer*, 21 May 1987.

60 See *New Law Journal*, 26 June 1987.

61 David Farrer and Anthony Spaight, 'Advertising and the Bar: Change the Rules', *Counsel*, Spring 1987, p. 4.

62 Ibid., pp. 27, 28; *Law Society's Gazette*, 25 February 1987, p. 573.

63 See 'Appointment to Silk and the Judiciary', *Law Society's Gazette*, 28 August 1985, p. 2335.

64 See W. H. Goodhart, QC, 'Time to Scrap the Silks', *New Law Journal*, 25 October 1985, p. 1048; Alec Samuels, 'Can the Silk System be Justified?', *New Law Journal*, 25 May 1984, p. 503; Social Democratic Lawyers Association, *Divided We Stand*, op. cit.

65 See, for instance, *Counsel's Guide to Computers for the Bar*, March 1986; Henry Brooke, QC, 'Competence for Chambers', *Law Society's Gazette*, 20 October 1985, p. 3081.

CHAPTER 2   Access to Justice

1 The origins of the state's involvement in legal services has been traced in a major scholarly article by Professor Mauro Cappelletti in 'Legal Aid: Modern Themes and Variations', 24 *Stanford Law Review*, 1972, p. 347. See also the multi-volume study entitled *Access to Justice*, edited by Professor Cappelletti published in 1978.

2 *Report of the Royal Commission on Legal Services*, 1979, Cmnd. 7648, Vol. 2,

'Survey of Users and Non-Users of Legal Services in England and Wales', para. 8.30, pp. 184-5. See similarly 'Awareness of Solicitors' Services', *Law Society's Gazette*, 16 April 1986, p. 1113.

3 *Report of Royal Commission*, op. cit., para. 8.20, p. 182.

4 Ibid., Table 8.4, p. 187. More than 20 per cent of that age group had seen a solicitor, compared with 15 per cent of those between 45 and 54, 12 per cent of those between 55 and 64 and only 9 per cent of those over 65.

5 Ibid. Table 8.8, p. 190.

6 Ibid., para. 8.52.

7 Ibid., para. 8.115, p. 205.

8 Ibid., para. 8.43, p. 186.

9 Donald Harris et al., *Compensation and Support for Illness and Injury* (Oxford University Press, Oxford, 1984).

10 Ibid., p. 65.

11 B. Abel-Smith, R. Brooke, M. Zander, *Legal Problems and the Citizen* (Heineman, London, 1973), Table 3.4, p. 156.

12 For discussion of these theories see M. Zander, *Legal Services for the Community* (Temple Smith, London, 1978), ch. 9.

13 Lord Chancellor's Department, *Report of a Survey of the Grant of Legal Aid in Magistrates' Courts*, October 1983.

14 Harris et al., op. cit., p. 65.

15 Ibid., p. 66.

16 Ibid., p. 67.

17 *Law Society's Gazette*, 3 December 1986, p. 3648; 1 July 1987, p. 1935. See also *Legal Action*, August 1987, pp. 8, 23.

18 *Legal Aid*, 36th Annual Report, 1986-87, p. 209-13.

19 Ibid., para. 117, p. 211.

20 *Judicial Statistics*, 1986, Cm. 173, Table 10.17, p. 82. See also the legal aid statistics in the Law Society's annual report. The latest was the 36th report for 1985/86. The report is accompanied by the report of the Lord Chancellor's Advisory Committee.

21 See Zander, op. cit., pp. 87-93.

22 The Law Society's annual legal aid report has for some years now called for secure governmental funding for law centres.

23 In 1976 the Lord Chancellor's Legal Aid Advisory Committee said that law centres were 'playing a vital part in making legal services available in the most deprived areas and on matters on which the poorer sections of the community most strongly feel the need for those services'. More centres should be established. Law centres had established themselves as 'an integral and essential branch of legal services'. (*Legal Aid*, 26th Annual Report, paras. 44 and 48). See also the 34th Annual Report, 1983-84, pp. 338-46.

24 See 'Law Centre Funding; the new regime', *Legal Action*, April 1986, p. 4.

25 The report was published in two volumes as *Legal Aid, Efficiency Scrutiny*, June 1986, available from the Lord Chancellor's Department.

26 *Legal Action*, October 1986, pp. 4-7.

27 *Legal Aid*, 36th Annual Report, 1985/86, pp. 198-208.

28 *R. v. Lord Chancellor, ex parte Alexander*, *The Times*, 21, 22, 24, 26 March 1986. The proceedings were withdrawn to permit negotiations to take place. These ended with an agreement to raise the rates an additional 5 per cent in the case of barristers and 6 per cent for solicitors over what had originally been proposed. (See *Law Society's Gazette*, 23 July 1986, p. 2811.)

29 See in particular the analysis of the implications by Cyril Glasser in 'Legal Aid — Decline and Fall?', *Law Society's Gazette*, 19 March 1986, p. 839.

CHAPTER 3   The Quality of Legal Services

1 See, for instance, M. Zander, 'Legal Advice and Criminal Appeals: A Survey of Prisoners, Prisons and Lawyers', *Criminal Law Review*, 1972, pp. 132, 154-

64. The results of the survey were hardly complimentary to the legal profession.

2 *New Law Journal*, 15 November 1979, p. 1117.

3 *Report of the Royal Commission on Legal Services*, 1979, Cmnd. 7648, para. 22.16.

4 Ibid.

5 Ibid., pp. 293-301.

6 *Law Society's Gazette*, 1 July 1987, p. 1943.

7 For a succinct account of the history of English legal education see the *Report of the (Ormrod) Committee on Legal Education*, 1971, Cmnd. 4505, pp. 3-20. The full history remains to be written.

8 *Report of the Select Committee on Legal Education*, 1846, Vol. X, British Parliamentary Papers, p. lvi, para. 3.

9 Ibid., para. 2.

10 Ibid.

11 J.F. Wilson and S.B. Marsh, 'A Second Survey of Legal Education in the United Kingdom', *Journal of the Society of Public Teachers of Law*, July 1975, Table 1, p. 249.

12 Ibid., pp. 241-2.

13 *Ormrod Report*, op. cit., p. 54.

14 Wilson and Marsh, op. cit., Table 6, p. 252, and Table 10, p. 256.

15 The Society of Public Teachers of Law, *Evidence to the Royal Commission on Legal Services*, 1977, para. 11.

16 *Law Society's Gazette*, 14 October 1985, p. 2904.

17 Avrom Sherr at Warwick is the leader of this development in British universities. His approach is now more widely available in his book *Client Interviewing for Lawyers* (Sweet & Maxwell, London, 1986).

18 *New Law Journal*, 15 November 1979, p. 1118.

19 *Ormrod Report*, op. cit., para. 85.

20 *New Law Journal*, 15 November 1979, p. 1117.

21 Bar, *Evidence to the Royal Commission on Legal Services*, 1977, Submission No. 7, p. xi, 23, para. A.23.1.

22 *Law Society's Gazette*, 27 May 1987, p. 1567.

23 *Law Society's Gazette*, 24 October 1984, p. 2894; Andrew Lockley, 'A Panel of Solicitors for Child Care Cases', *Justice of the Peace*, 30 March 1985, p. 199.

24 See *Law Society's Gazette*, 2 June 1985, p. 577; 20 November 1985, pp. 3316, para. 2.16.

25 See Alan Paterson, 'Specialisation and the Profession: Lessons from the United States', *Journal of the Law Society of Scotland*, January 1986, p. 8; see also by the same author 'Specialisation and the Legal Profession', *New Law Journal*, 25 July and 1 August 1986, pp. 697, 721.

26 *Law Society's Gazette*, 24 September 1986, p. 2818.

27 See John Ritchie, 'Specialist Qualifications for the Legal Profession: A Contrary Argument', *Law Society's Gazette*, 17 January 1987, p. 87.

28 *Law Society's Gazette*, 29 July 1987, p. 2238.

29 *Legal Aid in England and Wales: A New Framework*, 1987, Cm. 118, para. 58.

30 *Rondel* v. *Worsley* [1966] 3 W.L.R. 1666.

31 *Saif Ali* v. *Sydney Mitchell & Co.* [1978] 3 W.L.R. 849.

32 Clare Dyer, 'The high cost of protection', *Law Magazine*, 29 May 1987, pp. 28-9.

33 *Report of the Royal Commission*, op. cit., para. 25.23, p. 342.

34 Ibid., para. 25.18, p.340.

35 Ibid., para. 25.35, p. 345.

36 Ibid., para. 25.24, p. 342.

37 *Law Society's Gazette*, 18 June 1986, p. 1876.

38 *Report of the Royal Commission*, op. cit., para. 25.34, p. 345.

39 Ibid., para. 25.45, p. 347.

40 'Report of the Law Society Council's Committee of Enquiry into the Law Society's Treatment of the complaints of Mr L.A. Parsons against Mr G. Davies and Mr C. Malim', February 1984, (supplement to *Law Society's Gazette*, 22 February 1984), para. 43. For Law Society's response, see *Law Society's Gazette*, 4 April 1984, p. 938.

41 *Law Society's Gazette*, 7 May 1986, p. 1358.

42 See Report published with *Law Society's Gazette*, 10 July 1985.

43 Young Solicitors' Group, 'The Law Society — Time for Change', *Law Society's Gazette*, 17 July 1985, p. 2091, para. 3.2.

44 *Law Society's Gazette*, 26 February 1986, pp. 583, 592-9.

45 Sheila Kavenagh, 'Consumers and the SCB', *Legal Action*, July 1987, pp. 5-7.

46 Igor Judge, QC, 'Professional Conduct and the Bar', *Law Society's Gazette*, 29 October 1986, p. 3230.

47 *Law Society's Gazette*, 30 April 1986, p. 1303.

48 See M. Zander, 'Research as a Way to Improve the Quality of Legal Work', *New Law Journal*, 15 June 1978, p. 576.

49 *Law Society's Gazette*, 26 June 1985, p. 1840. Cf. the first draft, ibid., 2 May 1984, p. 1182.

50 *Law Society's Gazette*, 27 May 1987, p. 1567.

51 See D. Rosenthal, *Lawyers and Client: Who's in Charge?* (Russell Sage, New York, 1974).

52 Ibid., p. 152.

CHAPTER 4   The Judges

1 See generally Michael Zander, *The Law Making Process* (Weidenfeld & Nicolson, London, 2nd edn, 1985).

2 *Report on Top Salaries*, Report no. 22, 1984-85, Cmnd. 9225-I, paras. 121-8.

3 Ibid., para. 128.

4 Ibid., paras. 133-4.

5 'Judicial Appointment': the Lord Chancellor's Principles and Procedures, 1986; see also *Law Society's Gazette*, 28 August 1985, p. 2335.

6 See also *The Guardian*, 26 May 1986 for an account by Judge Pickles as to how Mr Justice Hinchcliffe had nearly wrecked his prospects of judicial preferment. Judge Pickles recounted the same story in his book *Straight from the Bench* (Phoenix, London, 1987), ch. 1.

7 *Counsel*, vol. 1, Easter 1986, p. 49.

8 *New Law Journal*, 6 June 1986, p. 525. See also Alec Samuels, 'Appointing the Judges', *New Law Journal*, 27 January 1984, p. 85 and 3 February 1984, pp. 107, 108.

9 JUSTICE, *The Judiciary* (Stevens, London, 1972).

10 Further data are set out in J.A.G. Griffith, *The Politics of the Judiciary* (Fontana, London, 3rd edn, 1985), pp. 25-7.

11 For the references and other statistics then available see Michael Zander, *The State of Knowledge About the English Legal Profession* (Barry Rose, London, 1980), pp. 22-3.

12 *The Economist*, 15 December 1956, p. 946.

13 Elizabeth Burney, *J.P. Magistrate, Court and Community* (Hutchinson, London, 1979), ch. 4.

14 Ibid., p. 72.

15 See Roger Hood, *Sentencing the Motoring Offender* (Heinemann, London, 1972), Table 1, p. 51; J. Baldwin, 'The Social Composition of the Magistracy', *British Journal of Criminology*, vol. 16 (1976) pp. 171-4; Burney, op. cit., p. 65.

16 Griffith, op. cit., p. 234.

17 Lord Devlin, 'Judges, Government and Politics', *Modern Law Review*, 1978, pp. 501-9.

18 For some examples see M. Zander, *A Bill of Rights?* (Sweet & Maxwell, London, 3rd edn, 1985), pp. 54-7.
19 P. O'Higgins and M. Partington, 'Industrial Conflict: Judicial Attitudes', 32 *Modern Law Review*, 1969, p. 53.
20 *Judicial Studies and Information*, Report of a Working Party, 1978, HMSO.
21 Ibid., para. 1.6. pp. 2-3.
22 John Baldwin, 'The Compulsory Training of Magistrates', *Criminal Law Review*, 1975, p. 634.
23 Burney, op. cit., p. 20.
24 Ibid., pp. 206-11.
25 Roger Hood, *Sentencing in Magistrates' Courts* (Stevens, London, 1962); Hood, *Sentencing the Motoring Offender*, op. cit.; Nigel Lemon, *British Journal of Criminology*, January 1974: Burney, op. cit.
26 See generally and on this case, S. Shetreet, *Judges on Trial* (Sijthoff and Noordhoff, Amsterdam, 1976), ch. VI.
27 *New Law Journal*, 4 October 1985, p. 976.
28 See to like effect, *Solicitors Journal*, 15 May 1987, p. 635.

CHAPTER 5 Justice in the Civil Courts

1 Civil Justice Review, 'Personal Injuries Litigation', Consultation Paper, February 1986, para. 12.5.
2 *Report of the Committee on Personal Injuries Litigation*, 1968, Cmnd. 369, paras. 520-25.
3 *New Law Journal*, 4 January 1985, p. 3.
4 D. Harris et al., *Compensation and Support for Illness and Injury* (Oxford University Press, Oxford, 1984), p. 105.
5 *Report of the Royal Commission on Legal Services*, 1979, Cmnd. 7648, para. 43.3., p. 723.
6 'LCD Rebuffed', *New Law Journal*, 28 September 1984, p. 324.
7 *Report of the Committee on Personal Injuries Litigation*, op. cit.
8 *Report of the Personal Injuries Litigation Procedure Working Party*, 1979, Cmnd. 7476.
9 Ibid., Appendix A and p. 2.
10 Ibid., Appendix B and p. 2.
11 Ibid., para. 8.
12 Ibid.
13 Ibid., para. 9.
14 Ibid., para. 10.
15 *Dwyer* v. *Roderick and Others*, reprinted in *The Times*, 12 November 1983.
16 Personal Injuries Litigation, Consultation Paper, op. cit., Table 3, p. 25.
17 Ibid., paras. 66-67.
18 Ibid., pp. 35-36.
19 Ibid., para. 69.
20 Ibid., Table 7, p. 29.
21 Ibid., Table 10, p. 31.
22 *Royal Commission on Civil Liability and Compensation for Personal Injury*, 1978, Cmnd. 7054, Vol. 2, Table 158, p. 207.
23 'Personal Injuries Litigation', Consultation Paper, op. cit., para. 81.
24 Harris et al., op. cit.
25 'Personal Injuries Litigation', Consultation Paper, op. cit., para. 88.
26 Civil Justice Review, 'Small Claims in the County Court', Consultation Paper, September 1986, Table 1. p. 12.
27 Ibid., para. 33, p. 13.
28 Ibid., Table 4, p. 15.
29 Ibid., para. 36, p. 14.
30 Ibid., para. 37, p. 14.
31 Ibid., para. 49, p. 17.

32 Ibid., para. 57, p. 18.
33 Ibid., Table 10, p. 24.
34 Ibid. para. 85.
35 Civil Justice Review, 'General Issues', Consultation Paper, March 1987, para. 172.
36 Ibid., para. 203.
37 See on this issue Sir Tom Bingham, 'The Judge as Juror', *Current Legal Problems*, 1985, p. 1.
38 *Law Society's Gazette*, 19 November 1986, p. 3479.
39 See R. Williams, 'Should the State Provide Alternative Dispute Resolution Services?', *Civil Justice Quarterly*, April 1987, p. 142.

CHAPTER 6   The Criminal Justice System

1 Criminal Law Revision Committee, *Evidence General*, 11th Report, 1972, Cmnd. 4991.
2 Ibid., para. 21, p. 12.
3 Ibid.
4 Ibid., para. 30, p. 17.
5 For a survey of reactions see M. Zander, *Law Society's Gazette*, 2 October 1974, p. 954.
6 *Report of the Royal Commission on Criminal Procedure*, 1981, Cmnd. 8092.
7 See, for instance, M. Zander, 'Investigation of Crime', *Criminal Law Review* (1979), pp. 211-13; P. Softley, *An Observational Study in Four Police Stations*, Royal Commission on Criminal Procedure, Research Study No. 4, 1980, pp. 75, 85, 86; B. Irving, *Police Interrogation: A Case Study of Current Practice*, Royal Commission on Criminal Procedure, Research Study No. 2, 1980, p. 149; B. Mitchell, 'Confessions and Police Interrogation of Suspects', *Criminal Law Review* (1983), pp. 596, 600.
8 D.J. Smith and J. Gray, *Police and People in London: IV. The Police in Action* (Policy Studies Institute, London, 1983), p. 205.
9 Zander, 'Investigation of Crime', op. cit., p. 214.
10 A.E. Bottoms and J.D. MacLean, *Defendants in the Criminal Process* (Routledge & Kegan Paul, London, 1976), p. 115.
11 There is a considerable literature on the subject including many books. See, for instance, V. Bevan and K. Lidstone (Butterworths) and M. Zander (Sweet & Maxwell).
12 Ian K. McKenzie and B. Irving, 'Police interrogation: the effects of PACE', *Policing*, Spring 1987, p. 4.
13 Ibid., p. 19.
14 *Police Review*, 2 January 1987, p. 18.
15 D. Steer, *Uncovering Crime, The Police Role*, Royal Commission on Criminal Procedure, Research Study No. 7, 1980, p. 67.
16 Ibid., p. 71.
17 Ibid., p. 78. See to the same effect Zander, 'Investigation of Crime', op. cit., pp. 205-8 where the police had enough information to identify the culprit from the outset in over 80 per cent of cases. See also Barry Mitchell, 'The Role of the Public in Criminal Detection', *Criminal Law Review*, August 1984.
18 M. Hough and P. Mayhew, *The British Crime Survey*, Home Office Research Unit, 1983, pp. 10-11.
19 M. Hough and P. Mayhew, *Taking Account of Crime*, Home Office Research and Planning Unit, 1985, pp. 11-13.
20 Steer, op. cit., p. 125.
21 Section 78 says that the judge may exclude evidence if it appears to the court that, having regard to all the circumstances, including the circumstances in which the evidence was obtained, it would have such an adverse effect on the fairness of the proceedings that the court ought not to admit it. For an

argument that the Police and Criminal Evidence Act should be amended to introduce something like the American rule see J. Driscoll, 'Excluding Illegally Obtained Evidence in the United States', *Criminal Law Review*, August 1987, p. 553.

22 D.A. Thomas, *The Principles of Sentencing* (Heinemann, London, 2nd edn, 1978), pp. 51-2.

23 *New Law Journal*, 27 October 1977, p. 1040.

24 J. Baldwin and M. McConville, *Confessions in Crown Court Trials*, Royal Commission on Criminal Procedure, Research Study No. 5, 1980, p. 14.

25 The grounds are set out in the Bail Act 1976, Schedule 1.

26 See a review by J. Vennard, 'Court Delay and Speedy Trial Provisions', *Criminal Law Review* (1983) p. 73. Following field trials in Avon, Somerset, Kent and the West Midlands regulations were made as from 1 April 1987 for those areas. See Prosecution of Offences (Custody Time Limits) Regulations 1987 (S.I. No. 299).

27 *Myers* v. *DPP* [1965] A.C. 1001.

28 Criminal Evidence Act 1965.

29 Police and Criminal Evidence Act 1984, s. 68.

30 *Fraud Trials Committee Report*, 1986, Ch. 5.

31 S. Moody and J. Toombs, *Prosecution in the Public Interest* (Scottish Academic Press, Edinburgh, 1982).

32 Now in the Criminal Appeal Act 1968, s.2.

33 See in particular *R.* v. *Cooper* [1969] Q.B. 267; *R.* v. *Spencer* [1986] 2 All E.R. 928, 940.

34 *Evidence in Identification in Criminal Cases*, 1976, House of Commons Paper 338, para. 6.22.

35 Sixth Report of the House of Commons Home Affairs Select Committee, *Miscarriages of Justice*, 1982, para. 24.

36 Ibid., para. 28.

37 *The Government Reply to the Sixth Report from the Home Affairs Select Committee*, 1983.

38 *Criminal Law Review* (1983), p. 577.

39 *Police*, July 1986, pp. 8-9.

40 See Report of the Home Affairs Select Committee, op. cit.

CHAPTER 7   The Jury

1 Seduction and breach of promise to marry are today no longer actionable.

2 *Ward* v. *James* [1965] 1 All E.R. 563 at 572.

3 *Hodges* v. *Harland & Wolff Ltd.* [1965] 1 All E.R. 1086.

4 *Report on the Law of Defamation*, 1974, Cmnd. 5709.

5 Ibid., para. 481.

6 Ibid., para. 484.

7 Ibid., para. 503.

8 Supreme Court Act 1981, s.69.

9 *Report on the Distribution of Criminal Business between the Crown Court and the Magistrates' Courts*, 1975, Cmnd. 6323.

10 'The distribution of business between the Crown Court and Magistrates' Courts', Home Office, 1986.

11 Jane Gregory, *Crown Court or Magistrates' Court* (HSMO, 1976), pp. 12-15.

12 J. Vennard, 'The Outcome of Contested Trials', in D. Moxon (ed.), *Managing Criminal Justice* (Home Office Research and Planning Unit, 1986), Table 12.1, pp. 131.

13 *Report of the Departmental Committee on Jury Service*, 1965, Cmnd. 2627, para. 42.

14 Jury Act 1974.

15 Juries Disqualification Act 1984.

16 See *The Times*, 4, 12, 15, 17, 18, 19, 20 and 27 June 1985.

17 *Fraud Trials Committee Report*, 1986, para. 7.37.
18 Ibid., para. 19.1.
19 Ibid., 'Note of Dissent', para. B4, p. 191.
20 Home Office, *Criminal Justice. Plans for Legislation*, March 1986, Cmnd. 9658.
21 Ibid., para. 35.
22 *Law Society's Gazette*, 18 June 1986, pp. 1885-6.
23 *Counsel*, Easter 1986, p. 2.
24 *The Guardian*, 31 May 1972.
25 Practice Note, [1973] 1 All E.R. 240.
26 *The Times*, 11 November 1981.
27 *Bansal, Bin, Mahio and Singh, Criminal Law Review* (1985) 151.
28 *Binns, Criminal Law Review* (1982) 522, 823.
29 *Danvers, Criminal Law Review* (1982) 680.
30 *McCalla, Criminal Law Review* (1986) 335.
31 J. Baldwin and M. McConville, *Jury Trials* (Clarendon Press, Oxford, 1979), pp. 104-5.
32 See, for instance, Harriet Harman and John Griffith, *Justice Deserted* (National Council for Civil Liberties, 1979).
33 See especially H. Kalven and H. Zeisel, *The American Jury* (Little Brown, Boston, 1966); Sarah McCabe and R. Purves, *The Shadow Jury at Work* (Oxford Penal Research Unit, 1974); M. Zander, 'Are Too Many Professional Criminals Avoiding Conviction?', 37 *Modern Law Review*, 1974, p. 28.
34 Zander, op. cit.
35 Baldwin and McConville, op. cit., p. 128.
36 Vennard, op. cit., p. 143.
37 See, in particular, Zander, op. cit., and Baldwin and McConville, op. cit., pp. 110-12.
38 'Improving the Presentation of Information to Juries in Fraud Trials', HMSO, 1986, p. 45.
39 *Fraud Trials Committee Report*, op. cit., para. 8.27.
40 Ibid., para. 8.34.
41 Ibid., 'Note of Dissent', p. 192, para. C5.
42 Ibid., para. C8.
43 Ibid., para. C11.
44 Ibid., para. C17.

CHAPTER 8   Who Are the Real Legislators?

1 R. Rose, *Do Parties Make a Difference?* (Macmillan, London, 2nd expanded edn, 1984), pp. 62-5.
2 Ibid., pp. 72-3.
3 Helen Beynon, 'Independent Advice on Legislation', 1982, unpublished Ph.D. thesis, Oxford University, Table II, p. 21.
4 Bruce Headey, *British Cabinet Ministers* (George Allen & Unwin, London, 1975), p. 36.
5 Peter Kellner and Lord Crowther-Hunt, *The Civil Servants* (Macdonald, London, 1980), p. 214.
6 Ibid., pp. 211-12.
7 Rose, op. cit., p. 71.
8 J.A.G. Griffith, *Parliamentary Scrutiny of Government Bills* (George Allen & Unwin, London, 1974), pp. 15-16.
9 Granville Ram, *Journal of Society of Public Teachers of Law*, N.S. 1951, p. 444.
10 Dorothy Johnstone, 'Role of the Administrator in the Preparation of United Kingdom Legislation', *Statute Law Review*, Summer 1980, p. 72.
11 Ram, op. cit., p. 450.
12 See National Consumer Council reports: *Gobbledegook*, 1980; *Small Print*, Plain English Campaign, 1983; *Plain English for Lawyers*, 1984.

13 Sir Derek Rayner, *Review of Administrative Forms: Report to the Prime Minister*, January 1982.
14 See also Richard Thomas, 'Plain English and the Law', *Statute Law Review*, Autumn 1985, pp. 141.
15 See especially the writings of Sir William Dale — particularly his *Legislative Drafting* (Butterworths, London, 1977); and Francis Bennion — see, for instance, his evidence to the Renton Committee published in *Statute Law: Renton and the Need for Reform* (Sweet & Maxwell, London, 1979), pp. 27-94. See also D. Miers, 'Legislation, Linguistic Adequacy and Public Policy', *Statute Law Review*, Summer 1986, p. 90; Lord Campbell, 'Law in Plain Language', *Law Society's Gazette*, 9 March 1983, p. 621.
16 Sir William Dale, 'A London Particular', *Statute Law Review*, Spring 1985, pp. 15-18.
17 Ibid.
18 T. Millet, 'A Comparison of British and French Legislation Drafting', *Statute Law Review*, Autumn 1986, p. 130.
19 *The Preparation of Legislation*, (The Renton Committee Report), 1975, Cmnd. 6053, para. 6.21.
20 461 *House of Lords Hansard*, 28 March 1985, col. 1175.
21 *Statute Law Review*, Autumn 1985, p. 137.
22 Ibid., p. 133.
23 Renton Report, op. cit., paras 18.39-41.
24 389 *House of Lords Hansard*, 7 March 1978, col. 776.
25 Dale, *Legislative Drafting*, op. cit., p. 336.
26 Renton Report, op. cit., para. 18.29.
27 See the special issue of the *Criminal Law Review* for May 1986.
28 Griffith, op. cit., pp. 15-16.
29 F.A.R. Bennion, 'Modern Royal Assent Procedure at Westminster', *Statute Law Review*, Autumn 1981, p. 139. The whole of the foregoing section on royal assent is based on this article.
30 J.E.B. Seely, *Adventure* (1930), p. 145 — cited by D.G.T. Williams in 'Statute Law and Administrative Law', *Statute Law Review*, Autumn 1984, p. 166.
31 Griffith, op. cit., see especially Table 3.6, p. 87; Table 3.8, p. 93; and Table 4.1, p. 146.
32 Ibid., pp. 206-7.
33 Ibid., p. 231.
34 Robert Baldwin and John Houghton, 'Circular Arguments: The Status and Legitimacy of Administrative Rules', *Public Law*, Summer 1986, p. 239. See also on the same phenomenon, Lord Campbell, 'Codes of Practice as an Alternative to Legislation', *Statute Law Review*, Autumn 1985, p. 127; Gabriele Ganz, *Quasi Legislation* (Sweet & Maxwell, London, 1987).
35 Baldwin and Houghton, op. cit., pp. 239-40.

CHAPTER 9 Bolder Perspectives for Reform

1 Leslie Scarman, *English Law — The New Dimension* (Stevens, London, 1974) especially pp. 18-21. The suggestion was made in the course of that year's Hamlyn Lectures.
2 *Report of the Select Committee on a Bill of Rights*, House of Lords paper 176, June 1978.
3 See for instance *House of Lords Hansard*, 29 November 1978; 6 December 1979; and 13 February 1981.
4 The lecture was published in *The Listener*, 6 November 1986.
5 For a list and references see M. Zander, *A Bill of Rights?* (Sweet & Maxwell, London, 3rd edn, 1985), pp. 102-5.
6 *Report of the Machinery of Government Committee*, 1918, Cd. 9230, p. 74.
7 Anthony Lester, 'Governing Law and Justice', *New Law Journal*, 17 February 1984, p. 138.

8 *Report by the Comptroller and Auditor-General, Home Office and Property Services Agency: Programme for the Provision of Prison Places*, National Audit, 1985, para. 2.

9 Vivien Stern, *Bricks of Shame* (Penguin, Hardmondsworth, 1987), p. 214.

10 Fourth Report of the Home Affairs Committee, Session 1980-81, vol. 1, para. 117.

11 Andrew Rutherford, *Prisons and the Process of Punishment* (Oxford Paperbacks, 1986), especially ch. 8.

CHAPTER 10   Is the Legal System Heading Anywhere?

1 J. Baldwin and M. McConville, *Jury Trials* (Clarendon Press, Oxford, 1979).

2 The fuss was *à propos* the study by J. Baldwin and M. McConville which resulted in *Negotiated Justice* (Martin Robertson, Oxford, 1977). For a commentary on the row see M. Zander, 'The Legal Profession and Academic Researchers — a Plea for a Better Relationship', *Law Society's Gazette*, 21 December 1977, p. 1121.

3 See further M. Zander, 'Promoting Change in the Legal System', *Modern Law Review*, September 1979, p. 503.

Index